1/94

D1161724

FOR THE SAKE OF ARGUMENT

FOR THE SAKE OF ARGUMENT

ARGUMENT

Essays and Minority Reports

———◆———

CHRISTOPHER HITCHENS

VERSO
London · New York

First published by Verso 1993
© Verso 1993
Individual essays © Christopher Hitchens
All rights reserved

Verso
UK: 6 Meard Street, London W1V 3HR
USA: 29 West 35th Street, New York, NY 10001-2291

Verso is the imprint of New Left Books

ISBN 0-86091-435-6

British Library Cataloguing in Publication Data
A catalogue record for this book is available from the British Library

Library of Congress Cataloging-in-Publication Data
A catalogue record for this book is available from the Library of Congress

Typeset by Leaper & Gard Ltd, Bristol
Printed in U.S.A. by Courier Corporation

CONTENTS

736205

6. Ideas and Interests

7. Rogues' Gallery

8. Critical Resources

INTRODUCTION

A feeble logic, whose finger beckons us to the dark spectacle of the Stalinist Soviet Union, affirms the bankruptcy of Bolshevism, followed by that of Marxism, followed by that of Socialism.... Have you forgotten the other bankruptcies? What was Christianity doing in the various catastrophes of society? What became of Liberalism? What has Conservatism produced, in either its enlightened or its reactionary form? If we are indeed honestly to weigh out the bankruptcies of ideology, we shall have a long task ahead of us.... And nothing is finished yet.

Victor Serge, 1947

When I was but a callow and quarrelsome undergraduate, my moral and political tutors used to think that, by invoking the gentle admonition of there being nothing much new under the sun, they had found an indulgent but quenching reply to all distressful questions. That the words cited above should have been written two years before I was born, and forty years before Fukuyama gave tongue, strikes me therefore as — in that most overworked of the language's most potent terms — an irony. And a pleasing irony at that, since it operates at the old foes' expense. A turn or two of history's wheel, a tug or so on Ariadne's thread, and sudddenly it is not the revolutionaries and idealists but the forces of reaction and tradition (to say nothing of the spokesmen for meliorism and compromise) who find themselves with much explanation due.

Not that Serge and his comrades ever sought to excuse or evade the crimes and illusions of the left, or to set these in any simplistic contrast to the horrors of the counter-revolution. On the contrary, they thought of social and cultural change, individual and collective emancipation, self-determination and internationalism, as subtly but surely indissoluble; for this reason they were the earliest and bravest opponents of Zhdanov, Stalin and all versions of the uniform and the correct. In dedicating these ensuing ephemera to the memory of the old brother-and-sisterhood of the left opposition, I'm conscious of a ridiculous disproportion which critics will easily be able to enlarge. But everyone has to descend or degenerate from some species of tradition, and this is mine.

If I may say it for myself, my last collection, *Prepared for the Worst*, ended on a slight premonition of the 1989 European and Russian revolutions: the axis, pivot and subtext of all commentary since. Even while I was writing about other matters (a ruling-class crime-wave in Washington here; a fresh calamity in the House of Windsor there; a fraudulent memoir; a power-hungry local intellectual) I was fighting to keep in mind that aspect of 'history' which, bewilderingly, both takes sides and fails to take sides. I swore off all metaphors that even hinted at the presence of owls, or the existence of Minerva. Still, I could see that it was wonderfully funny, as well as distinctly embittering, that our predominant culture, faced with one of the greatest episodes of liberation in the human record, chose to take it as no more than its due. Thus 'we' won the Cold War by the same exercise of natural right that 'we' enlisted in the Gulf War. Odd, this, when you consider that even the most Establishment teaching of history contains an inscription; the warning against hubris ...

Even if I had not spent much of that bogus triumphal period in the wastes of Kurdistan and Bosnia, I like to think that I would have seen the hook protruding from this drugged bait. In Kurdistan, an improvised socialism and *communitas* held tenuously against tribalism within, as well as against Saddam Hussein, Nato *à la Turque* and Western opportunism without. In Sarajevo, the onrush of Christian fundamentalism, military arrogance and racialist toxin was kept at bay by men and women honouring the remnant of the Partisan tradition. In both cases, the role of 'fascist' and aggressor was played by a ruling socialist party — the Serbian Socialist and the Arab Ba'ath Socialist, to be exact — but this did no more than lend point to the dysfunction between nomenklatura and nomenclature that had been apparent to any thinking person since approximately 1927. So I couldn't bring myself to see, in this or a score of other instances, the licence for Western liberal self-congratulation. And there has been something more than naïveté in those who affect surprise or shock at the release of impulses long-*nurtured* rather than (as the consoling sapience would have it) long buried.

Many things in this period have been hard to bear, or hard to take seriously. My own profession went into a protracted swoon during the Reagan–Bush–Thatcher decade, and shows scant sign of recovering a critical faculty — or indeed any faculty whatever, unless it is one of induced enthusiasm for a plausible consensus President. (We shall see whether it counts as progress for the same parrots to learn a new word.) And my own cohort, the left, shared in the general dispiriting move towards apolitical, atonal postmodernism. Regarding something magnificent, like the long-overdue and still endangered South African revolution (a jagged fit in the supposedly smooth pattern of axiomatic progress), one could see that Ariadne's thread had a robust reddish tinge, and that potential citizens had not all deconstructed themselves into Xhosa, Zulu, Cape Coloured or 'Eurocentric'; had in other words resisted the sectarian lesson that the masters of apartheid tried to teach them. Elsewhere, though, it seemed all at once as if competitive solipsism was the signifier of the 'radical'; a stress on the salience not even of the individual, but of the trait, and from that atomization into the lump of the category. Surely one thing to be learned from the lapsed totalitarian system was the unwholesome relationship between the cult of the masses and the adoration of the supreme personality. Yet introspective voyaging seemed to coexist with dull group-think wherever one peered about among the formerly 'committed'.

Traditionally then, or tediously as some will think, I saw no reason to discard the Orwellian standard in considering modern literature. While a sort of etiolation, tricked out as playfulness, had its way among the non-judgemental, much good work was still done by those who weighed words as if they meant what they said. Some authors, indeed, stood by their works as if they had composed them in solitude and out of conviction. Of these, an encouraging number spoke for the ironic against the literal mind; for the generously interpreted interest of all against the renewal of what Orwell termed the 'smelly little orthodoxies' — tribe and faith, monotheist and polytheist, being most conspicuous among these new/old disfigurements. In the course of making a film about the decaffeinated hedonism of modern Los Angeles, I visited the house where Thomas Mann, in another time of torment, wrote *Dr Faustus*. My German friends were filling the streets of Munich and Berlin to combat the recrudescence of the same old shit as I read:

> This old, folkish layer survives in us all, and to speak as I really think, I do not consider religion the most adequate means of keeping it under lock and key. *For that, literature alone avails, humanistic science*, the ideal of the free and beautiful human being. [Italics mine]

The path to this concept of enlightenment is not to be found in the pursuit of self-pity, or of self-love. Of course to be merely a political animal is to miss Mann's point; while, as ever, to be an apolitical animal is to leave fellow-citizens at the mercy of ideology. For the sake of argument, then, one must never let a euphemism or a false consolation pass uncontested. The truth seldom lies, but when it does lie it lies somewhere in between.

Christopher Hitchens
Washington DC, 4 January 1993

Dedicated by permission
to my son, Alexander Hitchens
and to my godsons
Jacob Amis and Henry Cockburn

1
STUDIES IN DEMORALIZATION

WHERE WERE YOU STANDING?˙

When people cease to believe in God, remarked G.K. Chesterton slyly, they come to believe not in nothing but in anything. When people cease to trust the word of the authorities, it might be added, they often become not more sceptical but more credulous. A truly hard-headed person could object that those who believe in God or in the benign ways of the government were *already* prepared to believe in anything. But this would be to overlook the dark and fascinating territory mapped by Richard Hofstadter in his endlessly consultable study *The Paranoid Style in American Politics*.

Don DeLillo could have had Hofstadter open before him when he sketched the in-tray of General Edwin Walker, real-life leader of the Kennedy-hating dingbat militia that convulsed parts of the South and West in the battle against liberalism and desegregation:

> Letters from the true believers were stacked in a basket to his right. The Christian Crusade women, the John Birch men, the semiretired, the wrathful, the betrayed, *the ones who keep coming up empty*. They had intimate knowledge of the Control Apparatus. It wasn't just politics from afar.... The Apparatus paralysed not only our armed forces but our individual lives, frustrating every normal American ambition. [Emphasis added.]

If one takes the normal American ambition to be the pursuit of happiness, and charts the ways in which that pursuit is so cruelly thwarted, sooner or later one strikes across the wound profiles of Dallas, Texas on 22 November 1963. In those 'six point nine seconds of heat and light' or those 'seven seconds that broke the back of the American century', some little hinge gave way in the national psyche. The post-Kennedy period is often written up as a 'loss of innocence', a judgement which admittedly depends for its effect on how innocent you thought America had been until a quarter of a century ago. But, while Presidents had been slain before, they had generally been shot by political opponents of an identifiable if extreme sort, like Lincoln's resentful Confederate or McKinley's inarticulate anarchist. Moreover, the culprits were known, apprehended and questioned. With Kennedy's murder, the Republic doomed itself to the repetitive contemplation of a tormenting mystery. Here is a country where information technology operates at a historically unsurpassed level; where anything knowable can in principle be known and publicized; where the bias is always in favour of disclosure rather than concealment; where the measure of attainment even in small-change discourse is the moon-shot. And nobody is satisfied that they know for certain what happened in the banal streets of Dealey Plaza. *Coming up empty....*

˙*Review of Don DeLillo, Libra*, New York 1988.

Then, as if to heap Pelion upon Ossa, the assassin is assassinated. Some years ago, Senator Daniel Patrick Moynihan, a man of whom it could be said that he was as free of the paranoid trait as any American politician or analyst, published a reminiscence of that weird November. He had spent hours, he wrote, calling around a somnambulant Washington with one single, practical, urgent injunction. We have to secure Lee Harvey Oswald, he beseeched. We have to get him out of Dallas, out of the world of the Walkers and the Birchers, and in a sense back into America. *We have to secure Oswald.* Federal jurisdiction must be reimposed. Moynihan feared that if anything happened to Oswald, the nightmare would go on for ever. His short memoir reads today as chillingly as anything in *Libra.* The nation's actual and hypothetical maximum-security prisoner was shot, while still handcuffed to his guards, by a fantasy-sodden huckster of showgirls. Once this mouth had been shut, every other one was free to open. The Warren Commission helped considerably, by its collusive, hasty emollience, to license the conspiratorial imagination and to turn every crank in America into a freelance investigator. Finally, the subsequent declension of the United States through Watergate, Vietnam and another series of murdered heroes has irrationally fixed 22 November 1963 in millions of otherwise unclouded minds as the moment when things began to go wrong. Early in this novel, the young Oswald is riding a shrieking, bucketing subway train and asks: 'How do we know the motorman's not insane?' One can be endlessly surprised at how often, in American life, a variant of this question comes up.

And then there is the other obsession: Cuba. The United States government has made its peace with 'Red China'; a demon which it went all the way to Vietnam to exorcize. It is in the process of thinking about making its peace with the Soviet Union. But somehow, the idea of a Cuban Embassy in Washington is unimaginable. This is oddness and denial raised to the power of objective political fact. Castro's depredations are trivial when compared to Stalinism or Maoism. Yet the hate he arouses is as near-pure as anything so long nurtured can be. And even those who wish to transcend this hatred are queasily aware of something coiled and smouldering in Miami; something that has several times taken revenge on the politicians who have first encouraged and then betrayed it. The Cuban underworld of Dade County was an energizing force in the Watergate burglary and the Iran–Contra network as well as in countless other minor *attentats.* It was on behalf of these exiles that Kennedy sent a lost patrol to the Bay of Pigs, and indirectly on their behalf that he got as near as any President has got to emptying the missile silos. In other words, Cuba represents high stakes gambled at high pressure. DeLillo has one of his assassins make this latent connection explicit. Discussing the morality and the likelihood of a successful 'hit', he says:

The barrier is down, Frank. When Jack sent out word to get Castro, he put himself in a world of blood and pain. Nobody told him he had to live there. He made the choice with his brother Bobby. So it's Jack's own idea we're guided by. And once an idea hits....

At the time of the Warren Commission, Americans did not know that Kennedy had approached the Mafia in order to discuss 'hitting' Castro, and had no notion that he was sharing a girlfriend with the mob leader Sam Giancana. Only the warped J. Edgar Hoover knew, and warned him privately that he was exposing himself to blackmail and worse.

In order to distinguish himself from the vulgar conspiracy theorists, perhaps, DeLillo arranges his narrative along two parallel tracks. Track one shows the intersection of Cuba and the paranoids, with a group of drifters, loners and fanatics having their grotesque imaginations manured, so to speak, by ambitious manipulators from the world of covert action. In this world we meet men like David Ferrie, deranged autodidact, his body denuded by *alopecia universalis* 'like something pulled from the earth, a tuberous stem or fungus esteemed by gourmets'. He is a bomb-shelter cultist fixated on the torsos of young men, and in his darkened brain he broods happily on cancer and war: 'It was heart-lifting in a way to think about the Bomb. How satisfying, he thought, to live alone in a hole.' In slightly too obvious contrast we have Nicholas Branch, a retired CIA analyst, who sits in a spacious air-conditioned archive trying to write the secret official history of the assassination. Like the rest of the country when confronted with the enigma, he finds knowledge dissolving in information. With all the resources of the Borgesian infinite library at his call, he learns that the tapes, documents and calibrations generate only theories and dreams. The forensic, DeLillo seems to say, is only guess-work. And you can never be sure that the Curator isn't withholding something. You might as well be a novelist.

It is in his evolution of the character of Oswald that DeLillo has excelled. Neglected child of a widowed, maundering, self-pitying mother, he leads an intense, dyslexic inner life. 'Most boys think their daddy hung the moon', says his mother, who watches the test-pattern on television. Pages later, young Lee is helping her to 'hang half-moon wall-shelves' — a scant substitute. Handed a leaflet on the Rosenberg case (another endlessly pickable scab on the national hide) at a subway station, he keeps it and forms an obsession around it. Brutalized in the navy brig, where every reminiscence from the grub-hoe to John Dillinger seems designed to evoke *From Here to Eternity*, he tries living in Russia, only to return to the grimy, scrabbling, subliterate American underclass. Except that, as Nicholas Branch concludes in his hygienic sanctum: 'After Oswald, men in America are no longer required to lead lives of quiet desperation':

> You apply for a credit card, buy a handgun, travel through cities, suburbs and shopping malls, anonymous, anonymous, looking for a chance to take a shot at the first puffy empty famous face, just to let people know there is someone out there who reads the papers.

Or, as DeLillo puts it earlier, in a reflection that might have been crafted for Oswald or Manson or Hinckley or some serial murderer or freeway sniper: 'How strangely easy to have a say over men and events.' It is *exactly* this ease, combined with the democracy and openness of America and its love of celebrity, that constitutes the national post-Dallas nightmare.

A novelist must commit himself to a hypothesis, and DeLillo tells the story of an assassination plot that was meant to fail but succeeded. He postulates a group of diehard rightist officials, disgusted by Kennedy's failure of nerve at the Bay of Pigs, who recruit from the zombie exile world of Miami. The idea is to fake an attempted murder of the President, which will not injure him but will 'lay down fire in the street'. A false trail will implicate the Castro Cubans, and will replenish the national will to destroy Fidel. The difficulty is that the recruits must be genuinely motivated enough to 'hit' the President, but must aim to miss him. They exceed their brief. On first reading, this seemed absurdly convoluted and strenuous. But then I reflected that the Contras, who had been recruited by Oliver North from a very similar milieu, were instructed, and instructed to say, that their mission was not to overthrow the government of Nicaragua but to 'squeeze' it. In the resulting folds of disinformation and self-deception, a whole strategy became chronically, crazily unravelled. In a bizarre column in the *Washington Post*, conservatism's arch-moralist George Will recently attacked DeLillo for writing a historical novel based on speculation and thereby creating alarm and despondency. He was answered by Anthony Hecht and others, who ridiculed this new 'responsible' standard for fiction. But the moment had its significance, in showing that there are subjects still considered too toxic and worrisome for any treatment save baffled, patriotic reticence.

The gruesome David Ferrie is given by DeLillo the opportunity to try an intelligent definition of paranoia. In a desperate bar in New Orleans he whines:

> There's something they aren't telling us. Something we don't know about. There's more to it. There's always more to it. This is what history consists of. It's the sum total of all the things they aren't telling us.

Nicholas Branch, of course, can afford no truck with plebeian rancour of this kind. For one thing, he is one of 'them' — the professionals who are paid to be in the know. For another, he has considered all the second-order stuff: the mysterious deaths and apparent suicides of witnesses; the missing files and the discrepant police reports; and has become 'wary of these cases of cheap co-incidence'. For him, the task of posing endless heuristic questions has to be sufficient even if the whole enterprise is futile and even if the accumulation of data thus far is just the raw material for 'the megaton novel James Joyce would have written if he'd moved to Iowa City and lived to be a hundred ... the novel in which nothing is left out'. The tendency of witnesses to die violently may indeed be a coincidence — no more than 'the neon epic of Saturday night'. But even this reflection, intended as it is to be partially reassuring, is in its way an unsettling one. Business as usual is often alarming, too. The proof of DeLillo's seriousness is the way in which he makes that uncomfortable thought occur without emphasis.

Particularly in the last two-and-a-half decades, Americans have become almost as repelled by conspiracy theories as they have by revelations of conspiracies or skulduggeries. Perhaps they are spoiled for choice: at all events a temperate belief in 'coincidence theory' has become almost mandatory in respectable circles. And the commonest thing said: by vulgar coincidence theorists in reply to vulgar conspiracy theorists is: 'There is no smoking gun.' This wised-up, handy term, in vogue since Watergate and lately much in demand, refers crudely to red-handed evidence or absolute proof. Yet, as metaphor, it has a crucial weakness. In Dallas, there *was* a smoking gun. Or was it two? — We'll never know. The main events took place on television and yet are still opaque. The official story was empiricism pushed to the point of obfuscation. No one will ever get beyond hypothesis — a term of abuse these days anyway — which means, as Moynihan feared, that the argument will go on for ever, coming up empty. Only a novelist can attempt to decode it now, and DeLillo has made the attempt with scruple as well as considerable dramatic panache. Cutting along the ragged seam that runs between politics and violence, between the *grandes peurs* of the century and the localized, banal madness of 'ordinary' life, he has shown what monstrosities result when reason even so much as nods off.

Times Literary Supplement, November 1988

ON THE IMAGINATION OF
CONSPIRACY·

Fine phrases about the freedom of the individual and the inviolability of the home were exchanged between the Minister of State and the Prefect, to whom M de Sérisy pointed out that the major interests of the country sometimes required secret illegalities, crime beginning only when State means were applied to private interests.

If ever a man feels the sweetness, the utility of friendship, must it not be that moral leper called by the crowd a spy, by the common people a nark, by the administration an agent?

(Honoré de Balzac, *A Harlot High and Low*)

Those who complain of the banality of American political life seem at first review to have every sort of justification. Political parties are vestigial; the ideological temperature is kept as nearly as is bearable to 'room'; there is no parliamentary dialectic in congressional 'debates'; elections are a drawn-out catchpenny charade invariably won, as Gore Vidal points out, by the abstainers; the political idiom is a consensual form ('healing process', 'bi-partisan', 'dialogue') of *langue de bois*, and the pundits are of a greyness and mediocrity better passed over than described. Periodic inquests are convened, usually by means of the stupid aggregate of the opinion poll, to express concern about apathy and depoliticization, but it's more consoling to assume that people's immense indifference is itself a wholesome symptom of disdain. Yet now and then, there are thumps and crashes behind this great, grey safety-curtain, and unsightly bulges appear in it, and sometimes great rips and tears. Politics here a bit trite, you say? Perhaps. But the following things really happened. President Kennedy was shot down in the light of broad day. His assassin was murdered on camera while in maximum security. Richard Nixon's intimates fed high-denomination dollar bills into a shredder in order to disguise their provenance in the empire of — Howard Hughes? Marilyn Monroe fucked both Kennedy brothers before taking her own life — if she did indeed take it. Frank Sinatra raised money for the Reagans and acted as at least a confidant to the First Lady. Norman Podhoretz's son-in-law Elliott Abrams, while working as Reagan's Assistant Secretary of State, dunned the Sultan of Brunei for a $10 million backhander to the Contras and then lost the money in a Swiss computer error. Ronald Reagan sent three envoys with a cake and a

·Review of Norman Mailer, *Harlot's Ghost*, London 1991; Theodore Draper, *A Very Thin Line: The Iran–Contra Affairs*, New York 1991.

Bible to Tehran to discuss an arms-for-hostages trade with the Ayatollah Khomeini. Robert Macnamara went to a briefing on Cuba believing that it was more than likely that he would not live through the weekend. The Central Intelligence Agency was caught, in collusion with the Mafia, plotting to poison Fidel Castro's cigars. Ronald Reagan's White House was run to astrological time, and its chief spent his evenings discussing Armageddon theology with strangers. Oliver North recruited convicted narcotics smugglers to run the secret war against Nicaragua. George Bush recruited Manuel Noriega to the CIA. As the Watergate hounds closed in, Henry Kissinger was implored to sink to his Jewish knees and join Richard Nixon in prayer on the Oval Office carpet, and complied. Klaus Barbie was plucked from the SS 'Most Wanted' list and, with many of his *confrères*, given a second career in American Intelligence. J. Edgar Hoover amassed tapes of sexual indiscretion in Washington, partly for his own prurient needs and partly for the ends of power. He caused blackmail letters to be sent from the FBI to Dr Martin Luther King, urging him to commit suicide.

Historians and journalists have never quite known what to do about these sorts of disclosure. They have never known whether to treat such episodes as normal or exceptional. It is, for example, perfectly *true* to say that the whole Vietnam intervention began with a consciously contrived military provocation in the Gulf of Tonkin, followed by a carefully told lie to the Senate. But can we tell the schoolchildren *that*? Then again, it now looks very much like being established that the Reagan–Bush campaign in 1980 went behind President Carter's back and made a private understanding with the Iranians about the American diplomatic hostages. But those hostages were the original cause of the yellow ribbon movement! Can a piece of fraud and treason really have been the foundation of the storied 'Reagan revolution'? Contemporary historians like Theodore Draper, Arthur Schlesinger and Garry Wills, or political journalists like Seymour Hersh, Lou Cannon and Robert Woodward, deal with this difficulty in various ways, but seldom succeed for long in firing the general consciousness. This is because they are either apologists for power (Schlesinger, Woodward) or its intimates (Schlesinger, Woodward) or politically conditioned to disbelieve the worst (Schlesinger, Woodward). Men like Wills and Draper, on the other hand, are almost too bloody *rational*. They are careful to speak truth to power and to weigh evidence with scruple, but they are wedded to the respectable and predictable rhythms of academe, of research, of high and serious mentation. They find and pronounce on corruption and malfeasance, and gravely too, but it's always as if the horror is somehow an invasion or interruption. This is why the permanent underworld of American public life has only ever been captured and distilled by novelists.

Mass culture in America, contrary to report, has no great resistance to believing in official evil. The citizenry stoically watches movies in which the cop is the criminal, the President is the crook, the CIA is a doublecross and the dope is dealt by the Drug Enforcement Administration. The great cult film of all time in this respect is George Axelrod's and John Frankenheimer's *The Manchurian Candidate*, withdrawn from circulation after the Kennedy assassination but now available again in cassette form. And the great artistic and emblematic coincidence of the movie is the playing of the good guy by Frank Sinatra — the only man to have had a real-life role in both the Kennedy and Reagan regimes, as well as a real-world position in the milieu of organized crime and disordered 'Intelligence'. *The Manchurian Candidate* began as a novel by Richard Condon who, with Don DeLillo, has done more to anatomize and dramatize the world of covert action than any 'authorized' chronicler. Before discussing Norman Mailer's magisterial bid for dominance in this field, I want to use Richard Condon to anticipate a common liberal objection — the objection that all this is 'conspiracy theory'.

One has become used to this stolid, complacent return serve: so apparently grounded in reason and scepticism but so often naive and one-dimensional. In one way, the so-called 'conspiracy theory' need be no more than the mind's needful search for an explanation, or for an alternative to credulity. If one exempts things like anti-Semitism or fear of Freemasons, which belong more properly to the world of post-Salem paranoia and have been ably dealt with by Professor Richard Hofstadter in his study *The Paranoid Style in American Politics*, then modern American conspiracy theory begins with the Warren Commission. There had been toxic political speculation at high level before, as when certain people thought that there was something too convenient about the *Lusitania* for President Woodrow Wilson, and too easy about Pearl Harbor for President Franklin Roosevelt — both of these, incidentally, hypotheses which later Churchill historians are finding harder to dismiss — but such arguments had been subsumed in the long withdrawing roar of American isolationism. The events in Dealey Plaza and the Dallas Police Department in November 1963 were at once impressed on every American. And the Warren Commission of Inquiry came up with an explanation which, it is pretty safe to say, nobody really believes. Conspiracy theory thus becomes an ailment of democracy. It is the white noise which moves in to fill the vacuity of the official version. To blame the theorists is therefore to look at only half the story, and sometimes even less. To take an obvious example: nobody refers to Keith Kyle as a 'collusion theorist' because he explodes the claim that Britain, France and Israel were not acting in concert in 1956. The term 'organized crime', which suggests permanent conspiracy, is necessary both to understand and to prosecute a certain culture of wrongdoing. And you may have noticed that those who are too quick to shout 'conspiracy theorist' are equally swift, when consequences for authority and consensus impend, to look serious and say: 'It's more complicated than that.' These have become standard damage-control reflexes.

In his Kennedy assassination novel *Winter Kills*, Condon's protagonist is Nick, the brother of the slain President. He has a grown-up adviser and protector named Keifetz:

Nick used to think that there was the Democratic Party and the Republican Party. It had taken Keifetz a long time to explain why this wasn't so, but after that, after Nick had been able to comprehend that there was only *one* political party, formed by the two pretend parties wearing their labels like party hats and joining their hands in a circle around their prey, all the rest of it came much easier.

That's put slightly cheaply: all the same, it makes more sense than the drear convention that two opposing parties contend in the 'marketplace of ideas'. Nick has two reflections on the way in which official truth is manufactured and promulgated in America, and on the 'Commissions' (one need only think of our Royal ones like Denning and Bingham and Pearce) which act as vectors in the process. First, he inquires:

> Was the history of all time piled up in a refuse heap at the back of humanity's barn, too ugly to be shown, while the faked artifacts that were passed around for national entertainments took charge in the front parlour? Could the seven hack lawyers of the Pickering Commission, with a new President for a client, decide that two hundred million people could not withstand the shock of history?

It was the argument of Chief Justice Earl Warren in 1964, and the Tower Commission members in 1987 when they 'reported' on Iran–Contra, that 'the American people' could not bear too much reality. And even the chief attorney for the farcical Senate/House inquiry into the latter affair, Mr Arthur Liman, conceded to Seymour Hersh that he and his colleagues had meant to find the President blameless, and thereby spare the masses the supposed agony of impeachment. Nick goes on to reflect that:

> The Pickering Commission had operated like arms, elbows and fingers upon a silent keyboard. They had played all the notes — the score was surely there to be read, but they would not allow it to be heard. The Commission had announced Stephen Foster when they were actually playing Wagner. Surely, critics who had followed the true score should have pointed that out?

A good question, but perhaps one that only literature can answer. 'Critics' — the press, the academics, the think-tankers — do not care to admit that they missed the big story or the big case. Nor do they get their living by making trouble for the Establishment.

A novelist, however, can listen for the silent rhythms, the unheard dissonances and the latent connections. 'Conspiring', after all, means 'breathing together'. Why not check the respirations? He can also do what quotidian academics and scholars are afraid to do — which is to ruminate on the emotions and the characters and the motives. Most instant reporters are so wised-up that they become innocent: taking politicians at their own valuation. Thus Kennedy the youthful and impatient, Carter the introspective, Nixon the driven, Reagan the folksy and so forth, *ad* — if not indeed well in advance of — *nauseam.* Then the scholars move in to give needed 'balance' and 'perspective' to these popular fables. A novelist need not do either. He can dispense with banality. He can raise intrigue to the level of passion.

> She would not have been a liberal; a courtesan is always a monarchist.
>
> (Honoré de Balzac, *A Harlot High and Low*)

I once got into trouble with Norman Mailer by asking him, on an every-man-for-himself chat-show with Germaine Greer, about his fascination with the Hubert Selby side of life. Boxing gyms, jails, barracks, the occasions of sodomy. The *practice* of sodomy. He appeared riveted, in book after book, by its warped relation to the tough-guy ethos. Had this ever been a problem for him personally? I miscued the question, and Mailer thought I was trying to call him some kind of a bum-banger. He later gave an avenging interview to the *Face*, asserting that he was the victim of a London faggot literary coterie, consisting of Martin Amis, Ian Hamilton and myself. (Amis and I contemplated a letter to the *Face*, saying that this was *very unfair* to Ian Hamilton, but then dumped the idea.) Now here is Mailer attempting the near-impossible: that is to say, a novel about the interstices of bureaucracy which, without any Borgesian infinite libraries or Orwellian memory holes, can summon the sinister and the infinite. Doing it, moreover, at a level of realism which vanquishes Condon and DeLillo while leaving spare capacity for the imagination. And here is Harry Hubbard, his outwardly insipid narrator. Hubbard is a white-collar type of CIA man, 'a ghost' writer of planted texts, who is vicariously thrilled by the knowledge that he is working with ruthless men. He meets this 'other half' of the agency, Dix Butler, a cruel exploiter of local Berlin agents, and has a gruelling soirée with him on the Kufurstendamm which culminates when:

> 'Let me be the first,' he said, and he bent over nimbly, put his fingertips to the floor and then his knees, and raised his powerful buttocks to me. 'Come on, fuck-head,' he said, 'this is your chance. Hit it big. Come in me, before I come back in you.' When I still made no move, he added, 'Goddamnit, I need it tonight. I need it bad Harry, and I love you.'

This blunt offer, which stirs Hubbard more than he wants to admit ('two clumps of powered meat belonging to my hero who wanted me up his ass, yes I had an erection'), enables him to summon the heft to take his first woman that very night. Ingrid turns out to have some qualities in common with her fellow Teuton, the German maid Ruta in *An American Dream*:

> She made the high nasal sound of a cat disturbed in its play ... but then, as abruptly as an arrest, a high thin constipated smell (a smell which spoke of rocks and grease and the sewer-damp of wet stones in poor European alleys) came needling its way out of her. (*An American Dream*)

> A thin, avaricious smell certainly came up from her, single-minded as a cat, weary as some putrescence of the sea ... pictures of her vagina flickered in my brain next to images of his ass, and I started to come. (*Harlot's Ghost*)

Berlin and *Bildungsroman*, you say. OK, so he's a camera: get on with it. But, self-plagiarism apart, I think that Mailer is distilling an important knowledge from his many earlier reflections on violence and perversity and low life. As Balzac knew, and as Dix Butler boasts, the criminal and sexual outlaw world may be anarchic, but it is also servile and deferential. It is, to put it crudely, generally right-wing. It is also for sale. (Berlin has seen this point made before.) Berlin was the place where the CIA, busily engaged in recruiting hard-core ex-Nazis for the *Kulturkampf* against Moscow, first knew sin. First engaged in prostitution. First thought about frame-ups and tunnels and 'doubles' and (good phrase, you have to admit) 'wet jobs'. More specifically — because this hadn't been true of its infant OSS predecessor in the Second World War — it first began to conceive of American democracy as a weakling affair, as a potential liability; even as an enemy.

Mailer strives so hard to get this right that he's been accused of not composing a novel at all. But as the pages mount one sees that this is one writer's mind seeking to engage the mind of the state. *The Imagination of the State* is the name of a CIA-sponsored book on the KGB, and fairly early in *Harlot's Ghost* its eponymous figure 'Harlot', a James Angleton composite, says of the agency: 'our real duty is to become the mind of America'. How else to link the Mafia, Marilyn Monroe, the media, the Congress, Hollywood and all the other regions of CIA penetration? 'The mind of America.' A capacious subject. As Harry minutes while he's still a green neophyte:

> In Intelligence, we look to discover the compartmentalisation of the heart. We made an in-depth study once in the CIA and learned to our dismay (it was really horror!) that one-third of the men and women who could pass our security clearance were divided enough — handled properly — to be turned into agents of a foreign power.

Which, in one sense, they already were. As Kipling made his boy spy say, you need 'two separate sides to your head'. The boy, of course, was called Kim.

A continuous emphasis, then, is placed on the concept of 'doubling' and division. It's expressed as a duet between 'Alpha' and 'Omega', which may not be as obvious as at first appears since 'Omega' was the name of the most envenomed Cuban exile organization. Homosexuality 'fits' here — even, on one occasion, androgyny — as being supposedly conducive to concealment and ambivalence. Other-gender infidelity, too, can be conscripted. So can the double life led by the 'businessmen' and 'entertainers' linked to organized crime. But Mailer calls his novel 'a comedy of manners' because it treats of people who have been brought up 'straight', as it were, and who need a high justification for dirtying their hands. One of the diverting and absorbing features of the book is its fascination with the WASP aesthetic. Not for nothing was OSS, the precursor of the CIA, known during its wartime Anglophile incubation as 'Oh So Social'. A proper WASP — former CIA Director George Herbert Walker Bush swims into mind — can have two rationales for entering the ungentlemanly world of dirty tricks. One is patriotism. The other is religion. Hubbard finds a release from responsibility in both.

> I eschewed political arguments about Republicans and Democrats. They hardly mattered. Allen Dulles was my President, and I would be a combat trooper in the war against the Devil. I read Spengler and brooded through my winters in New Haven about the oncoming downfall of the West and how it could be prevented.

Apart from its affinity with the Condon extract above about the irrelevance of everyday 'politics', this can be read as an avowal of Manicheism and thus as the ideal statement of the bipolar mentality. I've heard and read many CIA men talk this way, though usually under the influence of James Burnham (and Johnnie Walker) rather than Oswald Spengler, and found it easy to see that their main concern was sogginess on the domestic front – the enemy within. Hence the battle, not just against the Satanic 'other', but for the purity of the American mind. And, since the Devil can quote Scripture, it's an easy step to mobilizing the profane in defence of the sacred. *Facilis descensus Averno*. 'The agency' becomes partly a priesthood and partly an order of chivalry. Recall that James Jesus Angleton, though he detested his middle name for its Hispanic, mother-reminiscent connotations, was an ardent admirer of T.S. Eliot's Anglo-Catholic style and once startled a public hearing by quoting from 'Gerontion'. The norm at Langley, Virginia is Episcopalian, though Mormons and Christian Scientists and better-yourself Catholics are common in the middle echelons, and Mailer has a go at creating a Jewish intellectual agent who is also – perhaps avoidably – the only self-proclaimed shirt-lifter.

It is an intriguing fact, a fact of intrigue, possibly the most ironic fact in the modern history of conspiracy, and arguably the great test of all who believe in coincidence, that on 22 November 1963, at the moment when John Fitzgerald Kennedy was being struck by at least one bullet, Desmond FitzGerald was meeting AMLASH in Paris. FitzGerald, the father of the more famous Frances, was a senior executive at the CIA. AMLASH was the CIA codename of a disgruntled and ambitious Castroite. FitzGerald handed AMLASH a specially designed assassination weapon in the shape of a fountain pen, and discussed the modalities of termination. Emerging on to the wintry boulevards, he found that his own President had been murdered. A bit of a facer.

Conspiracy is, more than any other human activity, subject to the law of unintended consequences (which is why it should always be conjoined to cock-up rather than counterposed to it). Jonathan Marshall of the *San Francisco Chronicle*, who is in my view the most sober and smart of those who study conspiracy theory, has an elegant and minimal guess about CIA reaction to this disaster: 'Richard Helms asked himself: "Is my Agency responsible for this?" and answered: "I certainly hope not."' The CIA, in other words, knew that both Ruby and Oswald were involved in the febrile politics of Cuban exile resentment, and the scuzzy world of the fruit-machine kings. The CIA therefore prayed that this footprint would not be discovered. It did more than pray that this was not a 'blowback' from one of its own criminal subplots. By the neat device of Allen Dulles's appointment to the Warren Commission, it was able to postpone the revelation of its involvement by more than a decade. If the Warren Commission had known what the Church Committee later found out, American history and consciousness would now be radically different. But the meantime saw several more domestic assassinations, a war in Asia and the implosion of a felonious President who had also relied on Cuban burglars, and in that meantime the American mind had become in more than one sense distracted. This is ideal psychic territory for Mailer, who surveys with an experienced eye the Balzacian cassoulet of hookerdom, pay-offs, cover-ups, thuggery, buggery and power-worship from which the above morsels have been hoisted. 'Give me a vigorous hypothesis every time,' exclaims Harlot/ Angleton at one point. 'Without it, there's nothing to do but drown in facts.' His protégé Hubbard wonders whether it's ideologically correct to be too paranoid, or whether there exists the danger of not being paranoid enough. Mailer registers these oscillating ambiguities brilliantly in the minor keys of the narrative and in the small encounters and asides. He does less well when he tries to supply his own chorus and commentary, as he attempts to do by means of a lengthy epistolary subtext. Hubbard, 'on station' with the real-life E. Howard Hunt in Uruguay, writes long confessional letters to Kittredge, Harlot's much younger and brighter wife and a classic Georgetown blue- stocking. One sees the point of going behind Harlot's back, but this exchange is improbably arch and overly literal, bashing home the more subtle filiations and imbrications that are the real stuff of the novel.

'Large lies do have their own excitement,' as Hubbard shrewdly notices. There must have been CIA men who whistled with admiration at the scale of Adlai Stevenson's deception of the UN over Cuba, and disgustedly or resign- edly went through the motions of reassuring Congress that things were above board. There must also have been CIA men who enjoyed sticking it to the more earthbound, plebeian gumshoes of J. Edgar Hoover's FBI (more Baptists and Adventists than Episcopalians in that racket) and relished the freedom to travel, to make overseas conquests, to hobnob with Godfathers, to toy with death warrants and the rest of it. Mailer summons their sense of illicit delight very per- suasively. Crucial to the skill and thrill was, of course, knowing how far they could go and then going just that crucial bit further. There were laws and customs and codes to be negotiated and circumvented, and these were men with law firms in their families. As Cal, Hubbard's leathery old warrior WASP of a father, puts it, while seeking to lure President Kennedy into further complicity over Cuba:

'Always look to the language. We've built a foundation for ourselves almost as good as a directive. "*Subvert military leaders to the point where they will be ready to overthrow Castro.*" Well, son, tell me. How do you do that by half? ... Always look to the language.'

Two weeks later, Jack Kennedy sent a memo about Cuba over to Special Group. 'Nourish a spirit of resistance which could lead to significant defection and other by-products of unrest.' 'By-products of unrest,' said Cal, 'enhances the authorisation.'

I can just hear him saying it. By *looking to the language* you find that the secret state, in addition to a mind, possesses a sense of humour and a sexual sense also. The Agency knew, as Angleton's hero knew in *Murder in the Cathedral*, that potentates are very flirtatious and need to have their desires firmed up — hence the mentality, very commonly met with among intelligence agents, of aggressive self-pity. The public hypocrisy of the politicians convinces them that they do the thankless, dirty, dangerous tasks: getting the blame when things go wrong and no credit when they go right. (The CIA memorial at Langley has no dates against the names of agents missing in action.) Thus great fealty can be recruited by a superior who sticks by his thuggish underlings. As Kittredge writes to Hubbard, when the excellently drawn Bill Harvey, a psychopathic station chief, has run afoul:

> Helms did go on about the inner tensions of hard-working Senior Officers accumulated through a career of ongoing crises and personal financial sacri-fice.... Helms may be the coldest man I know, but he is loyal to his troops, and that, in practice, does serve as a working substitute for compassion.

Or again, annexing real dialogue for his own purpose, Mailer uses an occasion during the Commission hearings when Warren himself asked Allen Dulles:

> 'The FBI and the CIA do employ undercover men of terrible character?' And Allen Dulles, in all the bonhomie of a good fellow who can summon up the services of a multitude of street ruffians, replied, 'Yes, terribly bad characters.'
> 'That has to be one of Allen's better moments,' remarked Hugh Montague.

It's some help to be English, and brought up on Buchan and Sapper, in appreciating the dread kinship between toffs and crime.

Yet this gruff, stupid masculine world is set on its ears by one courtesan. 'Modene Murphy', who is Mailer's greatest failure of characterization here, is perhaps such a failure because she has to do so much *duty*. In the novel as in life, she has to supply the carnal link between JFK, Frank Sinatra and the mob leader San Giancana. (Ben Bradlee, JFK's hagiographer and confidant, says that one of the worst moments of his life came when he saw the diaries of Judith Campbell Exner and found that she did indeed, as she had claimed, have the private telephone codes of the JFK White House, which changed every weekend.) Because it's not believable that this broad would write any letters, Mailer's epistolary account of Modene takes the form of recorded telephone intercepts between her and a girlfriend. These are read by Harry, whose general success with women is never accounted for by anything in his character as set down. He both gains and loses the affection of Modene: the gain seemingly absurdly simple and the loss barely registered. Perhaps Mailer was faced with a fantasy/reality on which he couldn't improve, but one could hope for better from a friend of 'Jack' and a biographer of 'Marilyn'. Incidentally, what was Modene like in the sack? 'Its laws came into my senses with one sniff of her dark-haired pussy, no more at other times than a demure whiff of urine, mortal fish, a hint of earth — now I explored caverns.' This is perhaps not as gamey as *An American Dream* ('I had a desire suddenly to skip the sea and mine the earth'), but evidently Mailer's olfactory nerve has not failed him. Still, one occasionally feels ('Modene came from her fingers and toes, her thighs and her arms, her heart and all that belonged to the heart of her future — I was ready to swear that the earth and the ocean combined') that he is pounding off to a different drummer. At one point, losing his grip entirely, he makes Hubbard exclaim: 'I could have welcomed Jack Kennedy into bed with us at that moment.'

These elements — volatile, you have to agree — all combine to make Kennedy's appointment in Dallas seem like *Kismet*. It's a fair place for Mailer to stop, or to place his 'To Be Continued'. Ahead lies Vietnam, of which premonitory tremors can be felt, and Watergate, and Chile.... But the place of covert action in the American imagination, and in the most vivid nightmare of that imagination, has been so well established that it will be impossible — almost inartistic — for future readers and authors to consider the subjects separately.

> Louis XVIII died, in possession of secrets which will remain secret from the best-informed historians. The struggle between the General Police of the Kingdom and the Counter-Police of the King gave rise to dreadful affairs whose secret was hushed on more than one scaffold.
>
> (Honoré de Balzac, *A Harlot High and Low*)

It may seem astounding, after what happened to compromise the Kennedy brothers and Richard Nixon, and after what disgruntled CIA rebels almost certainly did to Jimmy Carter over Iran, that in 1980 a new President should decide simply to give the CIA its head. But in Ronald Reagan's warped and clouded mind, the fantasy world of covert action demanded such evil clichés as that hands not be tied, kid gloves not be used, and the 'stab in the back' over Vietnam be revenged. Thus it was only a matter of time before the crepuscular world of William Casey was exposed to view. 'Affair' is too bland a word for the Iran–Contra connection. Remember that it involved the use of skimmed profits from one outrageous policy — hostage-trading with Iran — to finance another: the illegal and aggressive destabilization of Nicaragua. This necessitated the official cultivation of contempt for American law and of impatience, to put it no higher, with the Constitution. It also entailed, since the funding of the racket had to be concealed from the Treasury and State Departments, a black economy. The arms-dealers, drug-smugglers and middlemen of this dirty budget were to furnish most of the 'colourful characters', as Americans found to their dismay that shady Persian *marchands de tapis* knew more about the bowels and intestines of the White House than, say, the Congress did. This more than licenses the plural in the title of Theodore Draper's book: one of the very few indulgences he permits himself. (The book itself has been abandoned by its English publishers at the last moment, in a flurry of unconvincing excuses.)

Draper's task may be likened to that of an anatomist or dissector, going coolly about his work while the bleeding and reeking corpse is still thrashing about on the slab. In his mild introduction, he confesses the 'horror' he felt when he saw the growing mountain of evidence and testimony that was heaping up in front of him. Nor was it just a matter of meticulous forensic investigation. Two elements of mania pervaded the case, and pervade it still. First, the principals in the conspiracy all claimed — and claim — to have amnesia. Second they all behave as if they had been working for King Henry II. It became a bizarre question of interpreting a President's desires: protecting that same President from the consequences of his desires, and then redefining knowledge and participation so as to elude or outwit the law. *Always look to the language.* In this case, the giveaway key word was the 'finding' — a semi-fictional document which conferred retrospective presidential approval for policies that had often been already executed. Ordinary idiom became un-usable in this context. Robert Gates, who is now George Bush's nominee to head the CIA, was at the material time William Casey's deputy. He told Congress in 1987 that when advised of the 'diversion' of funds from the Iran to the Contra side of the dash, his 'first reaction' was to tell his informant: 'I didn't want to know any more about it.' A strange response, at first sight, from a professional Intelligence-gatherer. And how did he know enough to know that he didn't want to know any more? This absurdity was easily lost in the wider, wilder cognitive obfuscation — did Reagan know? — by which the whole inquiry was derailed. One needs a separate brand of epistemology to attack the question of official 'knowledge', which has the same combination of Lear and Kafka that you sometimes find with British 'official secrecy'. Actually, what is required is the mind of a Mafia prosecutor. Once postulate a capo who tells his soldiers, 'I want the hostages out, and I want the Nicaraguans to say "uncle"', and I don't want to know how you get it done and if you get caught I never met you,' and the cloud of unknowing is dispelled. Fail to conceive of such a hypothesis — and the Congress could not bear that much reality — and there is a 'mystery'. This is not the 'thin line' of Draper's inquiry. Relying almost exclusively on the written record and his skill as a historian, he tries to compose a history of the present. But with knowledge, memory and desire left opaque, and without the promiscuity that is permitted to the freelance specu-lator, all he can do is show — employing their own words and memos — that the American Constitution was deliberately put at risk by a group of unelected, paranoid Manicheans. This in itself is one of the scholarly achieve-ments of the decade.

It's an amazing bestiary of characters, even when rendered with Draper's detachment and objectivity. Adnan Khashoggi, Oliver North, Amiram Nir, Michael Ledeen, Robert MacFarlane — the sweepings of the Levant meet the white trash of Washington. Reading Draper, one can discern the road-map that leads to BCCI — a banana-republic bank which acted as a laundry for both the CIA and Abu Nidal. Indeed, it is the use of banana-republic tactics and contacts, picked up in sordid engagements in the Third World, that has marked CIA intervention in American life. This and other considerations led Theodore Draper, earlier, to baptize Reagan's private government as 'the Junta'. In the turf wars between different police agencies, and the squabbling over the dirty money, the atmosphere became so fetid that a leak or discharge was inevitable. How appropriate, then, that the story blew, not in some pompous American journal of record, but in what Reagan angrily called 'that rag in Beirut' — city of so many recent American nightmares. Oliver North, with his puffed-out chest and his lachrymose style, his awful martial ardour and his no less awful sentimentality, is the perfect example of a Mailer figure — a superstitious fascist, whose whole entourage was full of self-hating, uniform-loving homosexuals. North's strong will to obey and his sadomasochism, his sense of betrayal over Vietnam and his need for revenge in Nicaragua, brought us as close to an American Roehm as was comfortable. It is still uncomfortable to reflect that he was not thwarted by law or by civilian authority.

Some critics have claimed to see a new maturity and acceptance in Mailer's novel, because it eschews polemic and treats its characters with empathy. I think that this misses the point. In *The Naked and the Dead*, Mailer was able to produce a fully realized character, General Edward Cummings, who, by making war on his own feminine 'side', was enabled to ready himself for the coming struggle for world order — by which, of course, he meant the postwar American Empire. This demonstrates, as does *Harlot's Ghost*, that there is a Mailer high and low, and that he can mobilize his feeling for the profane in order to bring himself to bear on more elevated subjects. 'What a man of the cloth he would have made!' says Hubbard of Harlot: 'The value of his words was so incontestable to himself that he did not question the size of his audience. I could have been one parishioner or five hundred and one: the sermon would not have altered. Each word offered its reverberation to his mind, if not to mine.' Harlot boasts of 'the Company's' ubiquity among 'bankers, psychiatrists, poison specialists, narcs, art experts, public relations people, trade unionists, hooligans, journalists ... soil erosion specialists, student leaders, diplomats, corporate lawyers, name it!' From the little world of *Encounter* to the more encompassing schemes of James Angleton and William Casey, all of us have been slightly deranged by the work of this giant cultural and political construct. And now, with the unsolved and unpunished penumbra and personnel of Iran–Contra, we have fuel for more and later conspiracy theories. But as the Cold War at last abates, having so wasted our lives and energies, we can blink our opening eyes at the monsters engendered in the long sleep of reason. It is Mailer's achievement to have summoned the ghosts of paranoia and conspiracy in order to demystify them, and in so doing to have raised realism to the level of fiction.

London Review of Books, November 1991

CONTEMPT FOR THE LITTLE COLONY

Whether or not you remember the riots in Washington that followed the murder of Martin Luther King Jr in the spring of 1968, you almost certainly can recall that imperishable photograph of the Capitol dome bathed in smoke and flame, with the National Guard in the foreground, hefting their weapons and gas masks. It is the starkest depiction I know of the relationship between the state and its capital — the actual workings of government and its notional seat — ever to be taken. I keep a grainy old black-and-white copy of the photograph near my desk — partly because the area shrouded from view by the angle of the shot is the mixed, imperfectly gentrified, northeast Capitol Hill neighbourhood where I have lived for nearly a decade, and partly because it serves to remind me that the affairs of the city of Washington and 'Washington affairs' are not as readily separable as some people wish — or choose — to think.

For a brief, jolting period in 1968, and for an even briefer but almost equally lurid moment in 1989, Washington the city became an emblem of sorts for the state of the nation. The allegory itself has changed a good deal over the years, however. In 1968 a moral lesson attached to the emblem, and there was a show of urgency and commitment — 'concern', in the argot of the time. In 1989 the emblem is but a warning sign, and concern is for 'us', not 'them'. While on his way home a few months ago, Senator Mark Hatfield of Oregon, one of the shining Republican dissidents of the 1960s, found that he had inadvertently driven into a shoot-out. He accelerated away and did not even bother to inform the DC Police Department, pleading later that there seemed little point in getting involved. Over at the White House, the Bush team tends to regard the city as a convenient demonstration case, like New York City in the 1970s or Willie Horton in 1988: Washington, symbol of the sickly folly of welfarism. (William Bennett, who has been 'responsible' for both education and narcotics control in the Republican regime of Presidents Reagan and Bush, is the most promiscuous exploiter for propaganda purposes of the stricken city's marginal utility.)

Today, no single image could quite capture the connection between the two Washingtons; it is too much a matter of mood and texture, and of these being shaped in back rooms, where cameras do not venture. Also, in 1968 the city of Washington was still governed by the other Washington: its chief executive and nine-member council were nominated by the President and confirmed by the Senate. Since 1974, under the Home Rule Act, the city has had not *a* government but two. One of these administrations, the District of Columbia government headed by Mayor Marion Barry Jr, is a debased relic of 1960s liberal and black coalitionism, left behind (as the nation and the other Washington swung right) to feast joylessly on the paltry fruits of office. Its rotting, indifferent public services make a nice counterpoint to the tacky luxuries its leaders demand for themselves. The corruption of the Barry entourage is at once so exorbitant and so pitifully small-time that it generates routine comparisons to that of some shifty, sweltering Third World kleptoc-racy. (For example, there was the 'consulting' tour of the Virgin Islands that Barry, an aide and a city public-works employee took, with shirts and dresses somehow added to the taxpayer-donated hotel bill.) Yet the fact is that although Barry crony (and DC's nonvoting congressional delegate) Walter Fauntroy has had close ties to Haiti, and other friends of the mayor have popped up in less notorious offshore and banana-republic hellholes, a truer analogy is to be found rather nearer home.

The Republican regime of the 1980s — whatever its attempts to distance itself from and exploit Barry and his problems — has much more in common with the torpid, feckless city regime than might at first appear. 'We don't rule this country any more,' says a bitter British policeman about late-colonial India in Paul Scott's *Raj Quartet*. 'We *preside* over it.' Presiding is what Reagan, and now Bush, have done. Presiding has been Barry's approach as well. Washington is really presided over. It is not so much an American city as a semi-colony, wherein neither the colonials nor the local administrators take much notice of the city and its problems, unless it is to make points by blaming each other for them.

Next to my home is Lincoln Park, which contains two statues. Until the bust of Martin Luther King was unveiled in the Capitol in 1986, they were the only two statues in memorial-infested Washington to show actual, identifiable black individuals. The first and most imposing of these commemorates Abraham Lincoln's emancipation of the slaves. It was put up in April 1876 and shows the late President and leader of the Republican Party making a generous and expansive gesture with his left hand. At his feet crouches a half-clad black man clutching a newly riven fetter. The figure of the freed slave looks like a generic one, but in fact it is a representation of one Archer Alexander. He is among the few slaves whose names we still know, and certainly one of the very few to have had his biography written — written by the man who rescued him, the Reverend William Greenleaf Eliot, a Unitarian minister from St Louis and the grandfather of the author of *The Waste Land*. 'There is nothing in all the scenes of *Uncle Tom's Cabin*', wrote the good Reverend in *The Story of Archer Alexander*,' to which I cannot find a parallel in what I have myself seen and known in St. Louis.' Alexander was nearly killed for giving a warning of ambush to Union troops in 1863; Eliot ransomed him and ensured that his features were immortalized. The Lincoln emancipation memorial — which, because it relied on purely voluntary subscription, took eleven years to be completed — saw Frederick Douglass himself speak at its dedication.

Across the park and facing Lincoln and Alexander is the statue of Mary McLeod Bethune, the great black woman educator — and seventeenth child of former slaves — who helped to discover and then to motivate Langston Hughes. (On his way to see Bethune in Daytona Beach in 1954, Hughes wrote from Missouri to a friend: 'The sun do move! I'm staying at a "white" hotel in St. Louis!' The Reverend Eliot would have been pleased by this evidence of progress in his home town.) On the plinth of Mrs Bethune's statue are the words 'I leave you hope.... I leave you racial dignity.' There is too little of either in the environs of Lincoln Park. Langston Hughes, at the end of his long, activist life, registered anguish at the tendency of black youth to uncouth language, separatism, and drugs. Still, he added, he would 'rather encounter several hundred reefer smokers than run into three drunks....' In Lincoln Park today, we could offer him a soupçon of both experiences, and more besides, within sight of Mrs Bethune's memorial.

The racial aspect of Washington's crisis — the crack epidemic; the drug-related murders, for a while averaging one a day; the drug-related AIDS deaths; the corruption of the Barry administration — cannot be dodged. It is the dimension that people are stressing even as they avoid doing so. Listen, for example, to the neo-liberal convener Charles Peters, speaking last May from his regular pulpit in *The Washington Monthly*, when the street-murder horror show was at its worst:

> Some people think that the District of Columbia's government is bad because it is black. That that explanation won't work is proved by the performance of the D.C. Metro system. Sixty-two percent of its employees are black and it is generally recognized as the best transportation system in the country....

Peters sounds — does he not — like a man who is trying to convince *himself* as much as other people. Prejudice says that Washington is a fucking Mau Mau land. But cool, objective surveys have shown.... The trouble with this kind of quantified liberalism is that it is vulnerable to another crop of figures, showing that the majority of indicted municipal aides is no less black than are the transport workers. Bigotry, in any case, doesn't yield to statistics. (If it did, you wouldn't remember Willie Horton's name — and little Mike Dukakis might be President even now.)

But let us stay on Peters's Metro for a while longer. For the DC Metro is rather a telling instance of the symmetry and asymmetry of the relationship between Bush's and Barry's Washington. It — the Metro — is basically a downtown loop, connecting elements of the bureaucracy with the suburbs and the airport (two stations for the Pentagon, one for Foggy Bottom). It's excellent for the commuter belt. But you can't get to the black town of Anacostia on the Metro, or to many places in Washington's black Southeast. And there isn't a Metro station in Georgetown, many of whose residents feel that a stop on their doorstep might make the place a little too — well — *accessible*. See the cleaning ladies as they leave work outside the concrete palazzi that house the great departments of state on Pennsylvania and Independence avenues. See them waiting for the bus that never comes, or for the cabs whose drivers can tell at a glance that they want to go to Southeast, and so keep on going. The sons of the cleaning ladies may work on the Metro and do very well, but the Metro won't take them home. All this talk of Washington transport brings to mind a comment by that well-known ornament of high Republicanism, the late John Mitchell. It was Mitchell — Nixon's jailbird attorney general — who, in 1984, compared the Barry government's workings to those of 'the Amos 'n' Andy taxi Cab Co.'. It was around this time, we now know, that Mitchell received $75,000 in consulting fees from the corrupt and slack-run Department of Housing and Urban Development — an agency whose budget Reagan had already slashed but which once harboured the idea that men and women shouldn't be spending the night in places like Lincoln Park.

Marion Barry tends to reward people who have done him personal favours — people like developer Jeffrey N. Cohen, with whom Barry had a secret real-estate deal in Nantucket, and from whom the city agreed to buy DC properties about to be lost through foreclosure. Ronald Reagan's cronies make thousands — in some cases millions — by acting as 'consultants' on federal housing projects. Marion Barry protects people who have protected him. He managed to find $4,034 in 'emergency' city funds for a loyal special assistant who fell three months behind on mortgage payments on her $200,000 house. In the same vein, George Bush makes sure that Donald Gregg and John Negroponte are rewarded with ambassadorships for keeping mum about their roles — that is to say, Bush's role — in the Iran–Contra scandal. It is true that Marion Barry used to wear a dashiki and that George Bush used to vote against the civil-rights programme. It is also true that Barry goes for things, like gay-PAC endorsements, that Republicans do not. But the bigger, sadder truth is that the 'fit' between White House and City Hall political degeneration is a remarkably close one. Both the Barry regime and the Republican regime believe in 'incentive' for those who are proven prosperous. (In the days of more blunt speech, this used to be known as socialism for the rich and free enterprise for the poor.) The results of this formula greet you and me each morning as we head off to work. Walking through downtown Washington today is like walking through any homogenized, supply-side-generated, post-Reagan city centre. A merciful city ordinance does forbid the building of any high-rise that would edge above the female figure, *Armed Freedom*, atop the Capitol dome, and nearer to Lafayette Park the great modern cult of 'security' forbids you to build in such a way as to overlook the White House; but allow for these local variations in scale and you have the standard 1980s American mix of pointless designer space surrounded by parking lots and building sites. This is development, Reagan–Bush style: fuelled by tax dodges, thick with condos for the young and credit-rich, replete with heating grates for the displaced and homeless.

In Washington, this national trend has been carefully and generously augmented by Marion Barry, the developer's friend, and is as much his memorial as are the crime rate and the crumbling services. The ubiquitous office blocks and expense-account hotels have been granted tremendous (local) tax holidays. For example, an indulgent City Hall levies no real-estate property tax on the occupants of new commercial buildings until the buildings are fully 'under roof', or entirely completed. This exemption, as you might have guessed, has allowed businesses to operate fully and profitably for appreciable stretches of time at addresses which, as far as the city is concerned, don't yet quite exist. The District, moreover, is rather shy about collecting property-transfer taxes. The Cafritz Group, for one, managed to acquire the Washington Harbor complex without paying a dime in transfer taxes, and a reporter from Washington's combative *City Paper* found that a partnership led by Chubb Realty of New York City had managed to acquire $64 million worth of property at Fourteenth and L streets, without paying such taxes. The Chubb-led partnership, you see, was buying not the property as such but a limited partnership at that address, and when the *partnership* is altered, it is not quite the same as.... Such are the loopholes through which, by judicious use of that tawdry euphemism 'incentive', the fat cats have been squeezing since the dawn of Reaganism. There is a corollary, too, that tends to hold. Even if you don't care to believe that there is a connection between private affluence and public squalor, you may have noticed that they often coincide. Last year, the Greater Washington Research Center found that between 1980 and 1986 there had been an 8 per cent rise in the number of poor people residing in the District. Terry Lynch, a spokesman for a coalition of downtown churches, puts it even more recognizably for any city-dweller in the late 1980s. Washington, he says, is a place of 'rising housing costs, minimum-wage jobs, downtown stores we can't afford, and hotels we can't stay at'. Here the relationship between Barryism and Bushery is not so much one of similarity as one of fraternity.

Neither Barry nor Bush (nor Reagan before him) has been particularly comfortable making the rich richer — comfortable, that is, at election time, when even they have been forced to stoop to democratic politics. Their shared solution has been to spend whatever time was deemed necessary in the costume of the populist, to be the regular guy and the people's friend against the faceless ones and the pointy-heads. Obviously, neither Bush nor Barry could bring himself to run against Washington — a feat that only Ronald Reagan managed to pull off after four years at 1600 Pennsylvania Avenue. But they have done their best: Bush with his NRA earmuffs and agonizing Joe Blow impersonations; Barry by appealing to the 'dream' of King and by hinting that there are anonymous white folks out to get him. In the nature of things, both these populisms are race-specific (though it is possible to imagine both men dumping on Harvard in a relatively colour-blind fashion). After a day spent pressing for a cut in the capital gains tax, George Bush munches pork rinds and listens to a country-and-western station. When Marion Barry is not amusing the developer community at testimonial lunches, he knows enough to go and hang out in bars and other places of public resort. (This, incidentally, is why it would be an excellent thing for Jesse Jackson to run for the mayoralty of Washington. A true national populist, who has at least tried to avoid racial populism, would finally be put to the test of running something – the something being a city that has so far been left prey only to parochial populists or irresponsible national ones.)

Among the things likely to tarnish one's populist image just now is being on friendly terms with drug-dealers, which both Bush and Barry are. Of the two, only Barry has suffered from his connection, perhaps because he is put at a disadvantage by the economies of scale. At his level, it is often necessary to go and meet your connection face to face. This is precisely what Barry did on 22 December 1988, in a downtown Ramada Inn. A convicted pusher was apparently offering narcotics to the hotel staff. The police were called to the scene. They were quickly recalled to base when it was learned that Hizzoner was in the relevant suite. George Bush, while CIA chief during the Ford administration, had on his payroll Panamanian drug merchant Mañuel Noriega. Vice President George Bush was in charge of the national drug task force at the time when a wild cover-up of drug-running for the Contras was being conducted with the connivance of the Justice Department. More easily protected at – and from – press conferences, Bush has never been subjected to the awkwardness of a question about the half-dozen known drug-dealers who were employed by the State Department to finance and nourish the Contras, and whose names and records may be found by the curious in 'Drugs, Law Enforcement, and Foreign Policy', a report of the Senate Subcommittee on Terrorism, Narcotics, and International Operations.

Interestingly – and by now, I hope you understand, not surprisingly – Bush and Barry take similar tacks to get themselves upwind of such scandal. Both, for instance, attack the *Washington Post*. Complaints can be heard from each regime that the *Post* is out to get their man, is on his case. If only it were so. Bush and his people regard the *Post* as a liberal sheet, even though it made no endorsement in the 1988 election and did endorse aid to the Contras. Barry and his crew are not above describing the *Post* as a white mouthpiece and propagandizing to this effect on their ceremonial visits to ghetto neighbourhoods. Acutely sensitive to this charge, which is a demagogic one in view of the many black editors and reporters on the paper, the *Post* has in fact been rather lenient with Barry, and has gone out of its way to appease his partisans by running 'balanced' columns and local uplift stories.

Press-baiting, phoney populist electioneering — such are the standard means by which the politically debased mask their corruption. And should these methods falter (they have not yet), there is always good, old-fashioned religion. Cleverly, both Barry and Bush profess an unctuous, ostentatious Protestantism. Of course they care, deeply; don't they say so before God? Bush has told of being reborn and has seldom, if ever, skipped a chance to intone about Christian values. Barry likes nothing better than a good prayer-breakfast, and has an outfit called the Washington Council of Churches more or less ready to endorse him on a day-to-day basis, wittily accusing his critics and detractors of being 'divisive'. Well, if Protestantism has a point — and I may not be the shrewdest judge here — it is surely its insistence on thrift, husbandry, and the deferment of gratification. The riotous hedonism of the possessing — or in Barry's case the governing — classes is not just a reproach in itself. It involves, by its reliance upon deficit spending, tax breaks, and speculative 'growth', an utter negation of the ideas of continence and proportion. In other words, the WASPs don't have a Protestant ethic, nor do the big-mouthed Baptist crooners and swayers. Simply look at what these men have done, and what they have failed to do.

When Lincoln Steffens was writing *The Shame of the Cities*, he had a regular question that he would put to new contacts in every burg he visited. The question was: 'Who runs?' This brusque inquiry has a special pertinence for the nation's capital. Washington is 'run' by the federal government, which 'runs' it as it wishes it could run the rest of the country; which is to say it runs it as a semi-colony, with some local buffoons nominally in charge. The point about the local buffoons is that if things go wrong, they can be blamed and scape-goated. And, with all the cunning of the subordinate, they in turn can blame the loftier powers for their own share in the colony's misfortunes. There is a sort of buck-passing symbiosis involved, with the national Establishment saying, in effect, Whaddaya expect? and the local operators claiming self-pityingly that the blue-bloods have a down on them that dates back to plan-tation days. During the street-murder mania of last spring, it was impossible not to notice this backing and filling, this reciprocal disowning of a city and a community. Mayor Barry made the imperishable observation that apart from the murders, the local crime rate wasn't all that bad (what might Archer Alexander or Mary McLeod Bethune or Dr King have said to *that* exhausted, craven rhetoric?), while the White House, in all its majesty, consulted the opinion polls, considered intervening directly in the policing of the District, and then decided to fight another day on more promising turf. After all, who was getting slaughtered, really? Mainly the hard cases in the Southeast, which saves on arraignments and committals and incarcerations, and could on one view of the 'invisible hand' be counted as a self-correcting market process in which risks and rewards come into fine alignment.

The minions of the Barry administration have been no less callous in their dealings with the underclass. During the last two years, Barry's people have been found in contempt of court on at least five occasions. District judges have cited contempt in cases involving overcrowding, understaffing, and inmate conditions at the ghastly Lorton Reformatory, in one instance for the city's refusal to comply with court orders about medical treatment for a wounded prisoner. The District has also been found in contempt for disobeying the result of a referendum on shelters for the homeless. In other words, the very people for whom the mayor claims to speak are the ones who receive the least reward of his attention.

   Contempt is a good and useful word, of which insufficient use is made these days. *Contempt* is what both Washington governments have for their citizens and voters. (If Jesse Jackson is smart, he will press hard and fast for statehood, so that he is a governor and not a mayor, and so that DC will have properly elected representatives on the Hill.) This contempt forces us to ponder an answer to the question: 'What sort of people do they think we are?' Much depends on the answer.

Harper's Magazine, October 1989

THE STATE WITHIN THE STATE

On the first day of August 1991, in Room 419 of the Dirksen Senate Office Building, there was a hearing that disclosed little to the eye but a good deal to the sceptical mind. The setup looked unpromising enough. With the exception of vast, choreographed numbers like the Iran–Contra waltz of the summer of 1987, congressional hearings are deliberately organized to militate against drama, and this particular hearing was no exception. Experts were on hand to speak in tones pitched to guarantee boredom. Committee members, typically half-prepared and distracted, would ensure monotony and torpor. The Subcommittee on Terrorism, Narcotics and International Operations of the Senate Foreign Relations Committee was taking evidence on the murky workings of an international bank – no big deal in our time. But the bank in question this day was the Bank of Credit and Commerce International, and the testimony, as it unfolded, had less to do, really, with the financial workings of BCCI than with the visceral workings of the government of the United States. Ranged in various attitudes of piety and relaxation were Senators Jesse Helms

(Republican, North Carolina), James Jeffords (Republican, Vermont), Claiborne Pell (Democrat, Rhode Island), Paul Simon (Democrat, Illinois), Alan Cranston (Democrat, California and a nice touch for an investigation of a bank), and John Kerry (Democrat, Massachusetts), the subcommittee chairman. The two witnesses were Jack Blum, a former investigator for the subcommittee, and William von Rabb, US Customs commissioner under Presidents Reagan and (until August 1989) Bush, and dull their declarations were not. As Blum and von Rabb got deeper and deeper into their testimony, reporters began to catch one another's eye; in the seats reserved for the public, quiet gave way to murmurs and even a few whistles of astonishment. I was a bit taken aback myself by the Q's and especially the A's:

Did the Federal Reserve possess a list of names of prominent Washingtonians who had taken kickbacks from BCCI? *Yes, it did.*

Had BCCI helped certain 'outlaw' states acquire American nuclear technology? *Yes, it had.*

Had payments been made through BCCI to drug-runners, gun-smugglers, death-squad leaders? *You bet.*

Had the Treasury Department known about BCCI? *Sure.*

What about Justice? (The department, not the concept — we're talking real world here.) *They knew what was up and seemed most concerned that no others would.*

Interesting. But in a way even more interesting (at least to the sceptical mind) than this long scroll of indictments was where the scroll suddenly screeched to a halt. Treasury, Justice ... what about the Central Intelligence Agency? I happened to know that the CIA had been politely invited to send someone to appear before the subcommittee. Its members had recently learned from investigators that the agency had stashed money in a number of BCCI accounts to use for covert operations in a number of countries. Senator Kerry's subcommittee — at any rate, Senator Kerry — wanted some answers. I actually have in my possession a letter from Senator Kerry — whose work on the connection between narcotics and the Nicaraguan Contras was so efficiently interred three years ago — to Judge William H. Webster, director of Central Intelligence. The letter was sent on 14 May 1991, weeks before regulators in several countries shut down BCCI and its worldwide $20 billion criminal operation. In the letter, Webster is asked to furnish a copy of a seven-to-ten-page memorandum about BCCI written in 1988 by the deputy director of the CIA, Robert Gates, and to provide as well a 'detailed explanation' of the nature and extent of the agency's use of the bank.

Kerry got no reply of any kind from Webster. Kerry *was* told by the agency that no CIA man would appear before his subcommittee unless the hearing was closed. The open hearing did produce an account of how the CIA knew, but failed to inform the Federal Reserve, that BCCI illegally controlled First American Bankshares Inc., the Washington-based holding company chaired by Clark Clifford; and Jack Blum did place in evidence a deposition from former

Contra bagman Adolfo Calero. (Very interesting, the latter – but its contents were not disclosed.) By the end of the day, however, no committee member had formulated a sentence placing in relation the terms BCCI and CIA. This day, as on all too many days since its modest inception in 1947, the CIA was the ghost in the machine. The ostensible processes of open, representative government were not to – and dutifully did not – reveal the agency's role, or its reach.

There exists a provision in the Constitution requiring of all branches of government 'that a regular Statement and Account of the Receipts and Expenditures of all public Money shall be published from time to time'. The CIA is exempted from this – hence its easy evasions with regard to BCCI. In truth, the CIA, citing national security, has managed to exempt itself from all manner of scrutiny, be it from the Congress, the press, or ordinary citizens. The BCCI scandal; the hubristic nomination of Robert Gates to head the agency, despite his umbral connections to the illegal funding of the Contras; the ongoing investigation by special prosecutor Lawrence Walsh into the Iran-Contra affair, now burrowing further and further into the CIA thanks to the attack of conscience and plea-bargains experienced by Alan Fiers, who headed the agency's Central America Task Force from 1984 to 1988; the trial of Mañuel Noriega, the CIA's torture-condoning, coke-dealing 'asset'; the mainstream attention given (finally) this past summer to allegations that the Reagan campaign team, led by spookmeister William Casey, sought to delay the release of the hostages held in Iran until after the 1980 election: the CIA, its awful role and lawless reach, is everywhere apparent in Washington just now. Everywhere, and nowhere: this fall there will be more sordid accounts of CIA operations and actions, to be sure, but I doubt there will be an accounting. It would seem to be no one's issue that the laws and institutions of government – that American democracy itself – have been, as they might say inside the agency, 'converted'.

'Our real duty is to become the mind of America.' Thus Hugh 'Harlot' Montague, the pseudo-intellectual spy who is the eponymous centre of Norman Mailer's recent epic novel about the CIA. Such airs – in life as in fiction – the agency gives itself! The mind of America, yet! But dare we repress the suspicion that there is something all too truthful in this arrogation? Even something that – if we keep in mind how the American political class has delegated numberless dark corners of its 'mind' to covert subcontractors – might explain the broadly felt sense of overwhelming political cynicism and disarray? Consider, if only briefly, the postwar role the CIA has played in bending the American mind. I am going to leave aside the overseas memorials – the graveyards filled by the noisy Americans in and around Saigon; the torture chambers constructed and used in Iran by SAVAK; the jail cell that held Nelson Mandela, in whose arrest the CIA played a part; the statues of dictators propped up by the agency – that mark the CIA's collusion with the most degraded elements in Third World politics. Let us confine the study to America's own internal affairs – including that area of 'police, subpoena, or law enforcement powers or internal security functions' that the CIA was, by its founding congressional charter, explicitly forbidden to touch.

Beginning at the beginning, we find the agency secretly finding homes and jobs in the USA for several hundred prominent Nazis and Nazi collaborators. Soon after begin the operational pacts with notorious American crime families. Drugs have had a special place in the CIA; it has, over the years, financed experiments with LSD and other hallucinogens and toxins on unwitting civilians, and worked in concert with pilots and middlemen who trafficked not only in information but in heroin and cocaine that wound up on the American market. As for that other American bogey, spendthrift government: the CIA may be mean, but never lean. Its exact funding, naturally, is kept from us, and anyway the 'intelligence community' is not only the agency but many agencies, which means only that the generally accepted estimate of the CIA's annual budget – no less than $3.5 billion, in support of 20,000 employees – is on the far side of conservative. In such a case, the smallest vignette may be quite instructive. In 1986, William Casey awarded a $20,000 bonus to Alan Fiers for his 'exceptional management' of the CIA's Central America Task Force – Fiers's chief 'task', as we now know, being that of circumventing congressional prohibitions on arming Contras and talking trade with hostage-takers.

Above and beyond the drugs and the wasting of tax dollars is the matter of American democracy, and the CIA's unrelieved contempt for it. It has bought and suborned senior American journalists and editors, and planted knowing falsehoods in the American press. It has established itself, by means of 'deniable' funds and foundations, in the belly of the American academy, although no doubt literature courses influenced by multiculturalism are infinitely more scandalous and threatening to the American way of life. Should I bring up the publishing houses the agency has subsidized to dispense disinformation? How it has further corrupted a political language – think of 'asset', 'destabilize', 'terminate' – already weakened by sordid euphemism? (This is not so much the American mind as the American id: down, dirty, sniggering.) What about the tainted money from overseas – from despots, mostly, as if to sharpen the irony – that, thanks to the agency, has entered the electoral process?

The damage the CIA has done to American democracy is most evident, I think, when we look to Congress. The Senate and House have been routinely deceived by the agency and by foreign governments assisted by the agency – this is the dark heart of Iran–Contra. What is more, the pornography of tough-mindedness, covert action, and preparedness for 'peace through strength' has had a predictably hypnotic effect on the legislative branch, turning it from legal watchdog to lapdog. As the agency's most famous counter-espionage man, James Jesus Angleton, once peremptorily told an 'executive session' of the Senate Committee on Intelligence: 'It is inconceivable that a secret intelligence arm of the government has to comply with all the overt orders of the government.' On that occasion – and note, please, the educated contempt with which the word 'overt' is employed – the CIA had refused to comply with a congressional call to destroy its supply of Castro-threatening shellfish poison. In recent years senior agency officials have grown somewhat more subtle in their disdain of lawmakers and the law. According to the 1987 report of the House and Senate Iran–Contra committees, Robert Gates testified, in answer to questions that involved the immediate space in front of his nose: 'We [the agency] didn't want to know how the Contras were being funded ... we actively discouraged people from telling us things. We did not pursue lines of questioning.' In his response to a question about how he was advised in October 1986 by an understrapper, Charles Allen, that there might be an Iran-to-Contra 'diversion' – bear in mind that this advising from Allen came a full month before the scandal broke – Gates testified that his 'first reaction was to tell Mr. Allen that I didn't want to hear any more about it'.

Lying? Yes, as it turned out. But in a sense what is more interesting, in an ominous way, is how Gates – how the agency, for it is true of it as well as him – claims the metaphysical power to negate knowledge, even cognition. This is intelligence work of a most peculiar sort. In the hands of the CIA, a well-known, widely reported, public fact – for example, Israel's early and crucial role in clandestinely arming Iran with American weapons when there was a congressional ban on such – gets classified a 'secret' and is never again mentioned by an elected official. (Israel, comically, went through the Iran–Contra hearings as 'Country One'.) Similarly, as with Gates and the diversion, a known phenomenon – profits from arms sales to Iran entering the Contras' coffers – becomes 'unknown' because a CIA official puts his hands to his ears when knowledge of the phenomenon is about to be uttered in his presence. (The obvious question for Mr Gates at his confirmation hearings: How did he *know* he didn't want to know any more about it?) It must be said that over the long haul such conjury does require an audience of almost doltish credulity. This has been furnished time and again by the aptly named intelligence 'oversight' committees on the Hill: juries of those not wishing to hear, nodding at witnesses not wishing to tell. In the mid 1970s there did flicker a moment when it was thought that perhaps the CIA should not be a law unto itself – I am thinking of the Church and Pike committees' work – but that moment was quickly extinguished, thanks in no small part to the work of then CIA director George Herbert Walker Bush. An outstanding example of current relations (that is to say, traditional relations) between oversight and the purportedly overseen can be discerned in the matter of the disclosure that Robert Gates, just days before the President nominated him to head the CIA, had been notified that he was a 'subject' of Lawrence Walsh's ongoing Iran–Contra investigation. Questioned about this troubling development (troubling even after so much overlooking, one might still think), the White House said it was troubled not at all – that 'through an intermediary' it had received 'some assurance' from the special prosecutor that Gates was not an actual target of the investigation. And the intermediary? Why, Senator David Boren (Democrat, Oklahoma), chairman of the Senate Intelligence Committee and the elected lawmaker most clearly responsible for overseeing, not facilitating.

If you had been at CIA headquarters in Langley, Virginia, last 4 March – in fact, youwould not, by law, have been allowed to have been – you would have witnessed a celebration of such facilitation, as Director Webster invested Republican Congressman Henry Hyde of Illinois and Democratic Congressman Anthony C. Beilenson of California with CIA Seal Medallions for their 'sustained outstanding support to the agency'. Both had served long and well (from the agency's standpoint) on the House Intelligence oversight committee, and Webster spoke of the 'high privilege' it had been to work with them. Ah, checks and balances. Congressman Beilenson made note at the ceremony of how the CIA had 'followed both the letter and the spirit of the law'. Congressman Hyde – you might recall his role in making absolutely sure the Iran–Contra hearings self-destructed – contented himself with saying that service to the oversight committee had been 'a rare adventure'. I dare say.

In its attempt to salvage the Gates nomination this fall and to fend off those, like Senator Moynihan (Democrat, New York), who have begun wondering aloud whether the CIA should not be subject to a full re-evaluation, what with the war it was set up to fight – the Cold War – now over, the agency has got the word around town about a 'new' CIA: no more plumbers, just computer nerds and specialists of the think-tank variety, white-collar types turning out economic forecasts and drawing up long-range predictions. The problem with this 'new' CIA is that it has been around for years. The tabulation of concocted figures and the drawing from these of fictitious conclusions have long been agency staples. The CIA's annual *Handbook of Economic Statistics* is a perfect example, and its 1989 edition makes for wonderful reading. My favourite number is the one putting the annual rate of growth in the USSR during 1981–85 at 1.9 per cent, significantly above the rate for those years in Western Europe. The CIA also cooked up the idea that the per capita GNP of East Germany was greater in the 1980s than that of West Germany – the agency's numbers are right there in the 1989 edition of the *Statistical Abstract of the United States*. To what end, this arithmetical fiction? Well, it wasn't intended to deceive the Russians or East Germans. They never toiled under the delusion that they were outstripping the West. The target here was the American lawmaker and, through him, the American taxpayer. The point was the maintenance of a national mood, one more deeply informed by fear. In such a climate, democracy might be overlooked here and there, and those in power might be given the chance to maintain it and exercise it in the shadows.

When the CIA predicted that the USSR would possess *10,000* antiballistic missiles by 1970, it was doing little more than giving an immense boost to the 'contractor community', as I once heard it unsmilingly called. The Soviet T-72 tank, recently demonstrated to have extremely combustive properties on the plains of Mesopotamia, was invested with magically sinister capabilities by one CIA report after another. Ditto the Scud. This wasn't the War Brought Home that the anti-Vietnam War demonstrators chanted of. This was the War Bought at Home. As for the agency's long-range forecasts, they have always been written ultimately with one thing in mind: assuring a continued and prominent foreign-policy-making role for the unelected government at Langley. With the Cold War in the past tense, this will not be easy: new enemies must be found, and fast. Drug kingpins? Terrorists? If joining them no longer pays off, one might as well beat them.

It would seem that the agency is also looking to develop *economic* enemies, beginning with Japan. The Rochester Institute of Technology in upstate New York, under the presidency of M. Richard Rose, has evolved into a satellite station of the agency, and last year in Rochester there took place a CIA-sponsored seminar on the Japanese economy. Among the participants were Kent Harrington, director of the CIA's East Asia Department, and former National Security Advisor Robert McFarlane (nice to have *him* back). Colonel Andrew Dougherty, a Rochester administrator, worked up a draft report based on the seminar, and I suspect it is something of a template for the 'new' CIA. We learn, for example, that the Japanese 'are creatures of an ageless, amoral, manipulative, and controlling culture'. They are poised to take advantage of Americans, whose natural 'optimism' forever 'creates a false sense of security and reduces the national will to act'. (Sounds here as though Mr Harrington cribbed a bit from the 1950s forecasts about the USSR.) In the not too distant future – the report is titled 'Japan: 2000' – there will loom the threat of 'an economic sneak attack, from which the United States may not recover'.

No 'new' CIA will be formulated from within the agency itself. Nor will pressure for such come from anywhere in the executive branch. Lest we forget, it was the CIA which moulded the plastic figure of George Bush and laid the trail of calamities and cover-ups that helped him along the road to the presidency. Appointed to the directorship by Gerald Ford supposedly as a technocrat – instructive, that, in getting a grasp on nominee Gates – Bush proved staunchly otherwise, beginning right off at his confirmation hearings with one of the more stupendous Freudian syntactical blunders of our time: 'I think we should tread very carefully on governments that are constitutionally elected.' During his tenure at Langley, the agency set up serious shop in Angola and Jamaica, American journalists continued to be hired on the sly, and General Noriega was even more generously cultivated. It was also Director Bush who used the agency to tighten the ratchet of 1970s anti-Commie paranoia by appointing 'Team B' to second-guess the annual intelligence estimates. 'Team B', made up of Paul Nitze, Richard Pipes, Lieutenant General Dan Graham and others of similar stamp, is perhaps best remembered for its belief in the unfalsifiable superstition that Moscow sought and could obtain strategic superiority. Out of this smoke came the atmospherics of Reaganism.

Bush will do nothing to bring either glasnost or perestroika to Langley. And he can be counted on to prevent Congress from doing so. Witness his demanding — and getting — from the Hill in August a new, post-Iran–Contra Intelligence Authorization Act which, formalities aside, permits the CIA to continue its unchecked, covert ways. This is not to say that some lonely congressional committee or two still should not make a thorough, concerted inquiry into the CIA a priority. Quite the contrary: there is here, as in the Soviet Union, an entire shadow history that must be brought to light if America is ever again to regain even a modicum of faith in Washington. One need look back no further than the 1980s — the 1980 presidential election, possibly tainted by William Casey and company; the arms build-up, under-taken on the basis of CIA-confected data; the Contra war, fuelled by the CIA against the will of Congress; the cover-up of the latter, smeared with agency fingerprints — to glimpse the breadth and depth of the shadow cast.

Can we take it? Capitol thinking says no; the people could not bear the grim news and do not wish to learn it. Credibility is said to be at stake. Well, yes, it is. The full exposure of the shadow government operating out of Langley is a necessary condition for — as people like to say — 'putting all this behind us' and 'moving the country forward'.

No candidate for the highest office in 1992 can be counted as genuine unless he or she announces that the elected government will be the only one.

Harper's Magazine, October 1991

VOTING IN THE PASSIVE VOICE

The Salem Screen Printers plant in Salem, New Hampshire, is like thousands of other factories in America. Set among various freeway intersections in a quasi-sylvan environment, and situated just off auspiciously named South Policy Street, it employs some dozens of friendly, partially educated young people who are delighted to have a job. The work itself, which involves putting blank T-shirts under a die stamp and then removing them with logos imprinted, is only notionally above the burger-flipping level of which we hear so much. But then New Hampshire's deep and lingering recession has at least assured a free market for cheap take-out food: in all directions across the state, the mall outlets for T-shirts with logos are putting up the shutters. (You haven't vibrated to the deep resonance of the word 'emptiness', by the way, until you have seen a dying mall in today's United States.)

It was a morning late in January when Arkansas Governor Bill Clinton arrived at the plant and stepped into an assemblage of workers — praying, I suppose, that nobody would make any jokes about pressing the flesh. His campaign for the presidential nomination was on this day poised awkwardly between the headquarters of this year's try at an early Democratic consensus and the hindquarters of Ms Gennifer Flowers. Numerous representatives of the Fourth Estate — which already, following the requisite week or two of Washington briefings, huddlings, and phone-arounds, had declared Clinton the frontrunner, and thus had a keen interest in keeping him so — were on hand. I circled the candidate, peppering him with questions, hoping to steer the conversation, however fleetingly, from his sleeping around to the quality of his sleep a few nights back after giving his personal okay for the execution of an imbecile Arkansas murderer.

Seeing Clinton scowling in my direction, I looked over my shoulder, hoping to hear a follow-up or two from my colleagues. It was then I realized that I was — photographers apart — alone. I had dutifully trailed the press corps from Washington to snowy Manchester to . . . *where was everybody?* The pack! Where was the pack!!? It was, as it turned out, ranged respectfully around a small, moustached man gesturing freely, confident of his hold on his audience. This happened to be Stan Greenberg, Clinton's storied pollster. During Clinton's entire two-hour visit to the Salem plant, Greenberg was the only one who did any serious talking. Clinton — just then the anointed Democratic 'frontrunner', and perhaps the next leader of the Free World — seemed content with the division of labour.

As why should he not have been? He had got this far by judicious study of 'the numbers', and by careful cultivation and propitiation of those who amass, decode and package them. Clinton's quietude in Salem, the acquiescence of the press in that quietude, Greenberg's centrality — here was the true picture of democracy in America *circa* 1992, no photo opportunity necessary. Before my eyes, as Greenberg carefully walked the reporters through the results of his latest instant survey of New Hampshire's electorate — his questions, his sample of voters, his interpretation of the results — impressions were taking shape as 'perception', perception beginning its brisk march to fact and on to truth — or, better, Truth. Here, indeed, was the quadrennial American political ritual — the reduction of the vast, varied, and increasingly restless polis to a poll.

Poll, poll, poll. Try reading a news story or watching one aired on TV without encountering the word. Readers of the *Washington Post* of 5 February, to take but one example, were offered seven stories on the front page, and of these, three – about the pessimism of Washington's residents, the souring of Poland on capitalism, and, it should go without saying, the Clinton campaign – were based on polls. Not content to wait a day or two for results, the Cable News Network pioneered the viewer phone-in poll, inviting nightly news-watchers to glimpse a minute-long story, then dial an instant opinion. And this year, just a few days before heading to New Hampshire, I was invited by CBS to take part (as were you) in a phone-in poll conducted in the fading moments of the President's State of the Union address.

But allow me to bring this problem down to an anecdotal level, which, of course, pollsters decry as unscientific. At a dinner party, one is seldom told – and one is never to ask – how, and especially why, a given guest voted in the last primary or national election. Instead, one spends the evening at a certain clever, cool remove from the stuff of democratic politics – swapping back and forth across the table numbers gleaned from the CNN or ABC or *Times/Mirror* poll. And these are only the most visible polls. Behind the drapery of the permanent plebiscite are the private, strategic polls of the Bush administration, of members of Congress, of all candidates for national office, as well as the daily digest of polling that is either modemed or hand-delivered to editors, producers, and reporters subscribing to *Hotline*, the political insider's ultimate data service. Gone are the days when newspapers like the *New York Times* debated whether they should commission polls of their own; and whether, if they did commission them, to put them on the front page; and whether, in that event, polls should carry a reporter's byline. Any newspaper – or news-magazine or TV network – which these days declined to make news in this way might stand accused of lacking 'objectivity' and also 'sophistication', which together are thought to attract readers, and are known to attract advertisers. Moreover, polls today no longer make only their own news; they colour the rest of it. A paper like the *Times* knows it is 'objective' and 'sophisti-cated' to publish a goofy photo of Bush, or run a bit longer with one of his train-wreck quotations when its CBS/*New York Times* poll shows the President's approval rating sagging towards the 50 per cent range.

Opinion polling was born out of a struggle not to discover the public mind but to master it. It was a weapon in the early wars to thwart organized labour and in the battle against Populism, and it later became rather a favourite in the arsenal of 'mass-psychology' parties of the European right. There was always money in it, and the term 'pollster' originated in a 1949 book by a political scientist named Lindsay Rogers, who coined it in order to evoke the word 'huckster'. Rogers was arguing against a seminal and pernicious book written by George Gallup in 1940 and pompously entitled *The Pulse of Democracy*. In its hucksterish pages Gallup sought to argue that James Bryce was wrong, in his *American Commonwealth*, to conclude that 'the machinery for weighing or measuring the popular will from week to week or month to month is not likely to be invented.' Not so, said Gallup. The opinion poll – or, as he grandly put it, 'the sampling referendum' — had the popular will wired:

> This means that the nation is literally in one great room. The newspapers and the radio conduct the debate on national issues, presenting both information and argument on both sides, just as the townsfolk did in person in the old town meeting. And finally, through the process of the sampling referendum, the people, having heard the debate on both sides of every issue, can express their will. After one hundred and fifty years we return to the town meeting. This time the whole nation is within the doors.

Lindsay Rogers wrote of this: 'The best thing about these claims is that they are completely false. If there were a modicum of truth in them, the outlook for popular government would be even grimmer than it is.' Rogers was particularly troubled by what he saw as the pollster's potential power to, in effect, wield the gavel at the town meeting — to frame a question in such a way as to limit, warp, or actually guarantee the answer. Wouldn't a practice of getting the right responses by asking the right questions (and only those) pose a grave threat to the ongoing and freewheeling conversation that is at the heart of democracy?

Rogers could not have imagined the way in which this particular malignancy would develop and advance. Early this past winter I sat and chatted in Los Angeles with Patrick Caddell, perhaps the most famous and successful pollster of the 1970s and 1980s. In 1988, Caddell recalled for me, he had been hired to do polling for Alan Cranston, the Democratic senator from California. 'He was in big trouble,' Caddell related. 'The Republicans were running Ed Zschau against him, a guy who was moderate and smart and young. All our figures showed that the voters were bored with Cranston and that the younger voters wanted a younger guy. It looked bad.' Bad, but not impossible. 'There was one other finding,' Caddell went on to say. 'The voters were alienated. They weren't strongly disposed to vote, and they were very turned off by negative campaigning. The fewer who voted, the better for Cranston.' The thinking went that because Cranston had more name recognition and was the incumbent, with the attendant organization to get out the tried-and-true voters, he'd squeak by in a low-turnout race. 'So I told them, "Run the most negative campaign you can. Drive the voters away. Piss them off with politics." It worked. Cranston just made it by two points. The day after, I realized what I had done and got out of the business.'

But the business, of course, lives on, growing ever more subtle and insidious. An admiring *Time* magazine profile of Clinton published early in 1992 described his campaign as being scientifically, masterfully 'poll-driven'. I learned the meaning of this term when I was told by the Clinton camp, very politely and candidly, that it would not be possible for me to watch a private poll being conducted. One of his senior advisers explained that that would be to give away the store. 'Our polling is predictive,' she said proudly. 'We're laying out the race, getting it to play out so that we'll be where the voters will be by, say, July.' Obviously, Clinton's people didn't want to expose their strategy any more than — and this was a comparison offered by a Clinton staffer — Lee Atwater did when he uncovered Michael Dukakis's 'vulnerability' on race and the flag in those legendary 'focus groups' of voters back in 1988.

There is an entire — and not unrevealing — pollster's argot to which one is introduced by hanging out with the professionals. A term that I came to love is 'forced choice'. This is where the questioner puts a firm, no-exceptions, yes-or-no proposition to the interviewee. 'You see, if you offer the people the *option* of saying "I'm not sure" or "I don't have enough information,"' I was told by Professor David Moore of the University of New Hampshire, who is a student and critic of polling, 'the number of them who will say it will go up by about 20 per cent. "Forced choice" means getting people to have an opinion.' Then there's 'choice or lean', which sounds oddly like something you'd see in a butcher's window. If you can't get computer-selected citizens to choose your candidate or his position on a given issue from a multiple-choice menu, you can at least ask them whether they 'lean' towards any one option. Together with 'tracking' (three-day rolling averages of the evolution of opinion) and 'panel-backing' (phoning up the same people you interviewed before and counting on their 'indebtedness' — *gee, if you drop out of the sample now, the whole tracking thing blows up* — to prevent them from hanging up on you), a flickering image of the state of opinion can be kept on the screen.

There is a dialectic of manipulation involved here. Not only must the 'poll-driven' campaign seek to shape and mould opinion, but its candidate must be ready at all times to assume the required shape and posture. The process is very far from being infallible — for example, George Bush's tracking geniuses must have completely missed the signals about the emerging salience last fall of the health-care issue — but it is *the process*. In effect, politics has become a vast game of simulation which it takes a lot of money to play — the most modest of tracking polls costs a candidate about $20,000 — and has replaced, for politicians, canvassing and, for journalists, basic reporting. See the eager seeker after the nomination as he meets the people. See his frozen posture and quacking, halting speech as he musters unfamiliar bonhomie. See him as he gets gratefully into his car and grabs the portable phone to call his pollster and find out what people really want. Now see the mackintoshed reporter as he calls up the latest findings on his green PC screen, writes them up, and puts his name on them. He has been out to test the temperature of the nation.

For one awful moment in January it had seemed that Bill Clinton's own god might fail him: He stood a sudden, deadly chance of being turned upon by the averages and the percentages — his own head, as it were, served up on a poll. A detailed study of this moment in New Hampshire — a scrutiny of a series of impressions as they strove to take form and shape, and to become a 'perception' instead of an impression — will, I hope, illuminate how polling is not a benign, detached mapping of the political landscape but, rather, a powerful means of cultivating and reshaping it. Far from being the mere study of intention and attitude, it is a profound intervention in the formative period of these things. From the Flowers flap one learns not about the supposedly undue influence of tawdry tabloids, or of the inability of Americans to remain focused on the crucial issues of the day (tax cuts of $60, $80; standardized testing by the year 2000 or 2010), but rather how a cunning campaign team and a compliant 'quality' press can do not everything yet many things.

If you exempt the polls done by the networks in conjunction with the big newspapers, and the private polling organizations of the individual candidates, there were in New Hampshire late this past January three polling organizations that *counted*, so to speak — and counted, or rather were counted, more than once. Results of these three polls — the *Boston Globe*/WBZ-TV poll, the poll taken by the American Research Group of Manchester, and that undertaken by the University of New Hampshire at Durham for station WMUR-TV in Manchester — were routinely extrapolated by columnists and broadcasters to say something on a national level about one or another candidate's standing or future chances. In turn, these impressions and analyses were *cycled back* into the state — by the media, the campaign staffs, and the candidates themselves — with further effects on fund-raising, on position-taking, on day-to-day campaign plans, and thus, again, on statewide and nationwide 'perceptions'. Here, beneath the clean veneer afforded by computers and cellular phones, we have the new smoke-filled back rooms, where the silent but crucial 'election' is held and the results are posted (war chests filled, pundits brought on board, 'electability' established) before even one citizen's vote has actually been cast.

On Monday 27 January — the day after Clinton's appearance with his wife, Hillary on *60 Minutes*, and the day his campaign people and supporters in the media thought he might be broken by a press conference held in New York City by Ms Flowers, during which scratchy recordings were played of purported Clinton–Flowers phone chats — the *Boston Globe* conducted its regular poll of 400 'likely Democratic primary voters' in New Hampshire. The *Globe*'s polling calls began going out to interviewees even as the Clintons could be glimpsed on the nightly news fending off reporters' questions about the scandalous tapes; and the polling continued as the crucial first edition of the paper — the edition that is sold, promoted, and studiously read by voters and opinion-shapers in *New Hampshire* — went to press. The early sampling turned up the result that Clinton was favoured by 33 per cent of those polled, roughly the same as earlier in the month, given the poll's acknowledged (that is, arrogantly *claimed*) 'margin of error' of plus or minus five points. These numbers, in turn, generated the front-page heading POLL SHOWS CLINTON'S LEAD UN-DIMINISHED and the instant front-page analysis (paragraph four) by Walter V. Robinson that 'so far, the poll suggests the news media — and not Clinton — have suffered from the intensive coverage of the Flowers charges.' The American Research Group, a private outfit that drops its market research practice every four years during election season and concentrates on polling, came away with different numbers after polling that night. The ARG had Clinton moving from a 39 per cent share to a 28 per cent share. Not so, says UNH's David Moore. Likewise polling on 27 January, Moore drew upon 'likely Democrats' who had been interviewed twice before. His findings can best be summarized in his own words: 'Clinton's support [on the twenty-seventh] is *not* from the same voters who supported him in the last poll.' Moore, in his polling, found that while Clinton remained the 'frontrunner', only 54 per cent of his original supporters stayed with him, while one-third went to other candidates and 12 per cent moved to the 'unsure' column. These statistics, in turn, were laid out by Moore in varying levels of intensity ('strongly believe', 'moderately believe', etc.), so as to licence his conclusion that 'these figures suggest how volatile the vote in New Hampshire still [was] at this time of the campaign.'

Now, one can attack the *Globe* numbers not only with other numbers but on innumerable theoretical and analytical grounds. For instance, I would agree with Robert Schmuhl, a professor of American studies at Notre Dame who specializes in the country's peculiar fascination with personality politics, when he said early in February that 'the real people up in New Hampshire are not acknowledging as openly as they might the doubts that a story like the Clinton story raises in their minds.' I might bolster this line of thought with — well, some rather volatile numbers. No more than 8 per cent of those polled by the *Globe* on 27 January said they definitely would *not* vote for a candidate who'd admitted to an extra-marital affair — and this number, or some rough approximation of it, was repeated through January and into February by pundits, editorialists, and Democratic movers/shakers as bracing proof that Americans (not simply New Hampshire's likely Democratic voters) were sick of supermarket sleaze, had matured as voters and citizens, were fully preoccupied with the issues. Interesting, and wholly uncommented upon, was the fact that fully 36 per cent of those asked essentially the same question five years ago by the *Times* at the height of the Gary Hart–Donna Rice furore said they could not vote for an acknowledged adulterer.

But let's return to the *Globe*, and its crucial first edition, with its declaration that Clinton remained the frontrunner and that the press, not the candidate, was in big trouble. This was the poll and conclusion trumpeted by David Broder, the capital's chronicler of received wisdom, in the *Washington Post* of 28 January; thus was established the 'take' inside the Beltway. The *Globe*'s early edition was also cited by ABC's *Nightline* on the night of the twenty-seventh, and no doubt steeled Joe Grandmaison, New Hampshire's former Democratic chairman and a Clinton supporter; he managed to keep Forrest Sawyer on the defensive by accusing *Nightline* of sinking to the level of the tabloids by devoting an earlier show to the Flowers allegations. The editors of opinion-shaping papers and magazines went to bed satisfied that they'd done the right thing by burying their stories about the scandal; and the fund-raisers and party bigs turned in resting easier now that their man had, at least for the time being, weathered the storm. But here's what poor Forrest didn't know, or couldn't know: by the time he was signing off, the *Globe*'s pollsters were uncovering a somewhat different response. Special calls placed to 229 additional likely voters found that Clinton's support had dropped enough to bring the entire sample down three percentage points. If my mathematics is right, Clinton was supported by about 25 per cent of those phoned up later rather than sooner — those, that is, who'd had an hour or two to reflect. Given the margin of error, it turns out that this later sample threw similar support to former Massachusetts Senator Paul Tsongas. These interviewees were particularly troubled not by the question of adultery but by the question of whether Clinton was telling the truth about his adulterous ways. To return to Mr Robinson: he would write in still another instant front-page analysis for the paper's *final* edition (paragraph four) that 'as the evening wore on, Clinton's support eroded ...'

We wouldn't know that. Nobody ever used the follow-up edition. Was it not Michael Deaver who said that getting the first version into print was half the battle? The other half was that nobody — by which I mean the party heavies, the consultants, the columnists, etc. — wanted to hear it. The last thing anyone in *the process* wanted to read was the kind of 'objective' headline the numbers truly called for: POLLS SHOW CLINTON SAGGING, TSONGAS SURGING, AMONG VOTERS GIVEN MOMENT TO THINK. With another candidate — one less firmly embraced by the party and the pack: a Gary Hart, say — one might have heard less about 'privacy' and more about 'credibility', ever an issue for the candidate from nowhere and very much one for Clinton, as, in the wake of his draft flap, fidelity to flag would commingle with fidelity to wife. However, with a nominating process constructed to ward off late entrants, with the filing deadlines by late January past for primaries that would choose nearly a third of the delegates, with the fund-raisers having taken their position with the 'frontrunner', with the press on board, a 27 January poll showing Clinton's support eroding had no place and was granted none.

Polls are deployed only when they might prove *useful* — that is, helpful to the powers that be in their quest to maintain their position and influence. Indeed, the polling industry is a powerful ally of depoliticization and its counterpart, which is consensus. The polls undoubtedly help to decide what people think, but their most important long-term influence may be on *how* people think. The interrogative process is very distinctly weighted against the asking of an intelligent question or the recording of a thoughtful answer. And, as all pollsters will tell you privately, the answers to poll questions are very greatly influenced by what has lately been defined as important by the television news. Since the television news, in turn, relies upon opinion polls to determine what is really going on, the range of discourse is increasingly constricted. Moreover, with polling one has the introduction of bogus, pseudo-objective concepts into politics. Example: Do you think of Governor Clinton as 'electable?' (a pseudo-objective criterion if there ever was one). If so, is your impression of his 'electability' derived to any extent from your reading of the polled opinions of others? In any case, would you like to say whether, in your own private, considered opinion, Governor Clinton is (a) Highly electable? (b) Moderately electable? or (c) Only slightly electable?

'It's all part of an attempt to keep order,' Pat Caddell commented, surprisingly but not inaccurately. 'It defines politics and politicians to suit those who are already in power.' And, of course, it is a great reinforcement of the spurious idea of the great national 'we'; from polls, we make 'our' rational-choice decisions on a basis of unpolluted and electronically delivered information. Is that Lee Atwater I hear laughing? Of course, in theory it would be possible to ask questions that put the consensus to the test. In the late 1980s, when official Washington was striving to 'put Iran–Contra behind us', it was common to hear the pundits saying that there was 'zero public support' for prolonging or deepening the inquiry, or for letting it become a threat to a President 'perceived' as popular. Analyses of this sort had their basis in polls that found a majority of interviewees assenting to questions such as 'Is Colonel North a real patriot?' But no pollster ever asked a sample group: 'If you were asked to choose between Ronald Reagan and the United States Constitution, which would you rather sacrifice?' Biased? Meaningless? More meaningless than the ABC News/*Washington Post* poll of July 1985, which actually asked interviewees whether or not they thought Ronald Reagan's cancer would recur before he left office? No fewer than 54 per cent solemnly responded that it wouldn't, and 33 per cent said that they thought it would, and only 12 per cent gave the sane reply that they had no idea — 'choice', on this occasion, not being 'forced'. Is not a plebiscite on the leader's health, reported on the front page, rather in keeping with the approach to politics and opinion exhibited by a banana republic?

It is because polls are very pricey that they tend towards broad, stark questions freighted with assumptions — questions that can 'hit a nerve' and bring a quick, thoughtless response. Polls get more costly the more they are 'filtered', filtering being a process of refinement that scrutinizes, separates, codifies, and 'breaks down' the 'don't knows'. So it's not surprising that you read questions like 'Are the poor lazy?' (*Los Angeles Times*) rather than 'Does the Federal Reserve's tight money policy favour the rich, the poor, or neither?' (nobody yet). A good pollster is like a good attorney, and fights for the result that the commissioning party expects or needs; in the parlance, such a poll is called 'client-directed'. Pollsters themselves make no bones about their influence on the outcome. In a 1988 interview Lou Harris boasted: 'I elected one president, one prime minister, about twenty-eight governors, and maybe close to sixty US senators'. Thus pollstering/huckstering is inextricably bound up with considerations of who will pay for the poll's results and the need to serve political clients who are winners.

'Fluidity' is what pollsters call the chaos and ignorance that they seek to influence. The leading student of fluidity is Professor Sam Popkin of the University of California at San Diego, whose book *The Reasoning Voter* tries to deal with the 'bandwagon effect', by which politicians in cahoots with pollsters seek to exert sufficient magnetism on enough scattered iron-filings to create a pattern and, with any luck, 'momentum'. In his book Popkin rehearses the way in which this was done the last time the Democratic Party 'found' that what it needed was a pragmatic Southern governor. In February 1975 Gallup asked Democratic voters to choose among thirteen Democrats who had been 'mentioned' (a key word for the consensus and the punditocracy. Mentioned by whom?) as potential candidates. Jimmy Carter, with 1 per cent, came in thirteenth. Pat Caddell remembers the networks leaving him out in order to reduce the field to a round dozen. After winning the Iowa caucuses in January 1976, Carter became the presidential choice of 12 per cent of Democrats, according to the February 1976 CBS/*New York Times* poll. He went on to take the New Hampshire primary, make the covers of *Time* and *Newsweek*, and win primaries in Florida and Illinois. Within *one month* the same poll made him the first choice of 46 per cent of Democrats. There are two views about this. The first is that of former Congressman Mo Udall, who, as a Democratic presidential candidate in 1976, objected to the pollsters' practice of 'defining' a 'front-runner' in this way before most voters had got near a booth and long before any real policy arguments had been heard. He later put it thus: 'It's like a football game, in which you say to the first team that makes a first down with ten yards, "Hereafter your team has a special rule. Your first downs are five yards. And if you make three of those you get a two-yard first down. And we're going to let your first touchdown count twenty-one points. Now the rest of you bastards play catch-up under the regular rules."' Contrast the cool Professor Popkin, who concedes that 'some voters *may* indeed have voted for [Carter] simply because he was shown in a positive light as a winner. But many more people felt that they had acquired enough information about him in barely a month to want him to be their president.'

Which of these views — Udall's or Popkin's — seems a more reliable analysis of the queasy experience of watching the Clinton effect and realizing that, in both a crude and a subtle way, some kind of fix was plotted, if not fully *in*, before a single ballot had been cast? Since, especially in primary season, money and press coverage follow the polls as doggedly as trade follows the flag, speed is of the first importance. 'Perceptions' must harden into 'numbers' and thus into 'news' (all three commodities often being supplied, for greater convenience, by the same networks and outlets) in order for the 'news' to keep the 'perceptions' sufficiently acute for the 'numbers' to build. As Popkin says excitedly of a later campaign:

> In 1984, it took three weeks of intensive campaigning in Iowa for Gary Hart to go from 5 percent in surveys to 17 percent of the actual [caucuses] vote. In New Hampshire, it took him five weeks to move from 5 percent to 13 percent in

surveys, but after news of his second-place finish in Iowa, it took him only five days to go from 13 percent to 37 percent.

And how long to go from that back to zero? Later developments in that same primary season reveal another factor: what the pollsters privately and euphemistically call a sample's 'inconsistency' on a given issue or candidate, but what has long looked to me like an interviewee saying, firmly if indirectly, 'Who cares about your stupid poll?' Asked by a *Times*/CBS poll in March 1984 about Walter Mondale — whether their opinion was 'favourable' — 47 per cent said that it was. Asked if they thought he had 'enough experience to be a good president', 75 per cent said yes. Yet asked if they had 'confidence in [his] ability to deal wisely with a difficult international crisis' or were 'uneasy' about this, 42 per cent said they were uneasy. Well, what *did* they think of Mondale? We learned in November 1984, when Reagan drubbed him. 'Garbage in, garbage out,' was the answer one pollster offered me without attribution, over the telephone, when I brought up 'inconsistency'. To him the problem is simply a technical one, a matter of refining the questions. He had no sooner said this when I distinctly heard his wife shout, 'That's because the American people are *stupid*.' In fact, that conclusion is tempting only to pollsters and other elitists. The answers may be stupid, but the voters are not. Stupid answers traditionally come from stupid questions. Stupid questions, however, need not come from stupid people.

Pollsters, for the most part, know perfectly well what they are doing. One thing they are doing is aggregating and averaging ephemeral spasms of 'mood' that may have commercial or political value. 'The "coding" process can be designed to prevent people from speaking their minds,' according to Caddell, who, of course, has needed to be swift in his time. 'They give you multiple-choice questions on, say, what motivated you to vote, and if your answer is not one of the choices on offer, you get dumped or written off as "other".' If you really don't fit, or conform, you can be dumped even if you are in the majority. Last fall the suggestive partnership of Peter Hart and Robert Teeter did its regular canvass on behalf of the *Wall Street Journal* and NBC. (I say 'suggestive' because Hart is a Democrats' pollster and Teeter polls for the Republican President, and both are friends of the *Journal*'s Washington bureau chief, Al Hunt, who likes to spread bipartisan joy when 'bipartisan' translates as 'consensus'.) As reported on the *Journal*'s front page of 1 November 1991, the findings made up a cheery salad of trivial, emollient morsels. 'Cutting taxes to spur the economy gets lukewarm support' (but support nevertheless!). 'Bad voter vibes rise towards [Jesse] Jackson.' '80 percent cite "drinks too much" as a disqualification for the Presidency.' Dan Quayle went up from 27 per cent to 35 per cent 'positive'.

Excluded entirely, and dealt with in a back-page story not until four days later, was the finding that 59 per cent of a specially sampled group assented to the statement 'The economic and political systems of this country are stacked against people like me.' The sampled group were defined as 'Democrats who say they voted for Bush in 1988 and independents with household incomes between $20,000 and $50,000' — that is to say, the group of so-called Reagan Democrats who might well decide this year's election. But 47 per cent of *all other voters* also agreed with the proposition, known in the trade as the 'alienation question', once it was put to them. It is revealing, to say the least, that pollsters will talk of such results as an example of polls that *don't come out right.* Careful evidence of this proposition can be found in a study undertaken by Professor W. Lance Bennett of the University of Washington. Entitled *Marginalizing the Majority: Conditioning Public Opinion to Accept Managerial Democracy,* it takes the unusually well-documented case of United States public opinion regarding the Nicaraguan Contras. Generally, public opinion is seen by the expert class as uninformed and unstable, and thus mouldable by, among other things, opinion polls. That a majority of Americans were against Contra aid, however, was one of those cases that the expert class characterized time and again as 'stable' and 'consistent'. In other words, the voters held, at a fairly steady two to one, against Contra aid throughout the 1980s. Moreover, their opinion appeared to be based on an informed and decided — if rather general — opposition to military engagement in Central America.

Professor Bennett observes that the White House news managers understood this very well, and that while they would trumpet official pollster Richard Wirthlin's discovery that the Reagan tax reform proposal was 'popular', they consciously downplayed popular wisdom in the matter of Nicaragua. The media, which commission polls and construct stories around them, generally followed suit. Between 1 January 1983, when congressional debate on Contra funding began, and 15 October 1986, when Reagan finally secured his Senate/House Majority for Contra aid, there were 2,148 entries for Nicaragua in the *New York Times Index.* Of these, only .6 per cent mentioned popular opinion on the subject and, according to Bennett's findings, only five references to the polls made it into the headlines affixed to *Times* stories on Nicaragua during that period. On one of the biggest and least popular policy campaigns of the Reagan administration, public opinion simply was not an issue. When what 'we' think jibes with the official and commissioning temperature-takers, we hear about it. Otherwise we don't get to know our own minds.

The final poll I studied was my own. Taking the University of New Hampshire questionnaire in hand, I dialled at random (other polls dial by computer, but it comes to the same thing) from the Manchester, New Hampshire, telephone book. The first three 'voters' hung up in my face when I announced myself to be from the 'New Hampshire poll'. ('We get 24 per cent refusals,' said Kelly Myers, a bright young graduate student at UNH. What are the politics of the phone-slammers? Hmm.) Making contact on my fourth call, I quickly established, at least to my satisfaction, that the 'respondent' was over eighteen and a likely Democratic voter. The trouble was, she was too smart for me. As I read her the multiple choice of candidates and asked how she 'leaned', she said it was equal between Clinton and Tsongas. There was no real provision for that answer.

'All right, who do you think is the "frontrunner?"'

'I guess Clinton has an edge there.'

'Who do you think is the likely winner?'

'Isn't that the same question you just asked me?' (I bit my tongue to avoid saying that as far as I could see it was.)

'Who do you think has the best likelihood of beating George Bush?'

'Who knows? It's only January. There might be another of his wars between now and November.'

No designated space for *that* answer either.

On the registers of present discontent and propensity to vote, she scored very high, but the only 'hard' opinion I was asked by the University of New Hampshire to solicit was about Clinton's alleged affairs. On this she said stoutly that she couldn't give a good goddamn. I was trembling when I hung up, and trembling too when I thought to what mush her spirited and warm answers would be reduced by a college student meeting his or her quota of calls from the telephone bank on a given evening with the presses and cameras set to roll.

On their own, one could argue, the opinion polls do no more than seek a common denominator among the demographics. But as practised, polling is a search for and confirmation of consensus, this to be exploited and reinforced by professional politicians. In alliance with the new breed of handlers, fund-raisers, spin-specialists, and courtier journalists, it has become both a dangerous tranquillizer and an artificial stimulant. 'Like many other technologies in politics,' says Pat Caddell, if I may again quote him, polling is essentially 'an instrument for deception whereby the truth is obscured and the public will excluded and ignored.' Which is a former pollster's way of calling polling an increasingly dangerous substitute for democracy, if not the precise negation of it.

Harper's Magazine, April 1992

THE HATE THAT DARE NOT
SPEAK ITS NAME

On 22 May 1985 Anthony Dolan, the President's chief speechwriter, took two full pages, at $2,800 each, in the Reverend Sun Myung Moon's *Washington Times*. He devoted this space to a long, confused diatribe about homosexuality in American politics and journalism. At certain points in his essay, he posed as the very model of tolerance and fair-mindedness, insisting that he did 'not countenance unfair discrimination or unkindness shown toward homosexuals'. At other points, he reverted to the traditional conservative style, saying that 'homosexual intrigue' in the newsroom of the *Washington Post* was so intense that 'poor Ben Bradlee has no one on whom he dares turn his back'. Referring to a recent feature story in the *Post*, Dolan added: 'Only if the story was vital to some issue of critical importance to the public should a man who had been dead for many months be dragged from his grave.' The purport of Dolan's article was the insistence, unusual for a 'family values' conservative, that homosexuality is a private grief and nobody's business except that of the immediate family. The readers of the loyalist *Washington Times* are confused enough as it is these days. Why, they may have had time to ask, does the President's principal scriptwriter go on so much about the fags? And, having decided to do so, why does he seem to be of two minds about them? Two reasons suggest themselves for Dolan's perturbation. The first is the recent death of his brother, Terry. The second is the existence — still awaiting honest acknowledgement — of a gay coterie among Ronald Reagan's bizarre network of lucre, guns, and Contras.

Terry Dolan was gay, and he died of AIDS. He died after a short but intense lifetime of ultra-conservative guerrilla theatre, during which he co-founded the National Conservative Political Action Committee (NCPAC) and helped to create the alliance between the Goldwater right and the blue-collar fundamentalists. It was Dolan's complicated life and AIDS-related death that, after considerable hesitation, the *Post* had featured. Carl 'Spitz' Channell is gay, and was one of Terry Dolan's political and personal protégés. Together they organized and raised funds for many 'negative campaigns' against liberal incumbents in Congress; and together they crafted many pieces of venomous right-wing direct mail. Distinctly a second-stringer while Dolan was alive, Channell has in recent months emerged as Oliver North's favourite fund-raiser. It was Channell who arranged the limos and auctioned the presidential photo opportunities for the phalanx of blue-rinse donors — 'Hamhocks', 'Dogface', and 'Mrs Malleable' to Channell — to the cause of Nicaragua. It was also Channell who took Western Goals — a whiskered front for the old John Birch Society that he inherited from the late Congressman Larry McDonald — and turned the organization (little more than a newsletter) into a frisky little dollar mill. As the first man to plead guilty to charges of fraud in the Iran–Contra affair, Channell may yet be the thread by which the whole web is unravelled. How amazing it is that this White House, normally so hysterical on matters of sexual continence and conformity, should have put its trust in men who wrote feverish odes to Lieutenant Colonel North, and lovingly referred to him in code as 'Mr Green' – the colour of money, and of boyish innocence.

Is the homosexuality of Dolan and Channell of the least consequence? It isn't, I suppose, if you can overlook the following:

- Channell gave a 'sizeable contribution' to Bert Hurlbut, a man whose name I have not made up. Hurlbut is one of those people cast in life as a 'Texas businessman'. In addition to being a Contra fancier, he runs what he calls an 'organization to oppose the homosexual expansion'. It was to that organization that Channell made his contribution. Hurlbut's plain-spoken view is that 'if AIDS had not come along to more or less do it for us, we would have been really in the middle of a vigorous opposition to what the homosexuals were doing to the moral structure of the country.' Thus did Channell put flowers on his friend Terry's grave.

- Channell's best-known pro-Contra outfit, the National Endowment for the Preservation of Liberty (NEPL), last year paid $17,500 to one Eric Olson. Olson has done nothing for NEPL, but he does share a lavish apart-ment with Channell. Terry Dolan was also a paid consultant to NEPL during the last, hospitalized year of his life.

- Daniel Lynn Conrad, executive director of NEPL, lives with Ken Gilman. NEPL paid more than $97,000 to a San Francisco consulting company named the Public Management Institute (PMI), of which Gilman is presi-dent. No other discernible relationship exists between NEPL and PMI. The NEPL gay network is notorious in Washington, but inhibitions of taste have prevented any outlet from alluding to it apart from National Public Radio, for whom Frank Browning filed a pathbreaking report.

- Terry Dolan founded NCPAC with Charles Black and Roger Stone. In the 1984 Texas Senate race, Black was a consultant to Phil Gramm's successful run against Lloyd Doggett. As Black put it, 'Doggett got the endorsement of the big gay PAC in San Antonio. That wasn't unusual, but then we got on to the fact that the gays had a male strip show at some bar and Doggett takes that money. That became a matter of his judgement, so we rolled it out there.'

It's one thing to be gay. But Terry Dolan belonged, as Channell does, to that special group of closet homosexuals who delight in joining the gay-bashing pack. Their friends and relatives often help to keep up this unpleasing pretence. Anthony Dolan we have already met, claiming special exemption from publicity for his brother. His sister, Maiselle Shortley, worked at the

White House for Morton Blackwell, special assistant to the President for public liaison. Blackwell gave lavish endorsement to a book called *The Homosexual Network*, offered by the Conservative Book Club. Its author, Father Enrique Rueda, says: 'homosexuality is a manifestation of the sinful condition that affects mankind and each man, and homosexual behavior is gravely sinful by the very nature of reality.' If the good father is right, then Anthony Dolan has some warrant for saying, as he did in the *Washington Times*, that his brother was not 'really' gay. Terry, he claimed, had 'had a deeply religious conversion and had completely rejected homosexuality'. But during Terry's lifetime, and even at his funeral service, Anthony denied that there was, or ever had been, anything to reject. He denounced the *Post* for accurately reporting the cause of death. Now he seeks to abolish the fact retrospectively by invoking the confessional.

Even in his purchased essay, Dolan sought to deflect blame for the publicity on to 'a certain former Congressman and a deeply committed partisan of homosexuality'. He was referring to Robert Bauman, the Maryland extremist whose career came to a sudden end seven years ago in the Chesapeake Bar in downtown DC, when he was busted by the FBI he had once so much adored for soliciting young male hustlers. No individual in politics had fought against homosexuality — his own and other people's — as strenuously as he did. And while Bauman flourished — as chair of Young Americans for Freedom, as one of the leading Reagan-team gadflies in the House, and as the darling of the New Right — Washington was his. Once he was caught, no conservative would take his phone calls. Bauman's most recent offence, in the eyes of Anthony Dolan, was to have helped organize (Bauman denies this) a memorial service for Terry. Held a week or so after the official event, this informal ceremony, at which Bauman spoke, allowed Washington's gay right to bid their late brother adieu. The officiatng priest was the Reverend John Gigrich, who has become the pastor for the capital's homosexual community. What objection could Anthony possibly have to this observance? Terry had been an undeclared member of Concerned Americans for Individual Rights (CAIR), which linked Bauman and others in a discreet pro-gay conservative caucus. CAIR has been shipwrecked by the AIDS crisis, but it still exists on paper, and still tries to hold up a mirror to homosexual right-wingers. As Bauman wrote in his memoir, *The Conscience of a Gay Conservative*:

> CAIR could fill a suburban Washington home for a cocktail party with nearly a hundred gay men representing positions from the White House staff, to offices of the most conservative Republican senators and congressmen, the Republican National Committee, and all parts of the Reagan administration. But only two of them, myself and one other, were willing to publicly acknowledge their role in the group.

(The 'one other' was Bruce Decker, adviser to Governor George Deukmejian of California. It was while Reagan was governor that he was 'shocked' to find a closet gay nexus operating under his nose. Lou Cannon's book *Ronnie and Jesse* quotes Reagan as responding to this revelation, 'My God, has government failed?' After Lyn Nofziger purged the gays, Reagan could joke about it. When Truman Capote visited him, to plead for men on California's Death Row, he lovably wisecracked: 'Perhaps we should trawl him [Capote] through the halls to see if there are any of them left.')

Why does the right torture itself about homosexuality? The flagellation is partly a consequence of the overlap between extreme conservatives and the more traditional wing of the Roman Catholic Church. Then there is self-protection — honesty means loss of power, so gays on the right toe the line and gay-bash. Bauman tells of sabotaging a Maryland fair-housing bill *because* it prohibited discrimination against homosexuals. And Terry Dolan mailed out a NCPAC fund-raising letter (he did object to it, later) that said: 'Our nation's moral fiber is being weakened by the growing homosexual movement.' There is, of course, self-hatred in all this, personal but perhaps ideological. The latter stems from the neurotic identification by some conservatives of homosexual conduct with weakness, cowardice, and even treason. To these people, the gay world is a lethal compound of E.M. Forster's morality, Guy Burgess's loyalty, and John Maynard Keynes's economics. See how Jim Bakker squeals, not at the accusations of attempted rape of a female teenager or the actual swindling of a credulous congregation or at Jerry Falwell's charge that he could not get an erection, but at the mere suggestion that he gave a man the eye! And remember, when William Buckley had just been called a Nazi, what the worst thing was that he could think of to hurl at Gore Vidal.

Yet history speaks of a long and not so surprising connection between homosexuality and the right. One can look to the Church and the military. 'Gay' has never necessarily meant 'left'. Before Yukio Mishima committed ritual suicide after failing to restore fascism in Japan, he wrote in *Forbidden Colors* that the homosexual should always hate democracy. He argued that gays should identify with the right because they had everything to lose by majority rule. This was also a big theme in the early stirrings of the gay right in Nazi Germany. Other ultra-conservative homosexuals have also ranged themselves with the snobs and the elitists, just as neo-conservative propagandists like Joseph Epstein and Midge Decter have crudely identified radical homosexuality with decadence and the effete.

The way through this morass is clear. It is marked by a simple signpost reading 'Out'. Once Bauman, Dolan, and others acknowledged their homosexuality, they began to evolve politically. Bauman developed a hitherto unsuspected sympathy for the civil rights of blacks and women. Dolan never quite made it that far. But we know that he was turning against the Moral Majority in his last years, and was disowned by Paul Weyrich and the other conservative barons for his pains. (Weyrich and his kind, and neo-conservatives like Decter, often give the pitiful impression that they don't number a single homosexual among their friends.)

There is no such thing as a coterie or conspiracy of declared homosexuals. Bigotry and denial are apparently opposing sides of an identical coin. The fear of being exposed is what spurs the witch-hunter. No one can or should object to Carl Channell's being gay. There were many crookedly raised donations, and many crookedly spent ones, and most of Channell's patrons, like Ronald Reagan, are not gay. Even so, many people might prefer that the money had been spent on gay lifestyles than on the Contras. It's the cheque to Bert Hurlbut that is hard to take.

Harper's Magazine, August 1985

A PUNDIT WHO NEED NEVER DINE ALONE*

Study and ponder the following lines written by George F. Will as Ronald Reagan went tottering back to his California estate in 1989:

> America was far less troubled in 1981 than in 1933, but it needed reassurance. It needed to recover confidence in its health and goodness. It needed to recover what was lost in the 1960s and 1970s, the sense that it has a competence commensurate with its nobility and responsibilities. Reagan, like Roosevelt, has been a great reassurer, a steadying captain who calmed the passengers and, to some extent, the sea.

Note, please, that as well as being perfectly inane in point of sentiment and unbearably hackneyed as to metaphor (the ship of state, for goodness' sake), this passage is wearily ill-written and repetitive — as if some flickering automatic pilot was at (you should pardon the expression) the helm. But quite probably, George Will was in some sort of suppressed panic on that day. Politically and journalistically, the Ron and Nancy show had been his meal ticket. After briefing Reagan for a debate with Carter, Will appeared on a top-dollar trash talk-show to make cool evaluations of the horse he had backed. Lunching with Nancy at costly, joyless expense-account hangouts in the capital, he played the courtier with everything except the courtier's

*Review of George F. Will, *Suddenly: The American Idea Abroad and at Home 1986–1990*, New York 1990.

accomplishments of wit and gallantry, mistaking the servile for the loyal.

As a stylist, Will is the idol of the half-educated. His blizzard of literary tags and historical allusions is a mere show of learning. To take one example: he rebukes Michael Dukakis for admiring Woodrow Wilson, who, as Will puts it, 'began by picking a moralizing amateur, William Jennings Bryan, as secretary of state'. Thirty pages later, we read a windy, populist quotation from Bryan, this time cited with approval, and the words: 'Today's supposed patrician has something to learn from The Great Commoner.' Good liars, it is said, must have good memories. The same goes for would-be successful impostors.

Will's imposture – an affectation of languid, mannered, pseudo-English judiciousness – had at least the merit of originality when it was at the service of an unashamed vulgar fraud such as Ronald Reagan. But in the Bush era, which *is* the Reagan legacy, Will must try to deny that his past positions have any connection with the present state of affairs. This gives him little to write about – or with. And a whole batch of mini-essays praising the supple brilliance of Robert Bork's legal mind do not serve to cover the nakedness. The rest is dotted with wrong-headedness or banality. 'A summit in Iceland (Gorbachev loves Iceland: few Jews and other disturbers of the peace) was Gorbachev's reward for releasing the hostage Daniloff.' Really? The late Sidney Hook, a profoundly interesting ex-Marxist scholar of Marxism, is described as 'anti-McCarthyite'; Hook may have been in many ways anti-McCarthy, but anti-McCarthyite he famously was not. On Panama, Will writes like an adoring hack in a one-party state:

> That is why, although the President's reasons for the invasion are sufficient to justify it, the first reason he gave is the one that explains it: It was an act of neighborliness.

As I.F. Stone once said of Theodore White's treacly prose, a man who can write like that need never dine alone.

It has to be said in fairness that Will has occasionally shown himself irritated by Bush's exploitation of bigotry and stupidity in American life. But even when he's right, he's wrong. He contributed to the foolish misreading of Bush as a 'wimp', a straw-man criticism which was set up – partly by Bush's own people – the easier to demolish it. During the whole of the Bush presidency, Will has been running on empty and failing to write a single memorable column. Increasingly he has turned to baseball, where for all I know he can keep a better score, or to episodes in his private and family life, which he depicts with excruciating archness. 'Let me tell you about our cat' is a one-line introductory paragraph that summons the instant response 'Hold it right there!'

Newsday, July 1990

HARD ON THE HOUSEBOY

Interesting how self-pity is becoming the predominant tone among the conservatives. The neo-cons faced at last with the indictment of Elliott Abrams (or Mr Kenilworth, as he preferred to be known when on money-laundering business), continue to grizzle about persecution and the cost in dollars of special prosecutor Lawrence Walsh's investigation, and are unwilling to concede that money could have been saved by old Kenilworth fessing up a lot sooner than he did. Clarence ('Bitch set me up') Thomas, naturally a bit stunned to have his theoretical dong handled in public by Joe Biden and Strom Thurmond, called it worse than a Klan raid and the toughest experience of his life as a black man.

Coincidentally, the Heritage Foundation journal *Policy Review* chose this month to reprint Judge Thomas's 1987 address 'The Loneliness of the Black Conservative'. In that speech, which was as turgid and clumsy as the judge's testimony before the Senate Judiciary Committee, he recalled an earlier bad moment in his lustre-free career:

> During my first year in the Reagan administration, it was clear that the honeymoon was over. The emphasis in the area of civil rights and social policies was decidedly negative.... The winds were not taken out of our sails until early 1982 when we changed positions in the Supreme Court to support a tax exemption for Bob Jones University which had been previously challenged because of certain racial policies. Although the point being made in the argument that the administrative and regulatory arm of government should not make policies through regulation was a valid point, it was *lost in the overall perception that the racial policies of Bob Jones University were being defended.* [Emphasis added.]

Our old friend 'perception' again. As you will remember, the racist practices of this tenth-rate degree mill *were* being defended. Other 'perceptions' proved similarly correct in the matter of the Voting Rights Act and, until an unmanageable and magnificent alteration in public opinion, in the matter of South Africa too. If Thomas thinks his Supreme Court nomination hearing was more humiliating than being a part of Reagan's civil-rights counter-revolution, that's all I want to know. On the first day of the hearings, he fatuously said that allegations like Professor Hill's were part of 'a high-tech lynching for uppity blacks who in any way deign to think for themselves'. Uppity? Clarence Thomas? It's too late for him to borrow the imagery of a movement of which he was never a part, and whose attainments he sought to belittle. And what's more worrying — that the judge doesn't know the meaning of the word 'deign', or that maybe he does? This will be the first lynching in American history to have ended with the victim holding a lifetime tenure in black robes on the highest court in the land. During the days of Thomas's yeoman service in the early Reagan bureaucracy, I had a television debate on the subject of apartheid with his young co-thinker and friend William Keyes. Keyes had also been a part of the black conservative milieu grouped around the Heritage Foundation, and at the time of our meeting he was being paid a fabulous sum by a South African lobbying firm. I opened mildly by saying that the South African regime could easily prove its legitimacy by releasing Nelson Mandela and holding an election. Keyes replied that to call for the release of Nelson Mandela was like calling for the release of Charles Manson. I remember thinking: You poor little ratbag, don't you realize that they're *laughing* at you?

Is it too imaginative to speculate on the psychic wounds that have been inflicted on black reactionaries? Look at the wretched figure of James Meredith, for instance, hired on as the first African-American aide to Jesse Helms's personal staff. Hired because he was a loudmouth racial separatist — the Helms people, I can assure you from private conversations, certainly saw the joke, even if he didn't — and finally 'let go' because he was an embarrassment. Given free rein for his twisted views in papers like *The Washington Times* and used as a disposable tool in the battle against the left and the civil-rights leadership. Now making television commercials for David Duke. There should be no forgiving forgetfulness of the humiliations visited by the New Right on its black puppets. The nomination of poor, stupid Clarence to the Court came from the same mind as conjured Willie Horton.

In his 1987 talk Thomas hinted at what he must have gone through to attain what he now openly describes as the proudest moment of his life — lunch at Kennebunkport with George Bush! The piercing pity that one feels is reinforced by his earlier reflection, which he has no doubt buried as deep as he can:

> It often seemed that to be accepted within the conservative ranks and to be treated with some degree of acceptance, a black was required to become a caricature of sorts, providing sideshows of anti-black quips and attacks.

You don't even want to think about the occasions — the shit-eating grins and forced bonhomie — that poor, stupid Clarence is remembering here. Perhaps he, too, was called 'Mr Mayor' and had to smile. Just reflect on what it takes to have been a sympathizer of Louis Farrakhan's 'self-help' *and* Ronald Reagan's version of 'colour blindness'.

But at least poor, stupid Clarence's massas have stuck by him in his tribulation. What about the friends of Mr Kenilworth? The whole boast of Norman Podhoretz, Charles Krauthammer, Midge Decter and the rest of the *Commentary/National Interest* crew was that their ideas and people really *mattered* in the Reagan revolution. Irving Kristol used to discourse about the shock of recognition when Jewish intellectuals at last met Republican businessmen and found that they could *do* things for each other. Hence, at least in part, the pathetic yearning for acceptance that is inscribed in Elliott Abrams's choice of a *nom de guerre*. Now he's deserted by his pal *and* his patron. If the President was asked what he thought of the plea bargain of one of his former hit men, I didn't read the answer. No doubt the White House spin-doctors think it clever that the exposure of one of their *Judenrat* was obscured by the humiliation of their houseboy.

The Nation, November 1991

NEW ORLEANS IN A BROWN SHIRT

Opinion-poll findings can be fascinating or absurd or misleading, but one of the discoveries made by the *Times-Picayune* about David Duke really made me sit up. The newspaper asked people after the vote whether they believed that the former stormtrooper and Grand Wizard had 'changed'. And 14 per cent of Duke's voters responded No. Allowing for low mentality and the degeneration of the white gene pool under the influence of a decade of Reagan/Bush, that still suggests an amazing number of eligible voters who chose Duke because of — or in spite of — his avowal of the most pornographic element in National Socialism. Probing into this, as I did in various New Orleans bars and dives frequented by Duke supporters, I found that the 'coding' of the Duke message was less subtle and more gross than I had been led to expect. Any fool can run by making innuendoes about the underclass — one such fool is now our President, after all — but most of them count the votes and make deniable noises and leave it at that. The Duke forces find the white underclass where it is already most vulnerable — in competition, or imagined competition, with the black underclass for jobs and entitlements — and go further. They want conclusions drawn, of which the decision to vote Republican is the least important. They want supporters to ask: Who is behind integration and race mixing? Who benefits from it? And they want them to answer, and to believe, that it is the Jews.

If you take all Duke's open and covert statements over his long career, it is clear that the black question basically bores him. Why stop at saying what Republicans can imply and Democrats can be shamefaced in not denying? The real energy of his theory and practice is provided by anti-Semitism. A hard evening's drinking with one young supporter materialized my suspicion. After the usual stuff about black muggers and dope-dealers and fast breeders, he became more animated: 'The niggers do all the crime, so you got to get theft insurance. And you can only buy theft insurance from the Jews.' He looked triumphant, as if a neat answer to a baffling mystery had been discovered by an

Aryan physicist. It was the same with this boy's peer group. Amazingly lacking in any sign of formal education, they were capable of being positively scholarly on the subject of the Holocaust, the Crucifixion, Wall Street's support for Bolshevism and the Jewish love for the mongrelization of the races. (I, who count only the last three of these as myths, often had to do some very fast talking.) Somebody, in other words, has been putting in some steady work down here. In a recent television debate with the Metzgers *père et fils*, who lead the White Aryan Resistance, I found the same. They take no time dismissing all nonwhites and Third Worlders as 'mud people' and a species without a soul. What gets them going is the stuff about Jewish doctors running the abortion business for genocidal purposes; Jewish involvement with disease; Jewish control over the media. Like Duke, they can't seem to decide whether the Final Solution was attempted and was a good thing, or wasn't attempted and is a propaganda fable; but it is at any rate their favourite subject. It allows for conspiracy, which the libel on blacks does not. In much the same way, Jean-Marie Le Pen had a nice racket in France, denouncing Arabs and Africans, until he blurted out his fouler thoughts on the Holocaust. At once, he was in all kinds of trouble with people who might otherwise have found him a bit rough but no more than a nuisance-value populist. So why did he do it? Because he couldn't *not* do it, and because the whole movement of French 'purity' is an attempt to reverse the Dreyfus decision.

I had this larger point put to me, but in a more guarded way, by a black New Orleans attorney with a fine civil-rights record. Thank God that Duke was a Nazi as well as a Klansman, the gist of his argument went; otherwise black voters would have had to face him more or less unaided (as they did in neighbouring Mississippi, against the ultimately victorious Fordice campaign). I couldn't disagree with the analysis, and I'd noticed that Duke supporters cited Fordice as an example of what might happen when the Jewish media were looking the other way, but I thought there was something wanting in the expression of the analysis. What my new friend was saying, in effect, was: It's okay to slander us, but lay off the Jews if you want to get elected. Might there not be a corollary just as true but more dynamic? Does the successful campaign to isolate Duke not give an impetus to the rebuilding of a black-Jewish alliance? The exemplary work of the Louisiana Coalition Against Racism and Nazism (Suite 915, 234 Loyola Avenue, New Orleans, LA 70112) indicates that it does. In Louisiana there were no black leaders suggesting that Jews are behind the AIDS virus, or that Jews run the redlining banks, or any of that Steve Cokely/Louis Farrakhan stuff. Nor were Jews saying that Duke was on to something when it came to 'quotas'. Confronted with the enemy in plain view, and with Jew-baiting as the father of lies, sectarianism was dispelled. Call me a sentimental old baggage if you will, but faced with Duke's socialism of fools, certain old socialist precepts seemed to me very much in order.

Gurgling horribly at a conference of Holocaust revisionists in 1986, Duke signalled his intention on tape, saying: 'I hate to be Machiavellian, but I would suggest that you don't really talk much about National Socialism. You need to leave your options open.' Reminded that Hitler started with seven men, he exclaimed: 'Right! And don't you think it can happen right now, if we put the right package together?' 'Options' and 'package' are the language of everyday marketing and spin-control and political correctness. They would be more easily exposed, and in more places, if authentic forces talked real politics and made real alliances.

The Nation, December 1991

RIOTING IN MOUNT PLEASANT

I had seen and reported curfews in my time, varying in their severity from East Jerusalem to Romania, but I had never lived in a curfewed neighbourhood until returning home to George Bush's Washington from a trip to Spain in the first week of May. In the morning I was in the Prado Museum, paying a last visit to view the exquisite triumphs of Hispanic culture, high among these the paintings of Velázquez, and of these my personal favourite, *Los Borrachos* – 'the drunken ones'. By nightfall I was being dropped on to a darkened Columbia Road, two miles from the White House, while helicopters thudded overhead and police cars cruised the streets and red-daub signs exclaimed *Justicia*. 'The Hispanics', it seemed, were in revolt.

Dumping my suitcase, I fared forth with my companion and tested the temperature. The local economy depends considerably on drink-selling establishments, and it appeared that the police had rather 'insensitively' shot a local *borracho* – actually the slang for a drunk is *bolito* hereabouts – after he resisted arrest and, depending on whom you believe, either had been handcuffed or, while being handcuffed, had pulled a knife. The authorities were faintly coy on the point, but it seemed that the person pulling the trigger was an African-American female officer, this perhaps marking the first underclass riot to be ignited by a black woman. Signs of black–Hispanic distrust and dislike are not difficult to come by locally, which made rather hollow the newspaper report saying that this was the most intense disturbance in the capital since the murder of Dr King. Destruction did not follow a strictly ethnic pattern, since a fair number of freelance looters came barrelling in from other neighbourhoods as the disorder spread, and Spanish and Korean businesses seemed hit more or less impartially. But where the rioting was in any sense political, it focused on the police. Slogans instructing them in detail on what they could do with themselves were usually signed *FMLN* or *FPL*. And here lies a clue.

The Adams-Morgan/Mount Pleasant district of Washington is heavily inhabited by recent arrivals from El Salvador. The population of one Salvadoran town, named Intipuca, moved here some years ago, having given up life back home as a bad job. (During the fall offensive in San Salvador in 1989, many Washington journalists got better information about the fighting by talking to locals who were using the telephone than they got from the newspapers and TV.) Conversation with these immigrants discloses, without much prompting, the most appalling tales of forced conscription, near-slave labour, the disappearance of family members and the general *miseria*. Nor are the victims often in much doubt as to the source of the hardship and the fear from which they fled. They blame the Salvadoran oligarchy and its patrons in Washington, who donate $450 million annually to the predatory armed forces and have no cash left to spare for Mount Pleasant.

Salvadoran immigrants, in other words, do not come to the United States with the same idealistic consciousness that draws other first-generation settlers. They have an ingrained suspicion, earned in a hard school, and they think of America not as the solution to their problem but in many ways as the source of it. An extra shove from a cop is enough to stir more memories and resentments than most officers are equipped to guess at, however 'community-orientated' they may be. Like all such events once they occur, the Mount Pleasant riot can easily be seen to have been coming for a long time. The District of Columbia is itself a colony, and feels like it. Its citizenry is highly segregated, has no right to vote in congressional elections and enjoys no meaningful self-government. Unemployment and dereliction are high, and though I live at the much nicer end of the curfewed area, I don't have to stroll far to see the rotting housing and badly paved streets with which the budget-conscious authorities can't be bothered. It's one thing to say, as local boosters do, that our quarter of town is so marvellously 'diverse', but this diversity will curdle if it is left in decay. And the reactions were so *dreary*. Friends in the sylvan suburbs said: What do you expect? Local merchants blamed the police for not acting more ruthlessly. 'Community spokesmen' talked of a lack of understanding – or was it a failure to communicate? *The Washington Post* started putting bylines like Escobar and Gomez, not heretofore conspicuous, on its front page. At the street level the Hispanic youths said the blacks were vicious, and the black youths said the Hispanics should learn to speak English. Epithets like 'lazy', 'dirty' and 'thief' were freely traded, showing how easy all that is.

The term 'curfew' derives from Old French – *cuevrefeu*, or 'cover fire'. It's an order from the lay and religious authorities to douse the lights, go to bed and leave the scene to those who know best. Two glimmers of this fire, however, remain hard to extinguish. The first is the sharp reminder of the international division of labour, and the way in which it is managed at both ends. Until now it has been the administration that has decided when we shall get excited about Central America — when we shall favour it with our 'advisers' and jets and mercenaries — and when we shall let it lapse back into a source of underpaid stokers and cleaners. The young Salvadorans who came out to play — *jugar*, as they put it — serve notice that they too want a role in this 'process'. The second point is, relatively speaking, much less obvious. It can be trite to say, as Dr King once did, that 'riots are the language of the unheard'. The initial revolutionary bravura of this riot very quickly degenerated into a sectarian brawl, a war of all against all, with tribal and racial overtones. Walking my own street, seeing the places where I drink being boarded up, being questioned by nervously polite black police officers, I could easily envision a *Blade Runner* future, with no solidarity except that of the block and the gang, with *lumpen* elements toughing it out while the remainder hire private security and practise 'self-defence' tactics. In a way, an exemplary consummation of the privatized, atomized society that, for more than a decade now, has relied on the politics of malign neglect.

The Nation, June 1991

BILLIONAIRE POPULISM

Tuning in to a stuporous *Crossfire*, which matched Ed Rollins and Robert Novak against my droopy liberal Beltway friends Michael Kinsley and James Glassman, I was amused to see Novak slump forward and say, with his customary sneering but off-balanced attempt at condescension, that if you wanted to take the real temperature of the Perot-struck American people, you should go to Ventura Boulevard in the San Fernando Valley and spend some quality time at the 'Ross for Boss' storefront HQ. This challenging recommendation came to me at the end of an exhausting day which I had passed at precisely that address. It's not often that I find myself so far ahead of the conservative–populist curve.

The storefront in question was part of that fragile span that now connects the activist wing or militant tendency of the American Association of Retired Persons to the guerrillas of *Soldier of Fortune* and the Liberty Lobby. (The name for this alliance between Middle America and Mad Dog America used to be 'the Silent Majority', and though I feel dated in mentioning it, Perot was an eager member of the Nixon gang and once hired the notorious Nixonian heterosexual Roy Cohn to persecute a too-pacific design of the Vietnam Veterans Memorial.) The first spokesman I met was Ed. In bold contrast to the contented oldsters who passed the day hanging out ever-larger versions of Old Glory and ever-cuter samplers ('We run on *Perot*-Pane'), Ed was farouche. His shaved head and aviator glasses bespoke the tripwire vet, or someone who didn't mind being mistaken for one. 'Are you aware', he asked me in suggestive tones, 'what the letters SONY stand for?' I said that I had no idea. 'Nobody does,' he replied with satisfaction, 'though a lot of people have tried to work it out.' This looked like my cue. 'What do they stand for, Ed?' 'They mean "Standard Oil of New York", which should give you an idea of what the Tri-lateralists and the Council on Foreign Relations are up to.' 'Uh-huh, and how do you know this?' 'Sources. We have our sources.' Above me was emblazoned a grand banner that said: PATRIOTISM NOT POLITICS. A very old and cherished illusion, dear to the heart of all those who think conservatism and jingoism are common sense. Lucky is the man who has found novelty in this stale idea. Innocent – or deeply cynical – is the man who takes his politics from it.

Let's quickly ink in the postage-stamp space on which the pro-Perot mani-festo can be inscribed. He has upset the rotten apple cart of the one-party 'bipartisan' racket. He has drawn attention to the deficit, and to the free ride hitched by debauched congressional hacks on the dollars of the toiler. He thinks and says that the high agencies of state lie about foreign policy. He inveighs against the influence-peddlers who have made DC into an exorbitant Eatanswill. And he may be the first serious populist who is not – or at least, not initially – toying with the race card. Anything else? Nothing that is con-spicuous, and much that is conspicuous the other way. The affection of certain 'progressives' for the bat-eared tsar conceals – and in some cases reveals – a species of moral exhaustion with democracy. So Perot's keen on the para-military style? Bush and Reagan gave us North and Singlaub. So he's a soldier in the 'war on drugs' and the lock-down state? Jesse Jackson endorses that, too. So he thinks the Constitution is a scrap of paper? What else did John Tower and Ed Muskie and Lee Hamilton do but wipe their butts with it? So he hates the press? What – do you love it?

The fact that a pro-Perot fanatic can so often seem to have the last word, and seem to imbue that last word with a kind of sincerity, is certainly a colossal condemnation of the consensus. But those of us who hated and despised the consensus long before Ross Perot reached for his bottomless pocketbook are more than any others obliged to be sceptical. What does the saviour-in-waiting think about Watergate? About Lieutenant Calley? About General Westmore-land? About the Shah of Iran? About Oliver North and the narcoterrorists he protected? There's a sort of mutual-assured-destruction calculus at work here. The frightened two-party/one-party Establishments dare not challenge Perot on these questions either, because they have good reason to keep quiet and to enforce quiet about the way the Republic has been run these many years.

Perot emerges, however, more as a man who keeps the secrets in a blackmailer's safe than as one who wants to tell the citizens where the bodies are buried.

And where did anyone get the brainless opinion that the super-rich are too wealthy to steal? Such naïveté! This is an illusion even more silly than its more attractive opposite — that the abolition of poverty would diminish crime. Since nobody in this abundant plutocracy has ever really tried to abolish poverty, we have no empirical test of the idealist proposition. But from Ford to Hughes to Iacocca and Trump and the other tycoon redeemers, we have an exact demonstration that nobody is more covetous and greedy than those who have far too much. If Mr Perot is an exception, he has chosen a bizarre way of proving it. In the course of my day spent among the Ross-fanciers, I found that despite their many charms and courtesies they want a revolution that is painless to them. They have the self-pity of the self-satisfied. They have no conception of self-criticism. They are, for the most part, those who thought Richard Nixon and Ronald Reagan were the tribunes of the little guy. One might call this the elitism of fools. The *summa* of this foolishness is to be found in Perot himself: a man who proudly and unoriginally shouts for the United States to be run like a private corporation without having the wit to appreciate that, as his own mediocre career testifies, it is run like one already.

The Nation, July 1992

THE CLEMENCY OF CLINTON

Bertie Wooster's Aunt Dahlia once warned him sternly against having anything at all to do with girls who spelled ordinary names in extraordinary ways: 'No good can come of association with anything labelled Gwladys or Ysobel or Ethyl or Mabelle or Kathryn, but particularly Gwladys.' Presuming this to extend to any Gennifers of the species, it seems that a failure to profit by Aunt Dahlia's counsel is the harshest verdict we are allowed to pass on Governor Clinton's ethical 'judgement'. All right, so these are lax times. That is why the name Gennifer Flowers is notorious and the name Rickey Ray Rector — surely just as euphonious — is not.

When Dostoyevsky wrote about the horrific torture of telling a man the date of his own death, and then keeping him waiting, he said that a man would endure any privation to escape that trap. This wouldn't be applicable in Rickey

Ray Rector's case, since he was lobotomized as a result of a self-inflicted bullet wound. So I suppose it could be said that Governor Clinton was sparing him some of the agonies of the condemned when he refused to grant executive clemency and had him destroyed by lethal injection on 24 January. This was the big *60 Minutes* weekend for the Governor, and you can well imagine that the last thing he felt he needed was idle talk about his softness on crime. One is tempted to be pontifical about this moral contrast – a temptress on one side and an execution on the other, and the mob turning from the medicalized gibbet to the exposed love nest – but actually the Rector case tells us nothing that we do not already know only too well. The lessons are that capital punishment is cruel and unusual, that especially in the South it is applied in a racist manner, that humane and defensible alternatives to it are within easy reach, and that Bill Clinton is a calculating opportunist.

The first point is easily established. As well as degrading the medical profession in a more intimate way than the use of gassing, hanging, shooting and electrocution, 'lethal injection' is just as barbarous as the submodern methods. As the US Court of Appeals for the DC Circuit was constrained to observe in 1983:

> There is substantial and uncontroverted evidence ... that execution by lethal injection poses a serious risk of cruel, protracted death.... Even a slight error in dosage or administration can leave a prisoner conscious but paralyzed while dying, a sentient witness to his or her own asphyxiation.

Point number two is as old as America, and older than Europe. It's well put by Clinton Duffy (another good name, by the way), who, as a San Quentin warden, was witness to more than 150 snuffings. Capital punishment, he said, is 'a privilege of the poor'. Is there any thinking person who does not know what this means in a state like Arkansas? The latest and the driest phrasing of the problem comes from the General Accounting Office, reporting to the Senate and House judiciary committees this very month:

> Our synthesis of the 28 studies shows a pattern of evidence indicating racial disparities in the charging, sentencing and imposition of the death penalty.... In 82 percent of the studies, race of victim was found to influence the likelihood of being charged with capital murder or receiving the death penalty, i.e., those who murdered whites were found to be more likely to be sentenced to death than those who murdered blacks. This finding was remarkably consistent across data sets, states, data collection methods and analytic techniques.

As for point three, it's pretty clear that Rickey Ray Rector met all the customary pragmatic objections to clemency. He had blown half his brain away after committing murder (I take it he was guilty, though miscarriages have been known), and he wasn't going anywhere. He was, by most standards, unfit to plead. He was, in any case, condemned by definition to confinement without parole. In short, by all the usual limiting cases his sentence would have been commuted. And in no other 'civilized' country – such as, for example, any member of the Council of Europe — could he have been condemned to death in the first place.

In discussion with partisans of Governor Clinton's decision to license the lethal injection, I have found myself more powerfully nauseated than in past arguments with rednecks and racists who really don't know any better. The strategic and tactical thinking displayed by his supporters — I asked Clinton himself, but he refused to favour me with a reply — convicts him of a base, hungry cunning. The last two executions he authorized — of John Swindler in June 1990 and Ronald Gene Simmons later in the same month — were both of white men. Thus, it is argued, by staying the execution of Rickey Ray Rector, Clinton would have opened himself to the charge of affirmative action. I cannot offhand think of a more contemptible reasoning. The mentally devastated Rector had to die because two men of a different shade had already been put to death? In other words, never act justly now, for fear you may have to act justly later. After all, justice can set that frightful thing — a precedent. It's also impossible to acquit Clinton of the charge of having people snuffed to suit his own political and career needs. In a candidates' debate on 19 January, the Governor bragged of his firmness in dispatching Swindler and Simmons, as if to pre-empt any Hortonizing of his future ambitions. And when he briefly lost the Arkansas Statehouse to a neolithic Republican named Frank White in 1980, Clinton was considered 'vulnerable' to White's demagogic charge that he was weak on law and order. The element of low calculation in the Rector decision is so evident and so naked that it makes one gasp.

So what is all this garbage about 'the new paradigm' of Clinton's forthright Southern petty-bourgeois thrusting innovative fearless blah blah blah? In a test of principle where even the polls have shown that people do not demand the death penalty, he opted to maintain the foulest traditions and for the meanest purposes. As the pundits keep saying, he is a man to watch.

The Nation, March 1992

CLINTON AS RHODESIAN

The Rhodes Scholarships at Oxford University were set up with the deliberate purpose of advancing the white imperial idea, and especially the Atlanticist version of it. (See, for an extended treatment of this strangely neglected topic, my strangely neglected *Blood, Class, and Nostalgia: Anglo-American Ironies*.) So it was rather a privilege to be at Oxford during the brief space in the late 1960s when the American cousins were less, rather than more, reactionary and clubby than the rest of the ancient institution. I remember the Bill Clinton set in Leckford Road, home base of the concerned Americans. (The rest of us on the left were very impressed that these guys had their own duplicating machine for the swift production of leaflets and bulletins.) Together we marched in the Vietnam War Moratorium parade, where I had the honour of being the speaker. Together we grilled visiting American Congressmen and members of the military–academic complex. Together we raised funds for the support of draft evaders and for the relief of the numberless Vietnamese victims, who still have no memorial. I didn't personally know Clinton, but I knew some in his circle. One of them, a super-serious youth named Ira Magaziner who is now a Clinton campaign adviser, once got me into trouble without knowing it. A telephone message in my shared home read 'RING IRA', and, alas, was still on the table when the cops came round on some bovine errand. I had to waste hours convincing them that I wasn't trying to unify Ireland by force that week.

So I read Clinton's 1969 Vietnam letter with keen interest. Obviously wasted on the colonel to whom it was addressed, it breathes with much of the spirit of those most defensible of days. A lot came back to me when I saw that Clinton had written of 'working every day against a war I opposed and despised with a depth of feeling I had reserved solely for racism in America before Vietnam'. Even more came back to me when I saw the objection to having to 'fight and kill and die' in such a war, with the verbs (as Todd Gitlin pointed out) not only in the right order but repeated as 'fight, kill and maybe die' lower down. Anyone who believes that the objection of the anti-war activists was to personal danger rather than to complicity in atrocity and aggression just wasn't there at the time. Also redolent of the period was Clinton writing: 'I decided to accept the draft in spite of my beliefs for one reason: to maintain my political viability within the system.' 'Within the system' is vintage 1960s, but now I wonder. Who else of that band of brave and cheerful young Americans, so apparently selfless in their opposition to their country's disgrace, was asking: 'How will this play in New Hampshire in around 1992?' The thought gives me the creeps, though perhaps it shouldn't. Someone had to be thinking about the long haul, I suppose. But I would bet a goodly sum that most of those concerned were not planning much beyond the downfall of Richard Nixon. A calculating young man this Clinton, at any event.

How dismal it is to realize that the standard for the Vietnam generation is now at the level of 'What did you do in the Great War, Daddy?' Nobody asks how people *thought* about the war, or what they did to stop it. Worse still, the dumb single-issue question is not being asked by the 'stab in the back' faction, which believes the war was lost by the press, the liberals, the faggots, etc. (No 'stab in the back' movement ever did emerge with any seriousness, if only because Saigon was evacuated, under shameful conditions, on Nixon's watch, thus robbing the 'Who lost Vietnam?' question of its complementary demagogy.) Instead, the question of who did and did not serve has been raised by liberals. It began with James Fallows's essay in *The Atlantic* some years back, where he intruded the matter of class and argued that, absent the *jeunesse dorée*, the war had to be fought by farm boys and blacks. I distinctly remember making this point about the draft, as did the whole of the anti-war movement and in particular the much-forgotten GI Coffee House and GI counselling groups, and I don't remember any other occasion on which a neo-liberal like Fallows has felt compelled to stress that America is a class society. Other liberals began crying before they had been hurt, and strove to pre-empt accusations of cowardice and want of patriotism. In a whole series of pieces, Jack Newfield in *The Village Voice* went after what he crudely called the chicken hawks, the right-wing drum-bangers who had either dodged the war or invented a record in it. Then came Dan Quayle, and a great cry of 'gotcha' from the massed ranks of the right-thinking media. The fools. By the time the jeering had died down, the conservatives had a new standard: Did you go to Vietnam or didn't you? If it's sauce for Quayle, it's sauce for everybody. So we had the degrading contortion of 'supporting the troops but not the war' in the Persian Gulf, and the no less cringe-making elevation of Senator Bob Kerrey for no better reason than that he had believed Richard Nixon until it cost him a limb.

The objection to Clinton ought to be that he is now ashamed of the fine paragraphs in his letter as well as the shifty ones. After all this time, and all the evidence about the conduct of the war, he apparently wishes that he could have borne arms in Vietnam, and perhaps brought back a medal or two. He should be faced with the same proposition that must be confronted by others who yearn for the 'moral authority' of the experience. You picture yourself coming back, perhaps slightly but honourably wounded, with mature reservations that can be cashed in for ethical credit. Do you ever picture yourself taking part in Operation Speedy Express or the Phoenix programme, or wading into My Lai on 16 March 1968? Never mind your own skin for a second; how about being forced to murder people who have done you no harm? Those who did do this, and those who made them do it and lied about the business, are the ones who should be arraigned and questioned. But so wonderful is the exercise of liberal masochism that it has decided to take the whole punishment on itself. Oh well, I suppose it *was* the liberals' war.

The Nation, March 1992

BILL'S BILLS IN MIAMI

Is there anything that Bill Clinton will not do? A few weeks ago, on 23 April to be precise, he came to Florida and, in return for a cheque for $75,000, attacked George Bush from the right. At a rally of Cuban exiles held at Victor's Café in Miami's Little Havana, he publicly endorsed the bill that calls itself the Cuban Democracy Act. Named for its sponsors — Representatives Robert Torricelli and Bob Graham — this legislation mandates the punishment of third countries and US corporate subsidiaries that do business with Cuba. It is opposed by the White House because, among other things, it violates the free trade agreements with Canada and Britain.

'I think this administration has missed a big opportunity', Clinton said, 'to put the hammer down on Fidel Castro and Cuba.' Before anyone had time to think what that opportunity might have been, he added: 'I have read the Torricelli–Graham bill, and I like it.' Not since Kennedy — Clinton's ostensible role model — ran against Nixon and Eisenhower from the right on the Cuba question has any Democrat given such a hostage to fortune. Election-year promises to Cuban ultras in Miami have a way of coming back to haunt those who make them. Not that Clinton as President would be able to stage his own Bay of Pigs. But it's worth being reminded that he's even now advertising his willingness to do so if called upon. Since nobody but a fool imagines that the Miami Cubans are going to vote for anyone but Bush and Quayle this year, one has to assume that Clinton made his rash and unprincipled commitment solely for the cash value. This proves, among other things, that he is cheap and small-time, a shakedown artist on an Arkansan scale. Admittedly, and in the irritating phrase of the moment, $75,000 'ain't beanbag'. But nor is it very much money in return for committing the Democratic Party to a harder line on Cuba than the Republicans are willing to take.

As everyone in Miami knows, the moral author of the Torricelli–Graham bill is Jorge Mas Canosa, the *caudillo* of the Cuban–American National Foundation. Mas Canosa is not a particularly sentimental or democratic fellow. He has recently added two new members to one of his advisory committees at CANF. They are the brothers Guillermo and Ignacio Novo, who were cited in the original indictment for the 1976 murder of former Chilean diplomat Orlando Letelier and his assistant Ronni Moffitt. The FBI considers the Novos to be dangerous, for this action and for others. Is this the kind of company that Clinton wishes to keep? Or does the money take care of that concern? While Clinton talks of bringing the hammer down on Cuba, and while the Castro regime sleepwalks towards an ideological meltdown, and while the right in Miami is sharpening its blades, the American left is apparently content to await developments in a fatalistic manner. One might have thought, given all that Cuba has meant in this century, that we could do better. An increasingly important choice is emerging. For actuarial reasons, let alone political ones, the Castro brothers cannot last much longer. That does not mean that Cuba ought to be abandoned to the Miami variety of counter-revolution, or allowed simply to lapse into misery, or saved up by some gruesome Republican strategist for a possible Mariel-style provocation sometime around October.

In her excellent new book *Cubans: Voices of Change*, Lynn Geldof conducts a series of illuminating conversations with Cubans on the island, in Miami and elsewhere, and with those who have made a study of the revolution. No single conclusion or strategy emerges, except on the matter of the embargo. In that case it is very clear that what we need is not a tighter embargo but no embargo at all. Wayne Smith, the former head of mission at the US Interest Section in Havana, puts it well when he tells Geldof:

> Cuba has the same effect on American administrations that the full moon has on werewolves: they just lose their rationality at the mention of Castro or Cuba.

There used to be, Smith reminds us, three administration conditions for 'normalizing' or 'thawing' relations with Havana. Cuban soldiers had to begin to leave Africa, political prisoners had to be released, and there had to be a reduction in Soviet–Cuban ties. Well, the Cubans have indeed left Angola (having earned warm thanks for defeating the South Africans at the Battle of Cuito Cuanavale, and thus speeding the liberation of the region from apartheid). The number of long-term political prisoners is now in the single figures. And there is only the most notional sense of 'Soviet–Cuban' relations. But the response of Bush and Baker is still No Dice. They and their class cannot forgive the impudence of the Cubans in expropriating American property and in outliving imperial warnings to cease and desist. This leaves millions of Cubans, including many of those interviewed by Geldof, stuck between the vindictiveness of Washington and the increasingly theatrical dogmatism of the autumnal patriarch himself.

Until now, Mas Canosa and the thuggish periphery of his organization have been able to repress dissent among Cuban-Americans, many of whom tell the opinion pollsters that they favour freedom of travel between Cuba and the United States, cultural exchanges, mail and phone service and other obvious and humane improvements. Against this must be set the domination of a faction, supported by the National Endowment for Democracy, that directly brought us the Bay of Pigs, indirectly brought us the Cuban missile crisis, twenty years ago gave us the Watergate burglars and has consistently supplied fanatics and hysterics to the national security state. This faction has now bought, with contemptuous ease, the Democratic nominee. A fine day's work.

The Nation, June 1992

2
THE POWER AND THE GLORY

REALPOLITIK IN THE GULF:
A GAME GONE TILT

On the morning before Yom Kippur late this past September, I found myself standing at the western end of the White House, watching as the colour guard paraded the flag of the United States (and the republic for which it stands) along with that of the Emirate of Kuwait. The young men of George Bush's palace guard made a brave showing, but their immaculate uniforms and webbing could do little but summon the discomforting contrasting image — marching across our TV screens nightly — of their hot, thirsty, encumbered brothers and sisters in the Saudi Arabian desert. I looked away and had my attention fixed by a cortege of limousines turning in at the gate. There was a quick flash of dark beard and white teeth, between burnoose and kaffiyeh, as Sheikh Jabir al-Ahmad Al-Sabah, the exiled Kuwaiti emir, scuttled past a clutch of photographers and through the portals. End of photo op, but not of story.

Let us imagine a photograph of the emir of Kuwait entering the White House, and let us see it as a historian might years from now. What might such a picture disclose under analysis? How did this oleaginous monarch, whose very name was unknown just weeks before to most members of the Bush administration and the Congress, never mind most newspaper editors, reporters, and their readers, become a crucial visitor — perhaps *the* crucial visitor — on the President's autumn calendar? How did he emerge as someone on whose behalf the President was preparing to go to war? We know already, as every historian will, that the President, in having the emir come by, was not concerned with dispelling any impression that he was the one who had 'lost Kuwait' to Iraq in early August. The tiny kingdom had never been understood as 'ours' to lose, as far as the American people and their representatives knew. Those few citizens who did know Kuwait (human-rights monitors, scholars, foreign correspondents) knew it was held together by a relatively loose yet unmistakably persistent form of feudalism. It could have been 'lost' only by its sole owners, the Al-Sabah family, not by the United States or by the 'free world'.

What a historian might make of our imaginary photo document of this moment in diplomatic history that most citizens surely would not is that it is, in fact, less a discreet snapshot than a still from an epic movie — a dark and bloody farce, one that chronicles the past two decades of US involvement in the Persian Gulf. Call the film *Rules of the Game of Nations* or *Metternich of Arabia* — you get the idea. In this particular scene, the President was meeting at the White House with the emir to send a 'signal' to Iraqi president Saddam Hussein that he, Bush, 'stood with' Kuwait in wanting Iraq to pull out its troops. After the meeting, Bush emerged to meet the press, not alone but with his national security adviser, Brent Scowcroft. This, of course, was a signal, too: Bush meant business, of a potentially military kind. In the game of nations, however, one does not come right out and *say* one is signalling (that would, by definition, no longer be signalling); one waits for reporters to ask about signals, one denies signalling is going on, and then one trusts that unnamed White House aides and State Department officials will provide the desired 'spin' and perceptions of 'tilt'.

On ordinary days the trivial and empty language of Washington isn't especially awful. The drizzle of repetitive key words does its job of masking and dulling reality. But on this rather important day in an altogether unprecedented process — a lengthy and deliberate preparation for a full-scale ground and air war in a faraway region — there was not a word from George Bush — not a *word* — that matched the occasion. Instead, citizens and soldiers alike would read or hear inane questions from reporters, followed by boilerplate answers from their President and interpretations by his aides, about whether the drop-by of a feudal potentate had or had not signalled this or that intent. There is a rank offence here to the idea of measure and proportion. Great matters of power and principle are in play, and there does in fact exist a chance to evolve a new standard for international relations rather than persist in the old follies of superpower *raison d'état*; and still the official tongue stammers and barks. Behind all the precious, brittle, Beltway in-talk lies the only idea young Americans will die for in the desert: the idea that in matters of foreign policy, even in a democratic republic, the rule is 'leave it to us'. Not everybody, after all, can be fitted out with the wildly expensive stealth equipment that the political priesthood requires to relay and decipher the signal flow.

The word concocted in the nineteenth century for this process — the short-hand of Palmerston and Metternich — was 'Realpolitik'. Maxims of cynicism and realism — to the effect that great states have no permanent friends or permanent principles, but only permanent interests — became common currency in post-Napoleonic Europe. Well, there isn't a soul today in Washington who doesn't pride himself on the purity of his Realpolitik. And an organization supposedly devoted to the study and promulgation of such nineteenth-century realism — the firm of Henry Kissinger Associates — has furnished the Bush administration with several of its high officers, including Brent Scowcroft and Deputy Secretary of State Lawrence Eagleburger, along with much of its expertise.

Realpolitik, with its tilts and signals, is believed by the faithful to keep nations from war, balancing the powers and interests, as they say. Is what we are witnessing in the Persian Gulf, then, the breakdown and failure of Real-politik? Well, yes and no. Yes, in the sense that American troops have been called upon to restore the balance that existed before 2 August 1990. But that regional status quo has for the past two decades known scarcely a day of peace — in the Persian Gulf, it has been a balance of terror for a long time. Realpolitik, as practised by Washington, has played no small part in this grim situation. To even begin to understand this, one must get beyond today's tilts and signals and attempt to grasp a bit of history — something the Realpoliticians are loath for you to do. History is for those clutching values and seeking truths; Realpolitik has little time for such sentiment. The world, after all, is a cold place requiring hard calculation, detachment.

Leafing through the history of Washington's contemporary involvement in the Gulf, one might begin to imagine the cool detachment in 1972 of arch-Realpolitician Henry Kissinger, then national security adviser to Richard Nixon. I have before me as I write a copy of the report of the House Select Committee on Intelligence Activities chaired by Congressman Otis Pike, completed in January 1976, partially leaked, and then censored by the White House and the CIA. The committee found that in 1972 Kissinger had met the Shah of Iran, who solicited his aid in destabilizing the Baathist regime of Ahmad Hassan al-Bakr in Baghdad. Iraq had given refuge to the then-exiled Ayatollah Khomeini and used anti-imperialist rhetoric while coveting Iran's Arabic-speaking Khuzistan region. The Shah and Kissinger agreed that Iraq was upsetting the balance in the Gulf; a way to restore the balance — or, anyway, to find some new balance — was to send a signal by supporting the landless, luckless Kurds, then in revolt in northern Iraq. Kissinger put the idea to Nixon, who loved (and loves still) the game of nations, and who had already decided to tilt towards Iran and build it into his most powerful regional friend, replete with arms purchased from US manufacturers — not unlike Saudi Arabia today, but more on that later. Nixon authorized a covert-action budget and sent John Connally, his former treasury secretary, to Tehran to cement the deal. (So the practice of conducting American Middle East policy by way of the freemasonry of the shady oilmen did not originate with James Baker or George Bush. As the US ambassador to Iraq, April Glaspie, confided to Saddam Hussein in her now-famous meeting last 25 July, almost as though giving a thumbnail profile of her bosses: 'We have many Americans who would like to see the price go above $25 because they come from oil-producing states.' Much more later on that tête-à-tête.)

The principal finding of the Pike Commission, in its study of US covert intervention in Iraq and Iran in the early 1970s, is a clue to a good deal of what has happened since. The committee members found, to their evident shock, the following:

> Documents in the Committee's possession clearly show that the President, Dr. Kissinger and the foreign head of state [the Shah] hoped that our clients [the Kurds] would not prevail. They preferred instead that the insurgents simply continue a level of hostilities sufficient to sap the resources of our ally's neighboring country [Iraq].

Official prose in Washington can possess a horror and immediacy of its own, as is shown by the sentence that follows: 'This policy was not imparted to our clients, who were encouraged to continue fighting.' 'Not imparted.' '*Not imparted*' to the desperate Kurdish villagers to whom Kissinger's envoys came with outstretched hands and practised grins. 'Not imparted', either, to the American public or to Congress. 'Imparted', though, to the Shah and to Saddam Hussein (then the Baathists' number-two man), who met and signed a treaty temporarily ending their border dispute in 1975 — thus restoring balance in the region. On that very day, all US aid to the Kurds was terminated — a decision which, of course, 'imparted' itself to Saddam. On the next day he launched a search-and-destroy operation in Kurdistan that has been going on ever since and that, in the town of Halabja in 1988, made history by marking the first use of chemical weaponry by a state against its own citizens.

By the by, which Realpolitician was it who became director of the CIA in the period — January 1976 — when the Kurdish operation was being hastily interred, the Kurds themselves were being mopped up by Saddam, and the Pike Commission report was restricted? He happens to be the same man who now wants you to believe Saddam is suddenly 'worse than Hitler'. But forget it; everybody else has.

Something of the same aplication of superpower divide-and-rule principles — no war but no peace, low-intensity violence yielding no clear victor or loser, the United States striving for a policy of Mutual Assured Destabilization — seems to turn up in Persian Gulf history once again four years later. Only now the United States has tilted away from Iran and is signalling Saddam Hussein. Iranians of all factions are convinced that the United States actively encouraged Iraq to attack their country on 22 September 1980. It remains unclear exactly what the US role was in this invasion; but there is ample evidence of the presence of our old friends, wink and nod.

Recently, I raised the matter of September 1980 tilts and signals with Admiral Stansfield Turner, who was CIA director at the time, and with Gary Sick, who then had responsibility for Gulf policy at the National Security Council. Admiral Turner did not, he said, have any evidence that the Iraqis had cleared their invasion of Iran with Washington. He could say, however, that the CIA had known of an impending invasion and had advised President Jimmy Carter accordingly. Sick recalled that Iraq and the United States had broken diplomatic relations in 1967 during the Arab–Israeli Six-Day War, so that no official channels of communication were available. Such contact as there was, Sick told me, ran through Saudi Arabia and, interestingly enough, Kuwait. This, if anything, gave greater scope to those who like dealing in tilts and signals. Prominent among them was Realpol Zbigniew Brzezinski, who was then Carter's national security adviser. As Sick put it: 'After the hostages were taken in Tehran [in November 1979], there was a very strong view, especially from Brzezinski, that in effect Iran should be punished from all sides. He made public statements to the effect that he would not mind an Iraqi move against Iran.' A fall 1980 story in London's *Financial Times* took things a little further, reporting that US intelligence and satellite data — data purporting to show that Iranian forces would swiftly crack — had been made available to

Saddam through third-party Arab governments.

All the available evidence, in other words, points in a single direction. The United States knew that Iraq was planning an assault on a neighbouring country and, at the very least, took no steps to prevent it. For purposes of comparison, imagine Washington's response if Saddam Hussein had launched an attack when the Shah ruled Iran. Or, to bring matters up to date, ask yourself why Iraq's 1980 assault was not a violation of international law or an act of naked aggression that 'would not stand'. Sick cautioned me not to push the evidence too far because, as he said, the actual scale of the invasion came as a surprise. 'We didn't think he'd take all of Khuzistan in 1980,' he said of Saddam. But nobody is suggesting that anyone expected an outright Iraqi victory. By switching sides, and by supplying arms to both belligerents over the next decade, the US national security Establishment may have been acting consistently rather than inconsistently. A market for weaponry, the opening of avenues of influence, the creation of superpower dependency, the development of clientele among the national security forces of other nations, and a veto on the emergence of any rival power — these were the tempting prizes.

How else to explain the simultaneous cosseting of both Iran and Iraq during the 1980s? The backstairs dealing with the Ayatollah is a matter of record. The adoption of Saddam Hussein by the power-worshippers and influence-peddlers of Washington, DC, is less well remembered. How many daily readers of The New York Times recall that paper's 1975 characterization of Iraq as 'pragmatic, cooperative', with credit for this shift going to Saddam's 'personal strength'? How many lobbyists and arms-peddlers spent how many evenings during the 1980s at the Washington dinner table of Iraq's US ambassador, Nizar Hamdoon? And how often, do you imagine, was Hamdoon asked even the most delicately phrased question about his government's continued killing of the Kurds, including unarmed women and children; its jailing and routine torturing of political prisoners during the 1980s; its taste for the summary trial and swift execution?

It can be amusing to look up some of Saddam's former fans. Allow me to open for you the 27 April 1987 issue of The New Republic, where we find an essay engagingly entitled 'Back Iraq', by Daniel Pipes and Laurie Mylroie. These two distinguished Establishment interpreters, under the unavoidable subtitle 'It's time for a U.S. "tilt"', managed to anticipate the recent crisis by more than three years. Sadly, they got the name of the enemy wrong:

> The fall of the existing regime in Iraq would enormously enhance Iranian influence, endanger the supply of oil, threaten pro-American regimes throughout the area, and upset the Arab–Israeli balance.

But they always say that, don't they, when the think-tanks start thinking tanks? I could go on, but mercy forbids — though neither mercy nor modesty has inhibited Pipes from now advocating, in stridently similar terms, the prompt obliteration of all works of man in Iraq.

Even as the Iraqi ambassador in Washington was cutting lucrative swaths through 'the procurement community', and our policy intellectuals were convincing one another that Saddam Hussein could be what the Shah had been until he suddenly was not, other forces (nod, wink) were engaged in bribing Iran and irritating Iraq. Take the diary entry for 15 May 1986, made by Oliver North in his later-subpoenaed notebook.

The childish scrawl reads:

— Vaughan Forrest
— Gene Wheatin w/Forrest
— SAT flights to
— Rob/Flacko disc. of Remington
— Sarkis/Cunningham/Cline/Secord
— Close to Sen. Hugh Scott
— TF 157, Wilson, Terpil et al blew up Letier
— Cunningham running guns to Baghdad for CIA, then weaps, to Teheran
— Secord running guns to Iran

This tabulation contains the names of almost every senior Middle East gunrunner. The penultimate line is especially interesting, I think, because it so succinctly evokes the 'two-track' balancing act under way in Iran and Iraq. That tens of thousands of young Arabs and Persians were actually dying on the battlefield ... but forget that too.

We now understand from sworn testimony that when North and Robert McFarlane, President Reagan's former national security adviser, went with cake and Bible to Tehran in May 1986, they were pressed by their Iranian hosts to secure the release of militant Shiite prisoners held in Kuwait. Their freedom had been the price demanded by those who held American hostages in Beirut. Speaking with the authority of his president, North agreed with the Iranians, explaining later that 'there is a need for a nonhostile regime in Baghdad' and noting that the Iranians knew 'we can bring our influence to bear with certain friendly Arab nations' to get rid of Saddam Hussein. Bringing influence to bear, North entered into a negotiation on the hostage exchange, the disclosure of which, Reagan's Secretary of State George Shultz said later, 'made me sick to my stomach'. North met the Kuwaiti Foreign Minister and later told the Iranians that the Shiite prisoners in Kuwait would be released if Iran dropped its support for groups hostile to the emir. When Saddam learned of the deal, which took place at the height of his war with Iran, he must have been quite fascinated.

It's at about this point, I suspect, that eyes start to glaze, consciences start to coarsen, and people start to talk about 'ropes of sand' and the general inpene-trability of the Muslim mind. This reaction is very convenient to those who hope to keep the waters muddy. It is quite clear that by the late 1980s Saddam Hussein had learned, or been taught, two things. The first is that the United States will intrigue against him when he is weak. The second is that it will grovel before him when he is strong. The all-important corollary is: the United States is a country that deals only in furtive signals.

It is against this backdrop — one of signals and nods and tilts and intrigues — and *not* against that of Bush's anger at Iraqi aggression (he is angry, but only because Realpolitik has failed him) that one must read the now-famous transcript of the Glaspie-Saddam meeting last July. Keep in mind, too, that at this point, just a bit more than a week before Iraqi troops marched into Kuwait, Glaspie is speaking under instructions, and the soon-to-be 'Butcher of Baghdad' is still 'Mr. President'. The transcript has seventeen pages. For the first eight and a half of these, Saddam Hussein orates without interruption. He makes his needs and desires very plain in the matter of Kuwait, adding two things that haven't been noticed in the general dismay over the document. First, he borrows the method of a Coppola godfather to remind Glaspie that the United States has shown sympathy in the near past for his land and oil complaints against Kuwait:

> In 1974, I met with Idriss, the son of Mullah Mustafa Barzani [the Kurdish leader]. He sat in the same seat as you are sitting now. He came asking me to postpone implementation of autonomy in Iraqi Kurdistan, which was agreed on March 11, 1970. My reply was: We are determined to fulfill our obligation. You also have to stick to your agreement.

After carrying on in this vein, and making it clear that Kuwait may go the way of Kurdistan, Saddam closes by saying he hopes that President Bush will read the transcript himself, 'and will not leave it in the hands of a gang in the State Department. I exclude the secretary of state and [Assistant Secretary of State John] Kelly, because I know him and I exchanged views with him.'

Now, the very first thing that Ambassador Glaspie says, in a recorded discussion that Saddam Hussein has announced he wishes relayed directly to the White House and the nongang elements at Foggy Bottom, is this:

> I clearly understand your message. We studied history at school. They taught us to say freedom or death. I think you know well that we as a people have our experience with the colonialists.

The confused semiotics of American diplomacy seem to have compelled Glaspie to say that she gets his 'message' (or signal) rather than that she simply understands him. But the 'message' she *conveys* in that last sentence is surely as intriguing as the message she receives. She is saying that she realizes (as many Americans are finally beginning to realize) that one large problem with the anomalous borders of the Gulf is the fact that they were drawn to an obsolete British colonial diagram. That fact has been the essence of Iraq's grudge against Kuwait at least since 1961. For Saddam Hussein, who has been agitating against 'the colonialists' for most of his life, the American ambassador's invocation of Patrick Henry in this context had to be more than he hoped for.

But wait. She goes even further to assure him:

We have no opinion on the Arab–Arab conflicts, like your border disagreement with Kuwait. I was in the American embassy in Kuwait during the late 60s. The instruction we had during this period was that we should express no opinion on this issue, and that the issue is not associated with America. *James Baker has directed our official spokesmen to emphasize this instruction.* [Emphasis added.]

I used slightly to know Ambassador Glaspie, who is exactly the type of foreign-service idealist and professional that a man like James Baker does not deserve to have in his employ. Like Saddam, Baker obviously felt more comfortable with John Kelly as head of his Middle East department. And why shouldn't he? Kelly had shown the relevant qualities of sinuous, turncoat adaptability — acting as a 'privacy channel' worker for Oliver North while ostensibly US ambassador to Beirut and drawing a public reprimand from George Shultz for doublecrossing his department and his undertaking, to say nothing of helping to trade the American hostages in that city. Raw talent of this kind — a man to do business with — evidently does not go unnoticed in either the Bush or Saddam administration.

Baker did not have even the dignity of a Shultz when, appearing on a Sunday morning talk show shortly after the Iraqi invasion, he softly disowned Glaspie by saying that his clear instructions to her in a difficult embassy at a crucial time were among 'probably 312,000 cables or so that go out under my name'. Throughout, the secretary has been as gallant as he has been honest. The significant detail in Ambassador Glaspie's much more candid post-invasion interview with *The New York Times* was the disclosure that 'we never expected they would take all of Kuwait'. This will, I hope, remind you that Gary Sick and his Carter-team colleagues did not think Iraq would take all of Iran's Khuzistan region. And those with a medium-term grasp of history might recall as well how General Alexander Haig was disconcerted by General Ariel Sharon's 1982 dash beyond the agreed-upon southern portion of Lebanon all the way to Beirut. In the world of Realpolitik there is always the risk that those signalled will see nothing but green lights.

A revised border with Kuwait was self-evidently part of the price that Washington had agreed to pay in its long-standing effort to make a pet of Saddam Hussein. Yet ever since the fateful day when he too greedily took Washington at its word, and the emir of Kuwait and his extended family were unfeelingly translated from yacht people to boat people, Washington has been waffling about the rights of the Kuwaiti (and now, after all these years, Kurdish) victims. Let the record show, via the Glaspie transcript, that the Bush administration had a chance to consider these rights and these peoples in advance, and coldly abandoned them. And may George Bush someday understand that a president cannot confect a principled call to war — 'hostages', 'Hitler', 'ruthless dictator', 'naked aggression' — when matters of principle have never been the issue for him and his type. On 2 August Saddam Hussein opted out of the game of nations. He'd had enough. As he told Glaspie:

> These better [US–Iraqi] relations have suffered from various rifts. The worst of these was in 1986, only two years after establishing relations, with what was known as Irangate, which happened during the year that Iran occupied [Iraq's] Fao peninsula.

Saddam quit the game — he'd had it with tilt and signal — and the President got so mad he could kill and, with young American men and women as his proxies, be killed.

Today, the tilt is towards Saudi Arabia. A huge net of bases and garrisons has been thrown over the Kingdom of Saud, with a bonanza in military sales and a windfall (for some) in oil prices to accompany it. This tilt, too, has its destabilizing potential. But the tilt also has its compensations, not the least being that the Realpoliticians might still get to call the global shots from Washington. Having taken the diplomatic lead, engineered the UN Security Council resolutions, pressured the Saudis to let in foreign troops, committed the bulk of these troops, and established itself as the only credible source of Intelligence and interpretation of Iraqi plans and mood, the Bush administration publicly hailed a new multilateralism. Privately, Washington's Realpols gloated: *We* were the superpower — Deutschmarks and yen be damned.

Generally, it must be said that Realpolitik has been better at dividing than at ruling. Take it as a whole since Kissinger called on the Shah in 1972, and see what the harvest has been. The Kurds have been further dispossessed, further reduced in population, and made the targets of chemical experiments. Perhaps half a million Iraqi and Iranian lives have been expended to no purpose on and around the Fao peninsula. The Iraqis have ingested (or engulfed) Kuwait. The Syrians, aided by an anti-Iraqi subvention from Washington, have now ingested Lebanon. The Israeli millennialists are bent on ingesting the West Bank and Gaza. In every country mentioned, furthermore, the forces of secularism, democracy and reform have been dealt appalling blows. And all these crimes and blunders will necessitate future wars. That is what US policy has done, or helped to do, to the region. What has the same policy done to America? A review of the Pike Commission, the Iran–Contra hearings, even the Tower Report and September's perfunctory House inquiry into the Baker-Kelly-Glaspie fiasco, will disclose the damage done by official lying, by hostage-trading, by covert arms sales, by the culture of secrecy, and by the habit of including foreign despots in meetings and decisions that are kept secret from American citizens. By Election Day the Gulf build-up had brought about the renewal of a moribund consensus on national security, the disappearance of the bruited 'peace dividend' ('If you're looking for it,' one Pentagon official told a reporter this past fall, 'it just left for Saudi Arabia'), and the re-establishment of the red alert as the preferred device for communicating between Washington and the people.

The confrontation that opened on the Kuwaiti border in August 1990 was neither the first nor the last battle in a long war, but it was a battle that now directly, overtly involved and engaged the American public and American personnel. The call was to an exercise in peace through strength. But the cause was yet another move in the policy of keeping a region divided and embittered, and therefore accessible to the franchisers of weaponry and the owners of black gold. An earlier regional player, Benjamin Disraeli, once sarcastically remarked that you could tell a weak government by its eagerness to resort to strong measures. The Bush administration uses strong measures to ensure weak government abroad, and has enfeebled democratic government at home. The reasoned objection must be that this is a dangerous and dishonourable pursuit, in which the wealthy gamblers have become much too accustomed to paying their bad debts with the blood of others.

Harper's Magazine, January 1991

CHURCHILLIAN DELUSIONS

According to the 11 February issue of *The New Republic*, the scene that follows occurred one day after the proud inauguration of Operation Desert Storm.

> Jack Kemp, the secretary of housing and urban development, brought a copy of *Winston and Clementine*, a book about the Churchills, to the Cabinet meeting on January 17, intending to give it to President Bush. Asked to deliver a prayer, Kemp read from the book instead. He chose a passage quoting from Churchill's diary after he'd become prime minister of a besieged England in 1940. 'As I went to bed at 3 a.m., I was conscious of a profound sense of relief. At last I had the authority to give directions over the whole scene.' Churchill felt as if he were 'walking with Destiny, and that all my past life had been but a preparation for this hour and this trial.' Kemp, looking up at Bush, didn't leave his point much in doubt. 'Mr. President, this is the moment you were elected for,' he said. 'Destiny made you our president for this crisis.'

The awful thing about this story is that it is almost certainly true. My own inquiries confirm it, and its author, Fred Barnes, is a reasonably reliable conduit and megaphone for the views of the administration and its membership. Quite clearly, Bush did not see anything extraordinary in the drooling tribute from Kemp. He thought it, on balance, to be no more than his due. So it's come to this. The little putz really does think that he is Churchill.

Further evidence for this preposterous delusion was provided in the State of the Union Message. In the very first paragraph, Bush spoke of standing 'at a defining hour', which is a conscious echo of Churchill's 'finest hour' address of 1940, and went on to speak of 'a great struggle in the skies and on the seas and sands', which is a rather clunky lift from the speech to the House of Commons on Dunkirk, given on 4 June 1940, in which the old man spoke of fighting 'on the seas and oceans ... on the beaches ... on the landing grounds' and, indeed, everywhere else including the streets. This tepid plagiarism was Bush's introduction to luminous, lapidary phrases of his 'own' such as (my personal favourite): 'With a few exceptions, the world now stands as one.' And of course, there was the customary claptrap about 'appeasement'. Judging from a cliché count conducted by *Congressional Quarterly*, Bush's understudies in the House and Senate are not much more fluent or original. In the course of the debate on 'whether' to go to war in Iraq — as if Bush had not already taken the decision — the nation's lawmakers came up with 289 references to Hitler, Chamberlain and Churchill. This compares with 413 mentions of Vietnam. (And those of us who remember Vietnam remember that Ngo Dinh Diem was described by the Kennedy administration as 'the Winston Churchill of Southeast Asia' before gorging himself so heavily on the blood of his own countrymen that he had to be removed from all life-support systems by the CIA.)

What is it about the figure of Churchill that makes him a cult figure on the American right? In the case of some devotees of the cult, such as Caspar Weinberger and, indeed, George Bush, one suspects a ghastly insecurity about their own lack of stature and courage. In the case of politicians in tight corners, Churchill can furnish a thesaurus of quotations far better than the average pinstripe speechwriter. Nixon was a great addict of this style, once remarking:

> 1972, as you know, was a very big year. A lot of things were going on. Winston Churchill once wrote that strong leaders usually do the big things well, but they foul up on small things, and then the small things become big. I should have read that before Watergate happened.

Breathtaking. Robert McFarlane, talking about his Iran–Contra suicide bid, self-effacingly claimed: 'I have to think about people who have overcome apparent near-catastrophic difficulty, from Jefferson to Churchill.' No doubt. And Admiral John Poindexter, caught in an official campaign of domestic disinformation, resorted to Churchill's remark that in wartime, truth is so precious that it must be protected by 'a bodyguard of lies' (of course, Churchill was talking about lying to the *Germans*). Senator John Tower, alleged to be awash in Wild Turkey before his confirmation hearings, had his defenders argue that Churchill was none the worse for a quart or two of cognac. And so it goes painfully on.

Two occasions upon which I know the Munich analogy did not work may be of interest. Plunging into Vietnam behind the French in April 1954, Eisenhower and Dulles sought British support, Eisenhower by writing to Churchill in these terms:

If I may refer again to history; we failed to halt Hirohito, Mussolini and Hitler by not acting in unity and in time. That marked the beginning of many years of stark tragedy and desperate peril. May it not be that our nations have learned something from that peril?

On Churchill's behalf, Sir Anthony Eden (who, whatever his innumerable crimes, had at least resigned over Munich in 1938) recorded:

I was not convinced by the assertion which Mr. Dulles then made, that the situation in Indo-China was analogous to the Japanese invasion of Manchuria in 1931 and to Hitler's reoccupation of the Rhineland.

Two years later, having abruptly discovered that *Nasser* was the new Hitler, Eden appealed to Eisenhower and Dulles for support in his deranged invasion of Egypt. He wrote: 'The West has been as slow to read Nasser's *A Philosophy of Revolution* as it was to read Hitler's *Mein Kampf*, with less excuse because it is shorter and not so turgid.' On this occasion, it was Washington's turn to tell London not to be so stupid. In other words, beware always of the Munich/Churchill rhetoric, as of the ignorant opportunists who make use of it.

On one point, though, Kemp is right. Bush's past life has been 'a preparation for this hour'. His shady years at the CIA, when he helped bury the Kurds; his dirty deals with Israel and Iran and Saudi Arabia when he was Vice President; his secret diplomacy with Saddam Hussein until 2 August last — these qualify him as the Neville Chamberlain, if not indeed the Pierre Laval, of the present disaster. Should he now be awarded 'the authority to give directions over the whole scene'?

The Nation, February 1991

NO END OF A LESSON

The future lay with Major Kitchener and his Maxim-Nordenfeld guns.... At any
rate it had all ended very happily — in a glorious slaughter of twenty thousand
Arabs, a vast addition to the British Empire, and a step in the peerage for Sir
Evelyn Baring.

('The End of General Gordon', in Lytton Strachey's *Eminent Victorians*)

In their anxiety to do nothing that can be construed as reminiscent of
Indochina, US military authorities are avoiding anything in the nature of a
'body count' for Operation Desert Storm. Saudi sources have spoken of Iraqi
casualties, for soldiers only, in the range of 80,000 to 100,000. Other estimates
put the toll as low as 50,000. We may — since nobody's counting — never
know. And it will be for the Iraqi people to decide how many of those deaths
are on what might be called Saddam Hussein's conscience. What interests me,
very much, is the butcher's bill presented to Iraq *after* its acceptance of UN
Resolution 660 and its offer to withdraw from Kuwait under international
supervision. That offer was made through Soviet mediation on 21 February.
On 26 February the following dispatch was filed from the deck of the USS
Ranger, under the byline of Randall Richard of the *Providence Journal*:

> Air strikes against Iraqi troops retreating from Kuwait were being launched so
> feverishly from this carrier today that pilots said they took whatever bombs
> happened to be closest to the flight deck.

The crews, working to the strains of the *Lone Ranger* theme, often passed up
the projectile of choice, the Rockeye cluster bomb, because it took too long to
load. Describing the scene on the jammed roads out of Kuwait, pilot Brian
Kasperbauer exulted: 'This was the road to Daytona Beach at Spring Break;
just bumper to bumper. Spring Break's over.' Others spoke of the massacre in a
predetermined vernacular, calling it a 'turkey shoot' and referring to 'fish in a
barrel'. So it seems odd that the President who ordered the assault should now
say, with that enthusiasm of his that seems so infectious, 'By God, we've kicked
the Vietnam syndrome once and for all.' I'd say that Lieutenant Kasperbauer
had the symptoms of the Vietnam syndrome pretty comprehensively.

The President should have a sharp word to say to Army Sergeant Roy
Brown, who was on the ground at Mutlaa at the scene that the pilots had
created. 'I got a little bit sick when I saw this,' he said. 'This' was mass burial by
the roadside and heaps of bodies. Pull yourself together, Sergeant Brown! This
is no time for sickly introspection and Vietnam masochism! Remember
Admiral Dewey at Manila Bay in 1898. 'You may fire when you are ready,
Gridley,' he remarked before sending the Spanish fleet to the bottom in a

leisurely fashion: what might be called the Philippines syndrome. As General Neal coyly allowed in his post-turkey shoot briefing of 1 March, 'We might have created a picture that they had a better capability than they really possessed.' No doubt.

On the night of the Soviet-brokered Iraqi acceptance of Resolution 660, I had a television debate with Senator John McCain, the Republican hawk from Arizona and (as well as leading Keating-fancier) a prominent enemy of the Vietnam syndrome. He thought the administration could, and probably should, accept the withdrawal offer. So did the moderators, Patrick Buchanan and Michael Kinsley. So let it be remembered that on the eve of the turkey shoot the political heirs of Barry Goldwater, Joseph McCarthy and Adlai Stevenson all thought that a solution short of slaughter was possible and desirable. I felt surreal and lonely as I argued that the Bush–Quayle team would reject the deal. Kuwait was a side-show to them. They wanted to give the troops some desert-fighting experience (after all, America is going to be in this region for a long time to come) and they wanted, in Bush's words, to show that 'what we say goes'.

It now seems that on their way out of Kuwait the Iraqi forces indulged in an additional saturnalia of looting and mayhem. Why shold this in retrospect license the turkey shoot? If they had been withdrawing under international guarantee, how would they have dared to behave in this fashion? But having offered to withdraw, and been told that, no, they had to be driven out, what disincentive existed? If Bush had cared for Kuwait and the Kuwaitis (and the families of the few slain American soldiers), might he not have tried to spare them this final paroxysm? Instead, Iraqis were told that withdrawal was not good enough because they had also to accept all UN resolutions enforcing 660 (such as Resolution 665, which calls on member states to allow the inspection of ships' cargoes; or Resolution 674, which calls for the release of foreign nationals and the protection of diplomatic and consular facilities; or Resolution 677, which mandates the Secretary-General to safeguard a smuggled copy of Kuwait's population register).

I look forward to the editions of *Sesame Street* and other special programming in place of cartoon fare in which American children will have the turkey shoot explained to them. I look forward to more statements from American peaceniks explaining how it is that they support the troops but not the war. I especially look forward to fresh Augustinian tautologies from our churchmen about proportionality in a just war. But perhaps we may be relieved of the necessity for these reassurances. After all, if no misgivings are expressed, where is the need for rationalization? I began with Lytton Strachey because this year of grace 1991 is the year in which the United States has become the direct inheritor of the British Empire in the Middle East. From ruling by unsavoury proxies (such as, before 2 August last, the vile Saddam himself) we have moved into a period of direct engagement and permanent physical presence. Moments like this are traditionally marked by some condign lesson being meted out to the locals. The fantastic, exemplary blood-letting that took place after the ostensible issue of the conflict had been decided was in that tradition. I can hardly wait for the parades. And I now know what the boring catchphrase of the day really means. It means an Order imposed by the New World.

The Nation, March 1991

BEFRIENDING THE KURDS

It was a bad day for the Kurdish nation when the American talking classes began comparing Kurds to Palestinians. Disposability could be the only outcome. At present, the *political* honours are about even; the Palestinians were never even promised any aid, let alone a state, by the administration. Faced, for the moment, with a denial of their right to self-determination, they made the stupid error of placing at least part of their trust in Saddam Hussein. The Kurds, faced with a serious challenge to their right to exist, put their faith in George Bush. And now Iraqi pilots and soldiers are presumably speaking in gross tones about the 'turkey shoots', 'fish-in-a-barrel' hunts and 'cockroach raids' with which they seek to erase the shame of the Kuwait syndrome. This horrific betrayal is remarkable for being one of the few instances of an almost exact historical replay. On my desk since August last has been a bootleg copy of the Pike Commission report, the 1976 findings of the House Select Committee on Intelligence, chaired by Representative Otis Pike. So damning were the disclosures of this report that the White House and the CIA convinced a more than usually supine Congress to suppress it until an executive censorship had been imposed on the text. The reason for this concealing action becomes immediately clear if one turns to the pages that deal with the Nixon–Kissinger programme, begun in 1973, of using the Kurdish insurgency in northern Iraq to destabilize the Baathist regime in Baghdad. With the help of the Shah of Iran and the Israeli Mossad, a policy of aid and encouragement was followed with these predictable results, according to the Pike Commission:

> The apparent 'no win' policy of the U.S. and its ally [Iran] deeply disturbed this Committee. Documents in the Committee's possession clearly show that the President, Dr. Kissinger and the foreign head of state [the Shah] hoped that our

clients [the Kurds] would not prevail. They preferred instead that the insurgents simply continue a level of hostilities sufficient to sap the resources of our ally's neighboring country [Iraq]. This policy was not imparted to our clients, who were encouraged to continue fighting. Even in the context of covert action, ours was a cynical enterprise.

After the Shah and Saddam had temporarily composed their differences at a summit of OPEC nations in 1975, the Kurds were dumped by the Peacock Throne and by its chief ally, the United States. The Baathists moved into Kurdistan in strength:

> The insurgents were clearly taken by surprise as well. Their adversaries, knowing of the impending aid cut-off, launched an all-out search-and-destroy campaign the day after the agreement was signed. The autonomy movement was over and our former clients scattered before the central government's superior forces.
>
> The cynicism of the U.S. and its ally had not yet completely run its course, however. Despite direct pleas from the insurgent leader and the C.I.A. station chief in the area to the President and Dr. Kissinger, the U.S. refused to extend humanitarian assistance to the thousands of refugees created by the abrupt termination of military aid. As the Committee staff was reminded by a high U.S. official, 'covert action should not be confused with missionary work.'

No indeed. The man who became Director of Central Intelligence at the time when the Kurdistan 'operation' was being hastily covered up and the findings of the Pike Commission censored was, of course, George Herbert Walker Bush. Having understood once that the Kurds were to be sacrificed for an alliance with the Shah, what could come more naturally to him than a later sacrifice, on a grander scale, for the sake of an alliance with Saudi Arabia?

In other words, all the drivelling liberals who regard the current nightmare in Kurdistan as a blot on the fine record of Desert Storm have got it exactly wrong. For Bush, the connection between his two public roles (Desert Storm-trooper and Desert Rat) is a direct one. The Saudis desire a Sunni military dictatorship in Baghdad, which could be five or fifty times as cruel as Saddam so long as it is one and a half times as compliant with Saudi Arabian and American desires. And as partner, paymaster and client, what the Saudis want the Saudis will get. How elevating it was to see my old friend Daniel Pipes arguing in *The Wall Street Journal* of 11 April that the United States should not now involve itself too much in inter-Arab and Kurdish disputes. Pipes is a perfect little register of administration opportunism — only a few months ago he was touting the 'Hitler' line and calling for air and ground war. Now he can live with the infliction of a Dresden on the Iraqi people, coupled with the simultaneous protection of the 'Hitler' himself.

Bear in mind what Bush and his 'people' have done. They have smashed the civilian infrastructure of an entire country, deliberately tearing apart the web of water, electricity and sewage lines that held it together. They have killed at least 100,000 conscripts (neatly sparing the 'elite Republican Guard' in order to conform to Saudi wishes) and a vast, uncounted number of noncombatants. They have prepared the way for the next wave of Apocalyptic horsemen in the form of famine and pestilence, described chillingly in reports from the UN and the International Red Cross. Their forces continue to occupy territory in Iraq. This is, perhaps, an odd position from which to declare that they have no interest in Iraqi internal affairs. Consider what has been done to a people with whom the President announced that we had 'no quarrel', and then consider what is now being done to another people in whose name, at least in part, the crusade for freedom was launched. Then do as I have been doing. Make a telephone call to the White House, or to your Senator and representative in Congress, or to the State Department, and ask what has happened to the proposal that there be a war-crimes trial at the conclusion of hostilities. I guarantee that you will derive some dry amusement from the response, though the amusement soon wears off, to be replaced by thoughts of quite another kind.

The Nation, May 1991

ARISE, SIR NORMAN

It seems scarcely worth mentioning, but if you should care to turn up sub-section 8 of Section IX of Article I of that neglected curio the United States Constitution, you will find the following lapidary stipulation:

> No title of nobility shall be granted by the United States; and no person holding any office of profit or trust under them shall, without the consent of the Congress, accept of any present, emolument, office, or title of any kind whatever from any king, prince, or foreign state.

Living as we do in a time when you want to take the poor old Constitution in your arms and just hug it wordlessly while kissing away its tears, the while swearing under your breath to balm and salve its grievous and undignified wounds, the point may seem a slight one. With such huge and garish violations of the spirit and letter of the Constitution as, say, the negation of the power of the purse (and the innumerable major and minor cuts anatomized by Theodore Draper in his book *A Very Thin Line*), who should care about trifles? The pompous answer I propose is that it matters to defend the Constitution in small things as well as big ones, and that the detail above, insisted upon by the

Framers, was a useful and thoughtful one.

To phrase the point in a different way: what the hell did General Norman Schwarzkopf think he was doing when he accepted, while he was still a senior serving officer, a knighthood from Queen Elizabeth II? When Ronald Reagan and Caspar Weinberger went to Buckingham Palace, all dressed up to resemble monkeys on a stick, and subjected themselves to the same ceremony, the emetic influence of the spectacle was the same, but the political implications were not. Both men were enjoying ill-earned retirements by then and could freely go about practising bows and even curtsies if it suited their fancy. The gallant general, though, is another matter. Having helped to reduce Kuwait and southern Iraq to rubble, and having inflicted six-figure casualties upon a people with whom the President said that 'we' had no quarrel, Schwarzkopf now feels qualified to lecture the Congress and the public on their — our — respective duties. He also appears to feel qualified as a historian. Listen to his windy address to a joint session of Congress, unloaded on 8 May:

> We now proudly join the ranks of those Americans who call themselves veterans. We are proud to share that title with those who went before us and we feel a particular pride in joining ranks with that special group who served their country in the mountains, and the jungles, and the deltas of Vietnam.... Finally, and most importantly, to the great American people: The prophets of doom, the naysayers, the protesters and the flag burners all said that you would never stick by us. But we knew better. We knew you would never let us down. By golly, you didn't.

This, even though it comes from a simple Spartan soldier content to do his duty with blind obedience, is a highly politicized speech. The direct invocation of the official White House line on the 'Vietnam syndrome' in the first paragraph can have been inserted only by political authority, and the second part reads (especially the 'by golly' bit) as if dictated over the telephone by George Herbert Walker Bush himself. Note, if you will, the barking reactionary insinuation about 'flag burning' — loony rallying point of two years ago and perhaps one year hence. The general knows, as well as any man living, of the superpatriotic exertions of the American 'peace movement', who seldom marched without a Saran-Wrap of Old Glory. His use of association is both crude and partisan.

There were many liberals and even leftists who, during the run-up to the conflict, pronounced themselves co-belligerents. A popular formulation was 'I prefer imperialism to fascism'. Now, with a ruined Iraq and a strengthened Saddam — not to mention a strengthened Al-Saud and Al-Sabah — we no longer have to choose between imperialism and fascism. By a near-miraculous synthesis, we can have both! While Congress may applaud such an outcome if it chooses, it is ominous that a senior general should give public boosts to this kind of politics and then go on to accept a knighthood from yet another foreign monarch. I called the clerks of both Houses, the library of the Senate and numerous other officials of the world's greatest deliberative body to inquire how, and when, General Schwarzkopf had sought or obtained the permission of Congress for his bauble. It was impressively dispiriting to register the surprise and confusion that were occasioned by the question. No one knew if he had — and indeed, no one knew that he was supposed to. Finally I was referred to a surreptitious little piece of public law, enacted in 1966, that empowers bauble-hungry Americans to accept awards for soldiering 'subject to the approval of the department, agency, office or other entity in which such person is employed and the concurrence of the Secretary of State'. Calls to all offices that are made relevant by this rubric have brought me up against similar bafflement. In other words, while it may not be possible to state with precision that General Schwarzkopf violated the Constitution by toadying to Queen Elizabeth, it is a sure thing that nobody in authority knows or cares whether he did or not.

Increasingly, Congress has become a machine for supplying standing ovations, and the presidency a machine for radiating monarchical waves. 'Checks and balances' refers to the exchange of bribes and emoluments on the floor of committee rooms. Television is a megaphone for the transmission of official wisdom. And the weeks between Memorial Day and 4 July are looking like a banana-republic or 'people's democracy' fiesta, with heavy weaponry being trucked past schoolchildren. The Democrats, according to our licensed pundits, must now search for a candidate who measures up not to the standard of Cincinnatus but to the vainglory of a 'Commander in Chief'. In this cluster of supposedly apolitical and patriotic symbolism, we can see the uses of imperial, military and aristocratic codes in the formation of government by elites and consensus rather than by Constitution.

The Nation, June 1991

JEWISH IN DAMASCUS

You would barely know it, what with the hectic press of nonevents, but Hafez Al-Assad was recently re-elected for a fourth seven-year term as President of Syria. I covered much of the campaign, which made up in colour and dash what it lacked in candidates. Every day and every city — Damascus, Aleppo, Hama — saw its rally, its motorcade, its pledge of allegiance — all of these reported with customary brio in the *Syrian Times*. As you may know,

Damascus has a friendly rivalry with Aleppo about which of them is the oldest continuously inhabited city in the world. Making a sporting allusion to this, President Assad at one point spoke of Damascus as the city in which human habitation had been the longest and most uninterrupted. I fear for the copy editor of the *Syrian Times* who, in next day's edition, quoted the leader as saying that Damascus was the capital in which human life had been 'more often interrupted' than any other. There are misprints, and there are mis-translations, and there is rank sabotage.

The city of Hama in 1982 witnessed its own share of life-interruption. Nobody knows quite how many men and boys of military age were made an end of during that year's uprising of the Muslim Brotherhood, but it could be as many as 20,000. Difficult to imagine now, with the city coated in portraits of Assad and a cluster of modern resort buildings looking out over the old Roman waterwheels. The veil, however, has not descended upon the local women, and the Brotherhood – potentially strong among Syria's Sunni majority – hasn't been heard from since. Indeed, a little farther north, among the Armenians of Aleppo, one heard nothing but praise for Assad's 'firm handling' of the 1982 unrest. Armen Mazloumian, who manages the city's famous old Baron's Hotel (T.E. Lawrence in the visitors' book, along with Agatha Christie and General de Gaulle – you know the sort of thing), pointed to the photograph of Assad in his dining room with some pride. It was not put up under any compulsion, he said, though during the 1982 revolt he had prudently taken it down. Syria's numerous Christians sense that Assad, too, is from a minority religious group – the Alawis – and believe that it is in his interest to protect the smaller confessions. 'I defy you', said Mr Mazloumian, 'to name a Syrian leader who has been better for this country and its minorities.'

So it was that a few nights later, on the biblical street called Straight in the old quarter of Damascus (where St Paul was healed by Ananias, as mentioned in Acts 9: 10–18, and thus gave rise to so many of our present discontents), I waited for the 'Syrian Jews for Hafez Al-Assad' demonstration to begin. I hadn't completely believed that it was going to come off, but Rabbi Ibrahim Hamra was prompt upon his hour. He led a large and well-organized convoy of vehicles (tactlessly described as 'fancy cars' in next day's *Syrian Times*) bearing slogans that were more than fulsome. 'Our blood, our souls, we pledge our lives to you, O Hafez.' That was one of the favourites.

I know what you're thinking. When the Syrian authorities suggest that a spontaneous manifestation of joyful support is in order, it's a case of y'all come, y'hear. Be there or be square. And I'm no dupe. I had been round the Jewish quarter (there are more than twenty synagogues in operation) a few hours earlier. Seeking the opinion of a Jewish pharmacist who was putting up his shutters, I had been asked to forget it in a torrent of words in which the term *mukhabarat* – secret police – had been unmistakable. I'd also heard of a community leader who had received a 'be there or be square' telephone call.

But the crowd seemed quite keen, honking and waving more than was necessary to the Arab passers-by. Then David was there. 'Are you a journalist? Have you been followed? Please come to my home for tea.' I followed the sudden David — not his name — through a warren of streets. Unlocking a door, he offered hospitality and showed me, in order, his collection of Torah books and his souvenir dollar bill, brought in from Brooklyn, from the Lubavitcher Rebbe. Now, I thought, for some uncoerced testimony. 'What do you think of Assad?'

'Well, I really like him.'

Was David a plant or an agent? It didn't seem likely. He told me that he was a religious Zionist who believed that the Third Temple would one day descend from heaven (bang on top of the Al Aqsa mosque, by the way) to herald the Messiah. He spoke warmly of Rabbi Schneerson of Crown Heights. He complained that Syrian Jews were not allowed to leave the country (although his sister had done so) without paying burdensome imposts. He told me the names of two Jewish families imprisoned for trying to leave on the quiet. I doubt that a *provocateur* would have said any of this. But he insisted that the regime was a protection to Jews against the fundamentalists, and that many people at the demonstration were perfectly sincere, including himself. But blood, soul, *life*? What about Assad's view of Palestine? 'The Palestinians should have a part of Palestine' — this said rather grudgingly, since David doesn't like the Palestinian neighbours who live near the Jewish quarter. I forgot to ask about Aloïs Brunner, the Nazi criminal who shelters in Damascus and whose extradition is refused by the government, but I doubt it would have made much difference. David and many of his co-religionists have made a wager in which Assad is, for the moment, the best imaginable leader of Syria. Indeed, many Jews and Christians say they are afraid of what would happen to them if he went. But has a one-man regime that creates anxiety about its successor really brought stability?

With shaloms and adieus, David walked me back to the Bab el Sharqui, gateway to the Christian and Jewish quarter. The streets were very quiet and I didn't see anybody, but I must have been lax because the next day David was at my hotel. 'The *mukhabarat* came round as soon as you left. They wanted to know if we talked about politics.' The true answer to that was — not really. David didn't seem to regret our conversation, but how was I to tell Syrian Baathists that behind closed doors they had unexpected Jewish support? If that support — or any other kind — was truly voluntary, they would have been completely baffled by it.

The Nation, January 1992

In the same week as the famous 'dogfight' between American F-14 fighters and Libyan MIGs, which had newspapers gloatingly headlining yells of 'Good Kill!' from the cockpit, I came into possession of a morbidly enthralling document. It is the recreational songbook of the 77th Tactical Fighter Squadron of the United States Air Force, based at Upper Heyford in England, just outside my old home town of Oxford. It was from bases in England, you will recall, that the gallant attacks on Tripoli and Benghazi were launched in time for the evening news on 15 April 1986. It is also from bases in England that US nuclear bombers and missiles would strike eastward if the day for which they were built should ever dawn. So it was good to have an insight into the minds of the boys who hang around awaiting for that day. Here, for example, is the song 'Phantom Flyers in the Sky':

> Phantom flyers in the sky,
> Persian-pukes prepare to die,
> Rolling in with snake and nape,
> Allah creates but we cremate.
>
> North of Tehran, we did go,
> When the FAC said from below,
> 'Hit my smoke, and you will find,
> The Arabs there are in a bind.'

The themes of this ditty, which are racism, sadism and infantilism (and which reveal the stupid confusion between Arabs and Iranians that is so reassuring to find in pilots who fly over the Middle East), are repeated throughout the book. And as you might expect, the attitude to death is expressed in some hateful attitudes towards women. Nobody likes a bit of filth more than the present author, but I'm not being hypocritical when I say that 'The Ballad of Lupe' strikes me as witless obscenity (punctuation as in the original):

> Down in Cunt Valley where Red Rivers flow,
> Where cocksuckers flourish and whore mongers grow,
> There lives a young maiden that I do adore
> She's my Hot Fuckin' Cocksuckin' Mexican Whore.
>
> CHORUS
> Oh Lupe, Oh Lupe, dead in her tomb,
> While maggots crawl out of her decomposed womb.
> But the smile on her face is a mute cry for more!!!
> She's my Hot Fuckin', Cocksuckin', Mexican Whore.

Intercourse with dead women is a recurrent theme. (Remember, someone went to all the labour of collecting these, writing them down and then committing them to print.) Here is the only quotable verse from 'I Fucked a Dead Whore':

> I fucked a dead whore by the road side,
> I knew right away she was dead.
> The skin was all gone from her tummy,
> The hair was all gone from her head.

The next two verses are so tough that I will break my resolution to spare you nothing. Then it's back to *Top Gun* stuff and the 'Upper Heyford Victor Alert Song', where the crucial stanzas are:

> Leaving the orbit our pits start to sweat
> We'll asshole those fuckers and that's a sure bet
> Burn all those Russkies and cover 'em with dirt
> That's why we love sitting Victor Alert.
>
> RHAW Scope is flashing, the floggers are closing
> SAM's all around us, the GUN-DISH is HOSING
> Flying so fast our hair is on fire
> Killing those Commies is our one desire.
>
> When the shit fills up your flight suit
> and you're feeling had, just simply remember that
> Big mushroom cloud and then you won't feel SO BAD ...

Let us not be too literal-minded about this puerile nastiness. But let us remember that these guys fly expensive planes on nuclear alerts and that, in the same way that some Jewish jokes are funny but Holocaust jokes are not, some versions of humour are not cathartic. In *The Washington Post* for 15 January, the paper's very conservative military correspondent, George C. Wilson, wrote an absorbing article about the lessons of the Iranian Airbus and Libyan MIG incidents, in which he said:

> After decades of extreme caution in the twilight zone between all-out peace and all-out war, the United States is now practicing a policy of shoot first and ask questions later.... It could yank the country into World War III. Gunners firing at radar dots, rather than an enemy they can see with their own eyes, can easily misread dials and screens. But, under current guidance, they are under pressure to act before they can verify a threat.

Wilson added that 'the attitude of our national leaders, especially during the Reagan administration, has evolved into one of "better to shoot first than second"'. If this is so, as it appears to be, then the macro-Reaganism of the commanders seems to be well matched by the micro-Reaganism on offer in the *77th Tactical Fighter Squadron Songbook*. The chief difference at mess level is that the singers evidently wish they *could* see their targets, if only in order to watch them burn up and die.

The songbook is larded with cute Rambo-like quotations and extracts, all of which are based on the conceited notion of pilots as an elite force who can screw all the dead and live women they want. One of these brash quotations reads: 'Only the spirit of attack, born in a brave heart, will bring success to any fighter aircraft, no matter how highly developed it may be.' That, in the age of the computerized 'kill', is of course untrue. But the source for the admiringly cited anachronism is given by the USAF compilers as Adolf Galland. Now, which do you think is more alarming — that the 77th Tactical Fighter Squadron is quoting one of Hitler's chief Luftwaffe pilots knowingly, or that it is quoting him without the faintest idea of who he was? What's the matter with me? Can't I take a joke?

The Nation, February 1989

HATING SWEDEN

The Cold War may wax and wane, China may move from being official enemy to official chum, the armaments industry may succeed in defining the strangest regimes as certified 'moderates', but through it all the American right maintains a permanent, visceral hostility to one small, durable country: Sweden. Ever since President Dwight Eisenhower made a demagogic, philistine attack on Swedish social democracy, contrasting its road to serfdom with the American way and saying that its citizens had an addiction to suicide and despair, Sweden has been a target of ignorant abuse from conservatives. A good recent example was offered by *The New Republic*, which seems more and more to aim at annexing the heavy sarcasm and witless sneering that were once the special signifiers of the *Commentary* style. Furious at Sweden's role in sponsoring talks between American Jews and the Palestine Liberation Organization, the magazine advised its readers that Sweden had been 'neutral' in World War II. So it counts as a minor but instructive irony of history that two recent foreign policy 'breakthroughs' — both claimed as successes by the Reaganites — were made possible partly by consistent, active Swedish diplomacy. Both the 'mutual recognition' strategy for the Palestine conflict and the 'mutual disengagement' solution for the Angola–Namibia one, imperfect as both are, owe a great deal to Swedish efforts and Swedish internationalism.

Sweden's role in the Middle East conflict goes back to 1948 and before, with the appointment of Count Folke Bernadotte as the United Nations' mediator in the partition argument. Bernadotte had been Raoul Wallenberg's deputy during the tense and bitter struggle to save the Jews of Hungary from the Final Solution, and he was personally responsible for securing the release of thousands of Jews from Bergen-Belsen in the closing months of the war. The use of Swedish passports and Swedish neutrality for this purpose would, I imagine, not be thought contemptible by *The New Republic*. I suspect that Bernadotte's exemplary role in the Wallenberg mission would be better known if he had not been murdered on the orders of Yitzhak Shamir in 1948. (Nobody could accuse Shamir of being neutral in World War II. His Stern Gang offered a military alliance to Hitler against the British.) After the 1956 invasion of Egypt, it was a Swede, UN Secretary-General Dag Hammarskjöld, who brokered the Israeli withdrawal from Sinai, thereby saving the stupid Eisenhower's bacon. After the 1967 war the UN mediator was Gunnar Jarring. Sweden's involvement in the question is thus a rather more mature and patient one than most countries could claim. When Sweden's Foreign Minister, Sten Andersson, sponsored the December meeting in Stockholm between Yasir Arafat and some American Jewish activists, he was building on a considerable tradition. One of those present at the occasion told me that the whole atmosphere changed when Menachem Rosensaft, founder and chair of the International Network of Children of Holocaust Survivors, introduced himself and said, 'I was born in a concentration camp. My life was saved by Count Folke Bernadotte.'

In the case of Namibia and Angola, pundits are already queuing up to award the palm to 'constructive engagement' and to the fearlessly soft attitude displayed by Chester Crocker towards apartheid. This is all nonsense. Credit for the agreement belongs to the South-West Africa People's Organization (Swapo), which has refused to buckle despite decades of foreign occupation and has created a movement that does not consider race or tribe when defining Namibian citizenship. Independence on these terms could have been won years ago if it were not for Crocker's procrastination and Reagan's attempt to change the subject to the presence of Cuban forces in Angola. Here again, the United States dogmatically extended diplomatic recognition to one side only – South Africa's. Here again, without 'neutral' mediators American policy would have deservedly become the victim of its own flagrant bias. An important participant was Bernt Carlsson, UN Commissioner for Namibia, who worked tirelessly for free elections in the colony and tried to isolate the racists diplomatically. Carlsson had been Secretary-General of the Socialist International, and International Secretary of the Swedish Social Democratic Party. He performed innumerable services for movements and individuals from Eastern Europe to Latin America. His death in the mass murder of the passengers on Pan American Flight 103 just before Christmas 1988, and just before the signing of the Namibia accords in New York, is appalling beyond words.

In Sweden a few years ago, it was claimed by social scientists and physicians that for the first time in history you could not tell the social class of a child by examining its health record and rate of growth. Ought this not to be considered a modest, even a boring, achievement? It is common sense, after all, that a child should not suffer for its parents' disabilities or misfortunes. (We have preachers and savants who dilate endlessly on the sanctity of family and childhood but who tolerate a system in which a casual observer can correlate a child's social origin with its physical well-being.) I must say that I doubt whether Sweden would be so trusted on the international scene if it did not have a citizenry which turns out to vote at a 90 per cent rate, and has abolished at least the major injuries of a class system. Yet the conservative intellectuals of a country poisoned by empire and riven by class have no shame in denouncing the Swedes. After Eisenhower's sneer came the hate campaign against Prime Minister Olaf Palme for his temerity in opposing the Vietnam War and sheltering draft resisters. (These were the years when Sweden was thought not to deserve an American ambassador.) Further insults were directed at Stockholm because of its opinion about a nuclear-free Europe, and because of its scepticism about the great American anti-'terrorist' crusade. You might think a country that had lost Bernadotte, Hammarskjöld, Palme and now Carlsson to violent death would require no lectures on how the world is a dangerous place, least of all from the forces who have done so much to make it so.

The Nation, January 1989

SQUEEZING COSTA RICA

Sitting in San José in the office of Eduardo Ulibarri, editor of the leading right-wing journal *The Nation*, I ask the usual foreign visitor's question about what makes Costa Rica so 'different'. Why, in an isthmus dominated by empire, reaction and revolution, do we find this contented little bourgeois Eldorado, celebrated for its Nobel Peace Prize, its pluralism and its social tranquillity? I get the usual complacent reply. Costa Rica did not have to fight for its independence from Spain. There was little slavery in the country and no *latifundia* landholdings. The United States Marines never troubled to occupy Costa Rica. So, by judicious balancing and trading, the country has been able to maintain neutrality without a standing army for most of the postwar period. Thus runs the anthem of self-congratulation. However, there was until recently one salient factor that negated all or most of the above. John Hull, a US citizen with Costa Rican nationality, operated a notorious *latifundium* on the border of Costa Rica and Nicaragua. From this vast ranch he ran a private army and airstrip on behalf of the US national security network. He worked tirelessly, in concert with elements in the Costa Rican Establishment, to bring the country into war with Nicaragua and to justify a US invasion. In 'Minority Report' of 8 May 1989 I set out what was known about John Hull: his regular stipend from Oliver North, his meetings with the Contra network in the office of then-Senator Dan Quayle and his eventual arraignment on charges of drug- and gun-smuggling by a Costa Rican court. Mr Hull has since been granted bail on grounds of age and health, and has used the opportunity to fly to his native Indiana. It is considered unlikely that Mr Hull will return for trial, even after having proudly maintained that he is a Costa Rican patriot.

Still, Costa Rican democracy and independence are not so utterly com-promised that nothing can be done. There are brave politicians and journalists here who have been pressing for a dignified inquiry in the face of some quite forbidding discouragements. This past July the Drug Commission of the Legis-lative Assembly presented a detailed report which has since been endorsed by a vote in the full legislature and which recommends that five citizens of the United States be barred permanently from setting foot in Costa Rica because their activities had led to the breaking of national laws and to the establishing of narcotics-running networks. The five are former Lieutenant Colonel Oliver North, Major General Richard Secord, Admiral John Poindexter; former US ambassador Lewis Tambs; and former San José CIA station chief Joseph Fernandez. This decision got barely a notice from the US press, although it might be thought a matter of public interest that five such well-known gentlemen are *persona non grata* on the soil of a friendly neighbouring state — and for involvement on the wrong side of the Drug War at that. Instead, we have an Attorney General who intervenes to protect Mr Fernandez and to argue that everything he did was classified.

The US Congress could learn a lot from its Costa Rican counterpart about the conduct of honest investigations of wrongdoing in high places. But it had better be quick. The Bush administration, which fought so valiantly against democratic invigilation both in Washington and in San José, is now intruding again in the affairs of Costa Rica to make sure that such impudent displays of independence do not recur. The National Endowment for Democracy has been busily pumping a flow of cash in the direction of the United Social Christian Party in preparation for next year's elections. This party and its affiliates were and are generally opposed to the tentative neutrality of Presi-dent Oscar Arias, and to the policies that led to his Central American peace plan. Modest though that plan certainly was, it did deprive the national security gangsters in Washington of some of their room for manoeuvre, and the support for Arias's political enemies looks very much like revenge for that insult. John Biehl, a former adviser to Arias, once described as 'a parallel state' the network of alliances and institutions created to serve US interests without the inconvenience of democratic scrutiny. Its sharpest symbol is the enormous fortified compound, surmounted by a rooftop helicopter pad, which houses the Agency for International Development operation in Costa Rica. AID subventions have been made conditional upon a hectic process of what is euphemistically termed 'privatization', with the beneficiaries tending to be tried and tested political allies rather than tried and tested going concerns. Given that Costa Rica received more than a billion dollars in aid between 1983 and 1987, more than in the three preceding decades combined, it can be understood that it was difficult for a relatively underdeveloped political establishment to resist 'quid pro quo' pressures aimed at its neutrality. A small example of the suggestive influence of foreign aid is provided by the $375,000 'business loan' advanced by the Overseas Private Development Corporation, a US lending agency, in 1984. The loan went to a Costa Rican farmer named John Hull.

A tap that can be turned on can also be turned off. As Frances McNeil, former US envoy to San José, told the House Foreign Affairs Subcommittee in 1987, when AID started suddenly to be less generous: 'It is impossible to avoid the suspicion that Costa Rica's "less favored nation" treatment is a form of revenge for having the temerity to disagree with us about the *contras*.' Costa Rica's most famous boast — its nonmilitary character — has also been compromised by this covert dependency. Between 1981 and 1985 the 'security forces' grew by more than 250 per cent, fuelled by a large US military aid programme and augmented by politically 'reliable' civilian elements such as the ultra-right paramilitary movement named Free Costa Rica. (Martha Hone's book *Undermining a Friend* has much new and connected detail.) The Costa Rican idyll, in other words, is under sustained attack from those who used to make the most noise about defending it.

The Nation, December 1989

THE SAVIOUR

The following exchange took place at President José Napoleón Duarte's press conference in San Salvador on 29 October, three days after the murder of Herbert Ernesto Anaya, who headed the unofficial Salvadoran Human Rights Commission:

Douglas Farah (United Press International): Mr President, I would like to know why you think you will be able to investigate the killing of Mr Anaya when there are tens of thousands of political murders in the past year you have been unable to resolve.

Duarte: The question is irrelevant. It seems to me rather to be an insinuation. I came to power three years ago and since that time I have been trying to reduce to a minimum the process of criminality that had opened in the country. You cannot demand of me investigations in a state which all Salvadorans recognize as a time of gigantic tension, as in the US you cannot demand — I do not know if you are North American, but tell me who killed Kennedy or who killed Lincoln? And I could mention many other cases of people who were killed and the case never solved.

One could make a number of observations about this reply. First, of course, we do know who killed Abraham Lincoln. And though many in the United States do go missing every year, it is rare to find that they have been kidnapped and murdered by the Highway Patrol or by an auxiliary police force attached to the IRS. Then one has to notice the uncharacteristic modesty of the third sentence. Duarte has been president for only three-and-a-half years, but before that he was the leading civilian member of the ruling junta. His time in office coincided with the death of no fewer than 30,000 of his fellow citizens. All these crimes, except for the murder of Archbishop Romero, have now been amnestied.

If Duarte were anywhere near as popular in El Salvador as he is in the United States, he would be a very successful politician indeed. What is striking about him is the extent to which he believes in his own image: an image reflected in the covers of *Time* rather than in the hearts and minds of Salvadorans. On his latest visit to Washington, in October, he embarrassed even his fulsome hosts by stooping and kissing the American flag. There is hardly a wall in downtown San Salvador that does not bear an ironic tribute, in poster or graffito form, to this abject gesture.

Duarte is suffering from an advanced case of the Sadat syndrome, an affliction for which there is no known cure. Typically, the victim begins to count political success in terms of the number of foreign celebrities visited or received. Cravings for US military aid are experienced, and become tragically harder to assuage even when the dosage is increased to life-threatening levels. One dinner at the White House is imagined to equal fifty meetings with domestic political groups. A dinner at the White House with wife equals a hundred such humdrum encounters. The sufferer begins to fetishize editorials in US newspapers while ignoring the humbler indigenous prints (an admittedly easy task in San Salvador, where *El Independiente* and *La Cronica del Pueblo* have been bombed and closed, and the latter's editor butchered). In the final stages of the syndrome the patient starts to make excuses for the US Administration that even the Administration is too shy to offer.

Before the flag-kissing photo opportunity Duarte had accused the Sandinista government in Nicaragua of being responsible for the civil war in El

Salvador, a claim that no Washington hawk has had the face to make. He has stated publicly that he was quite unaware of the use of Ilopango Air Force Base for the illegal supply of Contra forces. Ilopango is about twenty minutes by car from the centre of San Salvador and is the headquarters of the Salvadoran Air Force. If Duarte did not know that it was being used to attack Nicaragua, then he has effectively ceded power to an arrogant foreign patron. If he did know, while affirming the contrary and while arguing that the flow of arms was in the other direction, then he has effectively ceded power to an arrogant foreign patron.

In true Sadat style, Duarte has also 'written' a book, entitled *Duarte: My Story*. This volume was co-authored by Diana Page and published only in English. It is dedicated to, among others, the Boy Scout movement (a large statue to Baden-Powell is one of the unexpected delights of the capital's bourgeois district) and is not available in El Salvador. When Sadat produced a similar book in the aftermath of his Nobel Prize, he was careful to excise most of the shady political past he had described in an earlier volume. Duarte, who is jealous of President Oscar Arias's Nobel Prize and who claims credit for the Arias 'peace process', chiefly imputes shadiness to others. He contrives to imply that many of the death squad killings have been the work of the guerrillas, who seek to magnify the contradictions. Experience and investigation have shown that there is no need to simulate rightist atrocities in El Salvador. I had the opportunity to ask Maria Julia Hernández, the tireless head of the human rights office Tutela Legal at the archbishopric, if she thought that the left had indeed been shooting the civilian opposition as a provocation. Her pretended merriment did not mask contempt for the suggestion.

On 15 November, the last Sunday of my stay, Archbishop Arturo Rivera y Damas preached a homily in which he warned that the death squads were back in business. He gave details of several cases, including the murder of a church worker. Common to all the slayings, according to Tutela Legal, is the involvement of army and police personnel. President Duarte is forced to describe complaints of this type as 'irrelevant'. He has taken the side of the armed forces, and the armed forces have a short way with politicians who are halfhearted about them. When US Ambassador Edwin Corr, speaking from his bunker in the centre of the city, said that he saw his job in El Salvador as 'making sure the cattle get to Cheyenne', he had hit on more than a phrase with which to offend all Salvadorans. He was trying to say that there would be no military coup on his watch. In a way, there hasn't been one. The armed forces have annexed the Christian Democrats without the trouble or awkwardness of a seizure of the Presidential Palace.

The Nation, December 1987

TIO SAM·

A feature, not just of the age of the end of ideology, but of the age immediately preceding the age of the end of ideology, is that of the dictator who has no ideology at all. While Pinochet had a Manichean or Francoite anti-Communism to inform him, and Vorster and Verwoerd had the dream of white Christian destiny, and the Greek colonels the rather more insipid rhetoric of 'Greece for Christian Greeks', the decay of outright fascist systems was quite a rapid and complete one — much more rapid and complete than Nicos Poulantzas, for example, had envisaged in *La Crise des Dictatures*. On the other side of the Ribbentrop–Molotov hyphen, while it is true that men like Mikhail Suslov and Mao Tse-tung may have gone to their graves thinking of the Leninist state as history exemplified, it is not believable that Edvard Gierek or Milos Jakes or any of the other 'Vodka-Cola' general secretaries (Erich Honecker partially exempted) thought anything of the sort. When the Army deposed the Party in Poland in 1981, Susan Sontag was quite right to say that a new stage of decadence had been reached, though her ironic formulation of 'fascism with a human face' was misleading. By that stage, Ceauşescu and Kim Il Sung had taken the personality cult beyond the baroque, insisting on the study only of their own thoughts and lives.

In the Third World, where ideology was and is shaded by the exigency of competition for advanced weapons and aid, a crop of dragon's teeth was sown, and has sprouted into a toothsome harvest. I am writing this in the Saudi Arabian desert, just outside a gargantuan American airbase. The enemy across the border is the leader of a party, calling itself Baath or 'Rebirth', which blazons the sloganized trinity of 'Unity, Freedom and Socialism'. In *The Republic of Fear*, the pseudonymous Iraqi critic Samir Al-Khalil makes an eloquent case for regarding this 'Socialism' as National, self-consciously based on dogmas of *Führerprinzip* and total mobilization. Iraq has long enjoyed a friendship treaty with the Soviet Union, intimate contacts with China and trading relations with several capitalist states, notably France, the United States and Germany. Its own best claim is to represent thwarted Arab nationalism, but lately Saddam Hussein, once a stout secularist, has taken to posing as the special defender of pristine Islam against the unbelievers. If war comes, it will be a contest of weapons systems rather than of ideas and principles, and in the short term some hybrid of capitalism and feudalism will probably be the winner.

R.M. Koster and Guillermo Sanchez Borbon, respectively an American novelist and a Panamanian columnist, have done well to reinstate the antique

---

·Review of R.M. Koster and Guillermo Sanchez Borbon, *In the Time of the Tyrants: Panama 1968–89*, London 1990.

term 'tyrant' over the modern, purposeful word 'dictator'. Tyrants, after all, are in power in order to be in power. Like other human beings, they may desire to invest their actions with something of the noble and the grandiose. They may wish for commemorative poems and statues — the Ozymandias complex. But they are hopelessly old-fashioned, and any reader of Robert Graves could mentally update the plot as they expire in a chaos of money laundries, drug deals and palace feuds. Omar Torrijos and Mañuel Noriega, the two tyrants of this title, belonged to a specific breed that might be termed the unpatriotic or psuedo-nationalist. Even before Nelson Rockefeller reported to Richard Nixon that in Latin America the military was 'the essential force for constructive social change', the United States had ruled the Monroe Doctrine states by means of the purchased soldier — 'the officer with the trailing sword', as Neruda once characterized him — mostly commanding armies in countries that had no external enemies except the United States itself. The exceptional convenience of this arrangement, with arms sales in one direction, political compliance in another and Washington as broker in both cases, was best exemplified in the rule of the Somoza family. But the headquarters of the whole continental operation, the Escuela de las Americas, which served as the Sandhurst of every Latin American oligarchy, was always in Panama. And Panama was itself an American creation, or rather, invention — an isthmian limb snapped off from the territory of Colombia by Theodore Roosevelt in order to enable the building of an American canal to rival Suez.

The military parasites had to affirm *something*, and they also had to prove, perhaps even to themselves, that they were not mere hirelings and puppets. The cheapest form of radicalism and *dignidad* on offer was a species of anti-Yanqui populism, the option chosen by balcony-merchants like Perón and opportunists like Torrijos and Noriega. The authors are very acute in diagnosing this Panamanian version of the socialism of fools:

> Torrijos was going to play clever, bold Jack-in-the-beanstalk while Uncle Sam grimaced and growled, 'Fee, fie, fo fum!' and get all kinds of political benefit from the masquerade — in Panama, in Europe, in the Third World and (pricelessly) among liberals in the United States.
>
> But who had helped him become Panama's tyrant? ... Who'd helped his troops wipe out democratic insurgents? Who'd turned a blind eye when his troops 'mistreated' American citizens? And who was going to lavish AID funds on him and urge the banks to lend him more, even as he blustered against the yanquis? *El Coloso del Norte*, that's who, his gentle, mild, indulgent *Tio Sam*. And he never forgot which side of the bread had the butter. When the United States needed a favour, Torrijos came running. So let's have those hats off for the fake revolution.

Since the secret — of feigned defiance and real abjection in the face of the master — was actually a guilty one, woe betide anyone who blurted it out. Koster and Sanchez may at times seem too graphic in their account of the filthy cruelty visited upon dissidents, but there is a purpose to their detailing of it. The tyrants could not bear the ridicule and humiliation that came with exposure, and felt it as a challenge to the core of their masculinity — a core which, especially in Noriega's case, appears to have been rather shaky to begin with. A concentrated rain of pain on the testicles and prolonged rectal violation were the specific, repetitive means of tyrannical macho revenge. Dr Hugo Spadafora, the opposition leader, was martyred in this way during a feast of sadism which precipitated both these authors and others into a final contest with Noriega.

Dr Spadafora knew three things worth knowing about Noriega. First was his complicity in the regional narcotics cartel. Second was his involvement in the smuggling of weapons. Third was the fact that, despite much demagogy about Yanqui imperialism, he was doing both these things to oblige the national security *apparat* in Washington. Since Noriega's 'arrest' by US forces last January, it has been admitted with official embarrassment that he had at different times worked, for pay, for both the Drug Enforcement Administration and the Central Intelligence Agency. Koster and Sanchez expertly flesh out the nature of this commitment. Here is one of their best encapsulations:

> The very concept of a war on drugs became meaningless with Black Eagle and Supermarket, the CIA operations whereby weapons were secretly supplied to the contras in contravention of congressional strictures. In Black Eagle, Israeli stocks of captured PLO weapons were moved from Texas to Central America by means of Noriega's network of hidden airstrips.... Observe the delicate touch Noriega added: 'Instantly grasping that drug pilots would be sitting in the cockpits of empty planes for the return flights, Noriega alertly filled the void by arranging for them to carry narcotics.' The CIA, of course, was buying the gas, as well as protecting the whole operation against the impious meddling of law-enforcement organisations, which put the US Government in the cocaine trade — that is, in the war against drugs but on the wrong side.

Ultimately, and like many pimps and hired guns before him, Noriega got greedy and went into business on his own. He thought he 'had' enough on *Tio Sam* for protection, and for a time he did (all Koster and Sanchez's allegations are confirmed by congressional and other testimony). But at length Washington decided to put down its overmighty baron, who was getting ideas of his own about the Canal. Noriega, in extremity, reverted even more to the nationalist vernacular of Torrijos and even made some inept lunges at 'solidarity' with the Cuban and Nicaraguan revolutions against which he had worked. (They, in their turn and also in some extremity, made crass declarations of 'solidarity' with the foe of the gringos.) That did it. Just as the 1989 revolutions were removing post-ideological Communism from Europe, George Bush mounted Operation Just Cause. The authors neither endorse nor oppose the invasion, regarding it as the ineluctable outcome of the quarrel between senior and junior partners. In justifying Just Cause, Bush 'mentioned Mañuel Noriega and democracy. He was against the first and for the second — George Bush of the Reagan–Bush Administration that moved heaven and earth to help its protégé and accomplice Mañuel Noriega steal the 1984 Election.'

Even as I write, Mañuel Noriega is in a Miami prison, festooned with Miami lawyers like any other capo. The US government prosecutors have offered him the most amazing plea bargain in modern geopolitics, openly saying that he can use his own (temporarily impounded) foreign bank accounts to hire counsel if he will agree not to testify about his past service for the CIA and the Drug Enforcement Agency. A few stunned protests have been made about this, and about the recent disclosure that conversations between Noriega and his existing attorneys were illegally bugged. But more than one country's machismo is challenged and degraded by the revelation of a furtive collusion, and Just Cause has ceased to be celebrated. The more recent discovery of mass graves in Panama City, crammed with the uncounted civilian dead of the operation, likewise attracted little attention. All energies were concentrated on the spot in the sand where I am sitting: the bridgehead against yet another former official friend and new official foe.

A coda. Is this Torrijos the same genial populist who was hymned and wreathed by Graham Greene and Gabriel García Márquez? The plucky patriot who stood up for his people and his Canal? Yes, it is the torturer and traitor and bribe-taker himself. Nothing better illustrates the decay of ideology than the nonfiction composed for the General by these two fabulist heroes of the 'progressive' universe.

London Review of Books, December 1990

THE AUTUMN OF THE PATRIARCH

In a celebrated address to the Cuban writers' union just after the revolution, Fidel Castro claimed that his policy on the freedom of conscience and creativity was ample, generous, distinctive – and limited. 'Within the revolution – everything,' he said. 'Outside the revolution – nothing.' Over the years, this contradiction resolved itself, as it had to, into the even simpler proposition that Castro would decide what was and was not 'within the revolution'. The denuding of Havana's publishing houses, the flight of authors like Padilla, the decline of once-stimulating papers like *Revolución* and the sporadic heresy hunts against artistic dissent (often unpleasantly disguised as a campaign against homosexuality) all followed as a more or less mathematical certainty from this original misconception or fallacy. There have been some on the left — not as many as the neo-conservative demagogues suggest, but still a number — who have explained, if not exactly justified, this line. Their reasoning was not, as is often said too easily, of the classic Stalinist kind, because it was couched in tones that made allowances for the underdog rather than excuses or even paeans for the superpower. Cuba, ran the argument, was a small country that had repeatedly been invaded and despoiled by the United States (true). It had undergone an authentic popular revolution (true). As a direct result, it had been subjected to an unceasing campaign of sabotage and destruction, including the hiring of Mafia agents by American Presidents for the purpose of political murder (true). Therefore, it was entitled to impose censorship as a matter of wartime exigency, just as any capitalist country would do in similar circumstances. (The argument usually elided the historical attitude of the left towards wartime or 'national security' censorship in capitalist nations.)

I wonder what those who have flirted with this logic will make of a decision reported in *Granma*, organ of the Central Committee of the Communist Party of Cuba, on 4 August. Portentously headlined 'An Unavoidable Decision, Consistent With Our Principles', it announced a ban on the circulation of two foreign publications, both of which are indicted for 'justifying bourgeois democracy as the highest form of popular participation' and flaunting 'a fascination with the American way of life'. The names of the two foreign publications are *Moscow News* and *Sputnik*.

When Karl Marx was an editor of the *Rheinische Zeitung* he published some energetic essays on the stupidity of censorship, stressing the snivelling furtive-ness of the censor and lampooning the idea that such a cretinous practice should be employed against the circulation of ideas. (It used to be the fashion of Parisian Stalinists to say that this was just the immature, 'humanist' Marx; but I notice that this faction has lately been taking the opportunity to shut up voluntarily.) The Cuban comrades have now set out, paradoxically, to vindicate the young Marx. Cuba, they say in their statement, 'is fighting for socialism and communism, and therefore publications like these do not correspond with our reality or interests and are not for us'. In other words, we are menaced by Yankee imperialism on all sides; the revolution must be vigilant; therefore we forbid the publications of the Muscovite intelligentsia. Say what you will about this non sequitur, you are bound to admit that it is world-historical.

When I was last in Cuba, during the Havana film festival of 1987, the consensus among the braver souls in the writers' union was that things were improving. The cultural commissar atmosphere, so calamitous in the 1970s, was being dispelled. Everybody, not just the relatively privileged element with access to foreigners (if you call that privilege, which is itself an interesting question), mentioned the significance of *Moscow News*. Long a mouldering object in the bales of mediocre Sovet mags that had a shelf life of close to infinity, this had become the pick of the hundred flowers. Now, those in Havana who are curious about the great developments in the Soviet Union and beyond have been told, in one clumsy, casual edict, that it is none of their business. What an insult! Much graver, I would say, than the supposed offence often cited by Castroites, to the effect that 'outside' critics should not 'impose' their values on the Cubans.

I can anticipate one possible defence of the censorship. Since 1968, when Castro (I don't call him Fidel, as some people do, because I don't know the guy) supported the occupation of Czechoslovakia, Cuban partisans have resented the charge that their country is a Soviet stooge. Well, here's a fine disproof of that slander: Soviet papers can be banned as well as any other kind. Cuba takes orders from nobody! In the thoughtful silence that follows this pronouncement, who knows what uncontrolled ripostes may be forming. Actually, despite its sorry endorsement of the Brezhnev doctrine, Cuba very often did pursue a course independent of the Soviet Union. In the cases of Angola and Nicaragua it did so quite honourably, in my opinion, and in the case of Ethiopia very much less so. That can be debated. But the key soldier in all three campaigns was General Arnaldo Ochoa Sánchez, and if one year ago you had dared suggest that he was a drug cartel collaborator of Oliver North proportions you would, if you were a Cuban living in Cuba, possibly have been shot. Possibly on Ochoa's orders. Today, if you affirmed the contrary and said that Ochoa was a hero of the revolution, you would be jailed. Censorship is instituted precisely to mask distinctions of this kind, and to make sure that bad news can come only from the same source as good news, which is from on high. Remember Joseph Cotten in *The Third Man*, who keeps being asked why his hand is bandaged? 'A parrot bit me,' he says, with increasing exasperation. Living under censorship is like being permanently hectored by a parrot and occasionally savaged by it. Be ready to denounce tomorrow what we made you affirm yesterday.

Spare me the letters that remind us all that Cuba has a good health-care system and has abolished illiteracy. A healthy, literate people do not need to be told what they can read — least of all by those who once obliged them to read and revere the very output that is now forbidden.

The Nation, September 1989

THIRD THOUGHTS

There was something implicitly smug about the naming of the Second Thoughts Conference, just as there was something unmistakably sinister about its deliberations. The presumption of the title was that revisionism — in this case, post-New Left revisionism — is necessarily more thoughtful. The discovery made by those attending was that only one kind of thought is considered to be wholesome and hygienic. This came as a shock to those who signed up with genuine second thoughts about their former commitments. (Who believes everything that he or she believed in 1968? Back then, the Democrats were trying to save Vietnam from joining the Chinese empire.) In the category of 'genuine' I include David Hawk, a conscientious survivor of the movement against the Indochina war; Jeff Herf, a former SDS activist turned cautious military strategist; and Fausto Amador, half-brother of Carlos Fonseca and an original member of the Sandinista movement. These three were among the self-critical. But the tone was set by those who are now able to be critical only of others.

David Horowitz and Peter Collier, former editors of *Ramparts*, have come all the way from pink Pampers through Black Panthers to one-dimensional Reaganism. With a bit of effort, they could succeed in their current modest ambition, which is to become quite nasty. They make a good fit with the diagnosis offered by Isaac Deutscher in his 1950 review of *The God That Failed.* Speaking of a certain kind of former Communist, Deutscher wrote:

> He is haunted by a vague sense that he has betrayed either his former ideals or the ideals of bourgeois society; like Koestler, he may even have an ambivalent notion that he has betrayed both. He then tries to suppress his sense of guilt and uncertainty, or to camouflage it by a show of *extraordinary certitude and frantic aggressiveness.* He insists that the world should recognise his uneasy conscience as the clearest conscience of all. [Emphasis added.]

This disordered mentality got a chance to reveal itself at its most putrid on the afternoon of the first day. Ronald Radosh, announcing dramatically that we all face 'a massive Sandinista propaganda machine' in America, gave a lengthy account of how he had personally eavesdropped on a conversation in Managua between Alejandro Bentaña, director of the Nicaraguan Foreign Ministry, and Professor William LeoGrande of American University in Washington. Evidently thrilled by his own prowess as a fink, Radosh told the crowd that the two men had been discussing such dark matters as the political line of Michael Harrington and the editorial policy of *Tikkun.* Then, he alleged, LeoGrande had told Bentaña not to worry: soon, Reagan would be gone and the Sandinistas could do as they liked. At once David Horowitz was on his feet to shout, 'I know what I think of that! I say that's *treason!*'

It was a moment to savour. The spirit of Whittaker Chambers had materialized in the hall, and a rite of passage had been accomplished. 'Treason.' It has
a good, resonant sound, doesn't it? No matter that Professor LeoGrande (who
has issued a detailed denial) would never have said such a thing — for who
believes that Nicaragua will ever be allowed by the United States to do as it
pleases? Nor is it particularly relevant to point out that no formal state of war
exists between Washington and Managua. Nor does it make much difference
that Radosh, the patriotic eavesdropper, was on a trip financed by the United
States Information Agency. What is significant here is the full-throated roar.
Those who will not go the whole nine yards with the latest defectors are guilty,
not of naïveté or useful idiocy or the usual charges, but of treason. Whittaker
Chambers, as some people forget, was a considerable and complicated figure
who actually urged William Buckley, in vain, to have nothing to do with
Senator Joe McCarthy. He would have been denounced as a faintheart and
advocate of half-measures if he had made more than a spectral appearance at
this fervent gathering.

One sees the predicament in which Horowitz and Collier find themselves.
At the gala dinner of their event were Norman Podhoretz, Irving Kristol,
Martin Peretz, Hilton Kramer and William Phillips. That makes five editors of
five self-congratulatory neo-conservative magazines. It was an evening positively awash with pompous mutual esteem, punctuated only by a witty and
admonitory address from Kramer. So who needs yet another set of breast-
beating recusants, this time accusing themselves of a past mired in terrorism,
crime and family maladjustment? In order to make their point and stake their
claim, Horowitz and Collier had to exaggerate the zeal of the convert,
intensify the hunt for heresy. I can offer a trivial and amusing example, to take
away the taste of the LeoGrande episode. In private conversation the duo had
suggested a debate between themselves and your correspondent. They even
proposed that I contribute an article to the magazine which, with money from
yet another right-wing foundation, they propose to launch. But at the above-
mentioned dinner the toadying emcee, Marty (Hot Lips) Peretz, tried a flailing
attack on the 'loathsome' foreigner Hitchens. (Peretz is one of those tiresome,
unctuous types who thinks he's a wit and is half right.) At next day's session,
Horowitz took up this cry and made it more extreme. It was obviously
emotionally important for him not to be outdone by anybody.

The line of the conference was that a person who opposes the Contras is —
'objectively', of course — 'anti-American'. This must mean that the Contras
and their network of Norths and Channells and Singlaubs are, in some
essential way, the United States. What could possibly be more of an insult to
America? But the revisionism goes further still. According to the Horowitz-
Collier-Radosh school (I hope these people don't last long enough to need a
more convenient name), Franco should have won the Spanish Civil War, Cuba
would have been better off staying under Batista, the Sandinistas should have
been stopped in 1979 or earlier, the Vietnam War should have gone on —

presumably for ever – and the Chinese Revolution should have been aborted in Shanghai before Malraux got hold of it. These positions, which I do not caricature, are in the strictest sense idealistic as well as reactionary. They reduce the study of history to a mere working-out of conspiracies and betrayals. Suppose one were to say that the Russian Revolution *should* have occurred in 1905, that Rosa Luxemburg *should* have saved Germany from the right in 1919, that Gramsci's forces *should* have vanquished Mussolini's, that Sandino *should* have triumphed in 1929, that the French empire *should* have been allowed to expire in Indochina in 1945 or that the Spanish Republic *should* have arrested the rebellious generals and avoided the Civil War in the first place? One could properly be accused of utopianism, though God knows I wish all those possibilities had occurred. Instead, for refusing to indict the course of events and for seeking historical as well as moral reasons for the fate of revolution, one is accused of fellow-travelling and appeasement. Nice unironic going. You would scarcely guess that it is the Reaganites who now arm and endorse the Khmer Rouge.

Having rewritten it up to its present page, the H–C–R school now flatly announces that history has come to a full stop. To talk of change and evolution in the Communist world, for example, is to talk of something that is axiomatically impossible – a position that even Professor Leszek Kolakowski, who helped formulate it, now finds less tenable than he was wont to. This deaf, boring, fanatical opinion finds its ideal counterpart in the conviction that corporate, consumer, military capitalism is civilization's last word in the West. 'Aha!' exclaim the new zealots, 'You're ducking the question. Are you, or are you not, sincerely anti-Communist? Answer yes or no! Also, answer quickly!' In Stephen Ambrose's history of the political career of Richard Nixon, I learned that in 1950 Nixon was accused by Helen Gahagan Douglas of being soft on Communism in Korea. 'On every key vote,' said this silly, opportunist progressive, 'Nixon stood with party-liner Marcantonio against America in its fight to defeat Communism.' More recently, on 14 May 1986, I heard Robert McFarlane tell the Iran–Contra hearings why he had never checked on the legality of the Nicaragua policy: 'To tell you the truth, probably the reason I didn't is because if I'd done that Bill Casey, Jeane Kirkpatrick and Cap Weinberger would have said I was some kind of a Commie, you know.' Yes, I do know, and an auction in which Nixon and McFarlane can be outbid is too much for me.

I will say for David Horowitz that he urged me to speak with Fausto Amador. I did have a long discussion with Amador two days after the conference ended. He was blooded early as a Sandinista, experienced a great disillusionment in Cuba and became, successively, an ex-Communist, an ex-Trotskyist and an ex-Marxist. But he has stopped short of the full James Burnham apostasy. He now lives in Costa Rica, where he leads a grass-roots movement of the poor and was arrested not long ago for heading a demonstration in memory of the murdered Archbishop Romero of El Salvador. He is passionately opposed to the Contras and will have nothing to do with any Nicaraguan who supports them: 'They have burned down the possibility of civic opposition and become corrupted with American money. They are *shit!*' I asked him why he had not said so at the conference: 'Well, they cut my speech short — the only time it happened to anyone all weekend. I like David, but I don't know why he is getting involved with these people. He will soon learn what they are like.' I think Amador is an optimist. A very different kind of former revolutionary was also at the conference. Ndabaningi Sithole, the renegade black nationalist from the old Rhodesia, was a prominent guest. I used to interview him back in the days when he threw in his lot with Ian Smith and became a zealous prosecutor of the war against his people's insurgent majority. While in office he solicited the help of Idi Amin for his own private militia. He now beseeches Washington for aid to the South African-organized rebels in Mozambique. In the coming battle over South Africa he will provide some pathetic black decor for the pro-apartheid lobby. Is this what the Second Thoughters really want? All the available evidence about their mentality suggests that it is. For them, the demand to release Nelson Mandela and recognize the African National Congress is a demand that opens the door to Stalinism. And if Mandela dies in prison and the ANC comes to power in blood, the same geniuses will be on hand to say that they told us so. This is a cheap three-card trick, which any fool can see through while it is being played. The blacks who hate Mandela will meanwhile find good company with the Jews who supported the torturers of Jacobo Timerman. Who is travelling with whom?

Since I have never been a Stalinist, a Weatherman enthusiast or a Black Panther groupie, I may lack the imaginative sympathy that is required to analyse the H-C-R cult. But I know a dead end when I see one. The cult has changed ships on a falling tide. Every precept of Reaganism is coming to pieces before our eyes. And meanwhile in the Soviet Union, which was unmentioned at the conference, nobody any longer believes that glasnost is window-dressing (though Norman Podhoretz thoughtfully compared Gorbachev to Hitler in his most recent column on the subject). Of all the times to sign up for a simple-minded war on the socialist and revolutionary past, this must be the least propitious. But the absurdity of the H-C-R faction doesn't necessarily define it as innocuous. There will be further spasms of lunacy down the road, and fresh occasions for the paranoid style to express itself. As Deutscher put it so aptly in speaking of the penitent:

> His former illusion at least implied a positive ideal. His disillusionment is utterly negative. His role is therefore intellectually and politically barren.... He advances bravely in the front rank of every witch-hunt. His blind hatred of his former ideal is leaven to contemporary conservatism.

The Nation, November 1987

3
THE CUNNING OF HISTORY

CRETINISMO EROICO

I cherished only two modest ambitions for my visit to Prague, capital of the mummified baroque. The first was to be allowed to attend a legal meeting at which men and women from the human-rights movements in the East and the disarmament movements in the West would be attempting to establish a common terrain. The second was to be the first writer in modern history to compose an article from Prague that did not mention Joseph K or his equally imperishable creator. The latter ambition was repeatedly thwarted by the former.

You attend a meeting in a private apartment. An introductory statement is made by a man who was once Foreign Minister of the Republic under Alexander Dubček but is now an unperson in Czechoslovakia. There is a knock on the door. Into the apartment come uniformed and plain-clothes police, led by a man with eyes so close together that he could comfortably get by with a monocle. While one of his underlings sweeps the room with a video camera, he issues peremptory instructions to depart. At my request, the former Foreign Minister inquires politely if we may know what law has been infringed, and in what respect this law contravenes the Helinski Accords. He further inquires, on behalf of his foreign guests, if they may telephone their embassies. Neither request is exactly denied. Instead, the police official simply refuses to say on what charge, or for what cause, the Czechoslovaks or the foreigners are being treated in this fashion.

Still striving to avoid the easy resort to Kafka, I talk to one of the Hungarian delegates during the brief period of our segregation together. It reminds me, I say adventurously, of Nabokov's 1947 novel *Bend Sinister*. In this prescient and haunting book, a group of dolts and bullies takes power, under the leadership of the appalling Paduk, in the name of the Party of the Average Man. This pseudo-populist party understands the deadly combination of stupidity and cunning. It specializes in knowing the weak points of the human subject and possesses a ghastly, mediocre patience. My Hungarian friend nods in appreciation but proposes an alternative encapsulation. 'What we see here', he says, 'is what Gramsci described as *cretinismo eroico*.' Next day, while in detention at the police station, we read a crude and fantastic denunciation of one of our Czechoslovak hosts, Petr Uhl, one of the original signatories of Charter 77 and a man who has served almost a decade in prison. He is castigated across several columns of the rubbishy party paper *Rude Pravo* for being what he actually is — a dangerous leftist. The journal laboriously connects his ideas to those of a certain Trotsky, adding in brackets after this exotic name the explanatory word 'Bronstein'. Feeling against 'cosmopolitans' has never been especially strong in Czechoslovakia, but the view of the Party of the Average Man has long been that every little bit helps.

I have seldom been arrested by such pitiable people, and have never been detained in such distinguished company. Present with me were two women with exemplary records in the movement initiated by Edward Thompson and known throughout Europe as END (European Nuclear Disarmament). There was a representative of the Polish Freedom and Peace group; a leader of the Slovene dissidents in Yugoslavia; and the above-mentioned Hungarian, whose colleagues have recently succeeded in setting up flourishing and independent political clubs in Budapest. There was a woman from India, who has been energetic in the campaign for the victims of Union Carbide in Bhopal. There were two battle-hardened Puerto Rican socialists. The West German Greens, the Dutch anti-nuclear movement and some interesting revisionists from the Italian left were also in the bag. But our predicament, and its ironies, was a paltry one when compared with that of our hosts. And here, a simple point that also contradicts Kafka. None of the Czechoslovaks, when being grabbed and driven away, showed the least sign of fear. Jiři Hájek — who, as I said above, used to be Alexander Dubček's Foreign Minister — served five years in a camp under the Nazis and has every right to be unimpressed by the relative cretinism of the Czechoslovak quislings of today. But many of those who offered us bed and board were only three or four years old at the time of the Warsaw Pact invasion in 1968. And they went, quite confidently and cheer-fully, all the way to prison for the sake of our meeting. It is this, really, that spells defeat for the miserable regime established by Brezhnev two decades ago. As Isaac Deutscher was fond of saying: *'Plus c'est la même chose — plus ça change.'* Attempting to freeze and petrify society, the post-Stalinist *apparat* has created cynicism and disgust on a colossal scale. Talk to anybody — anybody — in a café in Prague and you will encounter that mixture of humour and contempt that negates all the efforts of the conformists.

It does not take a political genius to notice that *Rude Pravo* never mentions Mikhail Gorbachev unless it has to. It does not take a political genius to observe that the missile-flourishing Reagan of a few years ago was a free gift to *Rude Pravo* and its automaton propagandists. When the brave leaders of Charter 77 issued their invitation East and West (and South), they were expli-citly seeking to connect the struggle for democracy to the struggle against mili-tarism. Ever since Chernobyl, it has been easier and more urgent to make internationalist connections between the nuclear menace and the battle against political secrecy and the 'security state'.

At dusk on the Charles Bridge, small groups of young Czechs gather every night under the statues to play guitars and pass bottles of wine. They sing the forbidden 1968 songs of Marta Kubisova, and the police don't know quite what to do about it. The orders from the top, and from Moscow, are not as direct or as clear as they used to be. The Castle still looms above the city from the Hradčany Hill, but it is inhabited by pygmies who were fished out of the dustbin of history, and whimper in their sleep at the thought of going back to it.

The Nation, July 1988

THE TWILIGHT OF
PANZERKOMMUNISMUS

Although it has given rise to one of the century's great literary meditations on the political uses of amnesia, the striking thing about the August 1968 repression of Czechoslovakia is the continuing freshness and relevance of its imagery. Walk through Wenceslas Square today, where a banal regime has learned how to exploit the most tawdry aspects of the credit card and tourist culture, and the docile parties of Swedes and Germans with their guides are less vivid in the mind than those grainy old sequences of tanks parked under every balcony. The equestrian statue at the head of the square, with the National Museum of Bohemia looming behind, at once recalls its heroic period as the centrepiece of vast popular demonstrations, and as the site of Jan Palach's dramatic suicide by fire. Turn away towards the Old Town Square, and you come to the dingy splendour of the Klement Gottwald Museum, which houses the usual collection of leader-worshipping Stalinist memorabilia. There was a time when Gottwald exerted absolute power over every Czech and Slovak. There was a time when the largest statue of Stalin in the world looked down over the Vltava River. The statue is gone. Who outside the borders of Czechoslovakia remembers the name of Gottwald? Who, outside or inside those borders, has forgotten the name of Alexander Dubček?

For twenty years, Czechoslovakia has been the site of a planned stultification of society known as 'normalization'. This has been an almost fascinating exercise in the depoliticizing of life and thought, and the reduction of ideology to one dimension. It does not even possess the ironies and ambiguities of the original Communist seizure of power in 1948 when, as even a committed foe like Milan Kundera recalls, in *The Book of Laughter and Forgetting*:

> I took other Communist students by the hand, I put my arms around their shoulders, and we took two steps in place, one step forward, lifted first one leg and then the other, and we did it just about every month, there being always something to celebrate, an anniversary here, a special event there, old wrongs were righted, new wrongs perpetrated, factories were nationalised, thousands of people went to jail, medical care became free of charge, small shopkeepers lost their jobs, aged workers took their first vacations ever in confiscated country houses, and we smiled the smile of happiness.

Indeed, Kundera rather generously grants that in 1948 the Communist Party 'took power not in bloodshed and violence, but to the cheers of about half the population. And please note: the half that cheered was the more dynamic, the more intelligent, the better half.'

Nothing of this sort could be said about 'normalization'. It has been an

application of dull, crass, reactionary utilitarianism in the service of unsanc-
tioned power. Its chief features have been the rewarding of obedience, no
matter how conservative, and the punishment of opposition, no matter how
idealistic. Imagine a 'Scoundrel Time' that went on for twenty years, inaugurated by a post-invasion questionnaire from 'Education Minister' Jaromir
Hrbek, that asked all party members about their friends and colleagues:
'Which are honest and capable? (Name at least ten.) Which have been discredited by anti-socialist and anti-Soviet deeds and attitudes?' By the time this
inquisition was over, half a million Czechs and Slovaks had been purged from
the Communist Party, and an enormous percentage of the nation's intelligentsia had been forced to live abroad. Here, a word to certain anti-anti-
Communists. The authorities in Prague claim the support of the 'ordinary
people' against the pampered dissidents and elite scribblers who are so celebrated in the Western press. They take a special, sniggering pleasure in
punishing troublesome academics, for example, by demoting them to jobs as
truck-drivers, stokers and janitors. Certainly this shows a fierce contempt for
the pointy-heads and for intellectual labour. But does it not demonstrate a
revealing contempt for manual labour as well? It is notorious that in Czechoslovakia the bureaucratic class has reserved an almost Oriental privilege for
itself (that is what actually happened to most of those 'confiscated country
houses') while mouthing demagogically about 'enemies of the people'. As
Milan Simecka, a leading opposition essayist, puts it in his book *The Restoration
of Order*:

> However adaptable socialist ideology may be, it would be hard for it to justify
> with any credibility the fact that the socialist state behaves like a red-in-tooth-
> and-claw capitalist of the last century, that it establishes blacklists, and fires
> employees suspected of involvement in 'strikes', not to mention those who
> might be a source of trouble, or those who fail to show the right degree of
> respect to the management, and so on. You do not need ideological reasons to be
> disgusted by such practices; the good old socialist gut-reaction we inherited
> from earlier generations tells us they are wrong.

Trudging past the Gottwald Museum and coming to the Old Town Square,
there is no avoiding a confrontation with the statue of Jan Hus. In all of Czech
discussion, this Puritan martyr who died rather than recant is contrasted with
the figure of the Good Soldier Schweik, who made dumb obedience into a
form of passive dissent. Critical citizens incessantly debate this contrast in the
national character. They tend to reason defensively, and to say that long-term
organized resistance is made impossible by the country's geographic position.
It is true that Czechoslovakia has been condemned by geography. In this part
of the century, this is as much as to say that it is condemned by the Cold War.
In his enthralling memoir *Night Frost*, Zdenek Mlynar, who was Communist
Party Secretary in 1968, touched deftly on this point. The Czech leadership
had been taken hostage by the Red Army and was being hectored by Brezhnev.
He gloatingly told his prisoners:

I asked President Johnson if the American government still fully recognised the results of the Yalta and Potsdam conferences. And on 18 August I received the reply: as far as Czechoslovakia and Romania are concerned, it recognises them without reservation.... So what do you think will be done on your behalf? There will be no war.

The old 'spheres of influence' argument, put at the time of the heaviest American bombardment of Vietnam, has never been underscored to greater effect. Nevertheless there were those who preferred Hus to Schweik, even against these crushing odds. The Czechs have never forgotten Dr Frantisek Kriegel, chairman of the 'National Front' of Dubček's government, who alone refused to sign the Moscow Protocol legitimizing the invasion *ex post facto*, and maintained this refusal despite solitary confinement and threats to his life. As a veteran of the Spanish Civil War, a doctor in the Chinese Revolution and a militant in the anti-Nazi Resistance, he had not acquired the requisite habits of obedience. When he died a few years later, his body was seized by the secret police in order to prevent demonstrations at his funeral, and the basest anti-Jewish libels were circulated against his memory by functionaries whose record could not stand the least comparison with his. Now it is Brezhnev who is lampooned and reviled in his own country, while Kriegel is remembered with honour and respect. Those who made excuses for Brezhnev while he was alive should remember that, too.

Indeed, it was clear even at the time that the invasion of Czechoslovakia was a hinge event for Communism. *Panzerkommunismus*, said Ernst Fischer, leader of the Austrian Communists through the bleakest years of the Cold War and a man who had broadcast in German on Moscow Radio throughout the battle for Stalingrad. If the Italian, French, British and Spanish and other Communist Parties had not denounced the invasion, they would have split or suffered defections even more damaging than had occurred over Hungary in 1956. Those parties which endorsed the invasion — notably the Greek — saw some of their bravest militants disown the decision. In the long view 'Euro-communism' may have been only an episode in the historic eclipse of the Western Communist culture, but it can be said with certainty that this eclipse was hastened by the Prague events, which simply snapped the mainspring of belief in the Soviet Union as the bastion of socialism; more sinned against than sinning.

Developments in the East were less easy to monitor, but in the long run no less impressive. A Polish shipyard worker named Edmund Baluka once told me that he had been dispatched with his army unit to Czechoslovakia and told that a West German *revanchist* attack was under way. He and his mates were more than disgusted to discover the crude lie, and two years later he was a prominent figure in a strike in the Gdansk shipyard which is, in essence, still going on. Somewhere in East Germany in August 1968, a party official named Rudolf Bahro took the decision to leave the Party while remaining an ostensible member, and to begin work on a book. It took ten years for him to complete *The Alternative in Eastern Europe*, and throughout that time he continued to act as a dutiful servant of the regime. It has become more and more pertinent to ask how many unknown Bahros there are. Zdenek Mlynar, the above-mentioned Czech Party Secretary, wrote his memoirs without bothering to mention a critical and intelligent Russian he had known as a fellow-student in Moscow in the 1950s. This Russian had been a courageous exception to the conformist standard demanded by the late Stalin period, and had seemed impatient with the general stupidity and chauvinism that infected the atmosphere. Only two years ago did Mlynar, now in exile, read the papers and notice prominent photographs of his old schoolfriend Mikhail Sergeyevitch Gorbachev.

It is at least thinkable that we may have here an example of what Hegel liked to call 'the cunning of history'. Over the last two decades, Western commentary on Soviet Europe has been inclined to favour a certain ruthless pessimism, generally voiced by experienced ex-Communist émigrés. This tendency has spoken of a 'totalitarian' model of society, reinforced by Asiatic despotism, that is axiomatically *beyond reform*. Its style, whether in the elegiac later novels of Milan Kundera or the bitter essays of Professor Leszek Kolakowski, has been oddly resigned to the permanence of the Stalinist system, distinctly pitying towards those who entertained hopes of change, and therefore rather confirming and indulgent towards Western 'statesmanship' of the Reagan type. Eastern historians and essayists like Roy Medvedev, Milan Simecka, Boris Kagarlitsky and Rudolf Bahro have been left out of this account, with the consequence that the whole Gorbachev phenomenon has come to Western audiences as a more or less complete surprise; later claimed rather too hastily and opportunistically as a reward for 'Peace Through Strength'. (Doubters of 'Peace Through Strength', surely history's most exploded nostrum, have been accused, in a bizarre evocation of the Western capitalist betrayal of Czechoslovakia, of being the dupes of 'another Munich'.)

There is an intelligible case for saying that much of this was fatalistic mirror-Stalinism, which paradoxically believed that the Communist system was stronger and more self-confident than it actually was. Take, first, Milan Simecka's reply to Milan Kundera on the question of 'Central Europe'. This essay, written in 1984, was — as far as I know — published only in the *East European Reporter* of Summer 1985. It refers directly to Kundera's celebrated essay 'The Tragedy of Eastern Europe' in the *New York Review of Books* of 26 April 1984, which had discussed the possibility that the very identity of the Warsaw Pact nations might actually be obliterated by Russification. As Simecka says:

> The actual Central European tragedy is quite poignantly depicted by Kundera. He presents his American readers with a grandiose historical tableau of the Central European spiritual tradition, supported by all the names now familiar to us from his writing: Freud and Mahler, Bartók and Janáček, Musil and Broch, Kafka and Hasek, Gombrowicz, Milosz, Palacky, Dery etc.

Blaming 'Russia' for threatening to extirpate this tradition is, as Simecka says, unhelpful and ahistorical. For one thing, the nations of eastern Europe have not had their identity destroyed, despite the cultural desolation imposed upon them. For another, 'use of the term "Russia" as an expression has clear ideological overtones. We're all of us aware how much of a distortion it is. Most seriously, it involuntarily ignores the existence of all the other nations of the Soviet Union and tempts one to perceive Estonians and Armenians in terms of Pushkin and Dostoyevsky.'

Especially at a time when Baltic and Armenian peoples are asserting themselves with exemplary force, the consequences of this *Mitteleuropa* self-pity are more than just literary. As Simecka goes on to say:

> We should not disguise the fact that it was not Russia which ushered in the beginning of the end of the Central European tradition. It was Hitler who tore up by the roots that certain decency of political and cultural standards which the Central European nations managed to preserve more or less intact up to 1937. It was chiefly due to the insane acts of the Nazis that the nations of Central Europe became the victims and outsiders of history. It was Nazism, after all, which so effectively silenced the 'Jewish genius' which had been part and parcel of Central Europe's spiritual evolution. At the moment the tragedy of Central Europe began to unfold, Eastern influences were negligible or, at any rate, the Russian factor played scarcely any role. The cancer which finally put paid to what had gone before was nurtured on Western European history and fed on the decaying legacy of Western European intellectual innovations. That was the real succession of events: it was only the remnants of the old Central Europe that breathed their last in Russian arms.

Yet Kundera, and his admirers and emulators, seem to need the anti-Russian theme just as they need the 'totalitarian' one. Totalitarianism, as our home-grown theorists never weary of pointing out, is to be distinguished from authoritarianism by the state's need to conscript not just passivity but assent and even enthusiasm; by its determination to abolish the private life. Yet the private life, as Simecka explains in *The Restoration of Order*, is precisely what the Czechoslovak authorities encourage people to cultivate:

> In the renewed order, the unsupervised private sphere is quite extensive. The State allows adapted citizens to do what they like with the money they more or less honestly acquire. They may build houses, chalets and cabins, and fit them out as they wish. They may buy cars and travel in them where they will.... They may travel abroad, so long as they can afford the shocking tax on the purchase of hard currency.... They may not actually be able to read what they would like, but the State erects communal aerials to receive TV programmes from Vienna.

In other words, the life of the 'adapted citizen' may be hellish in its hypocrisy and in the mediocrity of its official standards, but it is not fascism or the Gulag. In 'normal' conditions, this exploitation of materialism and selfishness works reasonably well, allowing the regime to pick off troublemakers one by one or in small groups, without ever succeeding in crushing them absolutely. But how can the rulers be sure of 'normality'? Nobody predicted that the two 'hot' issues in Czech society would suddenly become military conscription — into an army that has never defended the country — and environmental destruction. But quite recently, the burdensome and stupid national service requirements, and the catastrophic acid rain situation in Bohemia and Moravia, have recruited new sections of the population into semi-opposition. Neither matter is exactly trivial, because the first raises the issue of the country's enforced militarization and the second the chronic inefficiency and waste of its economy. In both cases, intelligent citizens are asked to ignore, or even to disbelieve, the evidence of their own eyes.

This final contradiction is at the core of Rudolf Bahro's masterly book *The Alternative*. He began his detailed and practical critique by saying that 'snooping about Dostoyevsky-style in the moral atmosphere of the dictatorship' was all very well, but did not help in understanding what made it work, or what might make it break down. He proposed the daring and innovative idea of 'surplus consciousness': the realization that state socialist bureaucracy created a class of technically skilled people while requiring them to act without initiative, as serfs or robots. These people, in a historic sense, knew too much. And this could be as true of the theatre-director as of the supervisor in a power plant. This is how Bahro, in response to the Czech events of 1968, described the contradictions of 'surplus consciousness' in the Soviet Union:

> In the Soviet Union the contradiction between the apparatus and the surplus consciousness is particularly deep, since the polit-bureaucracy there is less cultivated and adaptable, as a result of the backward semi-Asiatic mentality it inherited, and less susceptible to assimilating the new social forces in compromises to various kinds and degrees. Soviet statistics claim that three-fifths of those working in industry now have either college or full secondary education. But the skilled elements are politically kept under tutelage in the same paternalist manner as the meanest *kolkhoz* peasant, who might still be living under the Tsars. Even those most qualified are treated in this respect as subordinate specialists, as cogs in the gigantic clockwork of the state economy, kept wound up by the anonymous activity of the bureaucracy.

In Marxist terms, Bahro has identified a conflict between the forces and the relations of production — a conflict that extends deep into the superstructure. As he goes on to say:

> Many millions of people have acquired, if only in a specialised field, the power of abstraction and differentiation that enables them to take part in decisions over the destiny of their country, and its perspectives of social development. But they are not allowed to use their heads for this purpose.

In the course of a seminar on the work of Bahro in 1979, I heard the late Raymond Williams describe this as 'a long look ahead'. Perhaps he was too sanguine. The remainder of that chapter, which I have no space to quote, now reads like a script for the post-Chernenko events in Moscow. It is becoming clear that Gorbachev is risking everything on a mobilization of 'surplus consciousness' and the release of intellectual and productive energy that is contained in it. In other words, he has decided to break with a tradition that is part Russian and part Stalinist, and to cease to insult the intelligence.

It is, as Confucians would have it, too early to say whether we can really thrive on reformism from above. The Czechs in 1948 and 1968 found that what can be given can also be taken away. But there has to come a point when 'surplus consciousness' takes on a life of its own. If it was to do so, it would drastically revise the assumptions upon which all theories of 'Communism' are currently based. The system is sterile; therefore it cannot reproduce itself. It wanted to emulate and overtake capitalism, but could not put its trust in innovation. In its self-inflicted difficulties with the cult of growth, with the burden of militarism and with the horrors of nuclearism, to say nothing of making an honest account of history, it may provide even smug Westerners with the opportunity for self-criticism, and may show 'Russia' to be more European than we think. That is all in the future. At any moment, though, the Moscow press may print a searching, revisionist article about the 'fraternal intervention' in Prague twenty years ago. Certainly, the process of reform will not be clearly and demonstrably under way until it does. The example of the Czechs has turned out to be an extraordinary one, both morally and practically. As Brecht put it in his poem on Czechoslovak history: 'On the bed of the Moldau, stones are rolling ...'

In the long run, Hus and Schweik made a historic compromise, with results that are neither laughable nor forgotten.

New Statesman, August 1988

POLICE MENTALITY

In Prague last Thanksgiving, for my first visit since I was locked up and deported in the dying convulsions of the Stalinist regime, I made haste to look up an old friend. Jan Kavan is the son of a Czechoslovak man and an English woman whose family travail during fascism, war, resistance, the Stalin show trials and the 'premature anti-Brezhnevite' period of the Dubček movement is excellently set down by his mother, Rosemary Kavan, in her memoir *Love and Freedom*. Exiled and stripped of his citizenship by the post-1968 occupation regime, Jan had set up the Palach Press in London and quickly made himself indispensable to scholars and journalists pursuing reliable information from Eastern Europe. He became the lifeline between the Charter 77 movement and the loose but influential collective of international groups working on human rights, disarmament and European unity. As soon as the Brezhnevites had been evicted from 'The Castle' in Prague, he returned home and ran successfully for Parliament as a deputy in Václav Havel's Civic Forum. Last year we dined in one of the beautiful squares of the Old Town, and Jan talked fluently about the internal politics of the new system, emphasizing the attempt being made to isolate the radicals who had kept up the clandestine opposition during the harshest years of repression. Then he took me to the memorial of the resistance in Wenceslas Square, and we talked about the past. He had always known, he said, that the regime would crack one day, but he had not been certain of living to see it. So his commitment to opposition, though it derived from socialist politics and family history, was in some sense also influenced by Havel's concept of moral resistance: of refusing, as a person, to live as anything other than a free man. I shook his hand, bade him good luck in the impending struggle against the one-note neo-Thatcherites who were trying to standardize politics, and departed.

In March 1991, a commission of the Czech and Slovak Parliament issued a report in which Jan Kavan was 'named' as having collaborated with the secret police forces of the former government. In a letter released on 15 March, Dr Jaroslav Sabata captures my reaction to perfection: 'All my experience cries out against the accusation. I regard the accusation as absurd and unfounded.' But since I lack the stature of a Sabata — he was a long-standing and brave opponent of the invasion, and is now a minister in Havel's government — I have had to take a close look at the evidence. The frame-up is even cruder than I had feared.

In London in 1969, Kavan was approached by the education counsellor at the Czechoslovak Embassy in London. There was nothing unusual in this, since Jan had been elected spokesperson for the Czechoslovak students then living abroad, and was empowered to deal with their consular and visa problems. However, the official, a Mr Zajicek, represented himself privately as a covert supporter of the deposed Dubček government. This too was not alto-gether improbable; in 1969 the great purge of state employees had not had time to get under way, and the hideous word 'normalization' was still unfam-iliar. Yet either at that date or at a later one, Mr Zajicek switched sides and became a conformist. He made a report of his meeting with Jan Kavan to the secret police. Then what? you may ask. That's it. That's the whole accusation. Through an exchange with a minor informer, logged by quisling bureaucrats two decades ago, Jan is deemed to have been listed as a contact for the secret police. The method by which the accusation was made public is as shabby as the accusation itself. Jan was given no chance to review the evidence against him and was peremptorily asked to resign from Parliament within fifteen days. He has been given no opportunity to confront or question the dubious Mr

Zajicek. The parliamentary commission both conducted the 'investigation' and, by a 6-to-5 majority, announced the verdict. Jeri Laber of Helsinki Watch does not exaggerate when, in a letter to President Václav Havel, she makes an allusion to the nightmare of Joseph K.

Jan's position, though, is preferable in many respects to that of Kafka's poor victim. He has numerous admirers and friends abroad, from the US Senate to the European Parliament, and many of these have written to Havel in the strongest terms. It was, after all, Havel himself who correctly opposed an early lynch-mob atmosphere by pointing out that 'those who in fact served the totalitarian regime ... are the very same people who are the loudest today. They shout so loudly to drown their own guilty conscience ... to compensate somehow for their own humiliation.' And it is a fact that many of the neo-conservatives now in positions of power in Czechoslovakia either kept quiet as mice during the occupation or accepted positions of minor responsibility. A genuinely guilty collaborator can now, it seems, easily save his or her own hide by 'naming names' and implicating independent-minded dissidents. So far, however, that prince of moralists Havel has not found the words with which to condemn this sordid and increasingly menacing process.

George Konrad warned at an early stage in the Eastern European revolution that the wrong people would get hold of police files and use them for coercive purposes. Kavan ruefully admits that he voted for the law that instituted a purge of the old collaborators, not realizing that it would be so cynically implemented, with so little safeguard. Given the extreme tensions in the new republics, with shock levels of unemployment, disputes over the distribution of former properties and privileges, and the frequent, highly toxic recrudescence of national and minority questions, it is tempting for demagogues and careerists to smear people who would make trouble for a new elite. Guilt by suspicion is easy to play upon in conditions of rumour, scarcity and instability. The resolution of the Kavan case will be an important demonstration of the way things are tending. It would be nice if those who were so eloquent and indignant in the past could find their voices again, and oppose the method of the witch-hunt and the Inquisition.

The Nation, May 1991

ON THE ROAD TO TIMIŞOARA

On Christmas night, stuck in freezing fog at the Austro–Hungarian border, I had telephoned my best Budapest friend and spoken across an insufferable line, fed with near-worthless *forint* coins cadged from a friendly guard. 'Have you heard?' said Ferenc. 'Ceauşescu has been *assassinated*.' The choice of word seemed odd. 'Murdered' wouldn't do, of course, in the circumstances. 'Killed' would have been banal. 'Executed' – too correct. And Ferenc always chooses his terms with meticulous care. No, a baroque dictator who was already a prisoner, and an ex-tyrant, had somehow been 'assassinated'. I took the first of many resolutions not to resort to Transylvanian imagery. Yes, there had been King Vlad, known as the Impaler, reputed to drink blood as well as spill it. Every writer and subeditor in the trade was going to be dusting him off. Still, I found myself wondering just how Ceauşescu had been 'assassinated' after his capture. A stake through the heart? I had read that the chief of Ceauşescu's ghastly Securitate was named General Julian Vlad, but I was determined to make absolutely nothing of it.

A sorry-looking shop-front, which was in one of the radial streets off Calvin Square in Budapest, housed the Alliance of Free Democrats (SDS), Hungary's main opposition party. It resembled the headquarters of every 'movement' I'd ever visited. The stickers and posters in haphazard pattern gave promise of an interior of clanking duplicators, overworked telephones and bearded young men in pullovers. One of the stickers was fresh and blazing with colours – the national colours, in fact. It read: TIMIŞOARA–TEMESVAR. To any Hungarian, it summoned an immediate, arresting image. On the plains of Transylvania, near the town the world knows as Timişoara, the Hungarian patriots of 1848 were scattered and cut down by the Tsar's Cossack levies, lent as a favour to the Austrian emperor. Near Temesvar, as the Hungarians call it, the national poet Sandor Petofi lost his life. At nearby Arad, the thirteen generals who had sided with the 1848 revolution were put to death. Now, under its Romanian name, this lost city so well-watered with patriotic Hungarian gore was again an emblem.

Today, the first day of the post-Ceauşescu era, the office was crowded to the doors with people of every class and category, standing around wearing intense expressions. Most wore buttons reading simply: TEMESVAR. Others displayed the more reflective symbol of two ribbons, one in the Hungarian colours and one in the Romanian, arranged over a black mourning stripe. Nationalists and internationalists, they were all waiting for the Romanian border to be declared open so that they could get to the stricken field of Transylvania and the wounded city of Timişoara. A volunteer convoy was in formation, with taxi-drivers, workers, housewives and students offering to donate, or to transport, food and medicine. As so often in the course of the astounding

Eastern European revolution of 1989, people seemed to know what to do. And they seemed to know, what's more, without being told. My companion and I, who continually needed and sought advice and instruction, felt this keenly. The Romanian Embassy in Budapest, scene of numerous protests (some of them cynically encouraged by the nearly defunct Hungarian Communist Party), had offered exactly the wrong kinds of reassurance. 'No problem,' said the greasy officials who had just run up a hand-stitched 'National Salvation' banner on the balcony. Had the border, sealed by Ceauşescu, been reopened by his death? 'No problem.' (I find these the two least relaxing words in the lingua franca.) Visas were said to be obtainable at the border. Or at the embassy, of course, with a wait on the cold pavement. And there would be a fee. In dollars. In cash. For some reason, we couldn't give hard currency to these soft, shifty figures, who were still dealing with the public through an insulting grille.

As the ten cars, one truck and one taxi that together comprised the Hungarian dissident convoy prepared to set off, I got an idea of how excited and intimidated they were by the whole idea of Transylvania. We had a short and cautionary talk from Tibor Vidos, an SDS organizer, who specialized in taking the romance out of things. 'There's to be no driving at night once we cross the border.... We pick up the blood supplies before we meet at the checkpoint.... No car is to pick up hitch-hikers, however innocent-looking they are. *Secu* men have been taking lifts and getting out while leaving plastic bombs behind....' Carrying blood to Transylvania? No, too glib an image, and indecent in the context. Dismissing Dracula once more, I went for a swift meal with Miklos Haraszti, author of *The Velvet Prison*, a book which relates the trials of writers and intellectuals in the 'goulash archipelago'. He had been to Timişoara/Temesvar years before, to see the now-famous Father Laszlo Tokes, and had been detained and tortured by the *Secu*. Haraszti comes from Leninist stock; his Jewish watchmaker parents left Hungary for Palestine in order to escape fascism, but quit Palestine in 1948 — the year of the proclamation of Israel — in order to come back to a people's republic. His own disillusionment had taken him through Maoism before fetching him up with the majority of Budapest's 'urbanist' intellectuals into the ranks of the liberal SDS.

Haraszti told us of something that had just happened to the convoy in front of ours: 'One of the volunteers was pulled from his car, not by the *Secu* but by the Romanian crowd. They said he looked like an Arab, and that Arab terrorists had been helping Ceauşescu's gangs.' This was an instance of the *grande peur* that infected Romania in those days, and was to poison the inaugural moments of the revolution. Not a single Arab corpse was found, nor a single prisoner taken. Yet the presence of Libyans, Syrians, Palestinians in the degraded ranks of the *Secu* was something that 'everybody knew'. The cream of the jest, as Haraszti went on to say, was that the 'Arab-looking' volunteer seemed exotic in appearance because he was a Budapest Jew. 'One of the few New Leftists we still have. He probably does sympathize with the PLO.'

Nobody knew what had become of this hapless comrade, because the convoy had been too scared to stop. As we concluded our meal, the waiter brought us the last of several predictions about the time at which Hungarian TV would transmit video pictures of the Ceauşescus' execution. At that stage, excited rumour was calling for an actual sequence of the bullets hitting the couple. Neither he nor his customers could wait for the event. I vaguely recalled seeing television pictures of the dead General Kassem after a coup in Iraq in the colonial fifties, but couldn't otherwise think of a precedent for a prime-time 'assassination' of a fallen leader. 'The genius of the Carpathians', as Ceau-şescu characterized himself, hogged the stage until the very last.

I describe this hesitation on the border of Transylvania because it shows, even in small details, the way that Hungarians felt Romania to be *in partibus infidelium*. Romania is much larger than Hungary, by virtue of having absorbed so much of it, and Ceauşescu was the perfect ogre neighbour from the point of view of the regime. Not only did he run a terrifying, hermetic police state, the weight of which was felt disproportionately by the Hungarian-speaking minority, but he flaunted a mad, grandiose, population-growth policy which overtopped the megalomania of a Mussolini. And, as he raved from his balcony, it seemed to ordinary Hungarians that the Bucharest crowd supported him, at least passively and at least in his 'Greater Romania' fantasy. I asked Haraszti if this had made him feel nationalist in turn. 'The fact that the Romanian revolution was started by Hungarians', he said firmly, 'is a miracle.' Almost at a blow, the mutual xenophobia had been dispelled. Neither regime could ever again easily mobilize or distract its people by fear of the other. This is no small issue for Hungarian democrats, who remember that their country took the Axis side in the stupid, vainglorious hope of 'redeeming' lst Magyar territory, and instead lost most of its Jews and decades of its history as well as its national honour.

As the convoy got on the move, and as people were allocating and being allocated their tasks and their cars, I was brought the news that Queen Elizabeth II had rescinded her award of the Order of the Bath to Nicolae Ceau-şescu. There were polite Hungarians who felt that I might wish to know this, and added that the decision was taken not a minute too soon. Bloody hell, I think, it's like Chesterton's definition of journalism — telling the public that Lord X is dead when the public didn't know that Lord X had ever been alive. I'm sure most people didn't know that Ceauşescu was sporting a Windsor honour. And, by the way, for what was the Order bestowed? The brute got 'most favoured nation' status from the United States, the Order of Lenin from Moscow, the moist thanks of international bankers for exporting all his people's food, pay-offs from Israel and the Arab League and solidarity from Beijing. He was the perfect postmodern despot — a market Stalinist.

Departure was announced for two in the morning, so that all night-time driving could be done on Hungarian territory, and everyone was ready to move out on time, and did move out, without being told. Our car was the property of a man who normally drove a beer-truck, and looked like it, and drove like it (the image of the SDS as an intellectual and elitist party is misleading). The freezing fog had thickened. At first light, after frequent stops and regroupings, and a detour for the blood pick-up at the border town of Gyula, all the cars met again at the border-point. Here people started to get nervous. It would have been a good thing to have had a leader or a commander. We knew that the previous convoy had been shot up, and had lost one of its Bohemian-looking members to the liberated populace.

The Romanian border guards were in the very act of revisionism when we turned up. A large blank space on the wall spoke eloquently of yesterday's *Conducator*, as Ceauşescu got himself called, and various party and state emblems were being hurriedly junked. Still, the place wore the dismal, dingy aspect of a little machine for the imposition of petty authority. Everything from the lavatories to the waiting room was designed for insult, delay and humiliation, and there was no one-day, quick-change cosmetic to disguise the fact. The unctuous, ingratiating faces of the guards, who were 'making nice' for the first time in their lives, only reinforced the impression they were trying to dispel. Eager to please, they overdid their hatred of the *Secu* to whom they had deferred the day before. They even suggested that we not proceed. 'They are firing from cars. There is no law, no authority.' Without orders, they had no idea what to do. When I said, quite absurdly and untruthfully, that I was given 'clear instructions' from the capital that visas were free of charge today, they gladly waived the fee. There was a pathetic relief in the gesture of acquiescence.

Quitting the stranded, irrelevant guardhouse, and holding perhaps the last stamps that read 'Socialist Republic of Romania', we fell back a few decades. The Hungarian town of Gyula had amenities, as Americans say. Shops and telephones, restaurants, street lamps. Across the border there were herds of pigs and geese, horse-drawn wagons and wayside hovels. The first cars to be seen were waiting in an abject queue, not because of the upheaval but because today was the day when the exiguous petrol ration was issued. The people at the side of the road looked like caricatures of Eastern European misery, in their shapeless bundles of coats and scarves. But there was a palpable lift in the atmosphere even so, because every person raised a hand in a V-salute at the sight of the Hungarian flag (or was it our reassuring Red Cross?). These villages had been the targets for 'systematization', perhaps the nastiest political neologism since 'normalization' in Czechoslovakia, and were saved from bulldozers and unheated tower blocks where the water-pressure sometimes got as far as the first floor, and the official cultural activity was praise for the *Conducator* and the denunciation of fellow-sufferers.

At the city of Arad, our first major stop, we found what we were to find everywhere: that the centre of activity had shifted to the gates of the hospital. The *Conducator*'s cops had been vicious and thorough in their last stand — whether from panic or from sheer professional pride it is hard to say. In the street an army lorry screamed to a halt, and I heard the sound of boots hitting tarmac. This forbidding noise heralded a squad of uncertain young soldiers, steel casques reassuringly askew, who held up traffic with large gestures before entering the crowd and fraternizing. In the Romanian attitude to the Army there was something of the Stockholm syndrome. The soldiery had changed sides at the last minute, and some of the brass (including the excellent-sounding General Militarescu) had been in touch with party dissidents when it was dangerous to do so. Thus there was a popular willingness to smile, to repress unease, to cry: 'Army and People'. It became an article of faith that the soldiers who had fired on crowds on Christmas Eve were not really soldiers at all, but *Secu* devils in disguise. To have armed men on your side at long last, for whatever reason, seemed worth the sacrifice of pride. So the classic photograph became that of old women handing scarce food and drink to tank crews. Which indeed happened, showing in the oddest way that Brecht was right when he said that every tank had a mechanical weakness — its driver.

The beer-truck chauffeur, who seemed to be a stranger to exhaustion, had had the idea of stuffing his back seat with bales of Hungarian newspapers, including the daily organ of the Communist Party he despised. To stand in the streets of Arad and hand out free copies of yesterday's Budapest editions was to court instant popularity. Every hand reached for a copy — probably because a good deal of Hungarian is spoken in these parts, and probably because there hadn't been any newspapers for days, but also and undoubtedly because the front page bore the death-masks of Ceauşescu and his wife Elena. Watching people rivet themselves to this photo-exclusive, I again fought down the impulse to Translyvanian cliché. They had to see the dead monster, had to know he was dead. The Ceauşescus' 'trial' had been a shabby, panicky business with unpleasantly Freudian overtones (Elena: 'I was a mother to you all.' *BANG!*), conducted by a tribunal which feebly refused to show its members' faces; but their execution had a galvanic effect on the morale of Transylvania and a correspondingly lowering effect on the fighting spirit of the *Secu*.

All had been festivity on the way to Arad, and as we left we met bystanders who were happy and eager to point the way to Timişoara. Wayside saluting and waving seemed inexhaustible. It was like being in Orwell's Barcelona, or in Portugal in 1974, or even like being on the skirts of a liberating army. But everything changed as we approached Timişoara. There were fewer people on the roads, and they seemed less keen and animated. As we found the outlying bits of the town, we noticed that our salutes were not returned. All the window-glass in the city seemed to have gone. Except for some flags with the now-famous hole cut in the centre (a borrowing from Budapest in 1956), there were no signs of anything except shell-shocked, sullen wretchedness. I felt almost cheated. Here was the town of the resistance, of the revolutionary epicentre; the town that had lived up to 1848 — and won this time. Where were the garlands, the proud slogans, the maidens in national dress, the gnarled old men with fierce tears in their eyes?

How could I have been so romantic and vulgar? Timişoara was the scene not of a triumph but of an atrocity — a sort of distillate of twentieth-century horrors. The inhabitants had been strafed from the air like the people of Guernica. They had been shot down in heaps like the victims of Babi Yar, and buried like refuse in mass graves in the forest on the pattern of Katyn. Many had been raped and mutilated like the villagers of My Lai. Before he left on a state visit to — of all places — Iran, Ceauşescu had given explicit orders that the city be punished. This was his Lidice; his Ouradour. At least the people who had been through such a digest and synopsis of horror could tell themselves that they were the last carnage of the last European dictator. But this obviously was not much of a consolation on the day after.

Again, it was at the hospital that everybody gathered. Timişoara is a superficially uninteresting town with a dull, routine Stalinist design. The box-like buildings even have generic names stencilled on the outside: 'Hotel', 'Restaurant', 'Cultural Centre'. It was a surprise to learn that the fateful, desperate demonstration in support of Father Tokes had taken place in Opera Square, because Timişoara doesn't look as if it rates an Opera House. Opera Square, on the other hand, doesn't disappoint your imagination of what a Transylvanian provincial city might boast after twenty-five years of philistine despotism. What a terrible place to die, I thought grotesquely, especially if you feared you might be doing it for nothing. On the other hand, a perfect place for concluding that you had little or nothing to lose. We entered the hospital, and were led through a morgue which perfectly misrepresented the proportions of casualties. It contained one-third civilians, one-third soldiers and one-third *Secu* men. I had come this far to see my first dead secret policeman — a great twentieth-century experience, and only partly an anticlimax. He lay in his scruffy black livery, balding but thickly furred like some once vigorous animal, and looked alarmingly intact, with no outward mark of whatever violence had taken him. One of his companions, however, had been got at by the crowd and given a thorough kicking — the more thorough, by the look of it, out of frustration at the fact that he was dead. There was a pure hatred in the way people spoke of the fallen regime and its servants. 'Our first happy Christmas,' said Dr Istvan Balos, without affectation, when I asked him for a reaction to the shooting of the Ceauşescus. Caligula once said that he wished the Roman mob had only one head so that he might decapitate them all at one stroke. The Romanian crowd wished only that the Ceauşescus had had a million lives so that everyone could have a turn at killing them.

Just before I left New York for Eastern Europe, I had been talking and drinking with Zdeněk Urbánek, original signatory of Charter 77, friend of Václav Havel and Czech translator of Shakespeare. Most of our conversation concerned the problem of vengeance, and the argument over amnesty and prosecution in newly emancipated Prague. Urbánek took the view that there should be no retribution, and his analogy was from Rome also. Remember, he said, that *Julius Caesar* is called *Julius Caesar* even though the eponymous character disappears after a few scenes and about fifteen minutes. 'But after he is murdered his influence remains over everything, pervading everything. That is the result of blood and the effect of revenge.'

The elevated sentiments of Prague and Bratislava were alarmingly remote from the Timişoara morgue. On a slab neighbouring that of the brutish-looking *Secu* man lay a dead young soldier, his eyes wide open and very blue, and on adjacent tables were two older civilians — man and wife, we were told — who had worked at the hospital. Their corpses were being processed in some ghastly way that involved the stench of formaldehyde. If it hadn't been for this stench, in fact, I might have been spared the moment I had in the corridor outside. My nostrils started to wrinkle only just as I felt my soles getting sticky, and the smell of drying blood hit me precisely as I realized what was gumming up my feet. A bloodbath has taken place here, I thought. A fucking *bloodbath*. All these people, killed like rats after leading such miserable, chivvied existences. Life-blood on my shoes.

'We have given the *Secu* another twenty-four hours to give up,' said Dr Balos, 'after which they are subject to a popular tribunal and a summary verdict.' As he was announcing this he dropped his voice. 'Do you see that man there?' — he indicated a tall and rather handsome man in a hospital housecoat who was talking easily with colleagues — 'He's *one of them*. We can do nothing now, because there is no law. But soon....' He spoke as if he was still living under occupation or dictatorship.

There appeared to be a delayed reaction in the Romanian psyche. It took the form of believing — not every rumour, but every rumour that had the morbid odour of pessimism or foreboding. This was where Caesar had his posthumous revenge. There were no apparitions exactly, but an unusual number of people said that they thought the trial video was a fake, the corpses were phoney, the 'live' Ceauşescu was a double. In his madness, it seems Ceauşescu had commissioned a few doubles for purposes of security (or perhaps of perverted vanity or repressed self-hatred). This is only a step away from having food-tasters and granting audiences while perched on the can, but it wasn't hard to believe about the *Conducator*. I began to soften in my anti-Dracula resolve when I learned from Transylvanian historians that Ceauşescu had forbidden all mention of the Bram Stoker book or the legend. The idea that he still walked seemed implicit in his entire cult of death, and in the haunting effect of his undead minions.

In Budapest, Miklos Haraszti had spoken with approval of the decision to kill the Ceauşescus and with enthusiasm of the proposal to ban the Communist Party. 'It proves that it's a real revolution,' he said decisively, adding, after a pause, 'in the dirty sense as well.' As Ryszard Kapuściński once remarked, 'Hunger revolutions are the worst.' The people of Romania, and especially of Transylvania, were starved in every sense of the term. Kept on short rations, kept in the dark, in the cold, kept from anything that could be called culture, screaming with boredom and groaning with humiliation; forced to applaud a mad gargoyle for whom they felt puke-making hatred. In Timiş-oara one could see all the bitterness and futility, as well as all the grandeur, of a hunger revolution. One could also get premonitions of the disagreeable things that lay ahead for the country — the crowd-pleasing decision to restore capital punishment, the hasty ban on the Communist Party (the only such ban in the 1989 European revolution), the evasive answers on the make-up and origin of the Council of National Salvation, the awkward hysteria about the body count, the ambivalence about the place of the Army in politics. People were — are — hopelessly rattled and furious and confused.

I had had the vague idea of finding out the true body count of the Timişoara massacre, because cynical reporters were already saying that there 'hadn't really been all that many' casualties. Nettled at this, many citizens of the town were staunchly reiterating unbelievable death tolls. I sickened of the task — not just because of the stench of blood around the morgue, but because it seemed vile to be disputing the statistics of something evidently awful and sacrificial. It gave one the same rather creepy feeling that is engendered by an argument with Holocaust revisionists about Dresden or Auschwitz. I cleaned the soles of my shoes, remembered the packets of Hungarian coffee sugar I had pocketed on leaving Budapest, distributed them to some ecstatic and unbelieving children, and made ready to leave the hospital. In the reception area, patients were sitting dully watching the television. All that could be seen on it was a test-card. But they sat passive and fascinated, gazing at the flickering, impro-vised logo that read: *Romania Libera*.

Granta, 1990

BRICKS IN THE WALL

Passing through the official hole in the Berlin Wall several years ago, I was impressed in spite of myself by the trouble taken by the East German guards to live up to their Hollywood reputation. Dull, surly, bored yet hostile — a combi-nation that takes a little police work — they confiscated everything in print, delighted in rudeness to women and seemed indifferent to the tatty slogans about people's power and peace that adorned their grim little post. One was reminded of what Marx said about Lassalle: that his socialism stank of the Prussian barracks. And East Germany is Prussia all right, as even a short stay will confirm. I was looking for Professor Robert Havemann, who had been in the same Third Reich prison as Erich Honecker but had developed uncomfortable ideas about political and social democracy, and was therefore a prisoner once more. I couldn't penetrate his house arrest and was trudging back towards Checkpoint Charlie when I saw a red illuminated quotation on a slab in the wall. It contrasted with the foul torpor of the guardhouse on the way in and read, in loose translation:

> Great Carthage fought three wars
> After the first it was still powerful
> After the second it was still inhabitable
> After the third, nobody could find it at all.

This laconic yet arresting observation (or was it verse?) was attributed to Bertolt Brecht. I've since learned, by reading Timothy Garton Ash's *The Uses of Adversity*, that it comes from Brecht's 'Open Letter to German Artists and Writers', composed in 1951. Not actually written as poetry, the letter called for the democratic and peaceful reunification of Germany, and for the abolition of censorship. I was reading it within a few feet of the ruins of the old Reichstag, and it was being pressed on me as East Germany's claim to be the guardian of peace and stability in Central Europe.

A lot of abysmal history had gone into the fabrication of this ironic and contradictory display. If it is possible to assign a date to the moment when European social democracy and European Communism became lethal antagonists, then 14 July 1927 is a date worth bearing in mind. On that day the powerful social democrats of Vienna were confronted by an open challenge from the clerical right-wing regime. A contemptuously rigged jury had acquitted those who had openly lynched three social democrats in the town of Schattendorf. Furious workers' leaders came to the offices of the Socialist Party, demanding action. They wanted to see the great Otto Bauer. They were told that protest should be verbal only. As Ernst Fischer, who was present at the meeting, records the argument in his marvellous book *An Opposing Man*, the militants from the power stations and factories were instructed: 'One can't demonstrate against a verdict returned by jury.... Trial by jury is a great democratic achievement. Even if the jury is mistaken, you can't come out into the streets.' The next day the workers of Vienna took to the streets anyway, and were fired on by the Austrian mounted police.

The failure of social democracy to challenge authority and legality on this and many other occasions meant that the pre-fascist right, which was cynical about its 'own' legal norms, had an easy time crushing Vienna's poor for good in the bloodbath of February 1934. (It was these events, brilliantly chronicled by Fischer, that led Elias Canetti to start thinking about crowds and power, and also led Kim Philby to join the Communist Party.) Fischer and many like him were so disgusted by the failure of nerve shown by Austrian and German reformists that when they fled, they fled to Moscow. They based their new-found Communism on the idea — vividly illustrated by experience and reality

— that 'bourgeois' freedom was a sham and a snare. This bifurcation of the European left — between those who cared for democratic proprieties no matter what and those who saw them as an ideological construct — led to disasters from which the Continent has never recovered. Even Fischer, by then a devout Stalinist, became a little upset soon after a talk he gave to the German and Austrian exiles in Moscow, defending the Hitler–Stalin Pact. The Nazis had invaded France, and he was in his room when 'suddenly the door flew open and a German Communist rushed in: "We've taken Paris!"' *Dummkopf.* How terrifying when the lessons of dogma are learned too well. One of the conformists at the meeting where Fischer spoke was Wilhelm Pieck, later President of the 'German Democratic Republic'. The German Communists managed to outlive Hitler, though not to live down their compromises with him, and when they came home it was as clients of the Red Army.

Given the utter historic discredit of the German right, the Cold War in Germany has basically been fought between two wings of the prewar German left: the Schmidts and Brandts on one side of the wall, and the Ulbrichts and Honeckers on the other. In one case we have NATO and hundreds of nuclear missiles as the price of 'pluralism'; in the other, a mediocre Sovietization as the price of an ideological commitment to 'the first socialist state on German soil'. Today, the polarities are being reversed. Red and Green forces in the Federal Republic are challenging the insanity of the nuclear state, and the citizens of the GDR are discovering for themselves that 'bourgeois' rights are human rights, and worth fighting for as such. The stupid but necessary conflict that began in the battle for Austria in 1927, and continued through Germany in 1933, stands a chance of being resolved. We should not be prevented, by the residual anti-German chauvinism that is such a morbid feature of our culture, from seeing the huge and hopeful opening. In an exhibition at the Reichstag, I saw an old leftist poster showing a horseshoe magnet spanning the German divide. The arm of the magnet planted in the East read 'Democracy' and the one planted in the West read 'Socialism'. A synthesis not unlike this one now seems a real possibility as the one-party state and the Cold War go to their graves together. Such a synthesis, in Germany of all places, would not be the end of history, but more like a new beginning for it.

The Nation, November 1989

THE FREE MARKET CARGO CULT

In a specially consecrated plot in Budapest's main cemetery the five most distinguished graves are the five which, until last year, were at once the most anonymous and the most defamed. Oafishly refusing to learn the lesson of Antigone, the regime of János Kádár wasted three decades by refusing to say where Imre Nagy and his fellow-combatants of the 1956 October Revolution were interred. Their names could not be mentioned in the press, and their last stand was described as 'counter-revolution', even as fascism. When they were properly mourned, named and given decent burial on 16 June 1989, most of the official party *apparat* were among the quarter-million silent mourners. To visit Plot 301 (as it has always been known in *samizdat*) at dusk, and to find the site heaped with fresh flowers and flags and candles, is to see the irreversible and dignified aspect of the slow-motion revolution that Hungary has been undergoing. A detail caught my attention. Nagy's grave is in the centre, and needs no stone. The markers erected for his four principal comrades — including the brave General Pal Maleter, who refused to turn his troops on the populace — all bear the same birth date. Every headstone reads 1917–1958. Each of these men, all of whom were executed as believing Communists, was born in year one of the Russian Revolution.

When I ask George Konrad whether he really means to say that the whole experience of Communism in this country has been a waste of time, he is significantly and usefully reticent: 'Ontologically, no detour can be utterly wasted. No human experience is completely void. Perhaps the values of socialism can only be realized by socialists in a nonsocialist society. Perhaps the search for a third way is not idealistic because we have already found the third way in the idea of Western Europe.' Certainly, it seems to me to be cynical and ahistorical to count the 1956 revolution a waste of time. Its example appears more pregnant and essential with the passage of years. By its coincidence with the Suez invasion and with the false dawn of Khrushchev's de-Stalinization, it shattered Communist unanimity and gave birth to the New Left — the first political movement to oppose the Cold War as a thing in itself. More recently, by announcing that they would automatically give refuge to anyone leaving Romania, and by allowing the transit of East German refugees, the Hungarian reformers did much to internationalize the Eastern European revolution and to ensure that it was, by and large, peaceful and democratic.

To appreciate the grandeur of the Hungarian resistance is to be very sensitive to anything that might vulgarize it. It was dispiriting to the utmost to see Budapest's Foreign Minister, Gyula Horn, return from an honourable visit to *Romania Libera* only to greet the Foreign Minister of South Africa. A smirking Roelof Botha announced that such matters as trade links and white emigration to Johannesburg were discussed. In an open session a few weeks before, the

Hungarian Parliament had eagerly taken the first offer it got from the IMF, as if it would be bad manners to show any reservations. Walking by the Danube after Christmas, I saw a queue outside a shop which, properly photographed by *Time*, could have illustrated any banal story about the miseries of Communism. It turned out to be the enormous daily queue for the Adidas store.

Of course it is true that under Kádár the Party built Hiltons and sold the workforce and the environment to Western concessionaires for hard currency, and did so while retaining a power monopoly. George Konrad told me that the fetishization of Western consumer goods was even more intense when there were fewer of them. And no doubt this is an emotional phase that must be gone through. But there is something uncritical about the cult of the 'free market' and of anything that might be termed 'Western', just as there was something repulsive in the earlier slavishness towards all things Russian. In Melanesia the islanders watched the Europeans build airstrips and jetties, and saw planes and ships arrive loaded with good things. They too built makeshift airstrips and jetties, hoping by this means to attract the envied riches. This 'cargo cult' led to intense disappointment for its practitioners — and not just because they didn't know the difference between production and consumption. So when Hungarians talk about von Hayek as if he had just been discovered, and about unemployment as if it were a new style of exercise therapy, about Thatcher and Bush as if they were innovators, and about South Africa as if it were simply another market economy, one has the dreary sensation of watching a second-rate old movie, and of realizing that one knows the ending.

Against this can be set the exhilarating fact that *politics* — not just the consoling consensus of of 'civil society' — is now possible once again in Hungary. The writer Istvan Eorsi, a leftist imprisoned after 1956, puts it very well in explaining his decision to join the Alliance of Free Democrats (SDS). The SDS is a coalition of neo-liberals and neo-conservatives for the most part, but it is a thinking organization that contains most of those who suffered in the battle for democratic change. It is denounced by the former ruling party, and by the right-wing populist opposition movement known as Democratic Forum, as being cosmopolitan, elitist and 'Trotskyist'. (Not much difficulty with the code words there.) As a consequence, the isolated, tough, ironic figures of the Hungarian left have had no choice but to join it. These individuals extend from Laszlo Rajk, son of the executed postwar Communist Prime Minister, to Eorsi, who says: 'In the end, I'd rather be comrades with people I trust but don't agree with entirely — we can argue — than with people to whom I'm ideologically close but can't trust.' Here is one of the most suggestive consequences of the depoliticization of a country by Stalinists who didn't believe a word of their own uplifting propaganda. Not for the first or the last time in history, the right people have the wrong line. At least that can change.

The Nation, February 1990

HOW NEO-CONSERVATIVES PERISH

I can now claim to have lived long enough to hear Ronald Reagan's chief foreign policy theorist, Jeane Kirkpatrick, defend a gradualist (read Gorbachevian) approach to independence for Lithuania, and this in the very week, late in April, when her former cheerleaders on Capitol Hill and the op-ed pages were crying 'Munich' and accusing President Bush of 'appeasement'. The place was Washington's Omni Shoreham Hotel, the occasion a weekend-long conference of the Committee for the Free World, the modestly titled *parapluie* of the movement styling itself neo-conservative. The advertised purpose of the gathering was to recast the long twilight struggle against the 'totalitarian' foe, but what actually transpired was a two-day confrontation between neo-conservatism and itself. The neo-cons do not *have* a style or a mood; they *are* a style and a mood. From the 'tough-minded' realism of *Commentary* and *The Public Interest* to the muscular 'family values' aesthetic of *The New Criterion*, the tone is one of 'I don't care if self-interest *is* unfashionable; I'm brave enough to affirm it.' And what holds for individuals and nations may be said, in this galère, to hold for ideas: the more strenuous the better, even if this means the more circular.

Words are watched and weighed carefully in this crowd, which makes them a pleasure to monitor. (I remember a neo-con speechmaker once saying that it was no accident the Russian language contained no word for détente. He was abashed, but by no means crushed, to be told that the English language apparently didn't contain one either.) It is not unfair to say that their politics have mainly consisted of key words and phrases, uttered with the proper sneer: 'Finlandization', 'disinformation', 'dupe', 'ripe fruit', 'choke point', 'fellow-traveller', 'strategic lifeline', 'fifth columnist', 'dagger pointed at the heart of', 'gullible', 'useful idiot', 'satellite state', 'infiltration', 'Chamberlain's umbrella', 'captive nation', 'peace through strength', 'moral equivalence', 'way of life', 'weakness and passivity', 'present danger'. This Scrabble of terms has suddenly tipped in chaos to the floor. And it has done so because of the demise of the neo-con Ur-word, the *echt* word: 'totalitarian'. What, in the wake of 1989, can it possibly mean? And, if it is deprived of its totemic power, how can one divine who, politically, is who?

The difficulty presented itself acutely at the first day's lunchtime session, when Kirkpatrick uttered her Baltic heresies. Norman Podhoretz, who first published Kirkpatrick's 'Dictatorships and Double Standards' in *Commentary*, and who thus applied the forceps at the birth of Kirkpatrick as a public nuisance, was joining with Jean-François Revel, author of the soothingly pessimistic *How Democracies Perish*, to arraign the West for its shameful cowardice over the captive Lithuanian nation. But the movement's one-time Jeanne d'Arc was having none of it. Quiet diplomacy, she averred, was the stuff. Realpolitik, not anti-Bolshevik outrage, was the method by which the people of Lithuania would win their place in the sun. Now, in the old days of, say, midsummer 1989, that is how Kirkpatrick might have responded to events in an 'authoritarian' part of the world (South Africa, for example) but never in the 'totalitarian' Soviet bloc. (Kirkpatrick won her post as Reagan's UN ambassador on the strength of this 'authoritarian–totalitarian' distinction.) Either the Soviet Union has metamorphosed from a 'totalitarian' to an 'authoritarian' state, impossible according to Kirkpatrick's theory — but earning it the right to a Kirkpatrick defence — or 'totalitarianism' had never been what it was thought to be; either way, the neo-conservative movement was now robbed of its theoretical undergirding; was an intellectual and moral shambles.

It is 'closing time in the playgrounds of the West', Cyril Connolly wrote of an earlier turning point. 'Does the "West" Still Exist?' inquired the rubric of the Free World conference, the very plaintiveness of the question echoing the combination of self-pity and grandiosity that has always informed the Free Worlders' bulletins and discussions. And all the Free Worlders were there. A table away at lunch I espied the smirking, perjured features of Elliott Abrams. Robert Bork made a rare, not-for-personal-profit appearance. Outstanding in the throng were the cheerful, joshing figure of Midge Decter, executive director of the committee, and the gorgeous, if acidulated, person of Hilton Kramer, looking as if he envied Midge her democratic manners, her wit, her panoptic world-view, and, perhaps above all, her marriage to Norman Podhoretz. All these people were ostensibly there to take personal credit for the final collapse of Communism. Why, then, did they look and sound so lost and deflated, like a herd of antis in search of a climax?

The old gruel was still being served up, lukewarm, by the panellists. 'Americans have *always* loved Soviet leaders.' 'Americans have *never* liked being a world power.' (These from Decter.) 'The Soviets are not giving up on their expansionist policy.' (This from Eugene V. Rostow, the man his father named for Debs, with a brother named for Walt Whitman.) My personal favourite came from a Thatcherite British delegate, who intoned, with heavy menace, 'Remember how nearly we had Henry Wallace as President of the United States.' Truly, the price of liberty is eternal vigilance. Somehow, though, the fizz had gone out of things. The house style of world-weary, superior sarcasm was still natural to most of the speakers, especially the ex-leftists among them. And there was always knowing applause for any jibe at the expense of the decade known as the sixties or the persons (noticeable by their scarcity, not to mention absence) one associates with affirmative action. But the lucubrations of *Commentary*, the *fatwahs* of the Ayatollah Solzhenitsyn, and the fervid search for the enemy within seemed as *passé* as — well, the Evil Empire itself. At the end of the opening session, which had featured Rostow and Decter, young John Podhoretz of the *Washington Times* ('Paper Moon', as I like to call it — and him) rose in astonishment to ask: Were none of the panellists going to *mention* the 1989 revolutions in Eastern Europe? A good question, none the worse for being asked in a tone of chubby filial bewilderment.

Should you be curious about the reticence of the neo-cons with regard to the astounding events of last fall in Prague, Bucharest, and Berlin, to say nothing of Budapest and Sofia, you might have the patience to turn up the essay written shortly before those very events by Jean-François Revel. (The neo-con right, so contemptuous for so long of the left's thralldom to Parisian sages, has picked itself a real lulu.) Discussing what the gullible had perceived to be the Soviet Union's ebbing international presence, he noted sapiently, for the readers of *Commentary*:

> Yet let us note that the pullbacks are all from conquests made since 1975, and even then only from parts of them, while others have not been put in question at all. So, although the instances of retreat do show that Moscow now regards direct territorial conquest in some cases as too costly and too risky, the balance sheet for the Kremlin for the entire period 1975–1990 will in the end be a positive one.

Revel was at his most acute and prescient when considering matters specifically European. About that continent he wrote:

> Gorbachev pursues the policies of his predecessors with prodigious Machiavellian charm, repeatedly intoning the magic word disarmament in the generation-old Soviet effort to separate Germany from the rest of Europe and Europe from the United States. Gorbachev aims to achieve by seduction what Brezhnev and Gromyko almost succeeded in achieving by threats.

There were some bold attempts, during the conference, at updating and surpassing Revel's majestic misreading of events. Gene Rostow darkly reported that a senior Gorbachev aide had spent seven years working on disinformation and that 'such habits die hard', and one felt, if only for a fleeting second, that Rostow ought to know. At the end of one discussion, Constantine Menges, former member of the Reagan–North National Security Council, stood to try his hand at spin-control: the Soviets, he maintained, had simply 'acquiesced' in the transformation of Eastern Europe. ('Acquiescence' is a word neither Erich Honecker nor Nicolae Ceauşescu would have chosen to describe what we now know to have been direct Soviet intervention against their regimes.) Josef Joffe, the neo-cons' favourite West German, inadvertently made a concession to reality when he remarked that short-range nuclear missiles, designed to obliterate places like Prague and Warsaw, had lost much of their allure these days in view of the fact that 'nice guys' like Havel and Walesa now lived there. Where, I wonder, did he think they lived before?

'Are we a gang of friends, a family?' Decter asked wistfully from the platform at one point. 'Or are we a long, sour marriage held together for the kids and now facing an empty nest?' Well, since you ask, however mawkishly.... There is in Washington a pervading sense that the neo-conservative movement has outlived its usefulness to the conservative Establishment. At the

reception preceding the conference, not one figure from the Bush administration could be seen, save for Irving Kristol's son, William, who works in Dan
Quayle's office and did a drop-by. The Reaganites had made good use of the
neo-cons, employing Abrams, Richard Perle, Kenneth Adelman, Linda
Chavez, and, most visibly, Kirkpatrick. But the Busheoisie has little need for
policy intellectuals of their sort, and little taste for their company. The only
prominent holdover from the Reagan era is Bernard Aronson, who now fills
Elliott Abrams's fetid shoes at the Department of State. By chance I ran into
him (Aronson, that is) at the White House Correspondents Dinner held the
weekend of the Free World conference and asked him why the folder bearing
his name still lay so forlornly uncollected at Decter's registration desk. He
replied that he hadn't even known that the conference was going on.

Since it was the demise of 'totalitarianism' as a useful term — useful in petri-
fying political opponents, in giving watery notions the strength of concrete —
that meant the demise of neo-conservatism, it might be instructive to trace the
history of its American usage, an undertaking not once suggested by the gathered Free Worlders. In America the key texts of the 'totalitarian' idea were
fully internalized during the early years of the Cold War. David Rousset's
L'Univers concentrationnaire, a difficult and interesting book more often cited
than read, was among the first to make the crucial identification between
Nazism and Communism, an identification that supplies the 'totalitarian'
concept with most of what it possesses by way of moral energy. A great deal of
popularizing was done for the notion by more readily available and intelligible
writers of imaginative fiction and poetry — Arthur Koestler, Czeslaw Milosz,
George Orwell, Stephen Spender. More recently, Milan Kundera has
performed the same function. Just as, in *The Captive Mind*, Milosz wrote about
the Baltic republics as if they had passed away, with their peoples, to join the
Mayas and the Incas, so Kundera wrote of the nations of East–Central Europe
that they had effectively ceased to exist as countries or as cultural entities. The
hidden appeal of the 'totalitarian' presentation has always been the powerful
and ruthless use it made of the idea of despair. It was this Spenglerian
pessimism that allowed people to think of Prague and Budapest as thermonuclear targets rather than as the vital, human European capitals they never ceased
to be.

Why was the audience for such pessimism so eager and rapacious? The
essential clue is to be found in the writing of James Burnham, the real intellectual founder of the neo-conservative movement and the original proselytizer,
in America, of the theory of 'totalitarianism'. Burnham was the first important
Marxist to defect all the way over to the right in his now-neglected masterpiece *The Managerial Revolution*, published in 1941. He was the first to generalize the symmetry between Nazism and Communism, appropriating the
anti-fascist term *fifth column*, for instance, and applying it adroitly to real or
supposed Communist fellow-travellers in the United States. In a 1945 article
in *Partisan Review* entitled 'Lenin's Heir', he set out in Neo-Platonic terms a

conception of the Communist grand design so necessary to Cold War thinking:

> The Soviet power, emanating outwards from the integrally totalitarian center, proceeds outward by Absorption (the Baltics, Bessarabia, Bukovina, East Poland), Domination (Finland, the Balkans, Mongolia, North China and tomorrow Germany), Orienting influence (Italy, France, Turkey, Iran, Central and South China) until it is dissipated in the outer material sphere, beyond the Eurasian boundaries, of momentary Appeasement and Infiltration (England, the United States).

Two years later Burnham published a book, *The Struggle for the World*, in which he showed his hand. Not content with repeating his grand, inclusive description of a Soviet global plot, he now declared what should be done to counter it:

> The reality is that the only alternative to the Communist World Empire is an American Empire which will be, if not literally world-wide in formal boundaries, capable of exercising decisive world control.

The connection could hardly be plainer. It was necessary, if one desired the latter (American Empire), to believe in the former (Communist Empire). The book was published in the same month – March 1947 – as the promulgation of the Truman Doctrine, and received enormous and flattering attention for its handy 'What is to be done?' properties.

Burnham had written *The Struggle for the World* while he was working for the Office of Strategic Services, the forerunner of the Central Intelligence Agency; in its original form, it was a briefing paper for the American delegation at Yalta. When the Congress for Cultural Freedom was formed in the early 1950s, Burnham was among its founders. He was successfully recommended to *Encounter* by Irving Kristol as 'a first-rate essayist on cultural matters'. In every important respect, he was the godfather of the Committee for the Free World – every respect save, perhaps, one. Burnham never shrank dishonestly from using the word 'empire'. He was always explicitly in favour of it, once writing:

> The first great plan in the third stage is for the United States to become what might be called the 'receiver' for the disintegrating British Empire.... The attempt is to swing the orientation of the Empire from its historical dependence on Europe to dependence on and subordination to the American central area. Success in the case of the English Dominion (Canada) and possessions located in the Americas is already at hand.... Along with the United States' receivership plan for the British Empire go still broader aims in connection with the rest of South America, the Far East (including conspicuously the Far Eastern colonies of formerly sovereign European states) and in fact the whole world.

'In fact the whole world ...' When the CIA trained local mercenaries in the art of torture, it would do so by pretending to teach them how to withstand it. In much the same way, by attributing the global design to the 'totalitarian' foe ('arc of crisis', 'soft underbelly', 'Southern flank') the Cold War propagandists were able to remain indirect and even defensive about a plan of their own. It was an axiom of 'containment' that no part of the known world could be considered neutral. 'Neutralism' was among the Cold Warriors' gravest curse words, applied with caustic hostility to India and even France. Those who were not with were against, subjected to intense economic and ideological — and sometimes military — pressure to fall into line.

Two further distinctive emphases were necessary to the all-enclosing world-view. It was proposed, first, that 'totalitarian' dictatorships were different from tyrannies of, say, the banana-republic sort because they were marked by a terrifying acquiescence, if not complicity, among their subjects. There was no such thing as a private life in the 'totalitarian' universe; every citizen was a member of the regiment, and every element in life a reinforcement of the conscription. It was argued, thus, that this very ruthlessness gave the 'totalitarians' a definite advantage in the global contest. While the decadent West pursued its democratic, self-critical, hedonistic path, fraught with emasculating influences such as homosexuality and investigative journalism, the tyrants were breeding a Spartan, manly phalanx, rejoicing in power and unanimity and force. How often were we told that the Red Army had a free hand in Afghanistan because 'there is no public opinion in the Soviet Union', while the United States had been undone in Indochina by snooping reporters, carping liberals, and gnawing, self-destructive introspection? Jean-François Revel, in *How Democracies Perish*, asserted that democracy gravely hampered the West, tying its hands and limiting its reach. Writers in the same key, from Michael Ledeen to Charles Krauthammer, moaned and whined about 'the imperial Congress', with its alleged habit of stymieing and miring the bold, heterosexual initiatives of a Henry Kissinger or an Oliver North. Our neo-con intellectuals, *pace* Burnham, time and again flirted with the idea that there was an essential incompatibility between democracy and survival.

The Committee for the Free World issues its pamphlets and screeds through something calling itself the Orwell Press, so it may be worth mentioning that George Orwell had Burnham's number from the start. In two long critiques of *The Managerial Revolution* and *The Struggle for the World*, he shrewdly pointed out Burnham's guilty secret — namely, that he was *envious* of the 'totalitarian' precept and had a strong, vicarious admiration for it. Orwell stressed Burnham's adoration for the full panopl of strength and cruelty, saying that his real desire was not to combat dictatorship and expansionism but to emulate them. The same tone is easy to discern in the neo-conservative voice. And it goes some way towards explaining the palpable melancholy with which the neo-cons have received the news from Eastern Europe. Not only have they lost an apparently unsleeping Soviet foe, whose very existence kept them on permanent moral red alert; not only have they lost the prime justification for American power and American empire; they have also lost the sheet anchor of an encompassing theory. The revolutions of 1989 negated *every single one* of the assumptions upon which the 'totalitarian' hypothesis rested. The Soviet Union did not intend to move its massed armour across the north German plain into Western Europe. The massed armour, which was always actually for the control of Eastern Europe, was even to be withdrawn from there. This was not done to impress the West, which had neither asked for nor expected the dissolution of the Warsaw Pact. And the population — ah, what can one say of the population? Cheerful, orderly, well-informed, happily familiar with all the values and procedures of democracy, anti-militarist, conscious of history — much more laughter than forgetting. Where had they all come from? How could such a people have been incubated under a 'totalitarian' system, where obedience and thought control were the norms?

In his sole reference during the conference to the actual peoples of the eastern part of Europe, Norman Podhoretz made a comment so shocking and awful that it was not until sometime afterwards that it sank in. Denouncing the 'shameful' Bush policy of appeasement with regard to Lithuanian independence, he predicted that if matters went on in this way there would be a recrudescence of guerrilla warfare in the Lithuanian forests, of the kind that had continued spasmodically after the Second World War. There was a definite relish in the way Podhoretz made this forecast, and in the way he name-dropped Vladimir Bukovsky as authority for it. (Bukovsky is one of those over-rated Russian exiles who have been writing for years about the axiomatic impossibility of a Gorbachev-style reformism.) Of all the conceivable outcomes for Lithuania, it is hard to picture a more gruesome one than a return to the futile 'resistance', often mounted and led by ex-Nazis, that it used to be the CIA's job to nourish and finance. To orate in these terms, at a time when independence parties are legal and electable in the Baltic states, is to betray the most morbid kind of nostalgia for the days when 'resistance' meant only clandestine and covert operations — funded from Washington, cheered on by Radio Free Europe, and wasting both time and life.

The neo-conservative movement is really a mentality, a mentality of refined pessimism about politics and rancid pessimism about human nature. As such, it is more or less impervious to new evidence or new experience, and increasingly obsessed with refighting battles of the past — such as the great triumph over George McGovern or the 'stab in the back' over Vietnam or the moral depredations of the counter-culture. It has also been centrally preoccupied with power and more explicitly concerned with its cultivation and exercise than any comparable intellectual movement. Writing to his son, John, in the 1979 prologue to *Breaking Ranks*, Podhoretz spoke with feeling about his ambition to be certified by the Establishment as having arrived. He described how, in an earlier generation:

old WASP families felt that the country was being stolen away and changed into a place that had no room for the likes of them. Edmund Wilson, who was probably the most important literary intellectual of his time, came out of just such a background, and in one of his essays he describes the difficulties his father and his uncles, educated at schools like Exeter and Andover and such colleges as Princeton and Yale and trained 'for what had once been called the learned professions,' experienced in trying 'to deal with a world in which this kind of education and the kind of ideals it served no longer really counted for much.'

This is the sort of angst that Wilson could handle and Podhoretz cannot. Having waited for years, as it seemed to them, to be admitted to the sanctum and the club, neo-cons like Podhoretz ingratiatingly squeezed in, only to find the place full of deconstructionists, historical revisionists and recreational drug-users, many of whom listened to rock music. (At the conference, incidentally, Hilton Kramer was eloquent in his disgust at the fact that Václav Havel admired John Lennon.) The choking hatred for 'the sixties' among this cabal — a hatred ultimately based on this failure to make it, WASP-style — has to be experienced in order to be believed. And against that Devil's decade, the surest prophylactic is the Establishment verities of the forties and fifties, when men were men and nuclear shelters were built to instil respect and discipline, and 'totalitarianism' was the clarifying antagonist. But alas, even the Establishment is now looking for a peace dividend. Can it be long before Olin and the other foundations that have bankrolled the neo-cons tire of paying for pessimism?

At last November's gathering of the Committee for the Free World, when things were already beginning to look a bit too bright for holders of the neo-con world-view, Frank Gaffney, a Richard Perle acolyte, announced that he and a few hard-liners were setting up the Center for Security Policy to resist appeasement tendencies in the weapons business. Seymour Weiss, one-time Reagan adviser, denounced Helmut Kohl as a dupe for lending money to the East Germans. You would not have guessed that the Berlin Wall was within hours of its fall. But if you had listened to the contribution of Bruce Weinrod, head Heritage Foundation military–industrial acolyte for much of the 1980s, you would have known why the idea was an unwelcome one:

> The first thing [Bush] ought to do is call Margaret Thatcher and try to talk some sense into her. She was recently quoted as saying the Cold War is over. That really is a problem if you have somebody who is tough-minded saying that. She may not understand that, at least with the American public, you have to create a sense of some urgency about what we are doing; *otherwise, the course of least resistance is followed and funding shifts to social programs.* [Emphasis added.]

There went the feline, screeching from the bag. In case of misunderstanding, Weinrod added:

> The Soviets have stated that one of their major objectives is to remove what they call the 'enemy image.' Unless something comes up that forces them to act in an overt way, making it clear that they have not changed, it is going to be a very difficult challenge to maintain our military expenditures.

How to maintain our military expenditures in a world without a Soviet enemy? Perhaps the Free Worlders will one day be honest enough with themselves to convene a conference to answer that.

Harper's Magazine, July 1990

APPOINTMENT IN SARAJEVO

The daily round in Sarajevo is one of dodging snipers, scrounging for food and water, collecting rumours, visiting morgues and blood banks and joking heavily about near misses. The shared experience of being, along with the city's inhabitants, a sort of dead man on leave, makes for levelling of the more joyous and democratic sort, even if foreign writers are marked off from the rest by our flak jackets and our ability to leave, through the murderous corridor of the airport road, more or less at will. The friendship and solidarity of Sarajevo's people will stay with all of us for the rest of our lives and indeed, at the present rate of attrition, it may be something that survives only in the memory. The combined effect of incessant bombardment and the onset of a Balkan winter may snuff out everything I saw.

On a paved street in the centre of town, near the Eternal Flame (already snuffed out by lack of fuel) which consecrates the Partisan resistance in World War II, is a bakery shop. Eighteen people were killed by a shell that hit a bread line a few weeks ago, and mounds of flowers mark the spot. Shortly after I paid my own visit, another shell fell in exactly the same place, randomly distributing five amputations among a dozen or so children. One of the children had just been released from hospital after suffering injuries in the first 'incident'. A few hundred yards farther on, as I was gingerly approaching the imposing building that houses the National Library of Bosnia, a mortar exploded against its side and persuaded me to put off my researches. All of this became more shocking to me when I went with some Bosnian militiamen to the top of Hum, the only high ground still in the defenders' keep. It was amazing, having spent so much time confined in the saucer of land below, to see the city splayed beneath like a rape victim. This sensation was soon supplanted by outrage. From this perspective, it was blindingly clear that the Serbian gunners can see exactly what they are doing.

Entering the handsome old Austro-Hungarian edifice that houses the presidency of Bosnia and Herzegovina, and that absorbed several hits that day,

I saw in the vestibule a striking poster. Executed in yellow and black, it was a combined logo featuring the Star of David, the Islamic star and crescent, the Roman Catholic cross and the more elaborate cruciform of the Orthodox Church. *Gens Una Sumus*, read the superscription. 'We Are One People.' Here, even if rendered in iconographic terms, was the defiant remnant of 'the Yugoslav idea'. (Pictures of Tito, incidentally, are still common in Sarajevo, in both public and private settings.) And here also was all that was left of internationalism. The display was affecting, and not only because it rebuked the primitive mayhem in the immediate vicinity. All across former Yugoslavia a kind of mass surrender to unreason is taking place, hoisting emblems very different from the Sarajevan.

Across the street from the Zagreb café where I am writing, there is a display of adoring memorabilia, all of it brashly recalling the rule of Ante Pavelic and his bestial Ustashe in Croatia, which was constituted as a Nazi and Vatican protectorate between 1941 and 1945. Young men in black shirts and warped older men nostalgic for fascism need no longer repress the urge to fling the right arm skyward. Their 'militia', long used for harassing Croatian Serbs, is now heavily engaged in the 'cleansing' of western Herzegovina, in obvious collusion with the Serbian Chetniks to the east and south. Miraculous Virgins make their scheduled appearance. Lurid posters show shafts of light touching the pommels of mysterious swords, or blazoning the talons of absurd but vicious two-headed eagles. More than a million Serbs attend a frenzied rally on the battle site of Kosovo, where their forebears were humiliated *in 1389*, and hear former Communists rave in the accents of wounded tribalism. Ancient insignias, totems, feudal coats of arms, talismans, oaths, rituals, icons and regalia jostle to take the field. A society long sunk in political stagnation, but one nevertheless well across the threshold of modernity, is convulsed: puking up great rancid chunks of undigested barbarism. In this 1930s atmosphere of coloured shirts, weird salutes and licensed sadism, one is driven back to that period's clearest voice, which spoke of:

> The Enlightenment driven away,
> The habit-forming pain,
> Mismanagement and grief:
> We must suffer them all again.

We must suffer them all again. But Bosnia, and especially Sarajevo, is not so much the most intense version of the wider conflict as it is the heroic exception to it. During respites from the fighting, I was able to speak with detachments of Bosnian volunteers. At every stop they would point with pride and cheerfulness to their own chests and to those of others, saying: 'I am Muslim, he is Serb, he is Croat'. It was the form their propaganda took, but it was also the truth. I met one local commander, Alia Ismet, defending a shattered old people's home seventy metres from the Serbian front line, who, as well as being a defector from the Yugoslav National Army (JNA), is also an Albanian from the province of Kosovo. There was a Jew among the entrenchment-diggers on Hum Hill. Colonel Jovan Divjak, deputy commander of the Bosnian Army, is a Serb. I shook his hand as he walked, with a Serbo-Croat aide-de-camp named Srdjan Obradovic ('Obradovic is a multinational name'), among the nervous pedestrians on the edge of the Old City, under intermittent fire at noonday. He was unarmed, and popular.

In the Old City itself, you can find a mosque, a synagogue, a Catholic and an Orthodox church within yards of one another. Almost all have been hit savagely from the surrounding hills, though the gunner is usually accurate enough to try and spare the Orthodox. ('Burn it all,' said General Ratko Mladic, the JNA commander whose radio traffic was intercepted, recorded, and authenticated recently. 'It is better to bombard Pofilici ... there are not many Serbs there,' replied his more 'moderate' deputy, Colonel Tomislav Sipcic.) The Jewish Museum is badly knocked about and closed, and perhaps one-third of the city's Jews have fled. An ancient community, swelled by refugees from Spain in 1492 and resilient enough to have outlived the Ustashe version of the Final Solution, is now threatened with dispersal. Even so, an Israeli Army Radio reporter, who had come hoping to cover the evacuation of Jews, told me that he was impressed by how many of them wanted to stay on and fight. The exquisite Gazi Huzref Beg mosque, set in the lovely but vulnerable Muslim quarter of wooden houses and shops, has a crude shell-hole in its minaret, and its courtyard garden is growing unkempt. The mosques, very important in the siege for their access to antique stone cisterns or *sadrivan*, normally used for ablution before prayer, have found even those old wells drying up. And thirst is a fiercer enemy even than hunger.

To speak of 'quarters' is not to speak of ghettos — or at least not yet. A good estimate puts the proportion of mixed marriages here at one in three, a figure confirmed by anecdote and observation. So to try to make Bosnia 'uniform' in point of confession or 'ethnicity' is not to put it together but to tear it apart. To call this dirty scheme 'cleansing' is to do grotesque violence to both language and society. To turn, for a moment, from the period's greatest poet to its greatest essayist, we find that in 1933, Leon Trotsky wrote in *Harper's*:

> The idea proclaimed by Hitler of the necessity of re-adapting the *state* frontiers of Europe to the frontiers of its *races* is one of those reactionary utopias with which the National Socialist program is stuffed. ... A shifting of the internal frontiers by a few dozens or hundreds of miles in one direction or another would, without changing much of anything, involve a number of human victims exceeding the population of the disputed zone. [Emphasis added.]

The 2.4 million refugees and the numberless dead *already* outweigh the populations of the various 'corridors' by which Serbian and Croatian nationalists seek to purify their own states and to dismember Bosnia. As before, their 'nationalism' has its counterpart in the axiomatic resort to partition by certain 'noninterventionist statesmen'. When Lord Carrington, the European

Community's mediator and a man obviously bored with the whole business, recommends 'cantonization', the Serbian puppet in Bosnia, Radovan Karadzic, and the Croatian client there, Mate Boban, both make a little holiday in their hearts. The British Foreign Office's favourite fetish has triumphed again. After Ireland, India, Palestine, the Sudetenland and Cyprus, partition – or ghettoization – ceases to look like coincidence. Cantons by all means! say the fascists of all stripes. They won't take long for us to cleanse! Near the town of Novska, on the Croatia–Bosnia border, I came upon a scene that illustrated the process in microcosm. An immaculate contingent of Jordanian UN soldiers was politely concealing its shock at the tribal and atavistic brutality of this war between the whites. It had done its task of separating and disarming the combatants in its immediate area. But here came six busloads of Bosnian Muslim refugees, many of them injured, who had taken the worst that Christian Europe could throw at them and were bewildered to find themselves under the care of a scrupulous Hashemite chivalry. They had come perforce to Croatia, but Croatia wants no part of these victims of 'Serbian terror', a terror that it denounced only when it was directed at Catholics.

A digression, here, on the etymology of 'ethnic cleansing'. Few journalists who employ the expression know where it originated, and its easy one-sided usage has maddened the already paranoid Serbs. José-Maria Mendiluce, the exemplary Basque who came to Zagreb from Kurdistan as the special envoy of the United Nations High Commission for Refugees, told me he thought he had coined the term himself (though he blushed to recall that he had used the word 'cleaning'). But of course there is no 'ethnic' difference among the Slavs, any more than there was between Swift's Big-Endians and Little-Endians. Nor is there a linguistic difference. And religion has not yet succeeded (though it has often failed) in defining a nationality. So 'cultural cleansing' might cover the facts of the case, if it did not sound more ludicrous than homicidal. At all events, a reporter for Belgrade TV described the gutted, conquered Bosnian city of Zvornik with the single word 'cist' (clean), after it fell in April. And the unhygienic Serbian militia which did the job, the self-described Chetniks (a name first used by Serbian royalist irregulars who, during the Second World War, could not decide whether they detested Tito more, or less, than Hitler) of the warlord Voytislav Seselj, also freely used the happy expression. The 'camps', which were the inescapable minor counterpart of this process, have at least served to concentrate a flickering European and American mind upon a fading but potent memory, though comparisons to Belsen and Auschwitz show not that people learn from history but that they resolutely decline to do so, and instead plunder it for facile images.

Who, if anyone, does play the part of the Reich in this nightmare? *Smrt Fasizmu! Sloboda Narodu!* (Death to Fascism! Freedom to the People!) say the wall posters of the Sarajevo Commune. In most of the Western media the role of fascist is assigned to the Serbs without hesitation. In order to try to comprehend the Serbian political psyche, I had to visit – and indirectly to loot – two highly significant museums. The first of these was the Gavrilo Princip Museum in Sarajevo, which stands by the bridge of the same name on the Miljacka River and is normally enfiladed by Serbian gunfire. Its wrecked appearance is deceptive, none the less, because although it has taken a round or two of Serbian mortaring, its actual destruction was wrought by enraged Sarajevan citizens. Gavrilo Princip, who stood quivering on this corner on 28 June 1914, waiting to fire the shot heard round the world at the fat target of the Austrian Archduke Franz Ferdinand, was a member of the Young Bosnia organization, which yearned and burned for the fusion of Bosnia with Serbia. No cause could be less fashionable in Sarajevo today, and the crowd had even dug up the famous two 'footprints' sunk in the pavement to memorialize Princip's supposed stance. Until recently this was the museum of the national hero, and it bore witness that Serbia, in alliance with Russia, was the historic guarantor of all Slavs. Princip appears to have chosen the date for the assassination to coincide with the exact anniversary of the Serbian defeat by the Muslim Turks at Kosovo in 1389, which testifies to the power of aggrieved memory and to the Serbians' conviction that *they* are the victims of regional history, under-appreciated by those for whom they have sacrificed.

The second museum I visited was the site of the Jasenovac concentration camp – a real one this time – where, during the Nazi period, some hundreds of thousands of Serbs and Jews, as well as Gypsies and Croatian Communists, were foully slaughtered by the Croatian Ustashe regime of Ante Pavelic. No Germans even supervised this 'cleansing', which was an enthusiastic all-volunteer effort to rival the butchery in Latvia or the Ukraine. Here is the Serbian Babi Yar, a piercing wound in the heart. It sits on a broad, handsome field where the rivers Sava and Una converge. During the appalling Serb–Croat combat last year, it was occupied for a while by Croatian forces. They methodically trashed the museum and the exhibits, and left only the huge, ominous mounds that mark the mass graves. As in Sarajevo, I was able to salvage a few gruesome souvenirs from the debris. My Serbian guide, a friendly metalworker named Mile Trkulja, told me: 'The world blames the Serbs for everything, but nobody writes about Jasenovac.' In other words, it was not so very difficult for the Serbs to become that most risky and volatile of all things – a self-pitying majority. (The man who commanded the now-notorious POW camp at Omarska, unearthed last month, had been born in Jasenovac. 'Those to whom evil is done ...') Faced with the mass expulsion of Serbs from the 'new' Croatia and laden with historical resentment, many of them fell for the crudest option, exemplified by the four C's on the Serbian emblem, which translate approximately to mean 'Only Unity Can Save the Serbs.' Here was a Versailles mentality, replete with defeat and fear on the part of the stronger side.

In an astounding speech given at the last Congress of Serbian Intellectuals to be held in Sarajevo, as late as March 1992, the Serbian academic Milorad Ekmecic was so daring as to phrase this consciousness directly:

The Serbian people do not want a state determined by the interests of the great powers and of European Catholic clericalism, but one which emerges from the ethnic and historical right possessed by every people in the world. In the history of the world, only the Jews have paid a higher price for their freedom than the Serbs. Because of their losses in war, and because of massacres, the most numerous people in Yugoslavia, the Serbs, have in Bosnia-Herzegovina fallen to second place, and today our policy and our general behavior carry within themselves *the invisible stamp of a struggle for biological survival.* Fear governs us.... Therefore the internal division of Bosnia-Herzegovina into three national parts is the minimal guarantee for the maintenance by Serbian *and Croatian* peoples of a partial unity with their national homes. [Emphasis added.]

Under the dispensation of Serbian leader Slobodan Milosevic, notional heir to a vestigial Socialist Party, this combined pathology of superiority/inferiority has become the equivalent of state dogma. With dismaying speed, and by a macabre metamorphosis, the World War II Partisan slogan of One Yugoslavia has mutated into yells for a Greater Serbia, and the army devised by Tito for defence against foreign intervention has been turned loose, along with various militias, against civilians and open cities. You could, without stretching things too much, describe this hybrid as 'national socialism'.

But it is also true that Croatia has a fascist ideology and a contempt for Serbian rights. President Franjo Tudjman does not quite affirm the Ustashe tradition, and can usually contrive to keep his right arm by his side, but he did adopt a near-replica of the Pavelic symbol for his national flag, and he did write a stupid revisionist book that said (1) that the Jasenovac camp had really killed very few Serbs; and (2) that in any case it was run largely by Jews! He coupled this crassness with a campaign against Serbs living in Croatia, 200,000 of whom 'relocated' as a result. Finally, he solicited support for his egotistical unilateralism from Germany, Austria and Italy, thus materializing the very geopolitical alliance that every Serb is taught by history to fear. Yet Serbs had never been persecuted in Bosnia. Nor had Croats. But now the Serbian and Croatian irredentists are allied in a sort of Molotov–Ribbentrop Pact against a defenceless neighbour. (Ekmecic was wrong. There will be *two* Bosnias, not three, and he knows it.) Each camp exploits its Sudeten minorities to establish 'pure' mini-states that will in time demand fusion with the mother- and father-lands. The Serbs have proclaimed 'republics' in Croatian Krajina, and in Bosnia. The turn of Kosovo and Macedonia is probably not far behind. Meanwhile, the Croats have begun the annexation of western Herzegovina, on Bosnian soil. There is no guarantee at all that this narcissistic subdivision will not replicate itself across international frontiers (involving Greece and Bulgaria in the case of Macedonia and Albania in the case of Kosovo) and attract the 'protective' interest of outside powers like Turkey, armed with NATO weapons. But then, that's what Balkanization is supposed to mean.

There is no need to romanticize the Muslim majority in Bosnia. But they have evolved a culture that expresses the plural and tolerant side of the

Ottoman tradition — some of this subtle and diverse character can be found in the stories of Ivo Andric, Yugoslavia's Nobel laureate — and they have no designs on the territory or identity of others. The Bosnian President, Alija Izetbegovic, is a practising Muslim, which makes him an exception among his countrymen. I have read his book, *Islam Between East and West*, a vaguely eccentric work that shows an almost pedantic fidelity to ideas of symbiosis between 'the three monotheisms' and the humanist tradition of social reform. In the rather surreal atmosphere of a press conference under shellfire, I asked Izetbegovic, who is accused by both Serbs and Croats of wanting to proclaim a fundamentalist republic, what he thought of the *fatwah* condemning Salman Rushdie. He gave the defining reply of the 'moderate' Muslim, saying that he did not like the book but could not agree to violence against the author. It is possible to meet the occasional Bosnian Muslim fanatic, and it is true that some of them made an attempt to sequester some Sarajevo Serbs in a football stadium. But that action was swiftly stopped, and roundly denounced in the Sarajevo newspaper *Oslobodenje* (Liberation). None of the Bosnian Serbs I met complained of cruelty or discrimination, and where they had heard of isolated cases they reminded me that it was the Serbian forces who had stormed across the River Drina, thus breaching a centuries-old recognition of the integrity of the Bosnian patchwork. If, however, that patchwork is ripped to shreds and replaced with an apartheid of confessional Bantustans, those who like to talk ominously of Bosnian Muslim fundamentalism may get their wish, or their pretext.

During the Tito and post-Tito years, one used to read *Praxis*, a journal of secular intellectuals, in order to find out what impended in Yugoslavia. Suppressed by the party–state in 1975, the magazine continued to publish as *Praxis International* under the aegis of Jürgen Habermas and other European and American sympathizers. Since the push for Greater Serbia began to ignite every other micro-nationalism in the region, I had not heard the voice of *Praxis* above the snarlings and detonations. But in Zagreb I did find the oldest and the youngest member of this apparently irrelevant collective. Professor Rudi Supek is a veteran by any definition. For his work in organizing resistance among Yugoslav workers in Nazi-occupied France, he was sent to Buchenwald and is now the last survivor of that camp's successful 'Liberation Committee'. He left the Communist Party when Tito broke with Stalin in 1948, and now tries to keep alive the ideas of secularism and internationalism in a Croatia that has grown hostile again. 'My family is an old Croat family, but I have no choice but to say I am still Yugoslav. In Buchenwald I was the chosen representative of Serbs, Bosnians and Croats, and they were Yugoslav in a way that I cannot betray.' Supek spoke with regret of the defection of some distinguished Serbian *Praxis* members. Professor Mihailo Markovic, on whose behalf I remember signing a petition or two in days gone by, is now a vice president of Slobodan Milosevic's Serbian Socialist Party and an ideologue of the diminished Serbian ideal. Svetozar Stojanovic, likewise, has become the personal secretary of 'Yugoslavia's' exiguous President, Dobrisa Cosic, whose stories about Partisan martyrdom have now taken on a distinctly Chetnik tone.

Zarko Puhovski, the younger *Praxis* adherent, teaches political philosophy at Zagreb University and bears with stoicism the anti-Semitic cracks that come his way as the son of a Jewish mother and a Croatian Communist father who did hard time in Jasenovac. 'If you say you are a Croatian atheist, given that there are no ethnic or linguistic differences,' he told me, 'the next question is: How do you know you are not a Serb?' For both Puhovski and Supek, the contest with their 'own' chauvinism was the deciding one. And for both of them, the defence of multinational Bosnia was the crux.

'Both the Chetniks and the Ustashe should be told to keep out of Bosnia,' said Supek. 'The fascists on both sides must be defeated and disarmed. If this needs an international protectorate, it should be provided.'

'The embargo on arms to "both sides" is pure hypocrisy,' said Puhovski. 'The Bosnians need arms to defend themselves, and the JNA has appropriated to itself the weapons that used to belong to everybody.' This, by the way, echoed the street opinion in Sarajevo, which roundly opposed the idea of foreign troops fighting their battles but bitterly recalled that the lavishly accoutred People's Army had been paid for out of the historic tax levies of Croats, Bosnians and Macedonians, and witheringly criticized the moral equivalence that the great powers are using as a handwashing alibi. Both Supek and Puhovski do their best to keep in touch with their Serbian counterparts, despite reciprocal jeers about 'treason' and despite wrenching breakdowns in ordinary means of communication. Supek gave me a printed statement from committed Serbian democrats, who denounced the ruin brought on their country by Milosevic's realm of delusion. Puhovski told me of the courageous Mirjana Miocinovic, widow of the great novelist Danilo Kis, who wrote to Milosevic renouncing her academic privileges and refusing the patronage of conquerors and occupiers.

For now, all these are no more than efforts to 'show an affirming flame'. But they may not be merely quixotic. Post-Communist Europe is hesitating on the brink of its own version of Balkanization, and Bosnia gives an inkling of the values of multicultural, long evolved and mutually fruitful cohabitation. Not since Andalusia has Europe owed so much to a synthesis, which also stands as a perfect rebuke to the cynical collusion between the apparently 'warring' fanatics. If Sarajevo goes under, then all who care for such things will have lost something precious, and will curse themselves because they never knew its value while they still had it.

The Nation, September 1992

4
NO CLASS: TORYISM TODAY

'SOCIETY' AND ITS ENEMIES

An underclass is a handy thing. In fact, no ruling class should be without one. It scares the middle class, and it arouses the contempt of the working class. These are powerful emotions: in the former instance the fear of crime, and in the latter the traditional dislike for the indigent and the unskilled. At election time, figures like Willie Horton — the products of an abandoned and demoralized stratum — can actually be run against. In the intervals the same imagery of the feral and the feckless can be mobilized, as if the inhabitants of the lower orders were just a given, to be put out of mind until or unless needed, like demons for a morality play. Margaret Thatcher did us the favour of putting this succinctly in a celebrated interview with a British women's magazine a year or so ago: 'And, you know, there is no such thing as society. There are individual men and women, and there are families.' Over the past decade and more, this attitude as applied to the British urban landscape has had results that it would be lazy to term predictable. A staple of middle-class conversation in London these days is the astonishing discrepancy between the classes, and the ways in which this discrepancy has been intensified by the poll tax. 'We've got a four-bedroom house, so we'll pay £500 less. But old Mrs Thing — she's our cleaning lady and we'd be lost without her — well, *she's* going to be £300 *worse off.*' Let the *lumpen* elements take the law into their own hands, however, and we soon enough find out that there is such a thing as society after all. In fact, this society is so definitely constituted as to have identifiable foes — 'enemies of society'. Loud and furious were Thatcher's rebukes to these enemies after the poll tax riots in London on the weekend of April Fools' Day. It turned out that we all had obligations as well as rights, a social contract to uphold, a duty to stand behind the forces of decency, and I don't know what else.

In the coverage of these disturbances in the American news media, I caught a distinct note of shock, as if the use of physical force were somehow axiomatically un-English. I've never understood why this illusion persists so doggedly. The British have a record of global violence second to few, and used to be celebrated throughout Europe as well as Asia and Africa for their willingness to employ deadly force. Until the present century, moreover, English social relations were extremely tempestuous, with the London mob very often used by Church and king against reform, and with the great British streetfighter called upon repeatedly in battles for the right to vote, to organize, to publish unlicensed newspapers and to be rid of arbitrary taxation.

The last issue is the germane one here. The Peasants' Revolt of 1381 may have been made easier by the shortage of labour that resulted from the Black Death a generation earlier, but it was ignited by a poll tax — a tax on merely being alive and having a head to count. Later, as Grafton's *Chronicle* put it in 1568: 'The people greatly murmured for the payment of foure pence the polle.' In 1637, John Hampden defied the subsequently executed King Charles I over the levying of 'ship money'. The Establishment learned little from this, publishing in the London *Gazette* for 1689 'An Act for Raising Money by a Poll, and otherwise, towards the Reducing of Ireland'. There is, in both the active and the passive repudiation of the Tories' latest impost, a social memory at work, and a historical one as well. Not all of this memory is to do with flagrant inequality and inequity. It also concerns the matter of democracy and representation. Just as poll taxes became notorious in the South as a means of keeping black Americans off the voting rolls, so the struggle against poll taxes in England has always involved questions of political justice. In the present case, Thatcher has made it plain that her real target is the autonomous local and city government system, which tends to return Labour and independent councils. The poll tax will throw the burden of revenue-raising on to this hard-pressed sector, and shift the responsibility for basic services and provisions. The temptation for voters will be to elect the party locally that promises the least crippling poll tax assessment, and this in turn will advance the coming of an atomized, anomic society in which private affluence and public squalor more or less necessitate each other. Those who wish to avoid the tax, as millions are already trying to do, will have to stay off the electoral register from which they and their dwellings can be identified. For them, there will indeed be hardly any such thing as society.

The recent pictures of the crowd versus the mounted police are a convenient, if stark, image of the 'free economy/strong state' project that has been the essence of Thatcherism. After more than ten years of it, Britain has emerged as the most reactionary country in Western Europe, with the worst unemployment, the most offences logged before the European Court of Human Rights, the largest relative expenditure on military and police forces and the second-lowest capital investment rate. The situation is so dismal, in fact, that a man like Michael Heseltine, who has spent all his career in the service of what is politely called 'venture capital' and who once donned a flak jacket to oversee the forcible eviction of peaceful demonstrators from a nuclear missile base, can be canvassed by apparently serious commentators as a healer and a moderate.

Thatcher is a much more durable and courageous politician than any member of her muted and neutered Cabinet, and it is always unwise to underestimate her. She does not care if she is liked so long as she is feared and respected. None the less it remains possible that, in the words one hears at every hand, 'The bloody woman's gone too far this time.' If so, we would do well to listen to the warning offered by Tony Benn, leader of Labour's vanquished left. The danger, he cautioned a few months ago, is that the Tory Party will change its leader and convince the electorate that there has been a change of government. It will take more than a shuffling of the personnel of the regime to reinstate the concept of society.

The Nation, April 1990

CREDIBILITY POLITICS:
SADO-MONETARIST ECONOMICS˙

It is rather a pity, considered from the standpoint of the professional politician or opinion-taker, that nobody knows exactly what 'credibility' is, or how one acquires it. 'Credibility' doesn't stand for anything morally straightforward, like meaning what you say or saying what you mean. Nor does it signify anything remotely quantifiable – any correlation between evidence presented and case made. Suggestively, perhaps, it entered the language as a consensus euphemism during the Vietnam War, when 'concerned' members of the Eastern Establishment spoke of a 'credibility gap' rather than give awful utterance to the thought that the Johnson administration was systematically lying. To restore its 'credibility', that administration was urged – not to stop lying, but to improve its public presentation. At some stage in the lesson learned from that injunction, the era of postmodern politics began. It doesn't seem ridiculous now to have 'approval ratings' that fluctuate week by week, because these are based upon the all-important 'perception' factor, which has in turn quite lost its own relationship to the word 'perceptive'.

When the Tories first hired a public-relations firm called Colman, Prentiss and Varley, back in the dying moments of the Macmillan regime, they got a fair bit of ribbing from cartoonists like the great Timothy Birdsall, and a certain amount of 'negative feedback' from their own more fastidious supporters. The Labour Party in those days was sternly opposed to the pseudo-science of PR and polling, and to the political hucksterism (such as the interviewing of candidates' wives) that went with it. Having won and lost a number of elections since then, and having seen Conservatism reinstated to an extent unguessed-at, Labour's leadership is now agreed on at least one big thing: that the battle of image, perception and credibility is what counts. Take Mr Hattersley, writing about the European election results in the *Independent* for 22 June. He went straight into it, even while pretending or affecting not to do so:

> Most commentators have concentrated on the statistics and confusion within the Tory Party that the arithmetic of the European elections has caused. Nobody should be surprised by that. The slump in Conservative support to its lowest percentage of votes in any national election this century is in itself an event – even without the BBC's extraordinary graphics and the mobile enthusiasm of Peter Snow.

˙Review of Gordon Brown, *Where there is greed ... Margaret Thatcher and the Betrayal of Britain's Future*, London 1989; John Lloyd, *CounterBlasts No. 3: A Rational Advance for the Labour Party*, London 1989.

Now, it's not especially surprising that the deputy leader of a historic social-democratic party should open an article with a sentence that reads as if it was hastily translated from the Albanian, or that he should close that article without a single mention of the European element in British and world politics. What is — or ought to be — surprising is his natural, unforced obsession with the media aspect of the outcome. Seeking for a split second to evade this judgement on his mini-essay, Mr Hattersley went on:

> But the facts behind the figures are more interesting. For several months, Labour Party workers have insisted that the opinion polls would soon begin to reflect a new national mood. There is a sea change in British politics — the sort of slow but irresistible movement which Jim Callaghan detected when the tide was flowing the other way in 1978.

Yes, I think that covers everything. First announcing, with his usual gift of phrase, that 'the facts behind the figures' are what count, Hattersley proceeds to list a series not of facts but of impressions. ('National mood' and 'sea change' are thought to be indispensable, in the trade, to the writing of analyses of this kind.) The most revealing reference is to 'Jim' Callaghan, who rested his whole career on the notion of credibility. Most of the time, he refused point-blank to listen to those who saw a Tory and right-wing revival in the late 1970s, but when he did listen he had an infallible prescription for staving off the menace. This prescription took the simple form of doing what the Tories would have done ten years before — but trying to square it with the unions. The end-result was a sort of Weimar without the sex: the country mortgaged to the IMF; placemanship and jobbery everywhere from the Washington Embassy to the Bank of England; and an indecorous last-minute vote-buying exercise involving both the Ulster Unionists and the Irish Republicans. On the night before the vote of confidence that put him out of office I met Callaghan at a party and, after being well patronized about the pessimistic little book that Peter Kellner and I had done on him, told him that he would lose the vote and the ensuing election. He was still blandly convinced that Thatcher lacked the credibility — it's difficult to remember now how popular it was then to dismiss her as a shrill suburban housewife. 'We *might* lose in the House,' he said, 'but we can't lose the election.'

If you take credibility to mean no more than 'plausibility' or 'electability', then it still somehow fails to correlate as the consensus journalists and poll-takers wish it would — which is to say, with 'moderation'. Gaitskell couldn't even beat Macmillan four years after Suez, and after repeated demonstrations of control over his own enfeebled left wing. Callaghan was humbled without the Falklands factor. The Tribunites Foot and Kinnock were walloped while in the process of 'finding the centre'. The only two Labour leaders to have unseated the Conservatives in such a way as to force a rethink upon them were Attlee and Wilson. Attlee was in conventional terms well to the left of centre, and in point of his electoral programme hardly less so. (Still, at the 1945

Labour Party Conference Ernest Bevin came raging up to those, including Ian Mikardo and — oddly enough — James Callaghan, who had called for public ownership to be in the Manifesto and yelled: 'Congratulations! You have just lost us the election.') Harold Wilson actually beat the Tories four times at the polls, which on the consensus calculus makes him the most 'credible' Labour politician of all time. Except that there is, is there not, something wrong with that last statement?

These two short books are both written by Scotsmen — Fifers, in fact — who express a regional and national resentment against Thatcherism as well as a more or less conventional Labourist one. Both men are of an age, and both have backgrounds in a harder left than the one they now espouse. Gordon Brown was one of the convenor/editors of the *Red Paper for Scotland* in the early 1970s, and John Lloyd saw the inside of the Communist Party before helping to found a pro-European Marxist tendency at about the same time. Rather touchingly, he uses the chorus of the 'Internationale' to supply the chapter headings of his 'CounterBlast', which is in fact not a polemic at all but a fairly dry tract of the sort put out by the Fabian Society.

Lloyd is prescriptive, while Brown is descriptive. *Where there is greed* is a terse, patriotic, businesslike compendium, stiffened with charts and figures, of British decline. As I read it, a line from one of Pablo Neruda's poems came back to me. After depicting the damage and humiliation inflicted on Chile by irresponsible rulers and unaccountable corporations, Neruda closed by saying simply: 'and the trunk of the tree of the country rots'. Brown is angered by the same sort of thing, though he would be more likely to call it infrastructure. It is said that Cecil Parkinson, asked what had happened to the fabled revenues of North Sea Oil, replied with perfect insouciance that they had been spent on the financing of unemployment benefit. This could well be the encapsulating anecdote of the Thatcher decade: at once an outrage to the Protestant ethic and a cynical negation of all the boastful claims about 'National Renewal'. Brown, who modestly describes his own book as a 'collection', and credits many researchers, has assembled within two covers the sorry account of an eroded manufacturing base, a neglected fixed-investment sector and an industry unprepared to face the brisk gale that impends in 1992. A rather candid reply to a parliamentary question, given early last year by Alan Clark, summarizes the whole position neatly. Mr Clark had been invited to say which OECD countries spent either more or less of their gross product on fixed investment than did the United Kingdom. He responded:

> Comparisons for most OECD countries are readily available only for 1986. In that year the following OECD countries spent a larger share of GDP on fixed investment than the United Kingdom: Australia, Austria, Canada, Denmark, Finland, France, Germany, Iceland, Ireland, Italy, Japan, Luxembourg, Netherlands, New Zealand, Norway, Portugal, Spain, Sweden, Turkey and the United States. Belgium spent a smaller share of GDP on fixed income than the United Kingdom. Comparable figures for other OECD countries are not available.

Plucky little Belgium our ally again. Once you untune the string of investment, as Brown argues, there are ineluctable consequences for innovation, for research and development, for the deployment of talent, and for anything describable under the heading of culture. As for welfare and education, it's exhausting to recount the long-term damage done by underfunding. And yet there seems always to be money — for Trident, for fortress Falklands, for computerized bunkers and bunkerized computers. When he touches on these contrasts — which he does mostly in passing — Brown should really give a tip of the *chapeau* to Andrew Gamble's earlier work on the 'free economy–strong state' calculus. (His book has no index or bibliography.)

Brown's critique is underlaid with strict moral sense. You cannot, he seems to say, eat the seed corn and hope to prosper. Without thrift and continence and thought for the morrow there is no firm foundation. Yet could this not be Thatcher herself talking? There is a fashion among social democrats for the expression of this paradox in its reverse form — in other words, for the accusation that Conservatism's high priestess is in reality an un-English and promiscuous radical. This tactic of irony — if it is an irony — perhaps too easily overlooks the undoubted fact that the Tories in 1979 were able to present themselves as the party of change against 'Jim' Callaghan's avuncular and dogmatic maintenance of a mediocre and deteriorating status quo. Will it be canny for Labour, ten years on, to be the voice of restraint and consensus once more?

A year or two ago, I was billed with Perry Anderson to give an evening to the not very influential New York Marxist School. We were to compare and contrast Reaganism and Thatcherism, both of which had been described as 'revolutions', and I drew the easy job of discussing the first. Reaganism, already a waning memory, was never much more than a fraud, based on a three-credit-card trick and appealing principally to hedonism and credulity. Taxes would not go up, but everybody would be better off and there would be a morale-boosting boom in military spending. The Brobdingnagian Federal deficit stands as the chief monument to this deluded interval. Just for the sake of example — to begin with but — as the evening went on, with alarmed conviction — I tried to contrast this with the Thatcher 'experiment'. First of all, Thatcher had promised that things would hurt. Her concept of sado-monetarism, anchored in some approximation of the work of Hayek and Friedman, was more aesthetic than economic, and couched in the language of sacrifice and struggle rather than of good times. Count up the changes wrought by her government and ask if Labour could have accomplished them *or* would now undo them if given a full majority. Would Labour restore the legal privileges of the unions? Would it buy back the new private sector? Would it stop recognizing the principle of council house sales? Would it restore exchange controls? Would it undo the Lancaster House or Hillsborough agreement, where the Tory Party rather impressively faced down emotional and political challenges from two of its traditional claimants and pensioners, the Rhodesian Front and the Ulster

Unionists? To ask these questions is to answer them. Labour would have botched all of the above, whether led by Callaghan–Foot or Kinnock–Hattersley. As a party it is, quite simply, happy that these risky structural changes were embarked on by somebody else. There is an important sense — not measurable by opinion polls — in which voters understand this perfectly well, and reward the Party which displays nerve and conviction.

Reverting for a moment to the free economy–strong state dialectic: it was Labour that began to use unemployment as a deliberate means of deflation, and it was Labour ministers who brought the most clumsy and brutal prosecutions of journalists under the Official Secrets Act. I feel almost like apologizing for mentioning anything so obvious, but neither Lloyd nor Brown gives the matter any space, and both show a wistfulness for the days of moderate Labourism that amounts almost to a rewrite of history. Cogent though Brown's facts and Lloyd's rhetoric may be, both authors show a fatal eagerness to please. How odd it is that a decade of Thatcher has not taught Labourites the essential distinction between being liked and being respected. The Prime Minister has demonstrated a willingness to take life and to risk her own in the forwarding of certain convictions, and by doing so has won the grudging admiration that is the sincerest compliment the British electorate can bestow. In Walworth Road, by contrast, anxious surveys are conducted in order to see how the electorate can be flattered and massaged by changes of emphasis. It reminds me of nothing so much as the high noon of the Dukakis campaign, with its stress on 'competence not ideology'. I quiver when I think of how much cogitation went into Gordon Brown's decision to publish with something called 'the Mainstream Press'.

Throughout, he shows an extraordinary deference to arguments from authority. In discussing the repeal of Fair Wages legislation and the phased abolition of Wages Councils, he describes these moves as 'changes that were made despite the findings of research commissioned from Cambridge University that showed no evidence that employment would increase if wages fell'. Cambridge University! The words must needs seem imposing enough in themselves, since we are not told which department or faculty or, indeed, private group in Cambridge reached the conclusion, or on what basis it did so. Then we have Sir Francis Toombs, chairman of the Engineering Council and an adviser to the Prime Minister, who says that 'normal market forces will not work to make up the severe shortfall and provide the skills base needed by modern industry and commerce'. To say nothing of Sir David Philips, Chairman of the Advisory Board for the Research Councils, who remarked in 1988 that 'decisions by the government were "progressively leading to an unstable situation"'. Fighting words, no doubt, but they have the unmistakably musty smell of the old days when quango chairmen were endlessly and pointlessly interviewed and quoted about this or that touch on the tiller of a corporate state. One gets the feeling that Gordon Brown cannot, in either sense of the word, credit Thatcherism. If he has any understanding of its appeal and its dynamic — and I suspect that he must do — he keeps it to himself. This reluctance is dangerous politically because it is, ironically, only a short step from vicarious envy of Thatcher and a wish to counterfeit her formula for victory.

I hope I will not be alone in objecting to another element of the Brown analysis, which is a faint but definite tinge of John Bullishness or John Bullshit. Am I supposed to take alarm at the fact that '23 per cent of the Fellows of the Royal Society now live overseas'? Am I to repine that 'a 1986 study' — another vague attribution, incidentally, to the anonymous authority of studies and surveys — 'found that the numbers living permanently outside the UK had risen from 161 in 1979 to 240 at the time of the survey. Between 1979 and 1986 the proportion living in America rose from 6 per cent to 8 per cent'? Horrors. Or what about this:

> To date, 40 per cent of Jaguar and 15 per cent of British Aerospace have ended up in the hands of foreigners. Control of the Royal Dockyard at Plymouth has passed to the American company Brown and Root. The foreign shareholding in Rolls-Royce, whose defence contribution is vital, reached an illegal figure of 21 per cent and, embarrassingly for patriotic privatisation enthusiasts, subsequently had to be reduced under a golden share provision.

Elsewhere, Brown argues persuasively that 'privatisation' is a synonym for the rebirth of monopoly. Why does he feel the need to cheapen his argument by attacking the one element of diversity that privatization does introduce? Moreover, by attacking the one element of diversity that is inextricably connected to the future of both capitalism and socialism — the internationalization of production? It reminds one of the grosser arguments employed by Labour spokesmen during the forgotten days of the 'great debate' over Europe, where once again there was an attempt to steal abandoned Tory garments and use them to deck out statist arguments in the redundant language of 'national sovereignty'.

Lloyd's pamphlet is replete with apparently tough-minded 'bottom-line' language, also pitched to the mainstream:

> Kinnock has grasped what other successful European socialist leaders such as François Mitterrand, Felipe Gonzales and Benito Craxi have: first get control of the Party — no matter how long it takes — for if you cannot control the Party, nothing else can be accomplished.

The punctilious cedilla under Mitterrand's first name makes it the odder that the surname of the Spaniard and the forename of the Italian are given wrongly, but the maxim of 'control of the Party above all' is one that has not recommended itself only to European social democrats. And it was not just his control over the French Socialist Party but his control over the French organs of security that allowed Mitterrand to conduct undercover military operations against a reformist Labour government in New Zealand, and to murder a member of the Greenpeace organization who was making a peaceful protest against French nuclear tests. In France, this operation is said to have enhanced Mitterrand's 'credibility'.

I want to raise the 'Green' issue for another purpose. By some law of unintended consequences which it would take the pen of a Dangerfield to describe, the very high noon of unfettered resurgent capitalism has been the occasion for a great and possibly historic revulsion against greed and rapacity. This revulsion differs from Luddism or Pre-Raphaelitism in the eminence of its practicality, and in the proven urgency of its presentiments. More important, the 'Green' movement indicts both the state-accumulation socialisms of the East and the short-term opportunism of private enterprise in the West, not to mention the Bhopal and Brazil horrors of the Third World. Inscribed in the idea of a planetary and holistic concern is the mandate for a humane collectivism and solidarity — the precise negation of Thatcher's crass assertion that there is no such thing as society. Is Labour capable of catching this favourable tide, and the strong currents of anti-nuclearism and concern for civil and constitutional liberties that are its partial corollaries? Not on the face of it. The lust for credibility, coupled with certain rather traditional attachments to trade-unionism and to Westminster forms, have impelled Kinnock and Hattersley to sneer at the Greens and at Charter 88, to repudiate the Campaign for Nuclear Disarmament and to make worried noises about foreign penetration at just the moment when a one-world sensibility is informing itself that the *nationality* of the corporation is close to irrelevant. This in turn makes a nice contrast with the surprising deference shown to the intolerant and unattractive face of other cultures, as in the smarminess demonstrated by the brave new leadership over the Rushdie affair — or, to put the same point in another way, when there were votes in it or votes thought to be in it.

Writing about the degeneration of the left in his own time, Arthur Koestler concentrated his fire on the Communists and fellow-travellers but took the trouble to notice, amid the hideous cynicism of the Hitler–Stalin Pact, that the British Labour Party had chosen precisely that moment to adopt a Vansittart resolution at its Party Conference. (The Vansittart theory, much in vogue at that period, simplified things by blaming Nazism on the German people, and thereby licensed total war against civilians. It was later adapted by its author to argue that the Russian people were the enemy in the Cold War.) In other words, having flirted with irrelevant pacifism and neutralism throughout the 1930s, Labour whole-hogged it for militarism when war actually impended. Or in still other words, it made the wrong change, and for the wrong reasons, in the hope of keeping up with events and keeping pace with public opinion.

Describing Kinnock's decision to live with the British bomb, John Lloyd lists it among his six most admirable achievements and can barely find the words to praise it sufficiently: 'Kinnock fought against his *own* grain, his *own* reflexes — the traits which had made *him* the most popular fellow in the Labour Party — fashioning a determined social democrat out of the clay of a left-wing neo-Bevanite.' This achievement may not be as remarkable as Lloyd's moist endorsement could suggest. For one thing, it was Aneurin Bevan himself who rather famously talked the Labour Party out of going 'naked into the conference chamber', and knifed his unilateralist admirers in the front. For another, the last person to go on endlessly about 'the mantle of Nye', and to employ that mantle as a cloak for political transmogrification, was Harold Wilson. The difficulty arises when you take Lloyd's test of statesmanship and maturity, which is the willingness or readiness to repudiate former comrades and former cherished convictions. It is never enough to take this test once. You will always be asked, like Arafat, whether you really mean it. *You will never be able to stop the auction.* You can never repudiate enough. If Kinnock didn't learn this from Foot, he will not learn it until it's far too late. Lloyd also makes it plain that the shift in nuclear policy is a matter of 'credibility', and that the unilateral credo was — or is — to be considered as a purely electoral liability. This isn't really a good enough reason to change such an important position. Either there is an excellent reason for Britain having its own nuclear war-fighting capacity, or there is not. And either there has been a change in the nuclear balance making this more or less true, or there has not. (Lloyd would have a hard time arguing the second, even if he believed in the 'deterrent' to begin with.) But perhaps more weighty will be the judgement of public opinion on a party which decides its stand on the nuclear question on — public opinion. Given the tendency of voters to trust the Tories more on military matters in the first place, the returns on media-guided indecision might show a tendency to diminish.

None of this will seem to matter if some pendulum effect brings Labour back to office, perhaps in coalition with its one-time deserters. But another defeat would expose Labour as the party that had tried everything — *everything* — to please, and still not got the mix quite right. That would be a historic humiliation. When the West German Social Democrats went to Bad Godesberg and renounced Marxism in 1959, they did so because they felt that the theory — with which, unlike Labour, they had had a genuine historical acquaintance — was no longer appropriate to the times. They did not do so in the spirit of a party which — to borrow a recent formulation of Austin Mitchell's — decided to find out what people wanted, and then give it to them. Still less in the spirit of a party which said, in effect: here are our policies and principles, and if you don't like them we'll soon change them. Kinnock may feel the lash of all this sooner than he thinks. All the available aggregates of data suggest that Labour would be up to 10 per cent more 'credible' without him. The average voter is apparently readier to trust John Smith, who certainly sounds credible enough. This would be a poor return for a career wagered on credibility, but then the ratchet of the credible paradoxically operates to the benefit of people who really mean what they say, which is why the facts of life have been Tory for so long.

London Review of Books, August 1989

UNION JACKSHIRT:
INGHAM'S CONSERVATIVE CHIC*

In the dismal mid 1970s Patrick Cosgrave, later to be Margaret Thatcher's adviser and biographer, took me to a Friday luncheon at the old Bertorelli's in Charlotte Street. Here was a then-regular sodality, consisting at different times of Kingsley Amis, Bernard Levin, Robert Conquest, Anthony Powell, Russell Lewis and assorted others, and calling itself, with heavy and definite self-mockery, 'Bertorelli's Blackshirts'. The conversational scheme was simple (I think it had evolved from a once-famous letter to *The Times* defending Lyndon Johnson's war in Vietnam and signed by all — or most — of those present). One had to pretend that Britain was a country where it was dangerous to hold conservative opinions. So that a sample sally might begin: 'I know it's *unfashionable* to say this' and go on to propose that, say, Hans Eysenck was on to something. Someone would lift a riskily brimming bumper and cry: 'Down with Oxfam!' Someone else might recommend a piece of samizdat from *Encounter*. And so the afternoon wore on agreeably enough, with daring satirical calls for South African port, Chilean wine, and so forth.

One of the number could never get enough of the joke. This was John Braine, whose special party trick was the skipping of ironic bits. When he said that England these days was run by the trade unions and the pansies, he meant it. When he went on about treason and the intellectuals there was grim, literal relish in his tones. Once, in dispute with Lord Soper — 'socialist, divine and peer of the realm' — he had been met with the naïve argument that he might not say such-and-such about absolute freedom in America if he were black. An incredulous pause, a bulge in the vinous features and then the outraged roar: 'But I'm *not* black, yer daft booger!' Fond — perhaps overfond — of recalling his days as a working-class Yorkshire socialist lad, he began to get the others down. After one too many of his excruciating hortations ('Call me old-fashioned if you will, but ah always say . . .'), the club began to break up. In the end it broke up altogether, with only Kingers and Conkers present on one dismal day, and Braine turning all chippy on them and saying, 'You 'ate me, doan't yer? 'Cos I've not bin to uni-i-*ver*-sity.'

Harris's portrait of the bulldog-visaged, anti-intellectual, aggressive, insecure, class-conscious reactionary tyke reminds me powerfully of old Braine and his blatherings. It's no surprise to find that Bernard Ingham, who failed to get to university and who, on internal evidence, has also been trying to compensate for missing his National Service, began his political life as a

*Review of Robert Harris, *Good and Faithful Servant: The Unauthorised Biography of Bernard Ingham*, London 1990.

boorish, hectoring columnist -- with the *nom de plume*, as he wouldn't have dreamed of calling it, 'Albion' — on the Labour machine mouthpiece the *Leeds Weekly Citizen*. From this anonymous pulpit he abused grousemoor Tories, metropolitan eggheads, unofficial strikers, disbelievers in the Yorkshire sage Harold Wilson, and all those too feckless to see the connection between muck and brass. Reading his reprinted stuff, which was mostly written out of a sort of turgid, inarticulate resentment rather than with real rage or outrage, one recalls the blustering world of George Brown, Ray Gunter and Robert Mellish — those Labour dinosaurs who used to invoke the common man but who, while envying the Tories their vowels and their ease of manner, would turn into RSMs when confronted with party dissidents like Bertrand Russell or even Aneurin Bevan. Then a sublimated loathing for the toffs would be vented on those who 'didn't know they were bloody born', 'didn't know how lucky they were', and so on. The mentality that Tories disdainfully call 'chippy', or christen 'the politics of envy', has very often been their secret weapon in the class war. Thatcher is probably the first senior Conservative to have understood this by instinct.

As an occasional jobbing hack for British newspapers, I had the opportunity to see Ingham in action a few times, and I'm annoyed that his rapid undoing cheats me of the opportunity to kick him while he's erect. Still, as he would be the first to affirm, down is better than nothing at all. During his time in office, Fleet Street took several steps towards an American system of presidentially managed coverage and sound-bite deference, without acquiring any of the American constitutional protections in return — and, indeed, while surrendering a few of the local and traditional ones. I have seen Ingham lie abroad for his Prime Minister (on the 'dual key' for Cruise missiles at a briefing in Washington in 1986) and bluff abroad for her (in Paris at the amazing dénouement last November). I have also seen him handle a breaking story which involved the 'credibility' of his mistress. This was in the think-tank territory of Aspen, Colorado, last August, on the first day of the invasion of Kuwait.

Scene: a briefing-room in a hotel basement. Ingham opens gruffly by saying: 'Usual rules. "British sources say."' He then gives a laboured digest of events, already well-known to any journalist who has had the wit to telephone London and talk to the desk. I ask a question about the Shia prisoners held by the Emir of Kuwait these many years. Their release is a demand made by many local fundamentalist factions including those supposed to be the captors of Terry Waite. They were also the subject of covert talks between Oliver North and the Ayatollah's men during a time when Mrs Thatcher was publicly exonerating Ronald Reagan of the charge of hostage-trading. So much is known. Any news of them today? Suddenly, HMG becomes HMV. I am fixed by Ingham with a dull Wackford Squeers look, combining ignorance with nettled hostility. 'I don't know what you're bloody on about' would be a summary of his reply. Other reporters look away and change the subject when I ask *sotto voce* why (a) he's so pig-ignorant, and (b) so hog-rude about it. Why their lack of solidarity? 'Bernard, can you tell us any more of the PM's thinking this morning?' *Bernard?* What is this Bernard? I swiftly learn that Mrs Thatcher is to make her keynote speech in Aspen on a Saturday morning, and that selected members of the 'Sunday Lobby' will be vouchsafed advance 'guidance' on its shape and content. Not being a member of the Lobby, but having still to meet the *Sunday Correspondent*'s needs by Saturday noon, with a seven-hour Rocky Mountain time-zone lag, I suddenly get the point.

It's an easy point, too, and one which Robert Harris understands very well and analyses very deftly. Who wants yesterday's papers? This relatively simple blackmail, which places the regular political staff of newspapers and networks at the mercy of the 'British source', also gives the 'First Among Equals' an advantage over other members of Cabinet. With 'leaking' made into a prime ministerial, taxpayer-supported state monopoly, a crucial 'edge' is available. Earlier figures like Chamberlain and Eden and Wilson were quick to see this advantage — Attlee and Churchill both rather despised it — but not until Thatcher and Ingham was it made into a fully politicized system *and* a major department of state. This is how it has evolved since the days of its founder, the well-named George Steward:

> Chamberlain used Steward repeatedly to bypass the Cabinet and promote his policy of appeasing Hitler. In the autumn of 1937, for example, Lord Halifax, the Foreign Secretary, had received a private invitation to visit Germany. The Foreign Office was anxious to play down the importance of the trip. Chamberlain's purpose was precisely the opposite. Steward briefed the Lobby with the Number 10 version. The next day the *Times* and the *Daily Telegraph* appeared with almost identical stories about the visit's vital significance in the eyes of 'the Government' — an interpretation which horrified the anti-appeasers and caused delight in Berlin. By exploiting his press secretary's contacts with the Lobby in this way, Chamberlain was able to raise 'news management', in the words of the historian Richard Cockett, 'almost to the level of an exact science'.

Obviously, it's a long march from making Lord Halifax look like an appeaser (which, Harris might have pointed out, he was already) to making Michael Heseltine look like a fool or a knave — which is, in Britain at least, a matter only within the competence of the libel courts. But between them, Thatcher and Ingham obviously employed the law officers of the Crown as well as members of the professional Civil Service and the daily press to win an inner-party faction fight over Westland helicopters. Heseltine had already enmeshed himself in the net that would choke him by agreeing to the hounding of Sarah Tisdall and Clive Ponting, and by not deploring Ingham's remark, made to the Meeting of Information Officers (MIO) on the eve of Ponting's trial at the Old Bailey, that the case should be heard by Judge Jeffreys. Nor had he dissented when Ingham told the IBA in crude and direct terms that the Official Secrets Act was a weapon which those in power might employ with almost feudal discretion: 'I must tell you that I — and I am sure my colleagues — have never regarded the Official Secrets Act as a constraint on my operations. Indeed, I regard myself as licensed to break that law as and when I judge necessary.' This pugnacious nastiness sits alarmingly well with a man who had laboured for too long under the (correct) impression that he was second-rate: doomed to obey instructions rather than issue them. Ingham is now convinced that as a no-nonsense son of a weaver he mastered the craft of journalism early, trudging through Hebden Bridge to cover weddings, traffic accidents, flower shows and industrial exhibitions, and falling victim to jealousy only when he came to London to be done in by city slickers on the *Guardian* labour desk, where he was indentured to Peter Jenkins: '"He was very nice to work with: extremely conscientious," recalled Jenkins, who was two years younger than his deputy. "He probably thought I was a bit flash and metropolitan."' One doubts that even our Bernie could have been so gormlessly provincial as *that*: even so, the psychic wound was obviously a deep one. And his grinding apprenticeship took its grisly revenge. For him, reporting had also been a cap-in-hand business – getting names right, flattering local worthies, taking down self-serving prose in shorthand, being impartial about tripe-fests and passing off the homo-geneous, conformist result as tough objectivity. This was precisely the mode of journalism that he sought to impose, with conspicuous success, on the Fleet Street national routine.

Here is an example of journalistic pluralism as given by Harris. After John Biffen, one of the few thoughtful and gracious members of the Thatcher front bench, had hinted at prime ministerial megalomania in a *Weekend World* inter-view in May 1986, Ingham summoned the Lobby and instructed them that Biffen, then Leader of the House of Commons, was an un-person. The phrase employed was 'semi-detached'. In the next day's *Times*: 'The sources said that Mr Biffen was a "semi-detached member of the Cabinet".' The same day's *Guardian* had him as 'a "semi-detached member of the Government" whose views were of little consequence'. In the *Financial Times*, 'Biffen was yesterday being authoritatively described as "a well-known semi-detached member of the Government".' The *Sun* was, if anything, more honest than the pack, writing that 'in an unprecedented bid to discredit Mr Biffen, Downing Street sources made it clear ...' before going on to repeat the *ipsissima verba*. But then Bernard Ingham always loved the *Sun*, because as well as getting his and her wishes down at dictation speed, it also behaved so disgustingly on occasion as to license his frequent attacks on press 'irresponsibility'. This leak–hate relationship between Thatcher and Murdoch, which gives the Tories two birds with no stone, would be a study in itself.

There isn't a single recorded occasion, in this book or in anyone's memory, of a real challenge to Ingham's assumption of news-management power, or to his replacement *at public expense* of the idea of accountability with the pseudo-science of deniability. When the BBC was bullied into sharing exclusive photo-op footage of Thatcher in the Falkland Islands, it caved in to one minatory telephone call. When reporters from the *Independent*, the *Guardian* and the *Scotsman*, whose editors had sought to modify Lobby practice very slightly, were denied privilege on an Ingham–Thatcher jet to Moscow, they whined at the withdrawal of his megaphone from their ears. Nor did any Member of Parliament — Tam Dalyell excepted — raise the constitutional point made by Harris:

> in the past, the rule which Prime Ministers had insisted upon was that the Cabinet could argue strenuously in private, but that in public a united front must be presented. Mrs Thatcher used the Lobby in precisely the opposite way: Cabinet discussions were kept to a minimum, whilst she reserved the right to make public her disagreement with her own ministers.

Harris has made an important and well-written book out of the study of an essentially nugatory individual, who was empowered by a surreptitious form of democratic centralism. Excellent on the suggestive detail, he is good at connecting with the more ample implication. Really, Bernard Ingham, with a staff of 1,200 at the peak of his power, four interlocking spokesmanships and a budget of £168 million, would, in a serious country, have been titled Minister of Information. But the amateur, informal British state has no such position, any more than it has a Director of MI6 or MI5 or a Ministry of the Interior. And without a democracy, there is always room at the top for an ambitious and obedient mediocrity.

London Review of Books, January 1991

NEIL KINNOCK:
DEFEAT WITHOUT HONOUR

In Michael Frayn's novel *The Tin Men*, media consultants go around asking members of the public what kind of news they would like to read in their papers. Would they like more airline crash stories, or fewer? If they would desire more, would they wish to read about children's toys found in the wreckage, or not? And so on. There is something touching, as well as something stupid, in the desperate effort to discover and predict the public taste. The recent defeat of the British Labour Party was an instance more of the stupid than the pathetic, and it may have implications for all of us who despise postmodern politics and postmodern journalism.

In the past the Labour leadership always had an explanation for the mauling it suffered at the hands of the Tories. It was invariably because there were too many people like me in the Party, people who gave a scrofulous and Trotskyist appearance to what would otherwise be recognized as a perfectly decent and respectable social-democratic racket. If it wasn't the association with supposed middle-class rabble, then it was the ghastly embarrassment of having to associate with all those greedy trade unions, combinations of working stiffs who had *no idea* of the slothful and acquisitive image they presented. Neither of those two explanations – both faithfully transmitted in the exiguous coverage of the British election that was mounted in *The New York Times* and the other guardians – will wash any more. Under the leadership of Neil Kinnock, Labourism took the Frayn route to its logical conclusion. Tell us what you want, it wheedled the voters, and we will agree to stand for it. Here are our principles, and if you don't like them, we'll change them. Labour tried everything to please. And, like the obedient servants of consensus that they are, the opinion polls reported that it was working. Why wouldn't they report such mindless disinformation? After all, Labour was doing what the opinion polls had said it must do. On that calculus, Labour jolly well *deserved* a spell in power and a taste of the fruits of office. Kinnock and his crowd had shown that they had earned it.

As everybody now knows, the eventual 'swing' to Kinnockism was on the statistical order that is represented in the suggestive term 'margin of error'. And what does a party do when it has tried everything – *everything* – and nothing works? It will take a long time to erase the spectacle of Neil Kinnock's ignoble resignation speech, in which he sourly blamed the influence of the very Tory tabloid rags whose favour he had courted these many years. Better still was the sight of the bloated face of Kinnock's deputy Roy Hattersley (a man so depraved that he had changed his mind on the Salman Rushdie case in order to ingratiate himself with Pakistani voters in his own constituency) as he came before the cameras on election night and wailed: 'I just don't *understand* it.' I was less inclined to jeer at my former comrades of the *New Statesman*, who, apparently believing that the polls had made an election unnecessary, committed the hubris of printing a premature victory issue. If Neil Kinnock had won, I know personally of more than one Washington pundit who had his *Zeitgeist* column already written: 'The triumph of a reformed, streamlined, neoliberal Labor Party is a happy omen for Bill Clinton's New Frontier style...' (fill in as applicable from existing boilerplate stocks). My own pre-recorded appearance on a PBS television show, in which I had said that the Tories would be back with almost no trouble, was snipped before transmission because 'the smart money' just didn't buy it and 'the numbers' didn't bear me out.

Why all this consensual concern for the fate of a mediocre careerist like Kinnock? I haven't yet absolutely established this with William Safire, but from my own observation I believe it to be true that the word 'electability' entered the political discourse as part of Kinnock's exciting, renovating, nonideological, thrusting New Frontier (draw down further boilerplate stocks) campaign for a new 'image'. Thus, a lot of dumb money as well as some smart stuff was riding on his putative path to power. This is why it didn't work. Apart from disowning scruffy leftists and trade-unionists, Neil Kinnock had also to disown his personal commitment to abolish Britain's nuclear missile capacity. This commitment had been so intense (we would now say 'defining') that he had once, and with typical exaggeration and sentimentality, said that if he ever wavered on the Bomb he hoped his wife would leave him 'and take the kids'. Well, he wavered on the Bomb all right and the little woman stayed by him, as political wives tend to do. (She's worth ten of him, by the way.)

What is the result? The electorate knows that you would change your mind on one of your cherished principles, and also change your mind on a crucial matter of defence and national security, because the opinion polls told you it was advantageous. Here is one of those unquantifiable things that opinion polls cannot measure. Can anybody *imagine* the Conservatives changing their position on nuclear weapons for anything like the same reason? The Tories believe that the so-called 'independent British deterrent' is the special symbol of their potency as a party and the survival of Great Britain as a post-imperial nation. They would not hesitate to lose an election rather than alter this preposterous and dangerous view.

So, as the real poll drew near, Labour had advertised, via its eagerness to please, that it was unserious about a serious question. Let all future Tin Men beware. The road from 'credibility' to 'electability' lies through plausibility, and people don't like you if all you want of them is to be liked. Now that it has ended in humiliation and utter disappointment, the authors of the disaster are already saying that all it proves is the need for 'new ideas' and 'new leadership' from the very same stable. At least I can't be blamed for the next debacle. Meanwhile, in America the Democratic Leadership Council is hoping that it has found a Teflon candidate with the skills of an Atwater, which says something about the generals who fight the last war and then blame the foot soldiers when they screw up.

The Nation, May 1992

BRIBING AND TWISTING·

British dirty-mindedness has contributed respectably to the humour and mental breadth of suffering humanity, as the postcards of Donald McGill and the routines of Benny Hill bear witness. British filthy-mindedness can also look the world more or less squarely in the eye, with the catharsis of *Monty Python* as its proudest claim. But British *foul*-mindedness — now there's another thing altogether. The snigger of a Myra Hindley, the cloacal chorus from the Millwall terrace, the focus on excrement through the letterbox, the ghastly innuendo about race and sex, the obsession with corporal punishment and the savaging of children ... you could turn over a stone in the yard of a charnel-house and fare no worse.

There is an obvious connection to be intuited between the grossly moralizing and repressive and the grossly prurient. Lear stumbled on something of the sort when, after observing crossly that 'a dog's obeyed in office', he exclaimed:

> Thou rascal beadle, hold thy bloody hand!
> Why dost thou lash that whore? Strip thine own back;
> Thou hotly lust'st to use her in that kind
> for which thou whip'st her.

George Orwell moved this intuition a little nearer towards our own day when he wrote of the subpornographic literature produced for the distraction of the proles, and composed almost entirely by specially programmed machines in the basement of the Ministry of Truth. In this dystopia, the relation between aggressive moralism and nasty sex was made painfully explicit. So let me now quote from the book under review. The scene is the relaunched Wapping newsroom of the *Sun*, the paper which has restlessly sought openings at the lower end of the British newspaper market ever since it simultaneously replaced and deposed the staid old Labourist *Daily Herald*. The 'editor', Kelvin MacKenzie, has just begun another working day by lining up all hands and shouting, as Peter Chippindale and Chris Horrie put it, 'C***! C***! C***!' Now read on:

> MacKenzie's power over the hacks had also been considerably strengthened by the ATEX computer system, which he had mastered immediately. MacKenzie christened the system the 'scamulator' and the terminals 'scamulator machines.' He would rush up to hacks slaving at their terminals, and slyly instruct them to 'give it a bit of that, eh?' while he mimed an exaggeration of playing the piano with an equally exaggerated nod and a wink. 'Get the old scamulator working, eh?' he would say.

·Review of Peter Chippindale and Chris Horrie, *Stick It Up Your Punter!: The rise and fall of the 'Sun'*, London 1990.

As many reporters were to find, it didn't especially matter which of them sat at which machine. This perfection of the concept of disposable employee and manufactured story had, it must be noticed, preceded the technology which made it simpler. According to *Stick It Up Your Punter!: The rise and fall of the 'Sun'*, the paper's reporter in Argentina during the Falklands conflict, David Graves, filed a story and was then called to the telephone. It was the newsdesk in London.

> 'Great exclusive! Kelvin's very pleased. But we want a blow-by-blow diary of the invasion. Can you do it?'
>
> 'Sure,' Graves replied. 'When it happens.' There was a short silence at the other end of the line. 'What do you mean "when"?' the voice demanded incredulously. 'We've just sent away the front page with your story on it. Listen, I'll read it to you: 'INVASION. Britain's counter-invasion forces swept ashore on the stolen island of South Georgia yesterday …'.

As it happened, there *was* an invasion shortly afterwards, so Graves was as fortunate in the falsification perpetuated under his byline as was the *Sun*'s favourite Prime Minister with the weather, the state of Her Majesty's opposition, and much else besides. The war, as well as supplying the authors of this book with their title, also gave MacKenzie the chance to scrawl 'GOTCHA!' in juvenile capitals as his jeering comment on the death of a large ship's company.

Speaking of Margaret Thatcher, who never tired of the theme of family values, it is worth being reminded that an earlier 'editor', Larry Lamb, liked her while she was in opposition and he still a commoner:

> All was sweetness and light as she and her 'boys', as key advisers like Geoffrey Howe and Nicholas Ridley were known at the *Sun*, began to drop in on Lamb's alcohol-smoothed 'chewing the fat' sessions after the first edition had gone away…. 'You know that's marvellous', she would say finally. 'If only I had people like you who really know how to communicate. Absolutely marvellous.'

One sees what she meant. There was a crying need, in the tentative early days of populist Toryism, for a voice that could bring the gospel to the *lumpen*. One of the first impressions made by Mrs Thatcher on the opinion polls was the direct outcome of her harsher line on 'New Commonwealth' immigration and the fear of being 'swamped by an alien culture'. The diary of a former *Sun* employee records MacKenzie's view that Prime Minister Botha wasn't ready for the moment when blacks came down from the trees, and the decision of his deputy: 'No, I'm not having pictures of darkies on the front page.' Subliminal advertising is easy to do at this level. It's important to bear in mind, though, that conscious thought and decision are involved as well. The mangling of Shakespeare into the caption 'Winter of Discontent' — another soaraway *Sun* coinage — may have been worth millions of votes on its own.

This is not to say that Labour would not have been defeated anyway, or that Arthur Scargill would not have been undone, or that the monarchy and the TV soap would not have exerted their own hypnosis. For that matter, it is not to say that immigration isn't a subject for intense debate. But bear in mind that 'Gotcha!'. And remember what the *Sun* said about Alan Bennett, when he had given a eulogy at the funeral of his much-hounded friend Russell Harty and complained at the *Sun*'s part in the story:

> By paying young rent boys to satisfy him he broke the law.
> Some, like ageing bachelor Mr Bennett, can see no harm in that.
> He has no family.
> But what if it had been YOUR SON whom Harty bedded?

This comes as close as makes no serious difference to incitement on the *Stürmer* model. It also raises an interesting question. MacKenzie appears in these pages and others as consumed with horror for homosexual behaviour. As the authors put it, none too delicately, he has an addiction to 'crude schoolboy wisecracks about "botty burglars", "shirt-lifters" and "bum bandits"'. In the case of individuals like Elton John and Peter Tatchell, he has been willing to make preposterous economies with the truth in order to actualize these obsessions. The *Sun*'s fabricated interview with a nonshrink about a nonanalysis of Tony Benn's psychology might, in another context, yield some horrid insights here.

There's no reason to be snobbish or prudish about British popular journalism and its appeal to the newly or the not-very literate. The *Daily Mirror* was a positively educational force at one time, as well as a training-ground for decent, witty columnists like Keith Waterhouse, who made distinct contributions to newspaper style. Pin-ups, nude or scanty, are also a great tradition. The *Sun*, however, is disingenuous in claiming to take the people as it finds them. It is not content to appeal to the lowest or the most base; it urgently seeks to exhort readers in that direction. But Chippindale and Horrie do some valuable work in showing (even though they confuse H.L. Mencken with Phineas T. Barnum) that there is a limit to gullibility and a diminishing return even on the lowest common denominator. At a certain point during the miners' strike:

> Previously it had mostly been a pleasure [for *Sun* reporters] to ring ordinary people who had popped up in the news. There would be a bit of light-hearted banter about bringing along a Page Three girl, and generally they would be told they were welcome and even that the kettle would be on when they arrived. But now they were detecting a new guarded note in the replies and their requests were being turned down with the standard evasion of 'Not today, thanks.'

It would be nice to record that this happened when the *Sun* featured 'Classroom Crackers' (underage girls with overage breasts), or when it called for rape and castration phone-ins, or in general when it smeared itself with sadism, pornography and masturbation. Still, it did happen after the paper invented a hate and scare story about the calamity at Hillsborough football ground. And the effect sometimes made itself felt on the staffers themselves. For Eric Butler, a reporter who finally refused Wapping, the moment came, according to Chippindale and Horrie, when he was approached by a vile thug with a story. Butler shudderingly offered to recommend him to another paper. '"No, they're no fucking good," the thug had replied angrily. "I want this in the *Sun* because it's the slag-off paper, innit?"'

MacKenzie and his team had worked long, punishing hours to din this idea into the public mind. He once screamed at his minions to remember that their target older reader was 'an old fascist'. MacKenzie would be — and probably will be — as disposable as the wretches he has put to the scamulator. He is typical of those who bully those beneath him while cringing at the voice of authority. The portrait of him that is rendered here will stand as one of the great Fleet Street profiles. The cretinization of the popular press — the replacement of gutter journalism by sewer journalism — is an enthralling story. But MacKenzie's role in the process has not been the deciding one:

> The hacks had always noticed how strongly influenced MacKenzie was by the Boss's day-to-day comments on his performance. Sometimes he would come charging out of his office with a broad grin, clap his hands, rub them together and announce: 'Rupert loves the paper!' ... but it was not always like that. To keep his total control Murdoch ruled by silence.

Thus this book, a rebarbative feast in so many ways, fails to answer the most absorbing question it raises: what does Rupert Murdoch want — out of politics, out of journalism, out of life?

Times Literary Supplement, November 1990

5

COACH INTO PUMPKIN:
THE FAIRY TALE REVIEWED

HOW'S THE VAMPIRE?[*]

'Uneasy lies the head that wears a throne.' This wistful schoolboy howler from *1066 And All That* is the essential summary of two related absurdities. The first is the intrinsic inanity of a Royal Family; the second is the ridiculous blend of deference and denial that goes into the making of public support for it. Philip Ziegler is a historian of uncommon candour and, especially considering the 'authorized' nature of his work, unusual humour. Yet in the very first paragraph of his very first page he pitches face-forward into the enduring fallacy that sustains our monarchical cult: 'To have been born in 1894, eldest son of the eldest surviving son of the eldest son of the Queen Empress, was to be heir to an almost intolerable burden of rights and responsibilities.' There you have it, even if expressed with Ziegler's manners and proportion ('almost' and 'rights' slightly qualify the supposed awesomeness of the burden). This is, still, the bleat of the drawing room and the drone of the saloon bar. 'I don't know *how* they do it.' 'I wouldn't have her job.' Yet the ensuing 560 pages contain conclusive and exhaustive evidence (a) that the Windsors are a burden on us, not the other way about; and (b) that the chief difficulty at every stage of Edward VIII's life lay in the finding and invention of things for him to do.

The same principle – of pointless duties joylessly undertaken – underlay his very conception. Prince Albert Victor, theoretical heir to the heir to the throne in the 1890s, appears here thus: 'Languid and lymphatic – "*si peu de chose*, though as you say a Dear Boy," the Grand Duchess of Mecklenburgh-Strelitz brutally dismissed him.' It was felt in court circles that a robust woman should be martyred to this nonentity, and the sturdy Princess Victoria Mary of Teck was led lowing into the ring. Between the betrothal and the match itself the futile Albert Victor expired, out of some combination of influenza and inanition, but it was decided to marry the same woman to the next in line. Accordingly, the biddable Mary was made over to Prince George, whom even Ziegler feels obliged to write down as: 'an arch-conformist; bored by books, pictures, music; wholly without intellectual curiosity or imagination; suspicious of new ideas; entertained only by his stamp collection and the slaughter of ever greater quantities of pheasants, partridges and the like'. Recovering himself – he has, after all, a whole reign ahead of him – Mr Ziegler adds: on 6 July 1893 'the couple, by now very much, if undemonstratively, in love, were married in the Chapel Royal.'

The fruit of this union might have been expected to be dull, bovine and pious. In point of fact, such fascination as the young Edward possessed lay in his febrile, restless and impetuous side. As far as books, pictures and ideas went he was a perfect chip off his father's block. But he didn't have the same,

[*]Review of Philip Ziegler, *King Edward VIII: The Official Biography*, London 1990.

appalling, unshakeable commitment to a lifetime of mediocrity and routine, to be endured for the apparent sake of a people upon whom it was actually inflicted. He wanted *only* the 'rights', and the 'responsibilities' be damned. When the world-historical quarrel between the Royal Family and its German relations broke out in August 1914, the Prince wrote to his brother:

> The Germans could never have chosen a worse moment, and serve them right too if they are absolutely crushed, as I can but think they will be. The way they have behaved will go down to history as about the worst and most infamous action of any govt!! Don't you agree? I bet you do.

He was just shy of twenty-one. No one, it appears, had taught him to think or speak any differently. During the 'Strange Death' period running up to 1914, he had freely given his views on the three great crises of Ulster, labour and women's suffrage. They were as one might have expected. 'I really think that at last some drastic measures are to be taken as regards those bloody suffragettes, whose conduct is becoming more and more infamous every day,' he wrote in the summer of 1914. Queen Mary herself encouraged him to take the side of the Curragh mutineers in the case of Home Rule, and to her he wrote: 'Although we aren't supposed to have any politics there does come a time when all that outward nonsense must be put aside, and that time has come.'

If it were true, as we are incessantly told, that the monarchy has 'no real power' but a strong sense of constitutional probity, then one might expect to find some evidence that the King-in-waiting was warned to be circumspect. But there's not a hint, in all of Ziegler's industrious fossickings, of any concern on that score. There was some royal pursing of the lips at his levity and laziness – despite costly tuition, he never achieved more than a subliterate standard of prose, spelling or punctuation, and despised English literature – but he seems to have imbibed his nasty politics from the milieu of royalty itself. Impatient to get close – but not too close – to the Western Front, he was allowed to make a pest of himself around the General Staff and the dressing-stations, and seems to have regarded himself as the patron and protector of the ex-serviceman ever after.

The experience of imperialist war and mass slaughter, which had a radicalizing effect upon so many of all classes, was also to interest some ill-assorted people in Fascism. Henry Williamson's later sympathy with the Reich, for instance, had much to do with his consuming horror of the trenches and his overmastering desire to avoid a repetition. Some years ago, I was interviewing Alan Clark MP about his book *The Donkeys*, a rugged study of British Great War generalship which became the script for Joan Littlewood's *Oh What a Lovely War*. He suddenly said to me: 'I dare say you've been told I'm a Fascist.' I admitted that I had heard something of the sort. 'Well, that's all balls,' he said briskly. 'I'm a *National Socialist*.' Obviously pretty well-used to the shock effect of this, he went on to explain that while Fascists were middle-class thugs who wanted to protect their dividends, National Socialists had a special responsibility to the worker and the artisan. 'We betrayed the British working class three times,' he told me sternly. 'First by using them as cannon fodder in the Great War, then by rewarding their sacrifice with a slump and mass unemployment, then by letting them in for another war.' (I was never sure, later on, whether to be impressed or disquieted when Thatcher made this hater of the brass hats and 'the old gang' into a Defence spokesman.)

My reason for this apparent detour is that the mystique of Edward VIII, still durable in some quarters, has to do with his alleged fellow-feeling for the Old Contemptibles, his related compassion for the privations of South Wales coal-miners and his consequent sincere – if muddled – antipathy to another war with Germany. It is a conspicuous merit of Ziegler's bibliography that it shows, without any scintilla of doubt, that Edward was – and not just in sardonic Clarkean terms – both a fascist and a National Socialist. In other words, as well as being a serf to stupid petty-bourgeois prejudices – against trade unions, against Indian nationalists and, indeed, Indians, against Jews and intellectuals – he was also an admirer of Nazi strength and power. His instinctive dividend-drawer's sympathies were loudly demonstrated during the General Strike when, as Ziegler records, 'he went out with the police, lent his car and chauffeur to transport the *British Gazette* to Wales, and resented the fact that he could do nothing directly himself to combat the Communist agitators, whom he believed to be behind the trouble.' On visits to India and Africa he repeatedly evinced racialist feelings which Ziegler terms 'probably even beyond the norm for his generation' – prompting one to venture the question: his generation of what? (He wrote to his mother about the disgust he felt at being offered the sacrament by a black clergyman in Sierra Leone; again we don't learn what, if anything, Queen Mary advised him in return.)

The Nazi seizure of power convinced him that at last something was being done to arrest the general rot. Count Mensdorff, a former Austrian ambassador to London, was surprised at how uncritical he was of Hitler during a conversation in November 1933: 'Of course it is the only thing to do. We will have to come to it, as we are in great danger from the Communists too.' During the same period he told Louis Ferdinand of Prussia that 'dictators were very popular these days and that we might want one in England before long'. He made similar remarks to Marshal Mannerheim at the funeral of King George V, gratified von Ribbentrop at every opportunity and opposed even Eden's modest proposal for a visit from Haile Selassie on the grounds that it might offend Mussolini. Ziegler writes that this convicts Edward of nothing that 'could not have been applied to Chamberlain or Halifax, Hoare or Simon', which is surely a point against the Princeling/King as much as for him. By his continued pro-Axis meddling he was, in effect, strengthening the future Munich party.

Ziegler, incidentally, does us the favour of clearing up the famous 'something must be done' incident in the stricken South Wales coalfields. The King visited the area laid waste by the closure of Dowlais steelworks, said of the workers that 'something must be done to see that they stay here — working', and hastened on to a dinner party in London, where he announced that 'agitation and Bolshevism' were at the root of the crisis. All this, and much besides in the way of callousness and dishonesty, was forgiven him. At the first, a special process of 'investiture' — a classic case of what Hobsbawm and Ranger have called 'invented tradition' — was contrived in order to make him presentable as Prince of Wales. Further elements of stage-management were added as it became more necessary to shield the British people from the true character of their monarch-to-be. This awkward necessity was laid upon the Establishment not by Edward's politics but by his penis, which was errant and capricious and was the only part of him inclined to disregard class distinctions (if not — as he made very plain in writing to his mother about 'black girls' — racial ones).

In 1916 he had been firmly but delicately relieved of his virginity by a French tart in Amiens, loaned for the purpose by an officer in the RFC with more clearly defined *droits de seigneur* over her. The pattern — of other chaps' girls and of the *mari complaisant* — seems to have been imprinted early. So, contrary to later vulgar rumour, does a taste for female society. Ziegler goes into the matter quite thoroughly and honourably, and dismisses all the sniggering stuff about Edward's impotence, homosexuality and inexperience. This staple of the smoking-room — I vividly remember being leeringly told that Wallis Simpson 'could make a toothpick feel like a Havana cigar' — is now dispelled. In fact, it seems that Mrs Simpson exerted the fascination of cruelty and authority; conceivably related to Edward's unwholesome yearning for men of action and power. Or perhaps something in his kingly training made him pine to bend the knee. At all events, several reports have him literally grovelling at the feet of Mrs S. (Did King George V, supposed to have said 'How's the Empire?' with his dying words, really say: 'How's the vampire?' Just a suggestion.)

There was something empty about Edward. He never, as Ziegler establishes with pitiless exactitude, made or kept a real friend. Cronies like 'Fruity' Metcalfe were as disposable, and as disappointed, as the equerries and stewards and private secretaries who all came to despise him. When he left England, not one of his former servants wanted to come with him. By the end, the Mosleys in their neighbouring château were his only reliable 'society', and you couldn't want it bleaker than that. Bleak is the word for the closing chapters of this story. Removed to the Iberian periphery by the Nazi invasion of France, the Duke chose his circle of acquaintances from among the most depraved Axis fans. Ziegler's own strained measure and fair-mindedness give out at about this point: 'Through the Spanish Foreign Ministry,' he writes,

the Duke had already requested that his house in Paris and at Cap d'Antibes should be looked after by the Germans for the duration of the war, now he compounded this already deplorable indiscretion by allowing his wife to send an emissary into the heart of German-occupied France so as to suit their personal convenience. The Germans can hardly be blamed for thinking that he must be in a mood to serve their ends in more important ways.

True, but then they knew that already. It's a toss-up whether Edward was trying harder to appease them for his wife, who, as Ziegler shows through innumerable eye-witnesses, delighted in exerting her supremacy over him. It must have been gruesome or her, later, cooped up in the petty hell of the Bahamas. Yet even in this fastness of colonial torpor, where they had specifically been sent to keep them out of range of Nazi temptation, the couple still managed to receive seedy, deluded go-betweens for the Germans, and continued to prosecute their pathetic campaign to have the Duchess styled 'HRH'. Strange, then, that anti-Establishment figures like Churchill and Kingsley Martin and Beaverbrook, a sort of distillate of the Rex Mottram set, should have been 'King's Men' of a kind in 1936 and have staked some part of their careers on defending this ugly little gargoyle. But perhaps not so strange, since in our own day there are radicals who flirt with monarchy as if it could provide a principled — or at any rate popular — alternative to a Toryism as apparently onerous as that of Stanley Baldwin and Cosmo Lang. A good thing that the Buck House short cut didn't work last time.

When Alan 'Tommy' Lascelles had had enough of his prince, and was about to tender his resignation from the household, he wrote: 'I am thoroughly and permanently out of sympathy with him.... His personal charm has vanished irretrievably as far as I am concerned, and I always feel as if I were working, not for the next King of England, but for the son of the latest American millionaire.' How far-sighted Tommy was. Edward was the first of the modern monarchs; the magic of the throne is now inextricable from Charles and the Annenbergs, Diana and Donald Trump — the extension of Edward's international white-trash habit into modern showbiz and celeb culture. The authoritarian trappings are less evident, true, even if you overlook the reactionary temper of Prince Philip or the quiet hard-heartedness of his wife in the matter of her sister and Group Captain Townsend. Still, the House of Windsor is a miserable, secretive family, claiming to stand for the nation and thereby inviting judgement on the model it represents to us. Do we really deserve — have we really earned — this kind of devotion and this level of sacrifice?

London Review of Books, November 1990

CHARLIE'S ANGEL

If you can imagine being force-fed a whole box of mint chocolate creams, you can catch a whiff of the intoxicating atmosphere that is England today. There is something about all Royal events which leaves a cloying taste. But a Royal romance is something quite else again. Overnight, the national press dissolves into a swamp of schmaltz. The BBC newsreaders adopt an unctuous tone and set their faces into a permanent smirk. Party leaders vie with one another in loyalty contests, and the grovelling Olympiad is usually won by Labour. Babes are taught to lisp a new name, and what name could come more trippingly than Lady Diana Spencer? Lady Diana was sixteen years of age when she first caught the eye of the Prince of Wales (a fact which might trouble mothers of other boys of thirty-two, but has not creased the brow of Elizabeth Windsor). She then survived a barrage of media attention, and passed the crucial test. Not to be too finicky about it, no callow youth could be found to say that he had bedded her. This was in bold contrast to Prince Charles's earlier escorts who, if they could not be said to be the nation's sweetheart, could at least claim to have been the sweetheart of a noticeable proportion of its adult male population.

Gone were the speculations about scandal. Lady Diana's father swore publicly that she was intact. Another relative, Lord Fermoy, told the press: 'I can assure you she's never had a lover.' Britain has never been specially fussy about pucelage, but virginity has now become a crucial issue. The whole thing might have been scripted by Lady Diana's step-grandmother Barbara Cartland, queen of romantic fiction, one of whose many tearstained bestsellers was entitled *Bride to the King.* As well as having reached nineteen without yielding, Lady Diana has been recommended on the ground of her breeding. She descends from the Stuarts on both sides of her line (if we allow for the interruption of King Charles's head) and has almost as good a claim to the throne as Prince Charles himself. She is a seventh cousin of Humphrey Bogart and (by marriage) an eighth cousin of Rudolph Valentino.

Her pedigree, then, is impeccable. And pedigree may be the word — the poor girl has been advertised as if she were a milch cow. One close family friend told the press about her first proper meeting with the heir to the throne: 'She taught him to tap dance on the terrace. He thought she was adorable. Who wouldn't? It was rather like being given a puppy, full of vitality and terribly sweet.' Indeed. There was a time when Prince Charles was being urged to strike out, to marry a girl from the Commonwealth, to found or enrich a line that in some fashion would keep the monarchy abreast of the century. Instead, he has opted for a girl nearly half his age, who was born on one of the Royal estates, has never passed an examination at any of her many schools, has never emerged from the warm bath of snobbery in which the English upper crust marinate their offspring and giggles when referred to as a puppy or a brood mare. One searches for ways to brighten up this picture. I can think of two. By the time the wedding bells ring out, there will be three million unemployed people in Britain who will badly need a splash of colour in their lives. And my old chum her stepbrother has, after a long wait, finally and suddenly succeeded in raising a loan from his bank.

The Nation, March 1981

UNHAPPY FAMILIES·

Racked as it is by under- and unemployment, ideological conflict, ecological woe, domestic breakdown, juvenile delinquency and resentment over taxation, and plagued the while by American white-trash imports, the Royal Family is more than ever fulfilling its role as a microcosm of all that is enduring about British values and traditions. Without the Queen, it must often ask itself, whatever should we do? If Her Majesty's calming, serene stoicism was ever needed and tested, surely now is that time. Can she act as a unifying force and moral figurehead to the fractious House of Windsor? Those who scoff that the monarch has no place in our go-ahead, modern, Europeanized society have yet again mistaken the real temper of the age. The Sovereign provides an essential pageantry and continuity in a clan which would otherwise resort to one long vulgar brawl. That the clan is her own clan is beside the point. We are all (and one means this in a very *real* sense) a part of that clan.

Every now and then, some colour magazine will do a feature on those remote islanders (Trobriand? Gilbert and Ellice?) who worship Prince Philip. With amused condescension, the reporter notes that the tribesmen — who wear status-enhancing penis gourds — will gather round photographs of the Royal consort and embark on elaborate propitiatory ceremonies. Once, the Royal Yacht *Britannia* cruised within hailing distance of the islands, and there was some talk of a possible 'putting in'. But, probably because of the awkward business of the gourds, the scheme was shelved *sine die*. By what right do we presume to mock this modest archipelago? If some Lévi-Strauss was to bring,

·Review of John Hartley, *Accession: The making of a queen*, London 1992; Phillip Hall, *Royal Fortune: Tax, money and the monarchy*, London 1992; Willie Hamilton, *Blood on the Walls: Memoirs of an anti-royalist from Miner's Row to Royal Palace*, London 1992.

not a Kwakiutl, but a Philip-worshipper to Royal London, the poor sod would feel embarrassed for us. Worship is a fine and pure thing, he might say. But *this* — this is a decayed idolatry. Even our arguments about monarchy have a musty, cobwebbed, time-worn air to them (is anything more dated than the phrase 'this day and age'?). The axis of tautology and contradiction — Why don't they pay taxes like the rest of us? They're *not* the rest of us, you fool! — is the preferred guarantee of a dialogue of the deaf. These three books, in distinct ways, perpetuate the stalemate.

Even when he was writing on top form, 'Peter Simple' in the old *Daily Telegraph* had two rather tiring standby sketches. One was 'the Socialist Royal Family', in which King Norman and Queen Doreen, and 'the Queen Gran', fought for special seats on a London omnibus amid coarse yells of 'All Right for Some!' The other was the dingy career of Mr Arthur Grudge, the boring and resentful MP for Stretchford, who was for ever demanding fair shares and the reintroduction of the ration book. And this Tory satire was a hit three decades ago. How dizzying is the pace of our progress. Now before me is a book on Royal tax evasion, a book by a self-satisfied 'prolier than thou' chippy Labour backbencher and a book with one of those fake-sonorous titles ('Majesty', 'Coronation', 'Investiture') that make one wince when they are reviewed in the American press. John Hartley, who was *The Times*'s man on royal tours of white dominions in the corking 1950s, has overegged the pudding by having a subtitle that actually adds to the fatuity of his one-word invocation. Like all crooked-knee chroniclers, he must understand better than most that hereditary monarchs are born, not 'made'. Succession, boy. *Succession*.

Can we not avoid the false antithesis of cringing and whinging? Phillip Hall's study of the Royal imposts and their studied evasion is easily the best of the three. It may begin as a straight Leveller's manual, but it goes up and down intriguing pathways *en route* to its easy target. For instance, the facile and cynical assertion of 'Victorian values' takes on an aspect of ambiguity when we learn that Queen Victoria did at least offer to pay her whack to the Revenue, and that 'her' Chancellor, Robert Lowe, was at any rate prepared for a sporting political contest with the republican Dilke in 1871, during which he asked Gladstone for permission 'not to confine myself to general remarks which would certainly lead to the belief that there was something behind that would not bear daylight'. Very few subsequent Chancellors have been either so gallant or so candid. Indeed, the point against monarchism is not so much that it expresses the belief that the Crown somehow owns the country. It is that it gives a potent, undeserved and unearned advantage to politicians and placemen who think that *they* should exert that privilege. As Hall smartly notes, when quoting a 1971 Select Committee which was bamboozled by Civil Service refusal to answer 'detailed information about tax of an individual':

> This deft switch from public to private, from the Prerogative of the Crown to claiming the rights of the ordinary citizen, and back again, is characteristically

employed as regards the financial affairs of the monarch. Faced with taxation, she is the Crown. Faced with disclosure, she is a private citizen.

What could be more agreeable for the secular arm, which revels in its 'Privy Council' discretion, its 'Orders in Council', its 'audiences' at the Palace and its appointments to 'Royal Commissions'? What if we were to speak our own language and properly describe the 'Privy Council' as the 'Secret Council'? That would be, as Bagehot feared and as Chancellor Lowe dared, to 'let in daylight', not upon the monarch only but upon those who amass and deploy power in 'her' name.

Hall specializes in a rather effective, dry, deadpan mode which, even if it masks his passion, yields him better results than chippiness would do. He cites Wigram, who had been private secretary to the fifth George, and Wigram's minute of the reading of the fifth George's will to the eighth Edward on 22 January 1936:

> Edward was much perturbed that his father had left him no money and kept on saying: 'Where do I come in?' We tried to explain that the late King felt that his eldest son, as Prince of Wales for twenty-five years, ought to have built up a nice surplus out of the Duchy of Cornwall and that there was no necessity to provide for him.

Poor, loyal Wigram. He had to stand mute like any grizzled Ruritanian game-keeper and keep his thoughts to himself while a spoiled, talentless princeling slobbered: 'My brothers and sisters have got large sums but I have been left out'. Though this kingly endowment was 'private', it brings us nearer to the complaint which, though often mouthed in humble saloon bars, actually originates with Sir Frederick Ponsonby. Ponsonby had been Keeper of the King's Privy (!) Purse during the period when the fifth George was asking a few thousand men a week to give their lives for him and country. (If he'd said 'For Me and Country', even the English might have cocked an eyebrow.) After the war, Ponsonby demanded an increase in the Civil List, menacing the Cabinet with the blackmailing conceit of 'the King going to open Parliament in a taxi-cab'. All *that* again, and even then. To Westminster Hall in a tumbril is an option. To Westminster to convene 'our' Parliament in a golden coach, itself confected from recently invented tradition, is another. The bicycle, the taxi-cab and indeed the skateboard are chimerical, time-wasting diversions explicitly designed, as with so much Establishment babble, to miss the point. Hall has shown that the immemorial tradition of Royal tax exemption originates more or less with the present 'reign'. In doing so, he has let in light on a system of crass patronage which wishes — as why should it not? — to be shrouded in 'mystery'.

Arthur Grudge, by contrast, spares us nothing except the main point. A long-standing and reliable member of the Gaitskell–Wilson–Callaghan–Kinnock lobby-loyalists, and a man who never gave the party machine any trouble, Willie Hamilton would still like to be mistaken for a russet-coated captain at the Putney debates. No such luck. Hereditary privilege won't get you to Putney either. I'm as likely as the next chap to be impressed by Hamilton's stories of his wretched childhood and schooling, but it's sad to discover that he has no notion of injustice except as it affects him in person. I also revolt against sentimentality and thus can't swallow Hamilton's tawdry account of a constituent giving him an old pair of wired-together pre-NHS specs:

> The glasses worn by that old man are still kept in the same little box in which he handed them over to me. I got far more satisfaction out of dealing with human problems like that than with getting all worked up about German rearmament or NATO's defences.

Fair enough, but why, in that case, be in politics at all? Better to answer grace and favour letters at Windsor or Sandringham, and be in touch with the pulse of real humans — a pleasure which Royal equerries know much more genuinely and intimately than most social-working MPs. Hamilton is even worse when he tries to reason his inchoate feelings into policy, as he did in a memorandum to the Labour Party National Executive in 1981:

> In my memo I accepted that it was unrealistic to propose the abolition of the monarchy. Instead, I suggested that a new Royal Department of State be set up, with its own Government Minister controlling all expenditure on the monarchy. All employees of the new Royal Department, from the Queen downward, would be regarded as civil servants, with special rates of pay for the Queen and her immediate family.

Hamilton records, with perfect humourless gravity, the reluctance of the left-wing intellectual types on the Benn–Heffer NEC to get back to him on this. Thank heaven for that. A plan for the worst of both worlds — a hereditary monarch encumbered yet sustained by a special, joyless new Ministry — could only have the effect of putting into turgid prose the embarrassment that generally comes in the even more forgettable form of Crown-sponsored pseudo-romantic poetry. At least this book makes it possible to quit Hamilton of the charge — republicanism — with which the royalist rags adore so unjustly to besmirch him — or rather, it.

No mere words are adequate to summarize John Hartley's exquisite deference. As he himself, not without an awareness of his own daring, ventures to put it:

> With the disappearance of the other major Monarchies of Europe, from Germany, Russia, Greece and France, for instance, the English Monarchy has been left as the only major 'traditional' royal ceremonial of ancient and genuine splendour. The honing and refining of these procedures has given the English Monarchy a somewhat exclusive presence in the world.

One loves the upper-case M for monarchy; the arch quote marks that hedge the word 'traditional', the euphemism of 'disappearance' and the astounding non sequitur that carpenters the closing sentence, illustrative only of survival, into a matter of refinement and exclusivity. This is exactly what is meant by courtier journalism.

Our monarchy is for ever being said to 'embody' certain things. One thing that it embodies for sure is the old, barely admitted alliance between the throne and the throng, or between Crown and mob. This alliance is expressly designed, as with all monarchies, to short-circuit and intimidate the educated, the sceptical and the ironic: the only class (precisely because it isn't a class) in whose defence I myself feel willing to be snobbish. When Buck House berates the *Sun* for going too far, it complains of a breach in a historic understanding between the two. In 1984, as Hall reminds us, a docker named Fred Adams got much tabloid attention for leaving all his life savings to the Queen. When the *Daily Telegraph* described the dead man's 'drab house', it filled in the sorry picture with Mr Adams's pin-ups of Royal magazines and his display of National Front slogans. 'Angels in Marble' was Disraeli's inspired term for this kind of plebeian credulity and superstition; long a secret weapon in the *lutte de classe*.

Our idiom is so conditioned that we even have to employ the term 'realm of freedom'. If that realm begins with our not living for others, and not having to have others live for us, why not declare that we release this unhappy family, not from our obligations to it, but from its onerous and unnecessary sacrifices for us? Who would not feel instantly relieved? More grown up? One begins to think that the republican choice is not so much a potential outcome of the debate on a constitutional future as an actual precondition for it.

Times Literary Supplement, March 1992

PRINCESS OF DYSFUNCTION·

The British public, renowned for its kindness to animals, apparently insists on the regular sacrifice of a human family. At least once every generation, a young princeling or princess is kept, like any Aztec or Inca monarch, in a gilded cage from which the only release is death. Our time of progress and improvement has, naturally, added certain refinements. The doomed Royal person may be faced with the hopeless choice: Give up your freedom and happiness for the

·Review of Andrew Morton, *Diana: Her True Story*, London and New York 1992; Nicholas Davies, *Diana: A Princess and Her Troubled Marriage*, London and New York 1992.

Crown, or give up the Crown for your freedom and happiness. And remember that your ordeal will be recorded in excruciating detail. Thus Edward VIII, a pro-Nazi wastrel and slob, was considered perfect monarch material by the Establishment until he craved a Baltimore divorcee. Thus Princess Margaret, sister of the present Queen, was told by the palace that she could not marry the love of her life, a dashing airman named Group Captain Peter Townsend, because he too had been married before. Thus Princess Margaret's nephew, Prince Charles, was told to find a wife before he was forty and hastily picked a disco-loving airhead who was, at the time of their first meeting, exactly half his age. Now mark the sequel. The same Queen Elizabeth II, who unsmilingly ruled against her sister's happiness and in favour of 'family values', has to face in the autumn of her life the fact that her own marriage is a notorious pretence; the fact that the marriage of her only daughter has ended in a messy divorce; the fact that her two eldest sons are involved in sordid and boring pre-divorce routines and the fact that her youngest son looks as though he may not marry at all. Score one for the hereditary principle, which is the font of monarchy, aristocracy and the British class system, and thus has graver implications than the bulimia and hysteria of the much-photographed Diana Spencer.

If you care to read about bulimia and hysteria, Andrew Morton and Nicholas Davies have done what Fleet Street reflexively calls a 'right royal' job. Thrill as the Spencer girl gorges and pukes. Gasp as she hurls herself, gravid with child, down the stairs of a palace that credulous taxpayers keep in business. Cringe as you realize that 'fairy tale' is precisely the right term for this romance scripted by the brothers Grimm. Morton is a specialist at the unintentionally hilarious. In *Diana: Her True Story*, he leans heavily on the breathless testimony of James Gilbey, 'a member of the distilling dynasty who has known Diana since she was 17', who told him: 'She said to me recently that she hadn't made any date in her diary past July because she doesn't think she is going to be there.' This, according to Morton, made him bring his book publication forward. And though it's never made clear whether 'there' is a reference to this vale of tears or the House of Windsor (the difference may be slight), what emerges is a picture of the perfect *mésalliance* between those two stock British characters, the buffer and the debutante; he, old before his time; she, a spoiled brat who sulks at the 'duty' part of her ostentation and privilege. What a symbol for an ancient and dignified people. The lineage of Mrs Simpson is carried on by this imperishable Mortonian observation: 'As Oonagh Toffolo, who once nursed the Duke of Windsor and regularly visits Diana for sessions of acupuncture and meditation, observes: "She is a prisoner of the system just as surely as any woman incarcerated in Holloway jail."' I haven't the advantage of having met Oonagh Toffolo, but I can tell that she's never been near Holloway jail (where convicts are kept, according to quaint English custom, 'at Her Majesty's pleasure'). Still, this passage and others make it clear that the fond illusion – of a vulgar war between the Royal Family and the gutter press

— is now quite unsustainable. Princess Diana is, for all intents and purposes, the author of Morton's servile and scandalous book. These are her friends, using her direct quotes at her express request. So much has been amply confirmed since publication. The Spencer girl wants us to know that 'there were days when she had her fortune read and her astrological traits analysed every few hours. She tried to live her life by their predictions; her volatile spirit clinging to every scrap of solace in their musings.' In other words (and to betray a well-kept national secret) it's not that the supermarket rags intrude into Royal doings; it's that there is an alliance between the two, and that the sort of people who adore astrology and supermarket trash also adore the dysfunctional House of Windsor.

Nicholas Davies, for instance, who became briefly famous a while ago as the Robert Maxwell journalist named by Seymour Hersh as an Iran–Israeli arms dealer, is also a polo-playing friend of Prince Charles. His rather more objective book, *Diana: A Princess and Her Troubled Marriage*, which contains very much the same grade of information, must therefore rank as one of the stoutest abuses of hospitality on record. I especially loved this vignette from the formative years of the Spencer girl: 'There were six servants, including a full time cook, and from an early age the children seemed to live on pheasant for lunch.' Small wonder, then, that Diana is now so keen on getting back in touch with her inner child, complete with tantrums, 'cries for help' and nursery orgies. The heir to the throne, meanwhile, pursues his own version of the New Age by holding conversations with shrubs and frequenting the company of dubious mystics. 'The firm', as the Queen stoically refers to the Royal Family, meanwhile runs badly to seed. Intended as it is for a mass family audience, this genre tends to hint rather than allege about the baser passions. Thus there is a hushed talk about 'separate beds' and 'constant companions', and a fine bestiary of double- and even triple-barrelled names. It's clear enough that Diana prefers the company of the more spirited members of the Travolta generation, where Charles inclines to the tried and tested wives of the various *maris complaisants* who sportingly gave him a start in these matters. Of our need to know this, or be told it by a publicly funded showbiz princess, I prefer to say nothing.

There's a fascinating subtext, which neither author is able to recognize or develop. We learn at one point that the Spencer girl has formed an attachment to Mother Teresa, but that she went straight from a meeting with her to 'promoting family planning issues'. Then it emerges that Diana 'asked the Pope about his "wounds" during a private audience in the Vatican shortly after he had been shot. He thought she was talking about her "womb" and congratulated her on her impending new arrival.' English law forbids the Royal Family to become Catholic or marry a Catholic, and appoints the monarch the head of the Church as well as the state and the armed forces in order to continue Henry VIII's vendetta against the Vatican. To talk family planning with Mother Teresa and wombs with His Holiness is surely pushing this tradition —

inherited, like the rest of it, from feudalism and sectarianism — a bit far.

Davies cites an opinion poll taken a year ago that found 22 per cent of the entire British population, and 60 per cent of the younger generation, giving more or less republican answers to the silly questions they were asked about their unhappy, spendthrift figurehead family. Random observation suggests that this proportion has not diminished in the meantime. Can it be that, faced with the ghastly alliance between Fleet Street populism and enervated royalism, the British public has finally done what the Spencer girl cannot do, and started to grow up?

Washington Post, June 1992

6
IDEAS AND INTERESTS

NEW YORK INTELLECTUALS AND THE
PROPHET OUTCAST ·

Each morning, the great, grey *New York Times* publishes a box headed 'Corrections', which box makes a sort of running auto-adjudication on the performance of the journal of record. On one day, there is a matter of spelling or nomenclature set right. On another, a date or a place. Occasionally, the correction goes so far as to specify what the paper might — or even should — have said. Some see, in this parade of scruple and objectivity, a Victorian combination of public rectitude and private hypocrisy whereby the more influential subscribers get their chance to 'set the record straight'. Others discern a sort of semiotic inquisition, useful for disciplining errant or overimaginative reporters into the uses of impartiality. (Alexander Cockburn comes right out and says that its purpose is to convince the public that everything *else* in yesterday's *Times* was historically and morally true.) Anyway, last November the paper ran a 'Correction' which is unlikely to be bested:

> An article on Saturday about Israeli efforts to control violence after the killing of Rabbi Meir Kahane included an erroneous identification, supplied by Israeli officials, for a man detained as a suspect in the killings of two Palestinians. The man, David Axelrod, is not related to Leon Trotsky. A man with the same name, who is a descendant of Trotsky, was questioned briefly by the police in a case of mistaken identity.

The arcane character of this item, which was at the top of that day's menu, might make it appear incongruous among the Saks and Bloomingdales ads, the opinion-poll findings, the Broadway listings and the remainder of the quotidian fare. But all across the Upper West Side of the city there is still a constituency, or at any rate a readership, to which any news of any relationship between Trotskyism and Judaism is as vivid and important as any dispatch from Trump Tower or Wall Street. In this circle, or set of interlocking circles, the names of Rudolf Slansky, Ehrlich and Alter, Max Schachtman, Andres Nin, Amadeo Bordiga and John Dewey are, still, names with which to puncture an argument, break up a friendship, revise an article or inaugurate a new and daring small magazine. Key words include 'Doctors' Plot', 'Deutscherite', and '*PR* Crowd', 'Vyshinsky' and 'neo-con'. New York is the last intellectual capital in history to concern itself with both the Surrealist Manifesto and the Platform of the Left Opposition.

Neil Jumonville's book contains rather more references to Trilling than to Trotsky, which, given the reverse emphasis in most discussions of his subject,

·Review of Neil Jumonville, *Critical Crossings: The New York Intellectuals in Post-War America*, Berkeley, CA 1991.

is by no means disproportionate. Mary McCarthy described the fell consequences of getting the proportions wrong in her essay 'My Confession'. Having
airily declared, at a fellow-travellers' publishing party, that Trotsky should be
allowed his day in court, she found her signature conscripted by a Trotskyist
'defence committee' that hadn't troubled to ask her permission. Before she had
time to object, she was pelted with so much obloquy by the Stalinists that it
seemed ignoble to remove her name. And then she began to look into the
matter:

> It is impossible to take a moderate tone under such conditions. If I admitted,
> though, to being a little hipped on the subject of Trotsky, I could sometimes gain
> an indulgent if flickering attention — the kind of attention that stipulates: 'She's a
> bit off but let's hear her story.' And now and then, by sheer chance, one of my
> hearers would be arrested by some stray point in my narrative: the disparaging
> smile would slowly fade from his features, leaving a look of blank consternation.
> He would go off and investigate for himself, and in a few days, when we met
> again, he would be a crackpot too.

Some of these people turn up in *The Group*. At approximately the same time as
Mary McCarthy was chivvying and being chivvied all over Manhattan, Saul
Bellow submitted his first short story for publication in the student magazine
of Northwestern University. (It took third prize in the competition.) Entitled
'The hell it can't', the story was intended to rebuke Sinclair Lewis's Popular
Front novel *It Can't Happen Here*. I once went to the labour of digging up this
un-anthologized tale, which describes an episode of vicious fascist violence,
and could see in it, if I chose, premonitions of Bellow's later impatient
pessimism.

Still, long after he had himself ceased to be a Trotskyist, Bellow had the
generosity to make his hero Augie March run into the Old Man in Mexico,
and to speak of him thus:

> I was excited by this famous figure, and I believe what it was about him that
> stirred me up was the instant impression he gave — no matter about the old heap
> he rode in or the peculiarity of his retinue — of navigation by the great stars, of
> the highest considerations, of being fit to speak the most important human
> words and universal terms. When you are as reduced to a different kind of navi-
> gation from the high starry kind as I was and are only sculling on the shallow bay,
> crawling from one clam-rake to the next, it's stirring to have a glimpse of deep-
> water greatness. And, even more than an established, an exiled greatness,
> because the exile was a sign to me of persistence at the highest things.

Augie March reports Trotsky as 'very gingery and energetic, debonair, sharp,
acute in the beard', which doesn't go all that badly with Mary McCarthy's
'small, frail, pertinacious old man who wore whiskers, wrinkles, glasses, shock
of grizzled hair, like a gleeful disguise for the erect young student, the dangerous revolutionary within him'. (Saul Bellow himself drove all the way to
Mexico to visit Trotsky and arrived just after the assassination.)

The variable elements that went to make up the unstable but attractive elements of Trotskyism might be summarized, through Trotsky's own personality and experience, as a register of the following: Intellectual, International, Jewish, Secular, Literary, Classical, Modernist. Moving from adjectives to nouns we would hit upon: Generalship, Dissidence and — perhaps above all — Exile. These are potent dialectical combinations: the stiff-necked atheist and the unapologetic Jew; the author of *Literature and Revolution* and co-signatory, with André Breton, of the Surrealist Manifesto; the companion of Frida Kahlo; the defender of embattled Einsteinians and Freudians; the founder of the Red Army and the pitiless opponent of great Russian chauvinism. What do we have here but the ideal-type — of the cosmopolitan, the modernist, the essayist and the man of action — that was yearned for by the diaspora of *Partisan Review*? We have one more thing: the most nerve-straining title of all, and the one discussed long ago by George Steiner in his *Trotsky and the Tragic Imagination*. Isaac Deutscher, the non-Jewish Jew *par excellence*, hesitated in calling his Trotsky trilogy *The Prophet*. There are messianic traditions after all, and there are messianic traditions. Yet surely Irving Howe, currently the very model of New York social democracy and of its literary counterpart, is not exaggerating when he calls the following excerpt from Deutscher 'Shakespearean in quality'. Trotsky, on the run from Stalin, is in Norway in 1936. The social-democratic government, quailing before Moscow's allegation that Trotsky is a Hitler agent, asks him to be silent. He replies:

> This is your first act of surrender to Nazism in your own country. You will pay for this. You think yourself secure and free to deal with a political exile as you please. But the day is near — remember this — the day is near when the Nazis will drive you from your country, all of you.

'After less than four years,' Deutscher writes, 'the same government had indeed to flee from Norway before the Nazi invasion; and as the ministers and their aged King Haakon stood on the coast, huddled together and waiting anxiously for a boat that was to take them to England, they recalled with awe Trotsky's worlds as a prophet's curse come true.' (Trotsky's persecutor in Norway, who was trying to appease Vidkun Quisling's local fascist movement, had been Trygve Lie, later first Secretary-General of the United Nations.) Prophet or not in the Old Testament sense — and his prescience about capitalism and Communism seems to have exhausted itself lately — Leon Trotsky was the first — and for some appreciable time the only — world-class figure to warn against both fascism and Stalinism. Even Churchill in his *Great Contemporaries* gives credit for some part of this achievement to the Old Man. Taking Trotsky's measure in this way, as human being and as theoretician, we see that all the strands of the 'New York intellectual' milieu are in some sense Trotskyist or post-Trotskyist. This is because, even if all Jewish imagery and emotion could be winnowed from the mix, and even if all Marxist terminology could be purged from the records of those concerned, he remains the century's most arresting instance of the aesthete and the intellectual in politics.

From the world of *Partisan Review* ('the *PR* Crowd'), which was the fountainhead magazine of the New York school (and never mind for the nonce that Bellow is from Chicago and Susan Sontag from Los Angeles), several streams have originated. The dissident left — as opposed to the proto-Communist left — symbolized by Dwight Macdonald, Philip Rahv and others. The Cold War hard-liners, such as Melvyn Lasky, Irving Kristol, James Burnham, Sidney Hook and later Norman Podhoretz. The 'End of Ideology' liberal professoriat: Daniel Bell, Nathan Glazer, Lewis Coser. And perhaps most enduring in their contribution, if only because they partook of all wings and of none, the Europeanized cultural and literary Modernists such as Clement Greenberg, Delmore Schwartz, Harold Rosenberg and, to a different degree, Malcolm Cowley — those who found *Partisan Review* an alternative to callow nativism, a transatlantic lifeline to Eliot, Malraux, Silone. To give the rollcall of magazines, as Jumonville does, is to tell off from the *New York Review of Books* by way of *Dissent*, the *New Republic*, and *New Leader*, *Commentary* and the *Nation*, without exhausting the list. And almost all of the above-cited writers knew one end of a Trotskyist internal disputation from another. Susan Sontag's short story 'Old Complaints Revisited' shows an easy, satirical familiarity with the argot and idiom of what Isaac Deutscher once termed the *Trotskisant* element in New York discourse. In their own worlds, however far they moved from the Old Man, they preserved the imagery of the faction-fight, the confession, the recantation and the necessity for long memory and sarcasm in argument. They also showed an occasional un-Trotskyist taste for historical rewriting. Professor Norman Birnbaum told me that in 1984, of all years, he asked the *PR* board what it proposed by way of a fiftieth-anniversary symposium. 'But Norman,' relied the now-thoroughly conformist William Phillips, '*PR* was *Stalinist* in 1934. We thought we'd wait until 1986 for our half-century. Why remind people?'

There is a related progression, involving upward mobility and assimilation, which fits the jagged pattern of class and ethnicity against the smoother curve of political 'maturation'. Many of the leading members of the New York group came from plebeian homes where English was not the first language. They educated themselves at places like City College and in Talmudic logic-splitting among the *groupuscules*. They sought to gain acceptance as Americans *and* as dissidents, as well as to better their lot. Not all of these objectives were strictly compatible — remember that as late as 1936 Lionel Trilling was being told explicitly by Columbia University that 'as a Freudian, a Marxist and Jew' he could not expect to be allowed to impart the great traditions of English Literature. His response was to make as little as possible of the 'accusation', or definition, and to metamorphose into a refined gentleman-liberal. His novel *The Middle of the Journey* is patterned on the classic Communist-into-ex-Communist evolution; effectively eliding the stage of Trotskyist anguish in which many of his contemporaries dwelt for longer than they now care to remember. These others were spikier, and did not seek 'tenure' in a time when credentials mattered less than they do now: a consideration well-caught by Russell Jacoby in his book *The Last Intellectuals*. But there was always a subliminal status-pressure at work. In a recent review in the *New Republic* of Christopher Ricks's *T.S. Eliot and Prejudice*, Irving Howe asks himself why he and his peer-group, who were ready enough to convict Ezra Pound of racialism, hesitated to attack Eliot in spite of his very crass and blatant attacks on 'free-thinking Jews'. First, of course, there was the intense excitement felt in *Partisan Review* circles at the first publication of *The Waste Land*. But was there not something else?

> Reading Eliot's poetry a half-century ago I felt so strongly (if not always lucidly) attuned to its inner vibrations that I had little desire to be critical, especially of what might be passed over as a few incidental lines of bigotry. With a supreme hauteur, Eliot had made the journey from provincial St Louis to cosmopolitan London. The New York writers could not match his hauteur, but perhaps they could negotiate a somewhat similar journey from Brooklyn or the Bronx to Manhattan. I doubt that this comparison occurred to many of the New York writers, but I am convinced that it figured in our feelings.

The intellectual in politics is always faced by the problem of elites, and by the much less precise notion of elitism. Should the masses or the intelligentsia be the proper target of enlightenment? Ought one to be a civilizing courtier or a *déclassé* agitator? Trotsky himself was celebrated for his panache and individualism, and his contempt for vulgar 'public opinion' and 'common sense'. In his raillery against the dull Stalinist hacks in Russia, and the even more stupid Communists in Germany who thought that Hitler would give them their chance, he made many a resentful bovine, 'ordinary man' type of enemy. (Though no snob, he was no populist — and he was a conspicuous member of the world's most visible minority. He became the first to write seriously about the role of anti-Semitism in the Stalin world-view, and the first to predict that Nazism might lead to an actual extirpation of Jewry.)

Consider how the New York school, itself committed to an integrated, mobile version of American society, for itself and others, interpreted the question of elitism. First, and perhaps above all, we have Clement Greenberg's 1939 essay in *Partisan Review*, entitled 'Avant Garde and Kitsch'. This was a trumpet-blast against massified, homogenized culture and was expanded by later writers into an attack on the political uses of conformity, nativism and provincialism. Without Greenberg it is almost impossible to imagine the Abstract Expressionist painters getting critical sympathy or attention and it is interesting to note, as Jumonville does, that he derived his position from an essay by Trotsky in *Partisan Review* which had stated that 'the struggle for revolutionary ideas in art must begin once again with the struggle for artistic *truth*, not in terms of any single school, but in terms of *the immutable faith of the artist in his own inner self*. Without this there is no art.' Take out the 'struggle' bits, and scale down Greenberg's own views of the 'revolutionary' potential of Pollock and de Kooning, and you have a defence of high-bourgeois artistic integrity; initially set against the barbarities of Zhdanov but equally to be wielded against Hollywood, advertising and Henry Luce. Even the postwar *Partisan Review* symposium 'Our Country and Our Culture', which in 1952 elected to celebrate, as the use of the possessive might indicate, a more rounded and reconciled view of America on the part of the intellectuals, was shot through with dislike for commercialism and manipulation.

Granted this distrust of the mass, and of the mass counterpart in intellectual public opinion (what Harold Rosenberg termed 'the herd of independent minds'), it became a question of what form elitism would take. It took, by my count, four distinct shapes. First, and easiest to dispense with, is the organized remnant of the Trotskyist vanguard. Dwight Macdonald, after his break with this outfit, wrote a scathingly funny article about the boast of James P. Cannon, leader of the Socialist Workers' Party, that 'the only really moral people' were the Trotskyists. He showed how this sub-Bolshevik arrogance had driven away the few influential sympathizers, such as the novelist James T. Farrell, that the SWP ever possessed. Some of these people, like James Burnham, retained elements of their Bolshevik identity when they offered their genius to the service of power. In *The Managerial Revolution* and *The Struggle for the World*, Burnham displayed a truly Trotskyist grandeur in his command of the twin subjects of productive relations and imperial rhythms. He merely altered some of the pluses to minuses, and argued in a third book, *The Machiavellians*, that power is always held by elites and that democracy is a sham. Victory goes to the elite that can best bewitch the masses. This ideology of conspiracy and manipulation, and its world-historical setting, outfitted Burnham admirably to become a CIA consultant and Cold War profiteer: a role in which he helped to evolve the Congress for Cultural Freedom and to recruit numerous intellectuals to an unfastidious interpretation of the *Kulturkampf*. His break with Trotsky was over the agonized question of Kronstadt: it was noticeable that those who had been most pure in this matter were later, as ex-Trotskyist and anti-Soviet campaigners, the least scrupulous about recommending the 'pacification' of Algeria, Vietnam and the Congo.

The third elite consists of those who remained broadly liberal on domestic questions and restrained on foreign-policy ones until the second, Reaganite phase of the Cold War. By that time, the issues of Soviet Jewry, Arab terrorism, Third World subversion and black-versus-Jewish urban American dramas had become emotionally — and to some extent intellectually — melded. The ethos of the group, which became known as 'neo-conservative', was never more happily expressed than by its leader Norman Podhoretz, who remarked with irritated sarcasm that American Jews still had the voting habits of Puerto Ricans and the income level of Episcopalians. Here one got a more rugged interpretation of the assimilation/mobility question, together with a marked decline in Jewish solidarity with current or former 'out' groups and, in the pages of *Commentary* and the *New Criterion*, a developed series of attacks on cultural decadence, homosexuality, pacifism and 'multiculturalism'. Vicarious identification with ruling and victorious WASPs culminated in the warm relationship between *Commentary* and the person of Ms Jeane Kirkpatrick, many of whose staff and advisers were drawn from a tiny group called 'Social Democrats USA', which had its origins in a Trotskyist sect led by Max Schachtman, most brilliant of the sectarian defectors after Burnham himself. (I remember meeting Melvyn Lasky in the street in London and hearing his part-shy and part-proud confession that he had just flown to New York expressly for Schachtman's funeral.) The condensed lucubrations of Schachtman and Burnham are lampooned by George Orwell in 'The Theory of Oligarchical Collectivism' — 'The Book' within the book in *Nineteen Eighty-four*. It should be added that not all of the *Commentary* set went all the way. Daniel Bell, for example, protested and resigned when *Partisan Review*, which in its dotage has joined the general rout, proposed to publish an open attack on democracy by an organizer of Reagan's Nicaragua and Iran policy, and Saul Bellow resigned from Podhoretz's grandly titled Committee for the Free World when it went overboard in defaming Norman Mailer.

The fourth classifiable group which can claim descent from the anti-Schachtman warriors in the great Trotskyist schism still holds the view that the intellectual must be an independent, critical person, neither a celebrant of the status quo nor a marginal propagandist. Writers like Irving Howe and the group connected with *Dissent* magazine, who in a sense constitute the right of the American left, do not desire to be part of a Kissinger-style *Judenrat*, at the service of the empire. They wish to maintain dialogue with supporters of the Reverend Jackson, say, and with the new immigrant populations who are re-enacting the Ellis Island saga. They dislike the rise of the Israeli ultras and the allegory this imposes on East–West and North–South, to say nothing of Brooklyn–Harlem, relations. But they are also out of sympathy with the part-green, part-red mishmash which is most of what remains of the New Left and the peace movement. This suspicion dates from the 1960s, when *Dissent* flirted with quietism on the matter of Vietnam because it thought the SDS leadership was unhistorical and potentially ochlocratic. And today, when the question of Palestine comes up, they wince.

In the recent crisis over the Gulf War, all these currents and tendencies were on view; not always predictable in their verdicts or diagnoses. Many of the Trotskyist sects opened the bidding by compromising the anti-war movement and declaring Saddam and the Baath to be anti-imperialist. *Commentary* and the *New Republic*, for reasons that are connected both to Israel and to their need for a demonstration of American will, would have struck Baghdad harder and earlier than Bush and Schwarzkopf did. The heirs of James Burnham, now more or less fully transferred to William Buckley's *National Review*, can see the shade of their founder in the grandiose rhetoric of the New World Order — which is, of course, an order imposed by the New World. The *New York Review of Books* published some learned pleas for a negotiated settlement and some consideration of 'linkage' but also more than one article justifying the use (if not exactly this use) of force. (The preferred authority in these circles was Samir Al-Khalil, author of *The Republic of Fear*, which laid bare the lineaments of Saddam Hussein's police regime and compared it both to Nazism and to Stalinism. Samir Al-Khalil is the pseudonym of Kanan Makiya, known to veterans of the Trotskyist movement as a one-time leading Arab member of the Fourth International.) From *Dissent* circles came a number of arguments which sought to find a left-liberal pro-war position by defining the conflict (as, unluckily for them, Bush had done) as essentially anti-fascist. Only the *Nation* (for which, I should say, I myself write a column) opposed the escalation and published regular reminders that America's role in the region is not that of a disinterested superpower. As I write, only the *Nation* has protested at the scale of Iraqi civilian and 'collateral' casualties.

The only quality exhibited in common by all four groups is a fixed attachment to the idea of minority, dissident status. When Whittaker Chambers (who appears as Gifford Maxim in Trilling's novel) decided to make his break with Communism, he still thought it morally essential to proclaim that he was deserting a winning cause rather than snuggling up to the Nixonites and the FBI. Meetings of the 'Committee for the Free World', lavishly funded and often attended by serving members of the administration, felt it necessary to talk as if they were a group of persecuted, reviled oppositionists. Many others signalled their acceptance of the mainstream by writing a confession entitled *Against the Current*, or words to that effect. Clearly the imagery of an embattled remnant does not lose its elite appeal even when it is politically metamorphosed.

Neil Jumonville's book, which is agreeably written and well — if narrowly — researched (there is no Burnham and no Schachtman), is an argument for pragmatism: for the solvent effect of the 'real world' upon grand or utopian systems. Pragmatism, indeed, was a theory and practice of John Dewey, who, after all, took years out of his life to defend Trotsky and to expose the gruesome frame-ups of the Moscow trials. But I detect a drift towards Bloomsburyization: the latest on a groaning shelf-full of reminiscence, self-reference and the multiple glossings of clique-think. Alan Wald's 1987 book *The New York Intellectuals* is a necessary companion volume and in the long run a more illuminating one, because it shows the germinal, contradictory force of revolutionary politics and the noticeable failure of those once singed by it to succeed, however much they may have tried, in escaping its implications.

In the rush of confession, revision, repudiation, self-advancement and mere ageing that has overtaken the New York crowd, the idea of the fearless unpublished, unimpressed and uncompromised intelligence has taken rather a beating. That is why, long after Trotskyism has become irrelevant, the admonishing figure of Trotsky himself has not. It just isn't possible to imagine him on some fortified kibbutz, with an anti-Arab pogrom down the road. As Mary

McCarthy wrote of him, keeping some part of her powder dry, 'his shrug before the unforeseen implies an acceptance of consequences that is a far cry from penance and prophecy. Such, it concedes, is life. Bravo, old sport, I say, even though the hall is empty.'

London Review of Books, April 1991

CLUBLAND INTELLECTUALS[*]

Let us now praise, and pity, famous men who did their thankless, almost unacknowledged best for the common weal. Let us begin by parsing 'Our Age', and by considering one instance of its operation as a historical concept and a literary device:

> Our Age was to see a reprise of the irrationality which Keynes so detested. In 1945 when the American and British governments were pondering what to do when they occupied Germany, there arrived in Whitehall the plan put forward by Morgenthau, the secretary of the US Treasury. It proposed Germany should be pastoralised and everyone in official and economic life down to the middle executive rank of, say, bank manager, should be expelled from their posts for having supported or connived at Nazism. Among the officials at the British Treasury was Edward Playfair who had been at King's. He saw at once that the proposals which had landed on his desk were like the settlement at Versailles, not only mad but bad. Why should Britain pay vast sums to feed the unemployable population of a deindustrialised and destabilised Germany in order to satisfy a demand, however comprehensible, for revenge? This time the forces of reason prevailed.

Where to commence? Let us admit, first, that this agreeable, freehand style has a charm of its own, and that despite an inclination to cliché ('forces of reason'; 'landed on his desk') it can still resonate successfully in parts. 'Mad and bad', which would have been more to the point if it were 'not only bad but mad', is rendered as it is in order to evoke the shade of Brian Howard out of Lord Byron. And could one have a name more exquisitely apt, for the circumstances, than Playfair of King's?

And yet, and yet. Henry Morgenthau's plan was actually defeated at the Quebec Conference between Churchill and Roosevelt in September 1944. It

[*]Review of Noel Annan, *Our Age: A Portrait of a Generation*, London 1990.

was defeated, having gained the assent of Churchill (who himself wrote in the word 'pastoral'), by the combined opposition of Cordell Hull and Henry Stimson. (Neither in 1944 nor in 1945, nor for many years thereafter, were any serious Washington plans being defeated by British civil servants of any college.) It was in the first instance a plan based on the racial theories of Sir Robert – later Lord – Vansittart, Permanent Secretary at the Foreign Office, who had declared that German culture, not National Socialism, was the essential enemy. Vansittart's concept, the adoption of which by the British Social Democracy prompted a protest from Arthur Koestler, was refashioned after the war to make Russia, not Germany, into the natural, ancestral enemy. And yet Vansittart does not once appear in Lord Annan's text, despite fitting at only a slight angle into his definition – appropriated from Maurice Bowra – of 'Our Age' as: 'Anyone who came of age and went to the university in the thirty years between 1919, the end of the Great War, and 1949 – or, say, 1951, the last year in which those who had served in the armed forces in the Second World War returned to study.' At least, by breaking with custom and by correctly giving the closing year of the Great War as 1919, Bowra and Annan concede the Anglo–American war of intervention in Soviet Russia (an episode which goes otherwise unmentioned in this and most other narratives). But in general the hinge events of recent times, such as the postwar emergence of Germany into what Norman Stone has proudly called '*the* successful modern European state' – and thus, clearly, *the* standing reproach to the British Establishment – are scanted unless they touch on the doings of a certain layer of the educated class. In other words, it must be doubted whether Annan would have dealt even as misleadingly as he has with something as momentous as the Morgenthau plan if it did not allow him to deploy Playfair of King's. There is also – to conclude our parsing of this randomly selected passage – that suggestive word 'comprehensible' in the penultimate sentence. It is, in its context, a rather weak compromise between the forgivable and the merely understandable: between *comprendre* and *pardonner*. This difficulty will recur.

Of course, Annan's text is self-limiting by definition. But it does attempt to use its subject as a prism for the study of politics and society. Which raises the intriguing question: can one have such a thing as collective solipsism? The placing of 'Our Age' at the centre of our age, the actual identification of a group or coterie with an epoch, and the use of the identical term to mean both things at different times, is evidence of a more than Hegelian or Weberian vanity. Clusters of persons within English society have always had protective resort to private vernaculars such as 'PLU' ('People like us') or the more cumbersome NQOCD ('Not quite our class, dear'), but these at least come to acquire, like the last Prime Minister's 'One of Us', an element of self-satire. Annan's usage of 'Our Age' is more like a concertina than a portmanteau, at once too capacious and too restrictive to serve in the nuanced, sophisticated sense that Bowra presumably desired. On one page, 'Our Age saw hundreds of

thousands of people come to exhibitions of abstract art'; on another, 'To Our
Age Henry Moore was the artist of international fame.' The first statement
could be made uncontroversially in the lower case, by any social historian or
journalist of the period. The second, whether given in upper or lower case, is
simply the expression of group taste. This deft switch of subject, object and
predicate recurs throughout, and bears watching as it alternates between the
active and the passive voice.

In his introductory passages, which are written with rather more *brio* than
their successors, Lord Annan seems to set out to prove that Anthony Powell is
a social realist:

> You did not have to belong to the intellectual aristocracy to realise that family
> connections and intermarriage were an entrée to Our Age. John Lehmann and
> Christopher Isherwood were cousins of Graham Greene; Evelyn Waugh of
> Claud Cockburn. Right-wing Roy Campbell married the sister of a communist
> whose other sister married a partner of Lawrence and Wishart, the publishers of
> the Communist Party. Kathleen Raine married the marxist apostle Hugh Sykes
> Davis and then ran off with Charles Madge who later married the first wife of
> Stephen Spender.

There is, depend upon it, more in the same vein. (Annan also follows Powell in
dwelling more on the delinquencies and absurdities of the thirties left, while
airbrushing the fellow-travellers of the Axis.) But this sort of effortless,
familiar, polymathic fluency is what makes Lord Annan and Sir Isaiah Berlin
into the intellectual and stylistic cynosure of the *New York Review of Books*: a
near-faultless meld of cosmopolitanism with English irony and European high
culture, marinated at the high tables of both ancient universities, and at ease
with — if at a decent distance from — metropolitan power. At its best, the
whole is crowned with a liberalism that both modifies and civilizes the institutions and privileges which sustain it. If asked to summarize the ethos, at least
as evinced by this book, I should stay with the upper and lower case and point
out that Marxism gets a small 'm' while Keynesianism, like the easy slang for a
knighthood, is awarded a capital 'K'.

Lord Annan has mapped part of this world before, with biographies of
Leslie Stephen and of his own public-school headmaster, Roxburgh of Stowe.
He probably captured his own poise and bearing to greatest effect and satisfaction by titling his best-known article, in 1956, 'The Intellectual Aristocracy'.
He is Jowett-like in the affectation of omniscience; his numerous small errors
are arguably the result of a tale worn too smooth by confident anecdotal repetition. Thus, in a discussion of Evelyn Waugh, Charles Ryder is said to have
failed to get religion, and Bratt's Club is both misspelled and wrongly characterized. Willi Muenzenberg, Stalin's whipper-in among the modernists, is
misnamed. Wilfred Owen's poetry is attributed to Siegfried Sassoon. Anthony
Powell's own Roland Gwatkin is absurdly misidentified. *Partisan Review* is
given the wrong founders. Sheila Rowbotham is placed in the wrong decade

and generation. And is it not flatly untrue, as well as fatally condescending, to write of Bertrand Russell: 'It was a blow to his vanity that the police failed to oblige by arresting him when he joined demonstrations'? These and other blunders would be less confidence-shaking if they did not come from a historian whose stock in trade is the minute observation and the telling detail: the detail in which God or the Devil is variously said to reside. They come, also, from a historian who embellishes his flyleaf with that grand old chestnut from Leopold von Ranke: 'The present essay is more modest. It merely wants to show what it was really like.' The modesty, of course, is false. Such an undertaking, even suppose it to be feasible in its own terms, would require a considerable scholarly and intellectual outlay, and would by no means be 'mere'. It would have to engage with regnant conceptions, instead of recapitulating thrice-told tales about Bloomsbury, the Cambridge spies and the trial of Lady Chatterley. (Incidentally, on the oft-related story of that landmark court case, which he says 'delighted Our Age', Annan writes of Richard Hoggart's testimony that 'the grammar-school extra-mural lecturer from Leicester had worsted the Treasury counsel from Eton and Cambridge.' In what sense of Bowra's definition was this a victory for the club which made up Our Age to begin with?)

Tautology is therefore as much a threat to the concept as is contradiction. But if we keep with von Ranke for a little longer, how did Annan and his peers test, or feel, 'what it was really like'? Make a vulgar calculus, and notice what merits attention and what does not. The Vietnam War is never discussed at all. Roy Jenkins's tenure as everybody's favourite Home Secretary is awarded several pages; Harold Wilson's crushing of the seamen's union gets nothing. Rhodesia — nothing. Northern Ireland — nothing. Public-school homosexuality — perhaps ten pages. The Official Secrets Act — one line. Suez — one sentence. ('Suez brought to a head the greatest of all issues since Munich: European Union.') In other words, on the end of Empire — nothing much. Kim Philby — perhaps five pages. Feminism — nothing (though Sylvia Pankhurst is written out of the record in the casual statement: 'Immediately war was declared the Pankhursts enlisted the suffragettes'). Bulldog Drummond — three pages. Salman Rushdie — nothing. Immigration from the former colonies — virtually nothing. It cannot be without significance that the three chapters dealing with outsiders, deviants and rebels are devoted to Evelyn Waugh, F.R. Leavis and Michael Oakeshott.

When Wickham Steed was editor of *The Times*, and was challenged on its editorial formulations, he replied loftily that the paper's policy was determined by 'a committee that never meets'. Much of British public policy has likewise been determined by committees which do indeed meet, but which are selected, it seems, by another committee that does not. (The policy of *The Times*, on the other hand, is now determined by influences far less opaque.) Annan is one of the most lofty and distinguished members of that 'list of the great and the good' which furnishes the active membership of Royal Commissions, the discreet invigilators of broadcasting, the guiding spirits in the administration of opera and university finance, and the occasional emergency envoy for diplomacy. This alone makes his omission of Northern Ireland and Southern Rhodesia very striking, since the record of institutional failure in those cases can be condensed into the 'Commission' names — Pearce, Devlin, Widgery, Bingham — by which the serial bungles and cover-ups were registered or euphemized. The Pearce Commission fiasco even compromised the once-unassailable Lord Goodman, who is elsewhere praised by Annan for — what else? — his contribution to the Opera Establishment, and otherwise described as 'the most skilled conciliator of the day', which is, perhaps, less of a garland than the most skilled conciliator of Our Age. Annan could have been illuminating about this subfusc world and its composition, and must have chosen not to be. But then, consideration — even mention — of these voluminous indices might perhaps have tended to qualify Annan's faith in the utilitarian, meliorist, *bien-pensant* hierarchy, and in the ideology that sustains it. We encounter two specimens of the ideal committee-man very early on:

> Such a man among Our Age, for example, was Lionel Robbins. Ostensibly Robbins was a professor at the LSE and an economist. In fact he was also chairman of the boards of the *Financial Times* and the National Gallery, and he sat on the boards of the Tate Gallery, the Royal Opera House and the Royal Economic Society. He served as President of the British Academy and was a life peer. Or consider Cyril Radcliffe, a lawyer who, without ever having been a puisne judge, was promoted direct to be a law lord. In the war he was director-general of the Ministry of Information and after it he was called in to determine the boundary line between India and Pakistan on partition and again in Cyprus; the chairman of two enquiries into taxation of profits and income; of the money and credit system: and of three enquiries into security. He was on the Court of the University of London and chairman of the British Museum Trustees.

'The stocks were sold, the press was squared, the middle class was quite prepared ...' But in this awed recitation of awesome credentials, unconsciously reminiscent of Betjeman's satire on 'first-class brains' and 'Rolls-Royce minds', there is no blood or fibre. What did Robbins and Radcliffe, these Whos of all Whos, *conclude* about the running of banks and colonies and museums? We learn nothing. When, in an earlier aside, it is laconically noted that Robbins put a stop to William Beveridge's invitation to the Institute for Social Research at Frankfurt, thus thwarting their escape from Hitler's impending 'New Order' and quarantining Houghton Street and England from Marxisant Continentalism, one almost starts from one's chair. A jagged point of conflict and interest! But it is fated to emulsify in the even flow of high-table reminiscence.

While defining the Robbins–Radcliffe type, however, Annan lets slip an illuminating formulation:

They were sagacious, believed themselves to be liberal, were in fact sound conservatives on most issues, were loyal to any institution with which they were connected, and regarded those who criticized it as ignorant, malignant or ill-informed. Yet as they grew older it was inevitable that some of Our Age, like myself, who had fancied themselves as needlers of the Establishment, began to run institutions.

Though this again somewhat dilutes Annan's ill-articulated 'Our Age' definition, and though it shows how his prose becomes more confused as the nub approaches, it does capture something of the mild but firm and unmistakable *dirigisme* with which the postwar consensus was administered. But Annan's taxonomy of men of goodwill, of the impartial expert and the disinterested academic and the broad-minded pedagogue, proves ultimately unsatisfactory even to himself. The book is almost three-fifths done when he first sounds the premonitory note: 'Unfortunately, Our Age were more concerned with how wealth should be shared than produced.'

Across this fragile pontoon — which at least serves to demarcate Our Age from marxism or Marxism more abruptly than any differences over The Souls or *Past and Present* — come at a canter the outriders of Correlli Barnett, 'Nico' Henderson and, gathering momentum, the apparently inevitable Thatcherite nemesis. In his review of Barnett and Henderson, Annan wavers in supporting their diagnosis. But in his assumption that Thatcherism was somehow a wealth-creating rather than wealth-distributing politics, he is unshakeable. It is as if nothing had ever been contributed from the left on the problem of investment, production and diversification, and therefore as if the liberal elite had been culpably charitable and indifferent to the imperatives of industry. Here is the unstated but latent crux for the self-assurance of Our Age. If the 'new' diagnosis convicted syndicalism, did they not form a most vulnerable *syndicat*? If the critique extended to cover corporatism, were not the Annanites a rather smooth and superior corporation, vertically and horizontally integrated into the quango business? More, such a pitiless diagnosis might turn out to be the wave of the future (Annan more than once confuses prescience with being on the winning side). Yet the chill exigencies of a renovated capitalism might disregard the civility, the urbanity, the *composure* with which Our Age had hoped to supply advice and consent. In a chapter of almost languorous masochism, entitled 'Was Our Age Responsible for Britain's Decline?' (which, by the way, could have read 'Were' if it was to be consistent with its more specific use elsewhere) Annan reviews the inattention to growth, competition and innovation that was exhibited by the British Establishment between, roughly speaking, the abandonment of the gold standard and the accession to the Treaty of Rome.

In a somewhat fractured attempt to deny the charge by affirming it, and in a related effort to demonstrate both prescience and retrospective depth, Annan shows that his heart lies with the Roy Jenkins–Anthony Crosland school of 'structural reforms', and with the later attempt to found a political party based on similar precepts. He is all too aware of the fact that this tendency has gone the way of Schweik's 'Party of Moderate Progress Within the Limits of Law', and he has no time for the Labour left; indeed, he pays an oblique homage to the unlovely but effective Thatcherites. He thus, like any good committee-man, makes an even distribution of honours. In effect, the established left was wrong about the Common Market and the trade unions, and the conventional right was wrong about the post-imperial illusion of a vast military outlay. This division of responsibility, which actually resembles nothing so much as Harold Wilson in 1964, is not as trite as perhaps I make it sound. What might have been accomplished by a left that was ungrudgingly European and accepted the analogous repudiation of corporatism/syndicalism at home and Stalinism and US imperialism abroad, while taking an internationalist position on inherited responsibilities such as Cyprus, Zimbabwe and South Africa? The one certainty is that we shall never know, because no such 'left' ever proposed itself. Nor did any principled centrism arise, such as would not have needed the permit of Washington and the opinion polls in proposing any of the above undertakings. By the logic of the *Eighteenth Brumaire*, then, it was a mutated Tory populism which moved to address the protracted stalemate. The result — nationalism *within* Europe, independence for Zimbabwe, facing both ways on South Africa (as does Annan when it comes to the sanctions issue), simul-taneous openness to Gorbachev *and* Beijing, a treatment of the United States almost as an equal, and a ruthless impatience with most forms of guild and municipal collectivism, including even some of the hereditary ones — has set Our Age to the unsettling task of 'catching up' instead of 'suggesting'. No doubt this accounts for some of the breathlessness of Annan's raconteurship. As a snapshot of the improvised, uneven, intolerant, wasteful but partially dynamic processes of Thatcherism, it serves reasonably well.

Annan is curiously reticent about the role of ideas in the evolution of the above compromise, even though he makes the requisite inclinations towards Hayek, Friedman and Walters. This is, first, because he can see the Peterhouse faction moving in behind them to take vengeance on the trimmers of Our Age; and, second, because he is wed of necessity to the maxim *Surtout, pas de zèle*. Valuable, at least until recently, principally against the radical left, the counsel also partakes of ancient wisdom: the soothing, civilized distillate of Isaiah Berlin. This is repeatedly contrasted by Annan with the unwholesome barbarism (he refers to 'irrationalism crossing the Channel') of the distasteful 1960s. His rebuke to Christopher Hill, borrowed from J.H. Hexter, shows the method at work. Hill is above all an exhausting fellow, credited with almost un-English prodigies of industry ('beyond doubt prolific'; 'also enormously erudite') but convicted of constructing 'boxes cunningly fashioned to fit his own conception of the past'. Indeed, he is triumphantly quoted as admitting that he works to a theory! This might be described as Annan's fork: what if Hill had *not* testified to his own methodology, or had artfully pretended to be a

FOR THE SAKE OF ARGUMENT

populist interpreter of the school of Bishop Stubbs? He could — and would — be accused of being surreptitious. How much better to praise Hugh Trevor-Roper, that contingent sympathizer of the *Annalistes*, who 'never wrote an inelegant sentence or produced an incoherent argument'. Dacre's validation of a sinister pro-Nazi forgery seems not to have ruffled Our Age; not enough to rate a mention in any event, which one feels sure a comparable Zhdanovite error by Hobsbawm or Hill would have done. More surprisingly, perhaps, given his strongly expressed residual sympathy for the Spanish Republic, Annan seems to have overlooked Dacre's view, offered in the *New York Review of Books* in the course of yet another discussion of the Cambridge traitors, that a Republican victory would have done no more than advance the date of the Hitler–Stalin Pact. That this conception of a *conjoncture*, which stunningly omitted any consideration of the other possible effects of a defeat for the Axis in Spain, might owe anything to a hidden conservative agenda does not seem thinkable to Annan. But his dislike of the 'ideology' of Hill and Carr, again expressed through the *dicta* of Isaiah Berlin, prevents him from appreciating the truth of Carr's old truism that 'to denounce ideologies in general is to set up an ideology of one's own'.

Long ago and in better days, Conor Cruise O'Brien observed that intellectuals who were too fastidious to sacrifice 'civility' and 'objectivity' for the revolution could quite often be induced to make these very sacrifices for the *counter*-revolution. Berlin, I suspect, might see the irony and pith of this in a way that Annan does not. It is difficult to imagine Berlin writing, as Annan did (*London Review of Books*, 24 January 1991): 'If we are to search for the progenitors of barbarism, where better than in those émigré circles in which Lenin moved and which were to institute the barbarism of Stalin's regime and its antidote Hitler.' Not only does this ill-wrought sentence, by its abysmal grammar, suggest that Lenin's émigré circle *instituted* Hitler; it also repeats without digestion the most vulgar recent insinuations of Ernst Nolte, Andreas Hillgruber and the new/old revisionist historians of the German right. And this crudity from an ostensible admirer of the German Renaissance! Carr could hardly have hoped for a neater posthumous vindication.

In his generalized and frequent application to Berlin, Annan seems almost to deprive the latter's work of its intended force. So keen is he to place him above the battle that he all but disarms him:

> He [Berlin] read the work of philosophers long dead, indeed of some who would not in Oxford have been called philosophers — weird German romantics or Russian revolutionaries, Herder and Hamann, Belinsky and Herzen. He read them not to convict them of error and contrast them with the truth as we know it today. He did not use them to illustrate the climate of opinion of a past age. Nor did he divide them into those who point the way to saner times and those whom tyrants have used to justify their cruelty.

This is a very odd and bland means of glossing Berlin's analysis of Herzen, for example — exhibited continually as a humane and tolerant (if defeated) alternative to Bolshevism. And it sits strangely with Berlin's opinion of Herder: 'For him men are men, and have common traits at all times; but it is their differences that matter most, for it is their differences that make them what they are, make them themselves, it is in these that the individual genius of men and cultures is expressed.' Above all, it seems inconsistent with the attempt, however loose and inconsistently applied, to establish an elite supra-category, which presumably stresses bonds, commonalities and solidarities, and also presumably attempts to impose structure and even to consider progress — a category such as Annan's *Unsere Zeit*.

If *Our Age* contains an argument, it is organized about the tension between utilitarianism and individualism. Individuals, of course, should not be considered as means, or sacrificed to what Annan scornfully terms 'teleology'. Yet there must be fiscal and other kinds of discipline, so that the mob does not eat the seed corn. To resolve this contradiction between the need for order and for postponement of gratification, and the need for the repudiation of ideology or teleology, it is as well to have a disinterested class of guides and mentors. Their disinterest, which it would be risky or arrogant merely to presume, is fortunately demonstrable precisely by their hostility to systems of thought. Thus the committee that never meets. Like the 'unwritten' Constitution, or the 'invisible earnings' of the City of London, this is a definition and a method of exceptional convenience to those interested in ruling discreetly.

The two greatest freehand exercises in English periodization, G.M. Young's *Portrait of an Age* and George Dangerfield's *Strange Death of Liberal England*, both survive because they showed what was to come, and why. Their method was paradoxical rather than dialectical, and rich in the illustration of unintended consequences. Annan's book, by contrast, is neither sufficiently complete to warrant a comparison with von Ranke, nor sufficiently adventurous to be set against Dangerfield. Rather, it expresses the uneasy conscience of an elite which has looked after itself whichever party or regime has been in power, and has somewhat blurred the distinction between doing good and doing well. It is torn between accounting, explaining and justification. An anecdote for Our Age was once given me by Simon Schama, who, while at Cambridge, was approached by Victor Rothschild (a man treated with much respect in the pages under review). Rothschild wished for a study of the role of his family in pioneer Zionism, and could supply original and authentic documents exclusively to the historian who took on the task. Would Schama accept the commission? Admittedly impressed by this overture from one so steeped in academe, diplomacy, think-tankery, security and the other special subjects of Our Age, Schama consented. While work was in progress on the book (which became *Two Rothschilds and the Land of Israel*), disagreements developed between the two about the shape and emphasis. Victor Rothschild did not mince words. 'Do you happen to know', he inquired, 'the Rothschild family motto?' Schama confessed that he did not. 'Our family motto', returned the Establishment veteran, 'is *Service.*' A respectful pause. 'And by God,' he concluded, '*we get it.*' Or to put it another way, unacknowledged legislators are one thing; unelected or unaccountable ones are another. Annan's narrative of debonair deniability is an imperishable tome in the growing library of decline.

New Left Review, January–February 1991

THE 'WE' FALLACY·

Lionel Trilling once wrote a short essay on the problem of 'we'. Apparently, whenever he said of a novel or other work under review that it engaged 'our' sympathy, or that 'we' felt repelled by the author's assumptions, he would receive letters of complaint. Who was this 'we', the letter-writers demanded to know, and what allowed Trilling to speak for 'us' in this way? The literary critic's experience may not seem immediately relevant to contemporary politics. But as one surveys the dismal field of political commentary, it is hard not to conclude that half the cretinism of the mainstream media is attributable to the 'we' fallacy. This is especially true in any discussion of imperialism. There is talk of 'our' interests, 'our' credibility, and 'our' will. Unexamined, this usage also infects the vocabulary and thinking of those who fancy themselves liberals. Watch some anguished isolationist as he or she shuffles across an op-ed page, for example, or listen to some Congressperson on *Nightline* struggle to make a case against aid to the Contras. Invariably he or she will end up apologizing and bleating meekly that the laying waste of Nicaragua is 'not in our best interests'. Occasionally the phrase 'the American people' is intoned: this, too, carries the suggestion that society is a family or a voluntary association. Unless one is armed in some fashion against the subtle operation on the mind of this consensus-fabricating syntax, one can end up saying, or letting pass without challenge, the most hateful and nonsensical things. What Democratic politician these days would think twice about referring to 'our' nuclear weapons?

Noam Chomsky's latest book has many merits, but I think its foremost virtue is the way in which it exposes this linguistic and ideological fraud. Chomsky writes ruthlessly and forensically about the operations of empire,

·Review of Noam Chomsky, *The Culture of Terrorism*, Boston 1988.

and about the cast of mind which underpins empire while simultaneously denying its existence. In a 1927 book, *Men of Destiny*, Walter Lippmann wrote:

> All the world thinks of the United States today as an empire, except the people of the United States. We shrink from the word 'empire,' and insist that it should not be used to describe the dominion we exercise from Alaska to the Philippines, from Cuba to Panama, and beyond. We feel that there ought to be some other name for the civilizing work which we do so reluctantly in these backward countries.

Most of what passes for educated opinion today is at a lower level of self-knowledge on this question than even Walter Lippmann (though you'll notice his grandiloquent 'we') half a century ago. Chomsky does not cite Lippmann on empire, but he does refer to an intellectual construct that Lippmann originated in order to cope with empire's domestic political consequences. That construct was 'the manufacture of consent'. This potent idea has been refined and developed with resources of propaganda and communication undreamt of by its pioneers. The novelist Ian McEwan has described watching audience behaviour on daytime TV as 'the democrat's pornography'. But what word should be applied to a public opinion that is, on one day, asked to get excited about Lebanon — a country of which it knows virtually nothing; on the next day, commanded to view the dispatch of American troops there as a test of will in a battle for the survival of the West; and the day after that, ordered to forget the whole episode? And in each case, complies? This is not so much the prostitution of democracy as its sheer negation.

The Culture of Terrorism is a sustained and rigorous engagement with this problem; and all those who hope to defeat the right by patiently educating public opinion have a duty to read and discuss it. The very word 'terrorism', of course, as ubiquitous as it is misleading, is an example of the power of official propaganda and the collusion of mass academia and the mass media with that power. In my view, 'terrorism' is a vacuous term, which trades on the cheapest moralism for its (diminishing) effect. I have serious doubts about Chomsky's persistent attempt to use the word ironically, and so turn it upon its manipulators. Still, he slays an impressive number of hypocritical pawns by playing his rather straightforward 'double standard' move against the official gambit. The following extract shows his method:

> Critics of Reaganite aggressiveness can perceive that Nicaragua may also have some concerns. Discussing the diplomatic alternative that he favors, Wayne Smith, one of the strongest and most consistent critics of the Contra option, urges that we enter into a bilateral security pact with Nicaragua as 'a corollary to the Central American treaty itself: 'Of course, we would want adequate means of verification. So would the Sandinistas, who have no more reason to trust us than we have to trust them. Compliance would be assured not by the Contras but by the strength and honor of the United States.'
> In short, our strength will assure their compliance, and our honor will assure

our compliance, thus allaying Nicaraguan concerns. Recall that we are
inspecting the outer limits of expressible dissent.

This is excellent, right down to its modest and proper use, in the last sentence,
of 'we' to mean no more than 'those who have followed my argument this far'.

I have tried once or twice in columns of mine to float the phrase 'superpower self-pity', in an effort to describe a mentality upon which Chomsky
expends much ink. My hope was to capture a pose that is very common
among neo-conservative intellectuals. These fretful types affect to believe that
mass academia and the mass media are instinctively un- or anti-American.
They write as though Congress spent all its time trying to thwart the purposes
of the military–industrial complex — in a particularly brazen instance, the *New
Republic*'s Charles Krauthammer referred to 'the imperial Congress'. They
even allege that the mainstream press has a bias against Israel. (I cite these
charges in ascending order of implausibility.) At one level, Chomsky has no
difficulty in refuting these warped and paranoid notions. He readily disposes of
canards like that propounded by Contra apologist Robert Leiken, who writes
darkly about the 'well-organized network of "opposition" figures, "witnesses,"
"correspondents," and professional writers of letters to editors'. Perhaps only
those of us who have toiled in this vineyard know quite how feeble a counter-
weight to state lying this 'well-organized network' has provided. As for the
inveterate oppositionism of the media — well, Chomsky has done his home-
work, as usual. In the first three months of 1986, as Congress deliberated aid to
the Contras, the *New York Times* and *Washington Post* published eighty-five
opinion pieces on the issue by their regular columnists and other contributors.
These articles, like a *Nightline* show, ran the gamut from A to C. Not one of
them failed to excoriate the Sandinista government, as a necessary prologue to
(or qualification for) taking part in the 'debate' in the first place. Small wonder
that by late in the year Congress had, in effect, arrogated to itself the *right* to
change the government of Nicaragua, and was wrangling solely over the means
by which to do so.

Chomsky is undoubtedly justified in his relentless harrying of this servile
conformity. Still, I am left with a question: If the media are such lapdogs, why
do the Reaganites dislike them so? This is not merely a matter of Leiken's and
other Contra supporters' absurd claims, but of a whole pattern of press-hatred
harking back at least as far as the 'stab in the back' fantasies of those who
believe that the liberals 'lost' Indochina. Chomsky might well reply that this is
no more than irrational ingratitude on the Reaganites' part, given the generally
patriotic way in which the press has played down such matters as the 'secret'
blitz of Cambodia. But while at many points he writes of the press 'obediently'
playing its 'allotted' role, at many other points he will cite a report from an
organ of respectable opinion in order to underline an argument of his own.
Many radicals, I suspect, have had similar experiences. I myself read nothing in
the left press in 1987 as damning about the Contras as Rod Norland's *News-*

week article (quoted by Chomsky). This first-hand report came complete with photographic evidence that US helicopters were flying illegal missions with false Red Cross markings. Elsewhere, Chomsky is hasty. He writes that the 1986 Reykjavik summit was 'widely portrayed in the United States as a great triumph for Reagan' and that there was no mention here of a USIA report which showed European opinion blaming Reagan for the Reykjavik break-down. Of his first observation, I can say only that I don't remember it like that. Of his second: I *can* remember a syndicated column of William Buckley raising the alarm at USIA's findings and deploring European gullibility. Those would be the merest quibbles, if Chomsky did not argue that there is an almost 'total-itarian' system of thought control in the USA.

Now of course it is true that a fair job of mind-bending gets done. I regularly win bets with 'experts' at dull Washington parties by asking which country has the largest military base in Cuba and which country is geographically closest to the USA after Canada and Mexico. (Answers: respectively, the USA and the USSR.) The very shape of the known world has had to be distorted, in a sort of imperial Mercator projection of the mind, in order to fit superpower delusions and to intensify their vulgar emotional counterpart, which is provincial fear. The United States has an isolationist and insular *culture*, combined with a global and interventionist *posture*. This highly dangerous and febrile mixture, which greatly facilitates the task of the fear-mongers and chauvinists, needs a very exact and nuanced diagnosis. I don't think that analogies from the totali-tarian model, however suggestive, are sufficient.

Another instance; despite a fantastic barrage of admittedly Goebbels-like broadcasts by Reagan and disinformation stunts by his underlings, the Ameri-can public has fairly consistently opposed aid to the Contras by roughly two to one. There have been some lurches on this chart, notably after Grenada and after North's televised free-associating; but in general, Reagan's favourite policy has been his least popular one with an electorate that allegedly trusts him. Why is this? Is it humane good sense? No doubt this counts for some-thing; but I suspect that on the day after an actual invasion of Nicaragua, opinion polls would favour the landing. Is it a legacy of Vietnam? Probably it is, in part, but this too cuts both ways — there are those who say: 'No more Viet-nams, unless we mean to win.' Why, then? Of this urgent question for demo-crats, Chomsky writes, in his treatment of the North spasm:

> But at a deeper level, the immediate public response illustrates the insight of the 18th-century European Enlightenment that the value and meaning of freedom are learned through its exercise, and that the instinctive desire of 'all free peoples to guard themselves from oppression' (Rousseau) may be repressed among a subordinated population, effectively removed from the political system, disen-gaged from the struggle against state and other authority, and in general, objects rather than agents. In the absence of organizational forms that permit meaning-ful participation in political and other social institutions, as distinct from following orders or ratifying decisions made elsewhere, the 'instinct for freedom'

may wither, offering opportunities for charismatic leaders to rally mass popular support, with consequences familiar from recent history.

That there is much truth in this analysis, it would be irresponsible to deny. There was more than a hint, from the few revelations offered in the Iran-Contra hearings, that the rulers of this country cherish a vision of the future that is modelled on their extensive acquaintance with juntas and plebiscites. But then why, despite an invertebrate Congress and a complicit press, did we witness the rapid collapse of North's public esteem? I think Chomsky's account of the 'manufacture of consent' falls short of being exhaustive here. His practice of saying 'the press' and 'the media', as if these formed an organic whole, leads to some of the difficulties I have sketched. Might it not make sense to regard the mass communications industry as an area of contestation, in which the ruling class naturally holds most of the cards, but no definitively or universally predictable result can be arranged? The regnant ideology, which is one of liberalism and 'objectivity', is difficult to read only because it denies that it is an ideology. Once one can parse the 'we' word, one begins to see through the near-automatic deference shown by the organs of news and opinion to the powers that be. And a large number of people – including some who work in the media – are shrewd enough to do this for themselves, at least some of the time. If they were not, then disinformation campaigns like the Reagan administration's 'Operation Truth' would be unnecessary.

I have assumed throughout this review that any likely reader will recognize international aggression when he or she sees it. Even so – and my criticisms notwithstanding – Chomsky has mustered evidence and argument that vastly extend and refine our understanding of the attack on Nicaragua. Several sections of The Culture of Terrorism approach the sustained brilliance with which he dismembered the report of the Kahan Commission, in what was perhaps the finest chapter of his earlier Fateful Triangle. Chomsky proceeds on the almost unthinkably subversive assumption that the United States should be judged by the same standards that it preaches (often at gunpoint) to other nations – he is nearly the only person now writing who assumes a single standard of international morality not for rhetorical effect, but as a matter of habitual, practically instinctual conviction.

Next time you are arguing about Central America and its 'crisis', ask your opponents when, in their opinion, the crisis began. It is a near certainty that they will date its advent from some time in the Carter administration. When Central America was 'our' sweltering, murderous backyard, untroubled by mass insurgency, the attention paid to it by the Establishment and the press was, quite simply, nil. The abundant coverage today is morally little better than the zero coverage of yesterday – almost without exception, it shares America's rulers' view that the USA owns the isthmus and need pay attention only when that ownership is in dispute. Inasmuch as he allows us to judge the political system by its effects rather than its self-image – and also because he reminds us of our civic duty, in a case of aggression, to take the side of the victim — Chomsky's dissection of this ideological pathology is exemplary.

Z, February 1988

SHOUTING ANARCHY

Once upon a time, a long time ago, I took a small part in a demonstration outside the South African Embassy in London. The Embassy is situated on Trafalgar Square, at a confluence of several slow streams of traffic ('The full tide of humanity', said Dr Johnson, 'is to be found at Charing Cross'), and there we pitched our picket. The idea was to satirize the apartheid pass laws. Some of our number had dressed up in South African police uniforms: a distinctive match of peaked cap, belt and boots quite alien to the 'London bobby' sensibility — at least as we knew it then. The plan was a 'see how *you* like it' happening, with these imposters rapping on car windows, accosting passers-by and saying, 'Show me your pass' in assumed Afrikaner accents.

I shall never forget the harvest of this piece of street theatre. Nervous, awkward grins and stupid excuses: 'I'm awfully sorry, officer, I seem to have mislaid it.' … 'I don't *actually* live in London, I'm visiting relations.' Nobody told us to fuck off. Everybody deferred to the strange uniform, and cursed the bureaucratic announcement they must somehow have missed. Partly, no doubt, this was the British folk-memory of rationing, queues and Civil Defence (so handy in manuring the ground for nuclear 'preparedness'). But it hinted at something else, ghastly and servile. When I later read, in a flimsy pamphlet from the Freedom Press, that the problem of humanity was not the will to command but the urge to obey, I felt that I had already come across the notion somewhere. The Freedom Press, based in a crepuscular Whitechapel alley, had once boasted Prince Peter Kropotkin himself as a patron and author. Yet what did this exponent of the chainless mind, this selfless, saintly, reflective and kindly old booby, do in 1914? Why, he declared for the victory of the 'Allies'. In faraway Australia, J.W. Fleming was hard hit by this apostasy. He had carried the black flag of anarchy along the Melbourne waterfront, and braved the toughest crowds in his speechmaking and soapboxing on the Yarra Bank. He was more than ready to risk prisons and goon squads for a trifle, like the opening of public libraries on the Sabbath. To oppose imperialist war, that special orgy of the state, he would go the limit. To Emma Goldman he wrote:

I regret to think that after all these years, having accepted Kropotkin as teacher and guide, he should so disappoint us. *I feel oppressed.* [Emphasis added.]

Fleming's choice of phrase might serve as the crux of Paul Avrich's charming and melancholy album of silhouettes, *Anarchist Portraits*. The tradition of which he writes so upliftingly must always be what he unintentionally reveals it to have always been — a lineage of losers. And this is not because of anything in the make-up of the volunteers, not all of whom were as brave as Fleming or as irritating as Kropotkin. It is because the anarchist must embody certain Platonic truths that are at once undeniable and unrealizable.

You can see this fateful, moving, necessary contradiction in the usages that reflect and express the stock of prevailing ideas about anarchy and anarchism. Even Shelley, whose *Mask of Anarchy* is one of the finest hymns of hate to authority to have come down to us, referred dully to the 'ship of state' as it veered between 'the Scylla and Charybdis of anarchy and despotism'. John Ruskin, who knew some sympathetic London anarchists, wrote that 'government and cooperation are in all things the laws of life; anarchy and competition the laws of death.' Yeats automatically referred to 'anarchy' as 'mere'. The primeval image is perhaps sustained from Milton, the old rebel who used it repeatedly as his allegory of Hell and Satan and chaos — 'the anarch old'; 'eternal anarchy amid the noise/of endless wars'. I can come up with only two compliments implied by the use of the term. One is Edmund Burke's, when he described *The Rights of Man* as 'a sort of institution and digest of anarchy'. The other, more subtle, comes in Auden's poem 'In Memory of Sigmund Freud':

> Sad is Eros, builder of cities,
> And weeping anarchic Aphrodite.

Just as you may — must — believe in the power of love but not know quite how to *institutionalize* it, so you may say with the anarchist that 'No one is good enough to be another's master' while believing or suspecting that this is a vital but impossible precept. Meanwhile, it is not just fear of freedom that makes the oppressed dread the idea of anarchy. There are other folk memories, and in the general recollection it is recalled that chaos, anarchy, what you will, meant the domain of the strongest, and necessitated appeals to kings and barons for blessed order. Probably for this reason, a more glib successor generation prefers the term 'libertarian', which has none of the crude, urgent tones of 'anarchist'.

Most of Avrich's subjects would have scorned any such emulsifying title. They were proud of their intransigence and careless of compromise. Fleming — who, I must say, is my favourite find in the book — didn't in the least mind addressing his fellow-workers (as Robert Tressell was later, and more successfully, to do in *The Ragged-Trousered Philanthropists*) as 'mutton-heads':

> The capitalist need only threaten, and obedience immediately comes forth.
> Conscription, the cherished weapon of the oppressors, is firmly rooted. Children

fourteen years of age are imprisoned in a military fort over a hundred miles from Melbourne. This is what Labour government has brought Australia to. Oh, hell, can these human weeds become virile? I am shouting Anarchy.

There is a non sequitur here, but it is a very exciting and excellent one, voicing the millennial human resistance to coercion, and the repudiation of the idea that man-made authority is part of the natural order. Would you have wished more, or fewer, anarchists around in the Thousand Year Reich or any of the other fantasies of hierarchy?

Avrich does not neglect the herbivorous anarchists: those who meant their peaceful and useful lives to embody harmony and order, or 'mutualism', as it was slightly depressingly called. Such a one was Benjamin Tucker, the mould and model of the New England gentleman-anarchist, whose life was the pattern of anarcho-fogeyism. As he put it, with refulgent self-regard:

> There are four lines of Emerson which I am fond of quoting.
> > When the Church is social worth,
> > When the State-house is the hearth,
> > Then the perfect state has come,
> > The republican at home.

Though there was nobility to Tucker — he called in his faithful housekeeper to witness the stubbornness of his deathbed atheism — his life and that of his family could have been drawn by an acidulated Miss Austen, and his insane fear of the motorcar and of vulgarity would have accoutred him ill for the Yarra Bank. His editions of the review *Liberty*, however, are accounted by all to have been both beautiful and scrupulous. And his friend Voltairine de Cleyre (about whose parents' christening theories one would have liked to know more) wrote of him significantly that he sent his 'fine hard shafts among foes and friends with an icy impartiality, hitting swift and cutting keen — *and ever ready to nail a traitor.*' (Emphasis added again.) The Saint-Just of an Emersonian ideal state is an arresting mental image.

One of the Freedom Press anarchists — George Woodcock, possibly — once said that the proper definition of 'anarchist' is 'something you are, not something you do'. If accepted, this would explain why those who profess or practise anarchism are so spoiled for choice when it comes to feeling 'oppressed' or detecting 'traitors'. But this also makes the anarchist personality a highly sensitive register. Take the famous case of Mollie Steimer, Jacob Abrams and their comrades. Scandalously persecuted for the promulgation of their opinions by mere leaflet during the scare set off by Attorney General Palmer in 1919, they mounted such a tenacious defence that Justice Oliver Wendell Holmes, in dissent, more or less restated the First Amendment as Americans know it today. The defendants, however, were deported *through* Ellis Island (another of those histories they don't teach you in school) to their presumed homeland of Russia. And who saw them off at the quay? The *Fraye Arbeter Shtime*, a Yiddish anarchist paper editorializing that there would be nothing but grief awaiting them on the other shore. Well, the *Fraye Arbeter Shtime* was right, and right about the Red Scare, too. It is this irreducible quality in anarchism, its attitude to power, however wielded, and to power-lovers, however enlightened, that lifts it above the eccentricities and the arcane factionalism and purism which are so often sneered at.

Robert Paul Wolff wrote *In Defense of Anarchism* to illuminate this very distinction:

> Taking responsibility for one's actions means taking the final decisions about what one should do. For the autonomous man, there is no such thing, strictly speaking, as a *command*.

Ah yes, say the conformists and the wise, but what if *everyone* thought like that? Passing over Yossarian's imperishable reply to that old taunt ('In that case I'd be a damn fool to think any other way'), consider Wolff's response:

> If someone in my environment is issuing what are intended as commands, and if he or others expect those commands to be obeyed, that fact will be taken account of in my deliberations. I may decide that I ought to do what that person is commanding me to do, and it may even be that his issuing the command is the factor in the situation which makes it desirable for me to do so. For example, if I am on a sinking ship and the captain is giving orders for manning the lifeboats, and if everyone else is obeying the captain *because he is the captain*, I may decide that under the circumstances I had better do what he says, since the confusion caused by disobeying him would be generally harmful. But insofar as I make such a decision, I am not *obeying his command*; that is, I am not acknowledging him as having authority over me. I would make the same decision, for exactly the same reasons, if one of the passengers had started to issue 'orders' and had, in the confusion, come to be obeyed.

Why does this take so long to say? Partly because it derives from a lengthy reasoning by Kant, and partly because it has to cut carefully against the grain of conditioning: the confusion of office and uniform with authority. As Wolff says, with an irony that is possibly unconscious: 'The responsible man is not capricious or *anarchic*, for he does acknowledge himself bound by moral constraints. But he insists that he alone is the judge of those constraints.'

This returns us to the figure of Tucker in Avrich's portrayal. There is a reason for the affected profession of 'anarchist sympathies' among Tories and grandees, and of 'libertarian principles' by Hobbesian yahoos of the right. Among the former, one sees the upholding of the view that a gentleman's business and property are his own, and none of the government's. Among the latter, a distaste for democracy, for taxation, and for the need to consult others about the planet. The unmolested gent and the selfish *commerçant* are not the models of autonomy that anarchists are supposed to have in mind, but then, there is a slightly arrogant tone even to Fleming's dismissal of the 'mutton-heads'.

Yet precisely because they deal in 'eternal verities', purist anarchists must operate independently of history and politics. There is, for them, no important distinction between sufficient and necessary conditions; no need to study the evolution of society or production. Their often religious and millennial attitude to the future derives in part from a religious attitude towards the past; towards some primordial and timeless hellhole of ignorance, innocence and simplicity such as Eden is reported to have been. Of all the anarchists I have read, only Noam Chomsky seems to have given any thought to the question of technology, and to the potentially liberating and counter-hierarchical possibilities of high-tech innovation. But these effects are democratic rather than anarchic, and for the anarchist the democratic notion of 'the consent of the governed' — actually a rather highly evolved concept — is only another form of acquiescence. This still leaves the indispensable anarchist who ought to dwell in all of us. The one who pushes away the proffered Kool-Aid even when it comes from the chalice of Jones the Redeemer, the one who asks the South African cop in Trafalgar Square for his name and number, the little boy in *Lord of the Flies*, noticed by E.P. Thompson, who gazes defiantly at the latest fetish of the gang and manages nervously to get out the words: 'Pig's Head on a Stick'.

Grand Street, Spring 1989

POLITICALLY CORRECT

Of what exhausting phenomenon are the following everyday terms an illustration? 'Bipartisan'; 'partisan'; 'divisive'; 'healing'; 'we look forward to working more closely'; 'I would need to see the full text of those remarks'; 'the business community'; 'the intelligence community'; 'put this behind us'; 'move the country forward'; 'define our agenda'; 'address our concerns'; 'appropriate conduct'; 'inappropriate conduct'; 'I cannot recall at this moment in time'; 'thank you for not smoking'; 'the American people'. These and many other routine fatuities represent the language of political correctness in our day, the prefabricated and conditioned phraseology by which 'we' (it's always 'we' in regular PC talk) express and imbibe the politics of the permissible. I had hoped to avoid writing about this room-temperature, pseudo-intellectual fad, but I realize that it's a fate not to be evaded. Just as those who call for 'English Only' believe themselves to be speaking English when they are mouthing a mediocre patois, and just as those who yell for 'Western civilization' cannot tell Athens,

Georgia, from Erasmus Darwin, so those who snicker at the latest 'PC' gag are generally willing slaves to the most half-baked jargon.

Obviously it's tiresome when some loud child who missed the sixties presumes to instruct us all about 'people of colour' or 'persons of gender'. Still, at least there's an element of self-satire in the business; even in the hopeless phrase 'politically correct'. But when every newscaster in the country uses the knee-jerk term 'peace process', or discourses about 'credibility', or describes some bloodsoaked imposter as 'a moderate', the deadening of language has gone so far that it's almost impossible to ironize. Yet this occurs every day, and it's accounted a wonder if the President himself can marshal the clichés in the correct order on his wooden tongue. A person intoxicated by political correctitude might say of capital punishment that it is racist, repressive, fascistic and reminiscent of the worst excesses of the Portuguese Inquisition (or whatever). He or she might even say it was sexist and homophobic — even though it doesn't seem to fall that much upon women and even though the contrived word 'homophobia', as we classicists know, means 'fear of the same', if indeed it means anything at all, which I take leave to doubt. However, all these positions would be preferable in their way to that of Clarence Thomas, who was asked, in a hearing of the world's greatest deliberative body, what he thought of the death penalty and replied that 'philosophically' he foresaw no problem in applying it in 'appropriate' situations. What could be more bipartisan than the use of the word 'philosophical' to mean 'no problem'? The beauty of consensus PC is that it makes differences on matters of principle almost unsayable. A bit of a blow, however, had perhaps been dealt to the Platonic foundations of our great Western Civilization.

In the nondebate over nonissues that goes on here, the hands-down winner is the culture of euphemism. Witnesses before Congress are actually awarded points for their expensively coached lying and emollience. Meanwhile, self-defined radicals sell the pass by announcing that anything is better than being 'offensive'. The two rivulets of drool merge softly and imperceptibly, and we end up with a public language by which almost nobody employs plain speech. One is almost rejoiced to hear a stupid, meaningless, barbarous emphasis — 'Fuck this shit' springs to mind — merely for the sake of its unadorned clarity. The disquieting thing about newscaster-babble or editorial-speak is its ready availability as a serf idiom, a vernacular of deference. 'Mr Secretary, are *we* any nearer to bringing about a *dialogue* in this *process*?' Here is the politically correct language of the consensus, which can be spoken while asleep or under hypnosis by any freshly trained microphone-holder. At least the PC felons are not trying — or not all the time — to 'bring us together' and make-believe we are all one family. However, the trend of their emaciated terminology leads in the direction of a mini-consensus that does not welcome dissent. The fact that this consensus is mostly a laugh doesn't make it, as an effort, any less potentially sinister. Morally, it may pose as a compliment to pluralism and 'diversity', which makes it feel superior to its white-bread senior partner. But politically and socially, it translates as 'watch what you say and don't give offence to anybody', which isn't a serious definition of diversity.

Senator Tom Harkin's kickoff campaign rally, I was interested to see, began with a mass open-air recitation of te Pledge of Allegiance, 'under God' and all, and a grand display of American flags. By these means Harkin hoped to show that Bush couldn't scare him! Yet what was this but a humiliating enactment of the mantras and gestures of official political correctness? A man who is still twitching from lashes inflicted more than three years ago is not a proud man, or an emancipated one. He is hoping, hypocritically, to stay within the admissible bounds of the politically safe (hypocrisy is not the least of the psychic wounds that result from enforced consensus) and to pass for white rather than as a possible friend of Willie Horton. What a country, and what a culture, when the liberals cry before they are hurt, and the reactionaries pose as the brave nonconformists, while the radicals make a fetish of their own jokey irrelevance.

It is not enough to 'have' free speech. People must learn to speak freely. Noam Chomsky remarked in the sixties about short-life ultra-radicals on campus who thought that Marx should have been burning down the British Museum rather than writing and thinking in it. The less political descendants of that faction have now tried to reduce life to a system of empowerment etiquette, and have wasted a lot of their own time and everyone else's in the process. But the real bridle on our tongues is imposed by everyday lying and jargon, sanctioned and promulgated at the highest levels of media and politics, and not by the awkward handful who imagine themselves revolutionaries.

The Nation, October 1991

FRIEND OF PROMISE*

When Tom Driberg died in August 1976, *The Times* ran an obituary which, as people used to say, broke with convention. The deceased, bleated the former *Thunderer,* had been: 'A journalist, an intellectual, a drinking man, a gossip, a high churchman, a liturgist, a homosexual ...' There was nothing precisely objectionable about this. Tom had, after all, been indubitably the most consecrated blow-job artist ever to take his seat in either House. But *The Times* had

*Review of Francis Wheen, *Tom Driberg: His Life and Indiscretions*, London 1990.

never before described a public figure as a homosexual, let alone *defined* him as one, let alone in an obituary. William Rees-Mogg had, apparently, decided that anything less would be anodyne. This same Mogg has written elsewhere of a psychic and political link between Maynard Keynes the homosexual and Keynes the promiscuous debaucher of the currency, tying this in turn to the homosexual propensity for treason, so his appalling frankness in the case of a known political and moral outsider was of a piece with his general tendency to ethical invigilation. With Tom safely below ground, others have crept forward to say that he was a shady player in the espionage milieu, thus rounding out the picture that Mogg had begun to sketch.

'Unacknowledged legislator' is an admittedly overfamiliar Shelleyan tag, but I think it describes Tom Driberg better than any other. He was more interested in, and adept at, influence than power. In barely any recognizable sense was he a politician at all. He once explained to me with customary pedantry that *Ruling Passions*, the title of his uncompleted memoir, was a pun on his service as an MP. The pun was at his expense, since he did precious little ruling and his passions did the rest. He was an uneasy, unhappy, inquisitive and voracious man, blessed with good taste and cursed by lack of means, for whom variety was not the spice of life but the pith of it. Well before the backbench existence ever occurred to him, he had given W.H. Auden his first reading of *The Waste Land*; had been the only witness as Evelyn Waugh was 'received' into Holy Mother Church; had been saluted by Edith Sitwell as the hope of English poetry; had been anointed as the diabolic successor to Aleister Crowley; had nearly interested John Betjeman in socialism and A.J.P. Taylor in incense. But he was one of those modernists who could have been formed only by an observance of tradition: he needed an anchor as much as he wanted a sailor.

I knew him only at the fag-end of his career, when the passions had been banked down a bit. He was tending to live off his store of anecdotes and acquaintances — making a point, for instance, of drinking only milk in Indian restaurants because 'Crowley — The Beast, you know — always advised it,' and dusting off filthy limericks he had collected from Auden or Constant Lambert. Every now and then, to pay some dun, he could knock out a piece on his friendship with Guy Burgess. In only one respect did he keep his old life up to speed. He would go anywhere and do anything for the chance to suck somebody off. Mark you, even this desire had been coloured, if that's the word I want, by advancing years. He tended to say that he did it on doctor's orders ('the potassium ingredient is frightfully good for one'). He did not, even when faced with decrepitude, much relax his exacting and minutely considered standards. The potassium donor should be heterosexual, proletarian, and — though this condition might be varied when demand outpaced supply — unknown to Tom before the encounter. I still wish I had listened more attentively to the stories he told about those who, like him, yearned for anonymous sex and its corollary, which was, as he hurried to point out excitedly, *dangerous* sex. (Certainly, I wasn't surprised at the nemesis that later overtook a senior politician I met in his company.) A taste for policemen, for uniforms, for dodgem-greasers and dockers and garage mechanics can be a version of cruising for a bruising, angling for a mangling, thirsting for a worsting, strolling for a rolling, aiming for a maiming, or what you will. Tom took his lumps philosophically, more or less along with the best of them. At its crudest, this can be a form of slumming, and he freely acknowledged the unattractive side of it when he mobilized 'friends in high places' to defeat a prosecution for indecency brought by two hunger marchers he took home one ill-starred night in the thirties. At its nastiest, the longing for tough male-on-male sex can be identified with uniform fetishism and fascism *à la* Mishima (who candidly wrote in *Forbidden Colours* that men of his kind were against democracy because they had a natural horror for majority rule). In Tom's case, though, there was something rather herbivorous and democratic about it. He wasn't a sadist or a masochist. He wasn't a coprophile. He didn't go in much for the anal end of the business, once telling me feelingly how he identified with Auden's 'Letter to a Wound' and with all those who had ever suffered a rectal fissure. He just liked to administer free blow-jobs to the masses. How many modern Members of Parliament can claim as much?

In this witty and combative portrait with background (to annex Tom's own title for his profile of Guy Burgess) Francis Wheen doesn't consider the social-democratic aspect of oral and homosexual promiscuity as much as he does the allegedly crypto-Communist angle that has lately been superimposed upon it. A whole flock of mediocre scavengers, from Chapman Pincher to 'Nigel West', have feasted on each other's leavings in this case. Unable to concert their stories with any intelligible sequence of dates or developments, and unable to prove that Tom was an agent of the Russians, they have concluded — quoting from each other with a high degree of discrepancy — that he was a double agent and well in with both Curzon Street *and* Dzerzhinsky Square. Not even this all-encompassing and unfalsifiable portmanteau theory is capacious enough to contain the multitude of its own contradictions, as Wheen shows very ably and amusingly in his chapter 'Honourable Members'. One day, the mischief done by hack writers and 'climate of treason' parasites will make a book in itself.

Is there any point, then, in Leo Abse's 'take' on all this, digested into one facile heading as 'The Judas Syndrome' and published in the *Spectator* in 1982? Abse began by mentioning something which I must say I recognize from recollection: 'Driberg walked all his life on a tightrope and gained his thrills in public and private by a never-ending series of adventures, courageously and foolhardily oscillating from one role to another almost every day of his life.' That's true-ish. Tom loved to come fresh from the potassium chase to some drear committee of the Commons or the Labour Party or the C of E, and to sit there beaming and replete, thinking: 'If they only knew,' while the cream was still drying on his whiskers. But, as Abse generalizes: 'The spy is a man of identities and each day he must act many parts.' Still true-ish, but tautological. Why aren't thespians thought to be security risks? And what about this deduction from the foregoing? 'Treachery is uncomfortably linked with disturbed homosexuals unable to come to terms with their sexual identity.... It was always so: did not Judas embrace and kiss Christ as he betrayed him?' The tie that binds disturbed homosexuality and treason, asserted Abse, is 'the child's lack of reconciliation between his hatred and his love of his father'. At this point, if not before, the non sequitur becomes the methodology of the witch-hunt. To take the most salient counter-example, there was nothing 'queer' (Tom's preferred term, by the way) about Kim Philby, who was the most dedicated and risk-taking agent of them all. For the matter of that, there wasn't anything famously fishy about Judas, though it's been argued that there may have been something a touch ambivalent about the Nazarene himself; no lady-killer, at any rate, and man with a distinctly odd relationship to *his* Papa. Tom emphatically did not get on with either his father or his mother, but he has — and had — that in common with many docile and patriotic heterosexuals. Moreover, as anyone with any Foreign Office or SIS experience will tell you, there were — and are — numerous confused homosexuals in the service who are well able to resist the blandishments of treason or Marxism. (One of them more or less incubated the Ultra Secret. Others we know have soldiered on in less obtrusive ways.)

I believe it's possible that Tom may have exchanged gossip and even information, at least for the hell of it, with fellow-journalists and even with officials who put things to him in a sympathetic way. But there are two persuasive reasons to disbelieve any specific or general suggestion that he was 'a spy'. The first is that he never had any money and was always painfully and chronically in debt. (Wheen has some gruesome exchanges of correspondence between him and the forbidding manager of the National Provincial in Liverpool Street, a banking address that is somehow amazingly lowering to the spirit.) The second — equally intuitive, perhaps, but more important — is that Tom had no desire to be on the winning or more powerful side. His fellow-travelling and Communist phases were marked not by Stalinist power-worship but by a rather sickly Christian sympathy for the underdog. At the end of his days he was still in agony about his decision to exclude the account of his blowing Aneurin Bevan from his memoirs. The reason he always gave me was the shock and hurt he judged this would cause to simple loyalists in his former East London constituency. This kind of sympathy *was* congruent with his disordered private life; continually invaded by mendicants, losers, dead-beats, schnorrers and wide (narrow?) boys needing one last chance. Many a time and oft, Tom would return to a flat picked bare of every last picture frame by some Borstal charmer, and count himself lucky that the charmer wasn't waiting behind the door with a cosh and a dildo. He even had the galley of his *Times* obit for Harold Wilson nicked by a smarter-than-usual short-stay guest, who flogged it to *Private Eye.* Any intelligence service reposing confidence in Tom's discretion and silence, in other words, would have had to be even more cretin-ously incontinent about secrecy than we know such outfits to be. (And any such outfit trying blackmail would have been wasting its time for the same reason. Like John Sparrow, Tom rather wistfully mourned the legalization of homosexuality because it removed some of the charge from the daily round.) The third argument for disbelieving such allegations against him is that there is, as Wheen points out disgustedly and in detail, not a shred of supporting empirical evidence for them. None of the pimps for Curzon Street — not Pincher, not 'West', not Boyle, not Costello — has ever dredged up more than an innuendo, and even those were third hand and posthumous. Pincher didn't even bother with the sub-Freudian niceties of an Abse, preferring to sink straight to Paul Johnson's level and to say that there is an axiomatic, Forsterian connection between homosexual and traitorous deportment.

To clear Tom on this charge, then, is a matter of journalistic and political hygiene. But it still leaves the matter of misogyny and cruelty. People like Paul Johnson are wearisome and sickening in their ceaseless complaint about the appropriation of 'that fine old English word "gay"'. (They never objected to the borrowing of that even finer old English word 'queer', which had to be reap-propriated by people like Tom.) But there *was* something grim and lugubrious in Tom's life, which he very often exposed in bursts of self-pity and sarcasm. And there was something a little depressing about his lavatorial stipulations: his positive preference for the dripping cistern and the reek of chemical disin-fectant. Wheen is wrong to say that Tom 'could hardly shake hands with a woman without shuddering', because he was popular with women and enjoyed their company, but it's fair to say that there was a marked element of disgust in his private attitude to them. 'That awful *wound* — I don't know *how* you can,' he would say, perhaps forgetting — or perhaps remembering — the cicatrice commemorated by Auden. If there had been scientific proof of vaginal fangs, he could hardly have been more cold on the idea. Once, when I declined dinner on the grounds that I had to visit a girlfriend in hospital, he feigned concern for a split second, moaning: 'Yes, there's a lot to go wrong with them, isn't there? I do hope it isn't her *clitoris* or anything like that.' Nice try, in a way. He made very occasional but very pungent reference to his bizarre and expired marriage, growling with irritation at the luckless woman's refusal to abide by their prenuptial agreement. 'She tried to seduce me! On our *honey-moon!*' But not until I read Wheen's book had I realized how wretched his treatment of the lady had been, and how anything can be pardoned except utter, ruthless indifference. I almost felt shabby in retrospect for laughing at his jibes — the one flat negation of his usually reliable humanism. It was a relief to turn away from that chapter and to concentrate again on Tom's career as a rebel.

His radicalism was unaffected and genuine, and reinforced by wide reading and extensive travel. He had an especial hatred for the vice of racial prejudice, a hatred which I really think was owed in part to his homosexual universalism.

He was the first Member of Parliament to argue against the postwar recoloniz-
ation of Vietnam, and the first to criticize Britain's unilateral acquisition of
thermonuclear weaponry. As a journalist, he put his pen at the service of anti-
fascism and did some original work in unmasking the now-forgotten Frank
Buchman and his 'Moral Re-Armament' racket, whose sole memorable
adherent today is, incidentally, Mrs Mary Whitehouse. Both in the Commons
and in Fleet Street, he was from the outset a stylist and an independent, of a
breed now etiolated to the point of near-extinction. (These days, if an MP can
be said to have 'outside interests' at all, they usually turn out to be in property
speculation.) In the sixties, he made a slight fool of himself by overidentifying
with the 'young'; by hanging out with Mick and Marianne and nodding while
floral-power nonsense was talked. These may be lapses, but compare the
repressed jealous attitude of Home Secretary Callaghan and the unsmiling
judges and policemen who panicked about marijuana, jailed Jagger and
snooped hysterically on campuses.

What this book conveys so well about Tom as poet, as columnist, as MP and
as individual is that everything about the old thing was bloody well manqué.
He had poetry in his make-up, but is mainly remembered for being the first to
notice that the Commons injunction 'The Clerk will now proceed to read the
orders of the day' had the same cadences as 'John Brown's Body'. He had a
talent for characterization and biography but squandered it on catchpenny
books, about Beaverbrook, and Hannen Swaffer, which didn't even catch
many pennies. He fought well for many good, brave causes but never sponsored any serious or successful bill. At his funeral there was a touching attend-
ance by diplomats from former colonial possessions, but his standing in the
Third World — last repository of reputation for many English leftists of that
generation — doesn't approach, say, that of Fenner Brockway. I can still see
him, though, rebuking the abysmal nosh in the House of Lords dining room
('the white wine is warmer than the food') and later showing up uncomplain-
ingly in the near-faultless squalor of Muriel's Colony Room Club or (is it still
there?) the Toucan in Gerrard Street. I still wish that Gore Vidal had had his
way with Hugh Gaitskell, and got Tom appointed — or at least nominated for
the post of — Archbishop of Canterbury. It would please old Tom, he argued at
A.J. Ayer's dinner table, and might help to extinguish Christianity in England.
Tom was thrilled at the scheme. He was not so much a snob as an elitist, and
helped me to realize that the two things are often wrongly confused. The path
of the rebel, as followed by Tom, was a protest against boredom and the ordinary, conformist, utilitarian precept. It was a hopeless search for a good life
where ugliness and need would not always be sovereign, and where there
would be wit and booze and wickedness, and it ended in a taxi between
Paddington Station and the Barbican.

London Review of Books, May 1990

BOOZE AND FAGS·

Hard by the market in Cambridge is — or was — Bacon's the tobacconist, and on Bacon's wall, if it stands yet, there's an engraved poem by Thomas Calverley of which I can still quote a stave or two when maundering over the port and nuts (before the brandy stage):

> Thou who when cares attack, bidst them avaunt and black
> Care from the horseman's back, vaulting unseatest.
> Sweet when blah blah in clay, sweet when they've cleared away
> Lunch and at close of day,
> Possibly sweetest.

Calverley goes on to heap scorn on those who impugn the habit, ridiculing the notion that it is torpor-inducing and fraught with disease. This was the first 'Thank you for Smoking' sign that I — playing truant from a Methodist public school up the road — ever saw, and I appreciated it. Round a corner or two in Petty Cury was King Street, where there stood a rank of pubs. A rite of passage in those days was to inhale a pint of suds in each within the space of an hour — the 'King Street run' — without puking, or without puking until the end. A novel and film of the period captures a proletarian version of this easy-to-grasp wheeze:

> The bartender placed a pint before him. He paid one-and-eightpence and drank it almost in a single gulp. His strength magically returned, and he shouted for another, thinking: the thirteenth. Unlucky for some, but we'll see how it turns out. He received the pint and drank a little more slowly, but half-way through it the temptation to be sick became a necessity that beat insistently against the back of his throat. He fought it off and struggled to light a cigarette.
>
> Smoke caught in his windpipe and he had just time enough to push his way back through the crush ... before he gave way to the temptation that had stood by him since falling down the stairs, and emitted a belching roar over a middle-aged man sitting with a woman on one of the green leather seats.
>
> (Alan Sillitoe, *Saturday Night and Sunday Morning*)

'Belching roar' is, I think, bloody good (you notice that Sillitoe is writing so plastered that it reads as if it's the poor old *temptation* that fell down the stairs), and I like the symbiosis of booze and nicotine that he brings off so cleanly. Anyway, at Bacon's one purchased the first illicit Perfecto — brand names mattered to the neophyte — and in King Street the first stoups of flat-as-ink Greene King ('drink your beer before it gets cold'), and it was an induction no less potent than the heated gropings in the Arts Cinema that was ready to hand.

·Review of V.G. Kiernan, *Tobacco: A History*, London 1991; Simon Rae (ed.), *The Faber Book of Drink, Drinkers and Drinking*, London 1991.

How did one get from that to this? From smoking after dinner to smoking between courses — the inter-course cigarette — to smoking between bites? From drinking to acquire a manly hangover to drinking to dissolve an inhuman one? From having a cigarette after the act to reaching blindly for one *during* it? From explaining, Lucky Jim-like, to a hostess that you have burned and soused her sheets to explaining that you have singed her shower-curtain? How did all *that* happen? Eh? The jammed, thieving fag-machine that I nearly kicked to death long after all the pubs had closed and the last train had gone and the glass looked wide enough to reach through. The hotel mini-bar that I unsmilingly up-ended into my suitcase, dwarf Camparis *compris*, when about to take a plane to Libya.The pawing through the garbage — through the fridge, actually — in search of the lost cigarette packet. The broad-minded, sneering assault on the cooking sherry when the interviewee says: 'No, in fact we don't keep it in the house but perhaps there's a glass of ...' Here are the milestones of shame, or a few of them.

Both of these books oscillate between praise and admonition, and come dangerously close at times to suggesting that drinking and smoking are all right in moderation. Victor Kiernan would be incapable of saying anything so trite. But his book is the record of a long farewell to a much-loved addiction, and he has not permitted his change of heart to make him into a fanatical opponent. The population is praised for puffing its way stoically through the shrieking pieties of King James I, whose pamphlet on the matter warned loyal subjects that it was 'a custom loathsome to the eye, hateful to the nose, harmful to the brain, dangerous to the lungs'. The tendency of those in authority to show who's in charge by issuing no-smoking edicts is detestable to Kiernan, who recoils instinctively from the martinet, the headmaster, the dominie and the bureaucrat. Weaving together an immense collection of quotations (though no Calverley, alas), he has one very heartening story which may be true even though it has Lord Dacre for its authority. After the suicide of the anti-smoking fanatic Adolf Hitler, it seems, all the bunker deputies began to light up: 'now the headmaster had gone and the boys could break the rules. Under the soothing influence of nicotine,' they could look facts in the face.

Engels is also prayed in aid, as having written that one of the worst privations of the workhouse system was that 'tobacco is forbidden'. And Marx reflected gloomily, as many a freelance scribbler has done whose stipend won't cover his humble snout bill, that '*Capital* will not even pay for the cigars I smoked writing it.' The political economy of tobacco, on which Kiernan touches, is rather iffy from the radical point of view. Colonial Virginia and Southern Rhodesia rested on forms of peonage, if not slavery, and Cuba is probably more disfigured than otherwise by its reliance on a tobacco economy. (Indeed, it would be interesting to study the degeneration of the Cuban revolution as a function of a semi-colonial system that produced only things — sugar, rum and cigars —that are supposed to be bad for you.) Pierre Salinger — or Pierre Schlesinger, as I always want to call him — once told me that he was telephoned by President Kennedy and asked to calculate how many Cuban cigars there were in all of Washington. He replied that he didn't know, but could discover how many cigar stores there were. 'Well, go to all of them, Pierre, and buy every Havana they've got.' The mystified underling completed his task, and learned its meaning only later that night, when Kennedy announced an embargo on Cuban cigars for everybody else.

Smoking is, in men, a tremendous enhancement of bearing and address and, in women, a consistent set-off to beauty. Who has not observed the sheer loveliness with which the adored one exhales? That man has never truly palpitated. It is the essential languor of the habit which lends it such an excellent tone in this respect, as Oscar Wilde understood so well when he described it as an occupation. Kiernan thrills to his own description of Greta Garbo blowing out a match in *The Flesh and the Devil*, and vibrates as he recalls Paul Henreid taking a smoke from his own lips and passing it to Bette Davis (*Now, Voyager*). With approval, he cites the mass meeting of young women at Tehran University; every pouting lip framing a cigarette in protest at a Khomeini *fatwah* against smoking for females. In spite of the misogyny of certain styles of smoking (pipes, of course, and Rudyard Kipling's hearty attitude towards cigars — 'a woman is only a woman, but a good cigar is a smoke') and Thackeray ('both knew that the soothing plant of Cuba is sweeter to the philosopher than the prattle of all the women in the world'), there is also a definite intimacy in the lighting ritual and in the mutual bowing over the flame. Nor, though it can catch you in the wind a bit, does smoking impair relations with the opposite sex in the way drinking has been known to do. ('No honey, we don't have a few drinks. We get *drunk!*' — *Days of Wine and Roses*; or: 'My god, my leg! I can't feel it! I can't move it!' 'It's *my* leg, you bloody fool.' I speak from experience.)

Kiernan's sweetest note is struck when he contemplates the wondrous effect of tobacco on the creative juices. Having reviewed the emancipating influence of a good smoke on the writing capacities of Virginia Woolf, Christopher Isherwood, George Orwell and Compton Mackenzie, he poses the large question whether 'with abstainers multiplying, we may soon have to ask whether literature is going to become impossible — or has already begun to be impossible'. It is increasingly obvious, as one reviews new books fallen deadborn from the modem, that the meretricious blink of the word-processor has replaced, for many 'writers', the steady glow of the cigarette-end and the honest reflection of the cut-glass decanter. You used to be able to tell, with some authors, when the stimulant had kicked in. Kingsley Amis could gauge the intake of Paul Scott page by page — a stroke of magnificent intuition which is confirmed by the Spurling biography, incidentally; and the same holds with writers like Koestler and Orwell, depending on whether or not they had a proper supply of shag. Kiernan suggests that both Marx and Tolstoy may have suffered irretrievable damage as writers from having sworn off smoking in late middle age; he has no difficulty in showing that Pavese also experienced great challenges to his concentration from trying to give up, and that poor old Charles Lamb (who took up smoking while trying to give up drinking) was stuck miserably, like the poor cat in the adage, between temptation and abstinence, to the detriment of his powers.

If I was to update Calverley I would include a stanza or two on the splendour of cigarettes as levellers and ice-breakers while travelling. Auden may have coupled 'the shared cigarette' with 'the fumbled unsatisfactory embrace before hurting', but if you are stuck with a language barrier and a high cultural hurdle there is no gesture more instantly requited than the extended packet and the shared match. This partly explains the popularity of the gasper among journalists, explorers and reporters. Now that most newsrooms ban the blue haze (and, in the case of the anal-sadist Murdoch, the agreeable fumes of booze as well), the atmosphere of most newspaper bureaux is like that of some sodding law firm. And, in the written outcome, it sodding well shows.

Searching unnecessarily for a socially conscious peroration with which to close his literate, broad-minded and considered guide to the history of a grand subject, Kiernan turns faintly censorious at the last. He says sternly that 'it is the poorer classes and countries that go on smoking', and mentions tobacco in the same breath and sentence as Aldous Huxley's 'Soma'. This allows him some boilerplate about the danger of drugs being 'utilised by dictators to manage public opinion', and a cry that 'mankind should throw physic of this kind to the dogs, and cure itself instead by radical reform of the worm-eaten social fabric, the moral slum we all inhabit today.' Och aye, or yeah, yeah if you prefer. One of the sterling qualities of tobacco leaf is its support for privacy and introspection; its reliability in solitary confinement and the dugout; its *integrity*. A long, slow expression of fragrant smoke into the face of the ranter and the bully has been the sound, demotic response since the days of King James the bad, and should be our continued prop and stay in these fraught and 'judgemental' times.

The hard stuff, of course, is a different matter. Uncollected in the Faber anthology is a moment in Michael Wharton's 'Peter Simple' memoir when one of the more heroic Fleet Street pub-performers kept a long-postponed appointment with his doctor. After tapping and humming away, the quack inquired mildly: 'D'you drink at all?' Well-primed for the routine, and knowing that doctors tend to double mentally the intake that you specify, our hero merely said that he did take a dram here and there. 'Well,' said the physician, 'if I were you I'd cut out that second sherry before dinner.' So intoxicated was the patient by this counsel that he went straight back to the boozer, bought sextuples all round on the strength of the story, and had to go home in about five taxis.

When the effects of drink are not extremely funny, they do have a tendency to be a bit grim. For every cheerful fallabout drunk there is a lugubrious toper or melancholy soak, draining the flask for no better reason than to become more repetitive or dogmatic. But there's a deep, attractive connection between the Italian for flask — *fiasco* — and the nerve of humour. When Peter Lawford or Dean Martin observed that it must be wretched being a nondrinker, because when you woke in the morning that was the best you were going to feel all day, they brushed that nerve. So did the porter in *Macbeth*. There are, of course, some who stand there pissed and weeping and give the porter an argument, to the effect that the male organ is actually rendered stouter and sturdier by drink, or at least by a hangover. Those who have found this are going to need K. Amis's terse but limpid chapter on the distinction between metaphysical and physical hangover. Bear in mind, first, as he says, that 'if you do not feel bloody awful after a hefty night then you are still drunk, and must sober up in a waking state before the hangover dawns.' Two keen reinforcements of this insight are included in the anthology. One is Adrian Henri's 'He got more and more drunk as the afternoon wore off.' The other is James Fenton on, if not in, 'The Skip':

> And then ... you know how if you've had a few
> You'll wake at dawn, all healthy, like sea breezes,
> Raring to go, and thinking: 'Clever you!
> You've got away with it.' And then, oh Jesus ...

These are the men who have been out and done the hard thinking for all of us. At all events, K. Amis compresses all the do's and don'ts of hung-over venery in a skilled manner which makes one bawl like a pub bore: 'Cheers mate! You said it!' (Those interested in cross-referencing the subjects of this review will need to note what he says about the nicotine ingredient in the modern hangover — something that was beyond the reach even of Jeeves's celebrated pick-me-ups.)

Smokers are in no real position to engage in denial, though I suppose there can be closet smoking, while drinkers can persuade themselves of practically anything between, as it were, cup and lip. It is amazing to read Byron's bemused speculations ('was it the cockles, or what I took to correct them?') about his insurgent interior, when 'what he took to correct them', after a heavy dinner of shellfish and wine, was 'three or four glasses of spirits, which men (the vendors) call brandy, rum or Hollands'. Of course, it could have been the cockles, couldn't it? And then there are always old saws, like my father's sapient favourite 'Don't mix the grape and the grain.' I never understood this until it was too late, by which time it translated absurdly as keeping Scotch and wine in separate compartments of the inner bloke. Stuff and nonsense! Still, you do get people whining on about this, like Sebastian's friend in *Brideshead* after he (Sebastian, not the temptation, you fool) had vomited copiously through Charles Ryder's window:

> His explanations were repetitive and, towards the end, tearful. 'The wines were too various,' he said, 'it was neither the quality nor the quantity that was at fault. It was the mixture. Grasp that and you have the root of the matter. To under-stand all is to forgive all.'

Arguably. The best variant of this excuse comes from Billy Connolly, in his impersonation of a lurching Glaswegian gaping down at what is known in that city as 'a pavement bolognese'. At length he concludes: 'It's no' the Guinness that does it. It's those diced carrots.'

I once saw the following manoeuvre actually performed, on the morrow of a Tory Party Conference in Blackpool, though the article employed was a necktie:

> O'Neill would prop himself against the bar and order his shot. The bartender knew him, and would place the glass in front of him, toss a towel across the bar, as though absentmindedly forgetting it, and move away. Arranging the towel around his neck, O'Neill would grasp the glass of whiskey and an end of the towel with his other hand. Using the towel as a pulley, he would laboriously hoist the glass to his lips.
>
> (Arthur and Barbara Gelb, *O'Neill*)

There's a very good 'Rock Bottom' section in this collection, designed for those who know what it's like to spill more than most people drink. Charles Jackson's maxim from *The Lost Weekend*, 'Never put off till tomorrow what you can drink today', might serve as a representative extract for much longer and more elaborate babblings, such as the full text of John Berryman's 'Step One' prelude to the general confession he made for Alcoholics Anonymous, wherein the sufferer relates all the harm he has done himself and others. If the day ever comes when I pin *that* document above my typewriter, it will be because the funny side just isn't enough. Extracts, for the flavour:

> Passes at women drunk, often successful.... Lost when blacked-out the most important professional letter I have ever received.... Made homosexual advances drunk, 4 or 5 times.... Gave a public lecture drunk.... Defecated uncontrollably in a university corridor, got home unnoticed ...

Unnoticed by whom? Of course, as this proves, and as the meeting of the United Grand Junction Ebenezer Temperance Association in the *Pickwick Papers* also illustrates, it's a sign of alcoholism to make rules about how much you drink.

There's a fatal attraction at work here (or don't you find that?) and it's to be found as much in the literature of dossing as in the pathetic fallacy which, as Waugh says, resounds in our praise of fine wine. Listen to the beauty of Peter Reading (who also found the beauty of *Perduta Gente*), in his poem 'Fuel':

> Melted-down boot polish, eau de Cologne, meths,
> surgical spirit,
> kerosene, car diesel, derv ...

This touches on a problem which, on a more refined plane, is understood even by merely social drinkers such as myself — namely: Where's the next one coming from? In one of its few klutzy decisions, this volume reprints the whole of Auden's '1 September 1939', presumably for no better reason than that it's set in a bar, and omits his poem 'On the Circuit', where he confronts a problem that's increasingly urgent in today's America, especially for those of us who fly and drone for a living:

> Then worst of all, the anxious thought,
> Each time my plane begins to sink
> And the No Smoking sign comes on:
> *What will there be to drink?*
> *Is this a milieu where I must*
> How grahamgreeneish! How infra dig!
> *Snatch from the bottle in my bag*
> *An analeptic swig?*

Or – and updating only slightly from 1963 – dash off to the gents for a smoke? Experiences like this and reflections like these teach one that only a fool expects smoking and drinking to bring happiness, just as only a dolt expects money to do so. Like money, booze and fags *are* happiness, and people cannot be expected to pursue happiness in moderation. This distillation of ancient wisdom requires constant reassertion as the bores and prohibitionists and workhouse masters close in.

London Review of Books, March 1992

7
ROGUES' GALLERY

NIXON: MAESTRO OF RESENTMENT*

We live, apparently, in a time of the composure of grievance, the forgiveness of transgressions, the putting-behind-us of the past. Ancient wrongs are righted, traditional conflicts resolved or dissolved. In the lees of this soothing tonic of lenience and euphemism, what is left for the bitter integrity of the radical personality? Well, there's always Nixon-hating. But as I read this, the latest of his awful 'books', I felt an uneasy slackening even in that usually taut string. On page 101, for instance, I hit upon the following:

> I particularly remember the time my mother served homemade ice cream topped with maraschino cherries for dessert. I had never had them before. My third-grade teacher ate the ice cream but left the cherries on her plate. People did not count calories in those days, and I always assumed that she left the cherries for me since she could not have helped but notice how much I had enjoyed my first exposure to that delicacy.
>
> Any program of educational reform should put the primary emphasis on the quality of teaching. . . .

Only pity, surely, can be felt for such an arid, constipated figure, who writes of his own childhood like a lugubrious bureaucrat and then makes it an occasion to inflict a moralistic cliché upon the reader.

'Now More Than Ever' was the slogan of the Nixon delegates at Miami, and it was only, I think, Renata Adler who noticed what was staring us in the face — that this boring chant was the unknowingly amputated first half of a lovely line from John Keats. The line positively cried out for its completion, which is, from the 'Ode to a Nightingale': 'seems it rich to die'. Today's moribund Nixon oppresses one with a similar emotion. Will he never acknowledge that there is a decent limit? Must he chatter and gibber for ever, dead but not recumbent, until at last our pity turns to loathing? Loathing may seem a strong word, but it came wholesomely back to mind before sickly compassion could gain any lasting hold. Just brood on this paragraph for a second:

> When I was first informed about the break-in, I did not give it sufficient attention, partly because I was preoccupied with my China and Soviet initiatives and with my efforts to end the war in Vietnam and partly because I feared that some of my close political colleagues might be somehow involved. Some have said that my major mistake was to protect my subordinates. They may be partly right. I believe that in any organization loyalty must run down, as well as up.

The paragraphs precedent and subsequent to this one are likewise larded with self-pity, untruth, and vengeful revisionism:

*Review of Richard Nixon, *In the Arena: A Memoir of Victory, Defeat and Renewal*, New York 1990; Herbert S. Parmet, *Richard Nixon and His America*, New York 1990.

Not taking a higher road than my predecessors and my adversaries was my central mistake.... What's more, I have paid, and am still paying, the price for it.... The Democratic National Committee was a pathetic target.... As a student of history, I should have known that leaders who do big things well must be on guard against stumbling on the little things.

The most agonizing chapter is undoubtedly the one entitled 'Friends', which more than fulfils the arch and dreadful promise of its title. 'I had often heard that real friends are there when you need them the most,' writes Nixon. 'After 1974, I saw that first hand.' He appears to be saying that until the abrupt end of his second term he had only heard this maxim but never seen it exemplified, and one fears that this might well be true. Pity breaks in again, to be dispelled again when the former President prints lists of 'friends' who stuck by him. Only on the second glance did I notice that these lists were in alphabetical order — a gruesome touch typical of a man who has no friends, only cronies and associates. (One list runs from Buchanan to Ziegler, which gives you an idea.) A ghastly lowering overtakes the spirit when one reads of the lonely, mistrustful half-lives that are led by our politicians these days; Reagan's printed recollections of 'friends' and family possess the same forced, insincere brightness and falsity. As a result, solipsism lurks in wait for the loveless, suspicious, unspontaneous professional pol. Literally everything reminds Nixon of himself and of his own bitter struggle to the top; to a summit which, once attained, did not bring him happiness or release. (On the night of his 1972 victory party, he angrily fired half his staff.)

> I remembered that when a superb group of black musicians had performed in the White House after one of our state dinners, the leader expressed his appreciation for the invitation and concluded his remarks by saying: 'You know, Mr. President, it's a long way from Watts to the White House.' I responded by thanking him and saying, 'It's a long way from Whittier to the White House.'

And, no doubt, sending him rejoicing on his way.

As a personal memoir, then, this is a cringe-making failure. It shows only that the unlived life is not worth examining. The interesting bits of Nixon's private existence — the foul mouth, the Jew-hating, the paranoia — all lie under a ban of denial and are bled out of the narrative. Politics, likewise, becomes an automatic exercise in boilerplate and retrospective self-justification. It's as if nobody ever heard the tapes. Ah yes, say a startling number of liberals, but Nixon made the *apertura* to China and put an end to the Vietnam War. He was always more sound on détente and foreign affairs. I don't need to tell the readers of *Dissent* what, or how, to think about Vietnam. And we know where the China policy has led, and why. But it may be worth recording what Nixon says about East–West relations in a book published in May 1990:

> Unfortunately, the INF Treaty has compounded the pressures on West European leaders, particularly in West Germany, to give in to Soviet demands.

This, in turn, has created sharp tensions within NATO. As Turkey's foreign minister told me in commenting on the treaty, 'Gorbachev has killed three birds with one stone. He has divided Europe from the United States, divided Europe against itself, and divided the German coalition.'

This amazing stupidity comes gift-wrapped, as if for reinforcement, with the inscription of NATO's only remaining dictatorship — a pungent reminder of Nixon's fondness, while in office, for regimes of this sort in Greece, Spain, and Portugal as well as further afield.

Herbert Parmet's well-written and well-organized study of this mediocre, wretched, warped, dishonest individual also makes the case that he is an American Everyman — the quintessential postwar politician enjoying the closest rapport with the ordinary voter. One needs the skills of a Brecht to resist this Arturo Ui presentation. Both Nixon and Parmet fail at some essential level to appreciate the distinction between the little guy and the small man. A small man, like Nixon, can appeal to the little guy, but only for so long and by so much. The little guy will not, in the end, stand for being told that he doesn't deserve or understand the sacrifices the small man has to make to stay on top. In this rejection of flattery lies our hope — there is a limit to the success of conservative populism and the exploitation of 'little guy' or 'silent majority' rhetoric, and it is very often reached because of the emaciated, corrupted personalities of the demagogues themselves. Nothing but disaster and disgrace comes of trying to accommodate to, or borrow from, the demagogic style. Parmet tells again a story that many left-liberal idealists are reluctant to believe (I first read it in Stephen Ambrose's *Nixon: The Education of a Politician*). In the celebrated 1950 campaign in California, it was Helen Gahagan Douglas who launched the red-baiting charge against Nixon, and not the other way round. 'YOU pick the Congressman the Kremlin loves,' she told the voters, adding with deliberate artifice and deceit that Nixon and 'Communist party-liner Representative Marcantonio' were in 'complete accord' on the selling out of our boys in Korea. Once that auction had been started, there could only be one long-term winner. Recall Walter Mondale deciding to attack Ronald Reagan from the right for his offer to 'share' SDI technology with the Communist enemy. A brilliant and profitable piece of post-'Missile Gap' centrism that turned out to be.

Every campaign, Garry Wills once wrote, 'taught Nixon the same lesson: mobilize resentment against those in power'. History taught the same to many conservative and reactionary populist movements, whose real attitude to those in power and authority was one of a servile, envious, vicarious adoration. Nixon, of whom this was also true, faced in smaller ways the dilemma that other such movements confronted on a sickeningly grand scale: how to redirect the resentment when 'those in power' are you and your 'friends'. Here, we need Wilhelm Reich as much as Bertolt Brecht. Still gnawed by hatred and jealousy, the small man must puff like a bullfrog to seem grand, but durstn't forget to slake the appetites that he aroused on the way to power. So — a bit of bombing here and a touch of destabilization there (never forgetting to treat Brezhnev and Mao with the utmost regard and respect) and at home a hateful drizzle of innuendo and spite against the press, the universities, the arts, the intellectuals, the outsiders, the you-know-whos. It's appalling to reflect that a version of this trick has been pulled at least four times since 1970, in the greatest constitutional democracy in the world. As I read Nixon's turgid, tenth-rate apologia, I found that I could see the unctuous features of George Herbert Walker Bush rise to greet my eyes. Nixon himself ushers him on to the stage, telling us of a call he paid on Eisenhower: 'When I saw him in 1967, among those he told me was a "comer" was a young Congressman from Texas named George Bush.' And, lest we forget, Bush was an exceptionally docile chairman of the Republican National Committee during the Watergate years.

Bush, of course, did not have to come from Whittier to the White House. But as a Yale Skull-and-Bones drone, he did not disdain to run against 'Harvard intellectuals'. Nor did he disdain the organizing energies of racists and creeps when they served his turn — like Nixon, prepared if the need arose to be adequately uninformed of the doings of his subordinates. Like Nixon also, he has spent too much time grinning agreeably as number two while the main man took the bows — a consumingly bad experience for a person of modest talent who combines the obsequious with the ambitious. Other similarities are certain to strike one. Bush, like Nixon, uses superpower posturings to offset his want of ideas on the domestic front. Bush, like Nixon, likes to see that domestic front as a field in something called the 'war on drugs'. Bush, like Nixon, had a long and torrid romance with the Marcos family. Bush, like Nixon, fears and hates what he laughably calls the liberal press (Nixon is so impressed by Bush's lying and blustering with Dan Rather in 1988 that he practically fouls himself with glee, telling the same story twice as an example of how to stick it to the media). Bush, like Nixon, has an exalted idea of the value of CIA and FBI heroes, and likes a chance to play the veterans' and hostages' card. In the latter case, indeed, by dealing direct with the kidnappers in return for money and guns, he actually surpassed Nixon's POW cynicism. Bush, like Nixon, is abject and adamant when it comes to the People's Republic of China, of whose decrepit hierarchy he will hear no ill. Again, he is slightly worse than Nixon on the point. In his memoir, Nixon relates how he told Mao Zedong: 'I think the most important thing to note is that in America, at least at this time, those on the right can do what those on the left can only talk about.' It might be argued that at least this degraded Realpolitik concerned the long-overdue establishment of diplomatic norms, rather than a limp handclasp over the hecatomb of Tiananmen.

Even as I write, the papers tell me of a certain Pierre M. Rinfret, Republican candidate for the governorship of New York, leaving the White House with an injunction from Bush to 'hit Mario Cuomo'. Thus empowered, Mr Rinfret attacked Cuomo for having been 'too chicken' to serve in Korea! How marvellously we progress. So, the apple did not fall very far from the tree. Bush is an unpersuasive patrician version of Nixon's authentic plebeian cult of resentment — drawing upon the same reserves of irrationality, selfishness, and bigotry but far too much at home among the fat cats. When he gets into trouble, he will bleat and moan rather than whine and snarl — the chivvied sheep rather than the cornered rat. When will we prove Professor Parmet wrong and raise politics above the level of these types? We might begin, as I may have said, by bewaring of pity.

Dissent, Fall 1990

KISSINGER: A TOUCH OF EVIL·

In a rather more judgemental time, history was sometimes written like this: 'The evils produced by his wickedness were felt in lands where the name of Prussia was unknown; and in order that he might rob a neighbour whom he had promised to defend, black men fought on the coast of Coromandel, and red men scalped each other by the Great Lakes of North America.' 'Evil'? 'Wickedness'? The ability to employ these terms without awkwardness or embarrassment has declined, while the capacity of modern statesmen to live up to them has undergone an exponential rise since Lord Macaulay so crisply profiled Frederick 'the Great'. Walter Isaacson's new study of Kissinger shows beyond doubt that he rose to power by intriguing for and against an ally, the South Vietnamese military junta, whom he had sworn to defend, and that in the process of covering his tracks, consolidating and extending his power and justifying his original duplicity, he was knowingly responsible for the deaths of hundreds of thousands of noncombatants in lands where his name was hitherto unknown. He also played an immense part in the debauching of democracy in the North America of his adoption. Walter Isaacson is one of the best magazine journalists in America, but he moves in a world where the worst that is often said of some near-genocidal policy is that it sends the wrong 'signal'. He accordingly approaches the problem of evil with some circumspection. At one point he correctly characterizes the Nixon regime as 'pathological', and he gives us a breathtaking passage in which Nixon conspires to have Kissinger put under the care of a psychiatrist — surely the great modern instance of what pop shrinks call 'projection'. But there is a limit,

·Review of Walter Isaacson, *Kissinger*, London 1992.

imposed by the tradition of New York–Washington 'objectivity', on his willingness to call things by their right names. It became very plain to me, as I finished the book, that if I were to employ the *argot* of popular psychology I could say that I had been reading the profile of a serial murderer.

Isaacson is probably right to begin with young Henry's abused German-Jewish boyhood. 'My Jew-boy', Nixon was later to call him – at least once on the White House tapes – and it's clear that many of Kissinger's traits were acquired early on in Fürth. His family was one of those which did not identify with the opposition in Bavaria, preferring to stress its patriotic character, its past loyalty to the Kaiser and its deep attachment to the *Kleinburger* class, and only when this failed choosing the option of emigration. Once across the Atlantic, young Kissinger avoided political anti-Nazi circles and found a mentor only in the shape of one Fritz Kraemer, a Spenglerian Prussian who flourished in the US Army perhaps not least because he was one of the few German exiles to criticize Hitler from the right. Isaacson's chapter on this man, who later disowned his famous junior for his total absence of any core of principle, is unusually interesting. Reflecting on Nazism, Kissinger placed it in the category of revolution rather than counter-revolution. Though it contained the essential doctrine of 'order', he identified it with disorder. He remains fond of mangling a phrase of Goethe's to make it appear that 'order' is to be preferred to justice, and has made this a rationale for more than one bloodbath. A mediocre dissertation that he wrote, seeking a place for himself in the conformist Harvard of the drear fifties, was entitled *Metternich: A World Restored*. In it, Kissinger wrote: 'The deviousness of Metternich's diplomacy had been the reflection of a fundamental certainty: that liberty was inseparable from authority, that freedom was an attribute of order.'

What causes a Jewish exile to give admiring expression to the precepts of German reactionary statecraft? We can only surmise Kissinger's mind as revealed again in this letter home from Germany after the war. He conveys what he considers to be the lesson of the death camps:

> The intellectuals, the idealists, the men of high morals had no chance.... Having once made up one's mind to survive, it was a necessity to follow through with a singleness of purpose, inconceivable to you sheltered people in the States. Such singleness of purpose broached [sic] no stopping in front of accepted sets of values, it had to disregard ordinary standards of morality. One could only survive through lies, tricks ...

This is fascinating. Though we know from the memoirs of survivors what is obvious – that the business of survival was a ruthless one – we also know that forms of solidarity, morality, decency and conviction were also of help both in motivating and in organizing survival and resistance. How else to explain the re-emergence of a leader like Kurt Schumacher, or the mere existence of a man like my friend Dr Israel Shahak? Of matters like this, Kissinger says nothing. Yet he presumes to write as if from experience, when in fact his war had been quite a cushy one. More than this, he writes with something like relish, as if he enjoyed imparting the brute lesson that morality and solidarity were mere feeble sentiment. This identification with the sub-Darwinist depravity of those who worshipped only 'strength' is unpleasant, as is the opportunity seized by Kissinger to lecture those back home on how little they knew. How often, in later years, were we to be bullied by him and by Nixon, and told that 'sheltered people in the States' were to be despised when great enterprises of bombing, destabilization and secret diplomacy were on foot. It's the unchanging, minatory rhetoric of the reactionary veteran and *Freikorps* man; doubly objectionable in one who had seen so little service.

Kissinger's fear of weakness and humiliation, and his pathetic adoration of the winning or the stronger side, has an interesting counterpart in much the same period. As he was working his way into Harvard, so we learn from Isaacson,

> in late-night bull-sessions, Kissinger strongly opposed the creation of Israel. 'He said it would alienate the Arabs and jeopardise US interests. I thought it was a strange view for someone who had been a refugee from Nazi Germany,' Herbert Engelhardt, who lived downstairs, said. 'I got the impression that Kissinger suffered less anti-semitism in his youth than I did as a kid in New Jersey.'

Mr Engelhardt is one of those simple souls who tends to blame American-Jewish paradox on self-hatred or, like Arthur Schlesinger, who — having in his time administered some wet smackeroos to the buttocks of the powerful — might be expected to know, on the 'refugee's desire for approval'. This is too simple. In 1989, Kissinger told a private meeting of the American Jewish leadership that the American media should be forbidden to cover the Palestinian intifada, and that the rebellion itself should be put down 'overwhelmingly, brutally and rapidly'. From being a foe of Zionism when it looked like losing in 1948, to becoming an advocate of its most racialist and absolutist application when it was a power to be reckoned with, is not second nature to Kissinger. It *is* his nature. There are no ironies to ponder here, unless you consider Hannibal Lecter an ironist.

The desire — or the need — for the death of better men is probably the special property of two groups — the chronically inferior and the incurably insecure. Kissinger belongs more to the second category. It took him a while to nerve himself, but having experienced the thrill of ordering and administering murder he was unable to get his fill of it. He grew sleek and satisfied, and more confident. He began to chafe at the status of number two. He began to slather his leaden monologues with heavy, fetid innuendo about power as 'an aphrodisiac'. He began to be gay, to be clumsily elegant — even safely and silkily indiscreet — and to seek out the salon life. Isaacson tells the story without fully intending to do so. Take, as Kissinger had to if he was going to cut himself a path, the question of nuclear annihilation. How he strove to get it right! How he laboured to achieve the right 'mix' of rigour and restraint! His first book on the topic, written in 1957 (Book-of-the-Month Club choice), spoke against the dogma of 'massive retaliation' and inclined to the oxymoronic concept, 'limited nuclear war', then in favour among anti-Communist liberals. This was published by the Council on Foreign Relations. Book the second was written for Nelson Rockefeller and called for 'tactical' nuclear weapons. Book the third, wisely entitled *The Necessity for Choice*, refined the case for massive conventional war with thermonuclear options only as 'a last resort'. In office, of course, Kissinger flung aside the mere nuclear pornography with which he had been disturbing and teasing himself, and went straight for the MIRV — a flat-out first-strike system designed for global extermination. To try and guess his work from his works, as Mr Isaacson gamely but irrelevantly does, is like poring for clues over the crabbed, cretinous scrawl of Ian Brady. Such a man needs scope. Scope! And scope is what, by relentless fawning on impressionable creatures, Henry finally got.

It's a tale well worth the telling. When the American elite divided over the war in Vietnam, Kissinger was in a quandary. He attended numerous private, blue-chip seminars and briefings in which the war was early on recognized as lost, and added his mite of conventional sapience to the pragmatic conclusions of the wise men of the tribe. But he also saw what they had not — that there was immense political capital to be raised by a candidate who exploited the resentment engendered by defeat. (He may have had in mind the efficacy of the 'who lost China?' fantasy of the fifties, but I don't think that the 'stab in the back' psychosis of his German boyhood can have been far from his mind either.) At all events, the year 1968 found him advising the ruling Democrats, who had long decided to cut the losses they had inflicted on both countries, while also covertly counselling Nixon's Republicans, who thought that perhaps both Vietnam and the United States had some lessons still to learn in the uses of pain. The accounts are basically congruent, whether you draw them from Clark Clifford's memoirs, Seymour Hersh's critique, Stephen Ambrose's judicious biography of Nixon or the recollections of Averell Harriman, Richard Holbrooke or Daniel Davidson. Mr Isaacson has added some extra but exiguous detail to the story. By shopping on both sides of the street, and betraying the side he notionally worked for, Kissinger helped the Nixon campaign in its secret effort to destabilize the Paris peace conference. He got credit for his guile from the incoming Nixonites, the South Vietnamese clients got the appearance of a better offer made *sub rosa* by Nixon, and the Democrats had the main plank of their re-election ripped out, by illegal covert action, on the eve of the poll. (Unbelievably, Kissinger did himself some harm as well as a bit of good by this even-handed subversion of both the Vietnam accords and the democratic process: Isaacson has later White House tapes with the pant-wetting conspirators wondering if Henry would do to them what they alone knew he did to his former Democratic confidants. But this might be described as the price of the omelette.)

There were more broken eggs than omelettes in the years to come. Having got elected on a false surreptitious promise to the Saigon regime, the Nixon–Kissinger team had to find a way of breaking said promise 'with honour'. As a matter purely of their own face, they instigated the secret bombing of Cambodia and followed that with a coup and an invasion; they rained bombs on the centre of Hanoi during the Christmas of 1972; they caused hundreds more American prisoners of (undeclared) war to be taken, thus furnishing the last hysterical pretext for continuing the fighting, and they presided over an additional 20,552 American battlefield deaths. Of the Vietnamese casualties, one might do better not to speak. All of this in order to accept the identical conditions for withdrawal, but under less shameful and deceitful circumstances, to which Johnson and even Humphrey had been ready to accede in 1968. Quite hardened men on Kissinger's own staff were able to see the hideous fallacy. 'We bombed the North Vietnamese into accepting our concessions,' drily remarked John Negroponte, a rough-stuff artist if ever there was one, and a veteran of Cambodia and later of Honduras. (Mr Negroponte was to offer his resignation from Kissinger's team a few years later over the Cyprus crisis. I once asked a close relative of his what had sickened such a strong stomach. 'Because', he replied after a silence, '*everything* you suspected was true.' But I'm moving ahead of the story.)

So many of the professional foreign policy Establishment, and so many of their hangers-on among the *lumpen* academics and journalists, had become worried by the frenzy and paranoia of the Nixonian Vietnam policy that consensus itself was threatened. Ordinary intra-mural and extra-mural leaking, to such duly constituted bodies as Congress, was getting out of hand. It was Kissinger who inaugurated the second front or home front of the war; illegally wiretapping the telephones even of his own staff and of his journalistic clientele. (I still love to picture the face of Henry Brandon when he found out what his hero had done to his telephone.) This war against the enemy within was the genesis of Watergate; a nexus of high crime and misdemeanour for which Kissinger himself, as Isaacson wittily points out, largely evaded blame by taking to his 'shuttle' and staying airborne. Incredibly, he contrived to argue in public, with some success, that if it were not for democratic distempers like the impeachment process his own selfless, necessary statesmanship would have been easier to carry out. This is true, but not in the way that he got newspapers like Rees-Mogg's *Times* to accept. Of what had this diplomacy consisted? Mr Isaacson describes Kissinger as 'an enabler for the dark side of Nixon's personality, someone who joined in his backbiting, flattered his ideals and never pushed him into a corner'. 'Enabler' is a weak word in the contemporary language of shrinkery and dependency. I began by saying that Kissinger demonstrated the profile of a serial killer. Let me make that case, *seriatim*.

1. Bangladesh. Often forgotten, but actually marking the inauguration of the puerile term 'tilt' to describe an abrupt change of policy or allegiance. In 1971, while still engaged in a war for his own and Nixon's faces in Indochina,

Kissinger overrode all advice in order to support the Pakistani generals in both their cilivian massacre policy in East Bengal and their armed attack on India from West Pakistan. In both theatres, this led to a moral and political catastrophe the effects of which are still sorely felt. Kissinger's undisclosed reason for the 'tilt' was the supposed but never materialized 'brokerage' offered by the dictator Yahya Khan in the course of secret diplomacy between Nixon and China. Often credited with that *rapprochement*, Nixon and Kissinger acted, as in Vietnam, only in the ways they accused their opponents and critics of being unpatriotic for recommending. (Also see under Tiananmen.) Of the new state of Bangladesh, Kissinger remarked coldly that it was 'a basket case' before turning his unsolicited expertise elsewhere.

2. Chile. As Isaacson reminds us (though in very lenient terms and mostly *en passant*), Kissinger had direct personal knowledge of the CIA's plan to kidnap and murder General René Schneider, the head of the Chilean Armed Forces and a man who refused to countenance military intervention in politics. In his hatred for the Allende government, Kissinger even outdid Richard Helms of the CIA, who warned him that a coup in such a stable democracy would be hard to procure. The murder of Schneider none the less went ahead, at Kissinger's urging and with American financing, just between Allende's election and his confirmation by the Chilean Congress. This was one of the relatively few times when Mr Kissinger (his success in getting people to call him 'Doctor' is greater than that of most PhDs) involved himself in the assassination of a single named individual rather than the slaughter of anonymous thousands. His jocular remark on this occasion — 'I don't see why we have to let a country go Marxist just because its people are irresponsible' — suggests he may have been having the best of times. Another occasion of his intimate involvement in the minutiae of conspiracy took place in the case of:

3. Cyprus. Deplorably seconding Kissinger's decision to omit discussion of this lethal episode from his own memoirs, Isaacson does not discuss the 1974 disaster at all. However, it can be — and has been — shown that Kissinger approved of the preparations by Greek Cypriot fascists for the murder of President Makarios, and sanctioned the coup which tried to extend the rule of the Athens junta (a favoured client of his) to the island. When, despite great waste of life, this coup failed in its objective — which was also Kissinger's — of enforced partition, Kissinger promiscuously switched sides to support an even bloodier intervention by Turkey. Thomas Boyatt, who was then State Department Cyprus desk officer, has since told me that he went to Kissinger in advance of the anti-Makarios putsch and warned him that it could lead to a civil war. 'Spare me the civics lecture,' replied Kissinger, who, as you can readily see, had an aphorism for all occasions.

4. Kurdistan. Having evolved the covert policy of supporting a Kurdish revolt in northern Iraq between 1974 and 1975, with 'deniable' assistance also provided by Israel and the Shah of Iran, Kissinger made it plain to his subordinates that the Kurds were not to be allowed to win, but were to be

employed for their nuisance value alone. They were not to be told that this was the case, but soon found out when the Shah and Saddam Hussein composed their differences, and American aid to Kurdistan was cut off. Hardened CIA hands went to Kissinger and asked at least for an aid programme for the many thousands of Kurdish refugees who were thus abruptly created. On this occasion, the *aperçu* of the day was: 'foreign policy should not be confused with missionary work'. Saddam Hussein heartily concurred.

5. East Timor. The day after Kissinger left Djakarta in 1975, the Armed Forces of Indonesia employed American weapons to invade and subjugate the independent former Portuguese colony of East Timor. Isaacson gives a figure of 100,000 deaths, or one-seventh of the population, resulting from the occupation, and there are good judges who put this estimate on the low side. Kissinger was furious when news of his own collusion was leaked, because as well as breaking international law the Indonesians were also violating an agreement with the United States. In the minutes, he is confronted by State Department legal adviser Monroe Leigh, who points out this awkward latter fact. Kissinger snapped: 'The Israelis when they go into Lebanon — when was the last time we protested that?' A good question, even if it did not — and does not — lie especially well in his mouth.

It goes on and on and on until one cannot eat enough to vomit enough. Angola: incite the Zaïreans to invade and give a nod to South African intervention. Portugal: summon Mario Soares and bully him about being 'a Kerensky'. The Iran–Iraq war: the policy of the United States should be that 'we wish they could both lose' — which meant sending arms and Intelligence to both to keep the pot boiling. A striking recent instance, discussed in some detail by Isaacson, is Kissinger's policy towards the dictatorship in Beijing. The day after the cleansing of Tiananmen Square in June 1989, Kissinger was respectfully interviewed for his response and surprised at least some people by counselling a policy of 'do nothing'. When Congress voted some minor sanctions against Beijing, he became even more eloquent and 'realistic', saying that Deng's regime had opened fire 'in reaction to events entirely within its domestic jurisdiction' (a condescension he had not extended to Allende) and adding, with the instinctive solidarity of one autocrat for another: 'No government in the world would have tolerated having the main square of its capital occupied for eight weeks by tens of thousands of demonstrators.' (Lucky he wasn't retained by the East German or Czech authorities a few months later.) It came out, of course, that Kissinger was at that time privily advising Atlantic Richfield, ITT, H.J. Heinz and others on their investments in China, and had succeeded in arranging many 'facilitating' meetings in Beijing for other like-minded American executives. When the *Wall Street Journal* printed this intelligence, there were two sorts of reaction. The first, unsubtle one was that our Henry was on the take. The second, expressed by that normally cynical gentleman Stephen Solarz, then Congressman from Brooklyn, was that

Kissinger always supported dictatorship whether he stood to turn a buck or not. Obviously the second view was the deep one. Since leaving active politics, Kissinger had been looking bored and ill, as if cut off from his death-support machine. He had made the occasional foray; warning that nuclear vigilance was even more necessary in the face of Gorbachev, for example, and memorably confiding his 'worry' that the United States would shrink from bombing Iraq. He had helped in the lowly task of briefing Dan Quayle for his vice-presidential debate. So here was a small chance to take part in something not for the squeamish.

There have, of course, been brutal and cynical statesmen in the past. But they were generally statesmen — Talleyrand and Bismarck come to mind — who could show something for the exercise of Realpolitik. Will anyone say what Kissinger's achievement was? Will anyone point to a country, not excluding his own, which is in the slightest degree ameliorated by his attention? And the old 'realists', of Vienna and Locarno and Yalta, though they may have looked at nations and peoples and borders as disposable and dispensable, did not axiomatically confuse crudeness and brutality with strength and (a significant Kissinger favourite) 'will'. They did not reach hungrily for the homicidal, self-destructive solution.

The masochism of the press in all this has been contemptible, and it forms a sort of repulsive minor theme of Isaacson's book. There have been other war criminals, law-breakers, phoneys and pathological liars during the long decline of the Empire and the Cold War, but they haven't had their memoirs ghost-written by Harold Evans, their consultancy retained by ABC News and their columns syndicated across the 'qualities'. They haven't been met, at every airport lounge, with an orgy of sycophancy and a chorus of toadying, complicit mirth at every callous, mendacious jest (Kissinger, I have noticed, loves and needs the sound of nervous laughter). This power-worship and celeb fetishism extends through the media into the dingy world of Oscar 'de la' Renta and the designer nonentities of New York and Hollywood with whom Kissinger likes to be seen, and who — bored, listless drifters that they are — like to be seen with him. Airhead television presenters like Diane Sawyer; conceited media-traders like Mortimer Zuckerman; salon-voiders like the Podhoretzes — you would need to be a spaced-out Visconti to capture the sinister tackiness of it all. These types seek the same rush as did Kissinger in his search for contact with the authentic thrill of death, and they exhibit the same spoiled, narcissistic contempt for democracy as something weak and inadequate. I wasn't surprised, though I was gratified, to have one of my old guesses confirmed by Isaacson, who is first-rate on Kissinger's social register. He may have taken out a dozen or so starlets in order to boost ugly overpriced restaurants and provide a few photo opportunities. But no business resulted. In his little nest in Rock Creek Park:

> The only decorative elements, other than books piled about, were pictures of Kissinger with a wide variety of foreign officials.... The bare room had two twin

beds, one of them used as a laundry dump. A woman who stole a glance later reported that socks and underwear were scattered about and the mess 'had so repulsive an aspect that it was hard to imagine anyone living there....' The dirty little secret about Kissinger's relationship with women was that there was no dirty little secret.

Repress the pang of pity. Recall what was said by James Schlesinger, former Secretary of Defense and yet another betrayed colleague: 'Henry enjoys the complexity of deviousness. Other people when they lie look ashamed. Henry does it with style.'

All over today's Washington there are men — Robert McNamara, William Colby of the CIA, George Ball of the State Department — who have written memoirs and given interviews which try to atone for past crimes and blunders. Kissinger, no doubt, would regard even the smallest exercise in atonement as sickly. When criticized, as in this book or in earlier work by Seymour Hersh, he reacts with great displays of rage and petulance. It is evident that he cannot allow any reconsideration of his own monstrous greatness. This may be a sign of instability rather than arrogance. Should we then say that he is 'in deep denial'? It would be more direct to say that Kissinger was the Albert Speer rather than the Adolf Eichmann of the crimes against humanity that he assisted in perpetrating, but that he lacked Speer's readiness to apologize. Nor, it must be recorded, was any attempt made to exact such a reckoning. That's not Isaacson's fault, but he has none the less written the biography of a murderer and largely left out the standpoint of the victims. So here we are again, invited to consider Kissinger as an essay in chiaroscuro, and not to make ourselves ill with the reflection of how many good people had to die so that such a man might prosper, and complain about profiles and book reviews, and remain 'controversially' in our midst.

London Review of Books, October 1992

BERLIN'S MANDATE FOR PALESTINE

In a column published in this space on 30 January, I made a glancing reference to the Nazi past of Yitzhak Shamir. This brought me a prodigious mailbag, with inquiries from people who didn't believe it and people who couldn't believe it, as well as from readers who wanted to know more. The chief organization on the right wing of the Zionist movement under the British mandate was the Irgun Zvai Leumi, which based itself on the ideas of Zev Jabotinsky. Jabotinsky was a relative moderate in that he acknowledged an admiration for Italian fascism rather than Nazism and nurtured the territorial aspiration only for 'both sides of the River Jordan'. At the outbreak of war between Britain and Nazi Germany, he agreed to suspend military operations against the British and was even prepared to co-operate with them as a last resort against the common enemy. This was too much for Avraham Stern, who broke with Jabotinsky over the question and founded the Stern Gang, later known as LEHI (a Hebrew acronym for Fighters for the Freedom of Israel), calling for a state that extended from the Nile to the Euphrates and proposing an alliance with Hitler to bring this about. One of his most loyal deputies, and successor as leader of the group, was Yitzhak Yezernitsky, now known as Yitzhak Shamir.

Stern began to put out feelers to the Axis in the fall of 1940, at a time when most of continental Europe was under the swastika, and Britain was resisting the Nazis alone. In September of that year Stern met one of Mussolini's agents in Jerusalem, but the discussions proved inconclusive. In January he dispatched an agent named Naftali Lubentschik to meet two of Hitler's emissaries in Beirut, then under Vichy control. One of them, Otto von Hentig, was chief of the Oriental Department of the Nazi Foreign Office. Stern's proposal, which was rashly put in writing, began by establishing his ideological common ground with Nazism, expressing sympathy with the Hitlerite goal of a Jew-free Europe and speaking of 'the goodwill of the German Reich government and its authorities toward Zionist activity inside Germany and towards Zionist emigration plans'. It then proposed the following:

> The establishment of the historical Jewish state on a national and totalitarian basis, and bound by a treaty with the German Reich, would be in the interest of a maintained and strengthened future German position of power in the Near East.
> Proceeding from these considerations, the NMO [i.e., the Stern Gang] in Palestine, under the condition [that] the above-mentioned national aspirations of the Israeli freedom movement are recognized on the side of the German Reich, offers to actively take part in the war on Germany's side.

It is important to note here that the Stern–LEHI approach was not based, like that of some Indian nationalists, simply on a rejection of Britain as the colonial enemy. The proposal clearly affirmed that the Stern Gang was 'closely related to the totalitarian movements of Europe in its ideology and structure'. Danny Rubinstein, a well-known Israeli journalist, remembers that the group's members would respond favourably, and publicly, to news of Nazi military victories. As 1941 wore on and the Nazis struck eastward, this policy was enough to sicken some of Stern's lieutenants. But Shamir did not leave the organization, and after the British killed Stern in a shoot-out he became its leader.

Let me give some citations for the curious or the incredulous. Two articles by Professor Israel Shahak in *Middle East International*, for 10 October 1986 and 18 November 1988, supply much useful background, especially on the ideological aspect. Lenni Brenner's book *Zionism in the Age of the Dictators* describes the German documentation of the meeting. In an interview in *Yediot Aharonot* on 18 July 1986, Professor Yeshayahu Leibovitz, former editor of the *Encyclopaedia Hebraica*, said: 'Within three months we will have a Prime Minister who was a leader in an organization which offered its services to Hitler.' He compared Shamir and Stern unfavourably with Kurt Waldheim, saying that Waldheim at least was mustered into Hitler's army, while LEHI volunteered. Shamir has never renounced his political past, and he keeps up many of his old associations. After the war LEHI members murdered Count Folke Bernadotte, the United Nations mediator in Palestine, who had earlier played an exemplary role in rescuing the Jews of occupied Hungary from Hitler's Final Solution. This act, too, is still justified by LEHI veterans.

Like a number of important facts about the Israeli–Palestinian drama, this aspect of Prime Minister Shamir's political evolution is well known in Israel but somehow occluded in the United States, where even liberal Zionists think nothing of accusing their critics of sympathy for Nazism if they dare to impugn the Holy State. Meanwhile, as was long ago foreseen by derided individuals such as Israel Shahak, there is a sinister fusion between the religious and nationalist right in Israel. Those who wish to force theocracy on the Jews, defining even their nationality by Orthodoxy, are making common cause with those who wish to force expulsion on the Arabs. In this menacing enterprise, the spirit of Avraham Stern — whose manifestoes called for the building of the Third Temple — lives on. It lives on, too, in Shamir's call for the collective punishment of the village of Beita after a Jewish settler child was killed by a Jewish settler vigilante. It lives on in the negation of the human and national rights of the Palestinians, a negation Shamir has fiercely supported all his life. And it lives on in Likud's anthem, which still calls for both sides of the River Jordan, if not the land between the Nile and the Euphrates. When will a single reporter challenge Shamir to renounce this 'covenant'? There were many hurt and surprised squeals last month when Shamir collapsed gratefully back into the arms of the racist, rejectionist right. But he was only continuing a long and ignoble tradition, of which the State Department and *The New York Times* have no reason to be ignorant.

The Nation, August 1989

GHOUL OF CALCUTTA

This column heartily endorses Governor Brown's campaign against Bill (Spoiler) Clinton for the Democratic nomination and urges its millions of loyal readers to call 1-800-426-1112. However, this column cannot sit idly by and tolerate Jerry Brown's repeated encomiums for the woman calling herself 'Mother' Teresa of Calcutta, a dangerous, sinister person who properly belongs in the caboose of the Pat Buchanan baggage train.

I first encountered M.T. in Calcutta in early 1980. While touring one of the less fashionable quarters of the city, I scheduled a drop-by at the Missionaries of Charity in Bose Road. Instantly put off by the mission's motto ('He that loveth correction loveth knowledge'), I none the less went for a walkabout with M.T. herself and had a chance to observe her butch style at first hand. There was something in the way she accepted the kisses bestowed on her feet, taking them as no more than her due, that wasn't quite adorable, but I held my peace until we got to the orphanage. Although built on a tiny scale in relation to the problem, this was in many ways an exemplary place. A small vacant cot told that one innocent hadn't made it through the night. I was about to mutter some words of praise for the nurses and was even fumbling in my pocket when M.T. announced: 'You see, this is how we fight abortion and contraception in Calcutta.' Squeamish as I am on the abortion question, I had seen enough of Bengal to know that the last thing – arguably the very last thing – that it needs is a campaign against population control. M.T.'s avowed motive somewhat cheapened the ostensible work of charity and made it appear rather more like what it actually was: an exercise in propaganda. Propaganda for the Vatican's heinous policy of compelling the faithful to breed, and of denying where it can the right of nonbelievers to get hold of birth control. I have met numerous relief workers in my reporting life, many of them battling in conditions far worse than Bose Road, but they have usually been doing the work for its own sake.

After this experience with the leathery old saint, I kept up an M.T. watch of sorts. I wasn't surprised to see her turn up in Haiti a few years later, as a kind of paid confessor to the Duvalier gang. When Michèle Duvalier started emulating Eva Perón in her enthusiasm for Potemkin clinics, M.T. was on hand to sanctify the vulturelike regime. 'I have never seen the poor people being so familiar with their heads of state as they were with her,' croaked M.T. approvingly. 'It was a beautiful lesson for me. I've learned something from it.' She then jetted off to Beirut to bind up Lebanon's wounds as a guest of the Phalangists. The 'beautiful lesson' imbibed in Haiti was soon to be shared with the long-suffering people of Albania. (M.T., whose family name is Bojaxhiu, was born in the Albanian-speaking Yugoslav province of Kosovo and has been, since the death of John Belushi, the world's most famous Albanian.) In August

1989 she made an official visit to the worst of all Stalinist tyrannies, as the personal guest of Nexhmije Hoxha, official widow of the dictator and a rival in tempestuousness to Michèle Duvalier herself. M.T., who has long been allied with the more fanatical wing of the 'Greater Albania' movement, laid a wreath on Enver Hoxha's tomb and made impassioned speeches about the 'brothers and sisters' of Kosovo. She certainly knew what she was doing. Ramiz Alia, Hoxha's successor, had in his younger days been a member of the ultra-fascist Albanian Youth of the Lictor. Under the direct patronage of Mussolini and the Vatican, this outfit stood for the twin objectives of Greater Albania and the forcible conversion of the Balkans to Catholicism. M.T., having lent her imprimatur to the most thuggish elements of Albanian irredentism, spent the rest of her visit as the guest of Health Minister Ahmed Kamberi, and made a number of affecting remarks about the beauty and spirit of the children in Stalinist orphanages. No doubt the motto about lovers of correction and lovers of knowledge was ready to hand.

Having prostituted herself for the worst of neo-colonialism and the worst of Communism, it was an easy and worldly step to the embrace of the worst of capitalism. During the heroic period of the S&L bonanza, M.T. nursed at the ample tit of Charles Keating, of Lincoln Savings and Loan of California. According to Nan Goldin, who made the splendid PBS *Frontline* documentary 'Other People's Money', the ghoul of Calcutta received '$1.4 million and use of a company plane' from the ascetic Keating when he was at the height of his charitable powers. Patricia Johnson, Keating's PR flack, recalls that Keating 'carried in his pocket a crucifix that Mother Teresa had given him when they first met. And he carried it always.' Another bargain for Mr Keating. I wonder where the money is now.

Brave and honest humanitarian workers are to be found all over the globe, and though I have never met one, there are conceivably some modest and self-sacrificing missionaries also. How has the extraordinary deception of M.T. come to be perpetrated so widely? As far as one can determine, the M.T. myth began after a British poseur named Malcolm Muggeridge found himself in the steps of St Paul. A likable old sinner in his way, Muggeridge took to piety and censure in his senescence and could usually induce the BBC to film him standing next to some phoney shroud or blubbering wooden statuette. Ready to spend time — but not *too* much time — among the lepers and beggars, Muggeridge got himself to Calcutta and struck pay dirt with a flying visit to Bose Road. And a star was born.

'The Pope is still fornicating with the Emperor,' wrote Dante in one of his pithier staves, and with M.T. one sees yet again the alliance between ostentatious religiosity and the needs of crude secular power. This is, of course, a very old story indeed, but when one surveys the astonishing, dumb credulity of the media in the face of the M.T. fraud, it becomes easier to understand how the sway of superstition was exerted in medieval times. Jerry Brown currently suffers from the 'perception' that he is somewhat rudderless intellectually. He couldn't make a better move than dropping the hell bat over the side.

The Nation, April 1992

THE LIFE OF JOHNSON

In a novel called *Left of Centre* which is now, to the relief of its publisher and author alike, safely out of print, Paul Johnson wrote what is generally agreed to be the most embarrassing spanking scene ever penned. The eclipse of that otherwise unreadable novel did nothing to dim the memory of the cringe-making episode, which was continually recalled to mind by Johnson's public and social behaviour. This often involved drunken and boorish conduct towards women, including his wife. On a famous occasion in a Greek restaurant in Charlotte Street in 1973, he struck her across the face for disagreeing with him in public and, when rebuked for this by a colleague of mine, threatened to put him through a plate-glass window. At a lunch given for the Israeli ambassador to Britain in the boardroom of the old *New Statesman*, I watched Johnson bully and barrack Corinna Adam, then the foreign editor, as she attempted to engage Gideon Raphael in conversation. 'Don't listen to her, she's a Communist!' he kept bellowing, his face twisted and puce with drink. 'Fascist bitch!' he finally managed, before retiring to a sofa on the other side of the room and farting his way through a fitful doze for the rest of the meal. The combination of his choleric, lobsterlike complexion and his angry mane of ginger hair used to excite comment. 'He looks,' said Jonathan Miller after witnessing one of his many exhibitions of dementia, 'he looks — *like an explosion in a pubic hair factory.*'

Long before he made his much-advertised stagger from left to right, Johnson had come to display all the lineaments of the snob, the racist and the bigot. 'The Portuguese are just *wogs*,' he yelled at me during a discussion of the Salazar dictatorship. Feeling himself slighted at the seating arrangements for a dinner one evening, he marched towards the door, thumping his walking stick and shouting, 'I won't have it. I'm going to my club!' His customary difficulty in fighting his way across a room was compounded on this occasion by his wife, who intervened to persuade him to stay and pointed out sweetly, 'Paul, dear, you don't *belong* to a club.' (He does now.) 'Fear of hellfire', he told me, kept him in the Roman Catholic Church. He added that all the same, he often broke the Church's commandments. I already knew that, or thought I did until he added wolfishly: 'You see, I quite often pray for people to die.' He has terrible trouble spelling and must carry a dictionary. I remember when he was utterly caught out plagiarizing a misquotation of Herbert Marcuse from *Encounter* — a sort of triple-crown howler. His knees, already weak, turn to a jelly of deference whenever a title or a country house is mentioned. Once at a cricket match he took out his displeasure at the arrangements on the family dog, Parker.

I really could go on (as he knows). But why drag up this wretched and distasteful stuff at all? I was quite prepared to go to my grave with it. Well, in his book *Intellectuals*, Johnson now rashly announces: *Le style c'est l'homme*. I wouldn't have done that if I were he. In a clanking, ill-carpentered sentence he begins: 'This book is an examination of the moral and judgmental credentials of certain leading intellectuals to give advice to humanity on how to conduct its affairs.' And he goes on, increasingly suffused with the odour of righteousness: 'How did they run their own lives? With what degree of rectitude did they behave to family, friends and associates? Were they just in their sexual and financial dealings?'

Having granted himself this licence, Johnson proceeds to employ it with extreme vulgarity and, I would say, imprudence. Seeking to discredit the theory of historical materialism, for example, he writes:

> One of Jenny's earliest surviving letters reads: 'Please do not write with so much rancour and irritation', and it is clear that many of his incessant rows arose from the violent expressions he was prone to use in writing and still more in speech, the latter often aggravated by alcohol. Marx was not an alcoholic but he drank regularly.

The entire book breathes with that sort of surreptitious, furtive, prurient mentality. Take this introduction to the thinking of Rousseau:

> His father Isaac was a watchmaker but did not flourish in his trade, being a troublemaker, often involved in violence and riots. His mother, Suzanne Bernard, came from a wealthy family, but died of puerperal fever shortly after Rousseau's birth. Neither parent came from the tight circle of families which formed the ruling oligarchy of Geneva and composed the Council of Two Hundred and the Inner Council of Twenty-Five. But they had full voting and legal privileges and Rousseau was always very conscious of his superior status. It made him a natural conservative by interest (though not by intellectual conviction) and gave him a lifelong contempt for the voteless mob. There was also a substantial amount of money in the family.

Notice how Johnson circles like some carrion bird, looking for the weak spot. If Rousseau had been born in poverty, he could have been accused of a lifelong envy for people more fortunate than himself. But the evidence on this isn't quite strong enough. So, a brisk *en passant* sneer at the father's difficulties before deciding to convict on the charge of pre-modern radical chic. If this simplistic method were pursued with the least elegance or discrimination, it might deserve to be called Johnson's Fork. As it is, it is merely Johnson's projection.

Or take the following, which shows the abyss of moral chaos into which Johnson's lurching footsteps have carried him:

> In his ascent to power, Hitler consistently was most successful on the campus, his electoral appeal to students regularly outstripping his performance among the population as a whole. He always performed well among teachers and university professors. Many intellectuals were drawn into the higher echelons of the Nazi Party and participated in the more gruesome excesses of the SS. Thus the four *Einsatzgruppen* or mobile killing battalions which were the spearhead of Hitler's 'final solution' in Eastern Europe contained an unusually high proportion of university graduates among the officers.

This slipshod, hysterical, clumsy passage (*Intellectuals* marks Johnson's final break with any claim to style) is a distillation of every fault and crime in the book: (1) It contains a stupid confusion between the notion of being educated and the notion of being an intellectual. This sort of lethal crudity was found among the cadres of the Khmer Rouge. ('Oh, you wear *spectacles*, do you ...?') (2) It contains what elementary logicians call an 'undistributed middle': certain intellectuals harboured illusions about Hitler, therefore intellectuals are Hitlerite. This puerile solecism is, in various forms, the whole scheme of the book. (3) It represents a dishonest rewriting of a dishonest earlier volume. In his turgid and apologetic *A History of Christianity*, Johnson made use of the same rather questionable survey of SS members to show that an alarmingly high percentage of them had been practising and confessing Roman Catholics. On that occasion he wrote that although the fact was uncomfortable, it didn't prove anything. (4) It is an insult to the exceptional number of German intellectuals, Jewish and non-Jewish, who went into exile or suffered gross persecution rather than compromise with the New Order. The most famous of these were secular leftists, the species of intellectual whose defamation is the principal purpose of this book. Still, in his witless hatred of the type, Johnson doesn't scruple to generalize, or to license the hatred of the intellectual and the university, which was the special contribution of fascism to modern discourse. I haven't the least idea whether Johnson considers himself, or wishes to be considered by others, an intellectual. But there is an element of self-hatred in these clotted pages that prompts the question. I don't just mean his sly, semi-conscious elision in point (3) above. On page 283 he retells the old story of the *New Statesman* and the suppression of George Orwell's dispatches from Barcelona in 1937. As it happens, I wrote about this episode in the *New Statesman* about a decade ago, saying that the editor at the time, Kingsley Martin, had acted deplorably. It was Paul Johnson, by then a well-paid-up member of the barking, foaming British right, who wrote in to attack me, to defend Martin and to call his censorship of Orwell a perfectly defensible exercise of the editorial prerogative. Yet here he is in 1989 making it seem as if Martin's decision was a classic symptom of the decline of the West.

There is a slightly unsettling emphasis on the sex lives of the great minds in this book. Edmund Wilson, it seems, was another spanker. Karl Marx was worried about boils on his Johnson. Victor Hugo and Tolstoy just could not leave their Johnsons in peace. You know the sort of ... thing. But it is in one of the few sex-free sentences in the chapter on Bertrand Russell that Johnson gives himself away. Describing some of Russell's many self-contradictions on the nuclear question, he says that the old philosopher 'tore off, following the howling banshees of logic'. I choose to regard this as a revealing criticism. Having condemned the educated, he despises the logical. What is next, if not an attack on reason itself? And sure enough, we get it. Evelyn Waugh turns out to be the model intellectual and the model of personal probity, because he 'was never a man to underrate the importance of the irrational in life'. Absurdly, Johnson tries to undergird this position by inept reference to the writing of George Orwell, already misrepresented and caricatured by him in an earlier passage. He suggests that Waugh, the friend of Franco and knee-jerk Jew-baiter (and, I must add, my favourite English novelist of this century), was on the way to annexing Orwell on his deathbed.

Well, facts are stupid things, as Johnson's favourite President once had the goodness to remind us. But on his deathbed, Orwell was actually working on a review of *Brideshead Revisited*. How I wish he had completed it. Still, the notes survive:

> W's driving forces. Snobbery. Catholicism. Note even the early books not anti-religious or demonstrably anti-moral. But note the persistent snobbishness, rising in the social scale but always centring round the idea of continuity/ aristocracy/a country house. Note that everyone is snobbish, but that Waugh's loyalty is to a form of society no longer visible, of which he must be aware.

For Johnson, who appears to be ignorant of this commentary, awareness comes in altogether different guises. As he says on page 72, in his flailing and pitiful account of the life of Karl Marx: 'An unusually intelligent Prussian police agent who reported on him in London noted ...' And again, five pages later: 'On 24 May 1850 the British Ambassador in Berlin, the Earl of Westmorland, was given a copy of a report by a clever Prussian police spy describing in great detail the activities of the German revolutionaries centred around Marx.' It's difficult to know whom Johnson admires more: the Prussian police spy or the Earl of Westmorland, whose mere name is a magic caress to him. But this book is written by a would-be informer and stool pigeon, who would gladly sniff the sheets and snoop through the drawers and run lolloping drunkenly back to dump the trophy at his master's feet. On every page there is something low, sniggering, mean, and eavesdropped from third hand. How right that it should have drawn an enthusiastic endorsement from Norman

Podhoretz, another moral and intellectual hooligan who wishes he had the balls to be a real-life rat fink.

Two words have, of course, been dishonestly elided from the title of this book. They are 'secular' and 'left'. If an 'intellectual' is motivated by religious or conservative convictions, he or she is exempted axiomatically from Johnson's picknose inquisition. Writing his elegy for one whose emotions *were* conservative and spiritual, W.H. Auden observed with generosity that:

> Time which is intolerant
> Of the brave and innocent
> And indifferent in a week
> To a beautiful physique
> Worships language and forgives
> Everyone by whom it lives.

He went on, rather suggestively, to propose that:

> Time which with this strange excuse
> Pardons Kipling and his views
> And will pardon Paul Claudel
> Pardon him for writing well ...

Auden had what Johnson cannot guess at — which is to say he had at least the ideal of the whole man, to be contemplated and evaluated with irony and complexity. (One can imagine Johnson replying with a sneer that Auden had excellent personal reasons to hope for forgiveness.)

The relationship between a personality and a set of ideas or precepts is, in other words, an important and delicate consideration. Most often, the relationship is disclosed by way of contradiction. (One thinks of Sir Isaac Newton's addiction to unscientific superstitions, or Evelyn Waugh's invitation to his friends to imagine how much nastier he would be if he were not a Catholic.) These contradictions repay study. But the study is made impossible if, like Johnson, you propose that personal failings are the essential clue to inquiry and analysis. Even at the philistine public schools which Auden satirized so beautifully, there is a handy injunction that the real gentleman tackles the ball, not the man.

Something occurred to me as I put *Intellectuals* on the chuck-out shelf. It is a book so sordid and comical that it discredits even its ridiculous author. Yet apparently nobody — family member, colleague, publisher, drinking companion — told Johnson to pull the chain on it. It seems, then, that he can't have a true friend in all the world. Perhaps it is this that makes his prose so hateful and lunging. 'Look at me. I'm fouling myself again!' Sorry, Paul. Now that I remember, I suppose I always knew that this was going to happen.

Critical Quarterly, 1989

A GRAVE DISAPPOINTMENT
ALL ROUND·

On 22 February 1965, the fifth month of Harold Wilson's first ministry, Richard Crossman recorded the following in his *Diaries of a Cabinet Minister*:

> Then Harold Wilson raised the issue of Anthony Howard. He has just been appointed by the *Sunday Times* to be the first Whitehall correspondent in history, looking into the secrets of the Civil Service rather than leaking the secrets of the politicians. His first article had been an analysis of the relationship between the DEA and the Treasury. The PM said this was outrageous and he was going to accept the challenge of the *Sunday Times*. In order to kill Tony Howard's new job he forbade any of us to speak to him.

Uncharacteristically, Crossman did not follow this entry with any comment or aside, and the remainder of the six-year narrative does not include any 'off the record' meetings with his friend, whose job was indeed 'killed', by the combined malice of Whitehall and Wilson and the inanition of Thomson Newspapers, after one more sporting try at a piece on the Ministry of Technology. (Ah! The DEA! The Ministry of Technology! The tantrums of George Brown! Later that same day, Crossman dined with 'Wedgwood Benn' to discuss the menace of Radio Caroline. There is a decomposing madeleine wedged between every leaf of those diaries, which I have just reread.)

In his lenient and chivalrous biography of Crossman, Mr Howard gallantly does not mention the *Sunday Times* incident. And indeed, whenever the old suggestion of 'double-Crossman' comes up, he is at pains to put the case for the defence. He even says that the nickname itself derives from schooldays at Winchester rather than from Labour politics, and it may well be true that Crossman bore the title all his life. Still, I'm quite clear that he earned it afresh, as it were. There's an old Claud Cockburn doggerel that goes (from my memory):

> Here lies the body of Dick Double-Crossman.
> Classical don with political flair.
> Favoured of fortune he yet took a toss when
> Out with the hounds, he ran with the hare.

This was widely quoted; and quoted because it came often to mind rather than, as Howard implies, because his name happened to lend itself to the joke. In spite of his declared friendship and admiration for his subject, Howard, too, gives the evidence for thinking of Crossman as one of Labourism's apparently inexhaustible corps of ambitious phoneys.

·Review of Anthony Howard, *Crossman: The Pursuit of Power*, London 1990.

We are hurried fairly smartly through the obligatory formative scenes: Crossman at Winchester giving every sign of exemplifying Cyril Connolly's 'theory of permanent adolescence'. A nasty David Benedictus-like episode, with prefect 'Dick' going too far in wielding the Ground Ash, leads to a new school mandate for the lighter but more efficient cane: much relish here in the details. 'Dick' moans to Stephen Spender: 'Even if I become Prime Minister, I'll never again be as great as I was at Winchester.' 'Dick' is immortalized by John Betjeman:

> Broad of Church and Broad of Mind,
> Broad Before and Broad Behind.

'Dick' competes with Auden for the affections of a rugby-player — I cherish this bit because years later, in a villainous wine bar called the Bung Hole, Crossman told a group of *New Statesman* staffers about the *amour*, and all present were so flabbergasted that afterwards no one could recollect the name. (It was Gabriel Carritt, whose actual tastes impelled him towards the future Countess of Longford.)

Politically, his thirties seem to have fitted a conventional anti-fascist and moralistic description. I say 'seem' because Howard gives us some reason to think that Crossman had a furtive admiration for the Nazis, acquired during his sojourn in Germany, and for their unswerving singleness of mind. In 1934 he told his BBC listeners that 'the spirit of the youth movement still inspires many of the young officers in the labour camps and fills many students with the belief that they are digging the foundations of a new German socialism.' Not that Crossman, in praising what he called the 'idealism' of the Hitler Youth, shared these ideals himself. More likely, on the available evidence, he was drawing upon his traditionalist, Wykehamist zeal. True to his thesis in *Plato Today*, which located the totalitarian principle in ancient Athens, he identified the new Germany with Sparta. He was also doing something that ambitious intellectuals have been known to do before and since, which is to say that he was rating the 'practical' and the 'hard' above the merely contemplative or hesitant. In Labour politicians this often manifests itself by way of a kind of aggressive/defensive 'realism'. Asked in later years why his 1937 election campaign in Birmingham had largely ignored the fascist threat to Republican Spain, Crossman replied: 'I had never seen such slums and poverty in my life and as a result perhaps it never occurred to me to mention Spain.' This is a demonstration example of intellectual populism — a tone in which Crossman was to be something of a specialist.

During a fairly good war, which he spent in the weird and suggestive interstices of the Political Warfare Executive, Crossman seems to have become an early private fan of the emerging 'special relationship': admiring the broader American resources and broader American minds, and getting himself posted to the Eisenhower–Macmillan joint command in North Africa. He also developed, according to Howard, a marked preference for the active-service officer over 'the trained diplomats or elected politicians with whom he had been accustomed to deal in London'. After the war, though sharing much of the general resentment at nascent American power, he was to take the American side in the Commission on the future of Palestine, and thus to signal one commitment on which he never gave up. This decided preference for the winning side and the man of action appears to have been the steering principle on which he operated in Labour politics for the next three decades. Having been, in a generally centrist 1945 parliamentary intake, a member of the mildly radical Keep Left Group, Crossman began to trim as Labour's tide receded. On 25 February 1950, just after a calamitous slump in Labour's majority, he wrote in his *Sunday Pictorial* column: 'Herbert Morrison got his way, as he usually does, and persuaded the Party to water down its Socialism in an effort to appease the middle-class vote.... Enough confusion was created to prevent the nation from taking the decision which was required and which I am firmly convinced would have been taken if it had been presented with a clear-cut choice.' That was for the comrades to read. Within days, he was writing privately to the puissant Morrison, saying meekly: 'I doubt if anyone denies that the proposals for new nationalisation in our election manifesto — whatever their individual merits — looked very silly in the election campaign. Frankly, they were irrelevant. If they were calculated to appease left-wing socialists, they certainly did not accomplish that purpose; and they certainly lost us floating votes.' Howard describes this manoeuvre as a tribute to 'the primary allegiance which Dick continued to yield to the Labour Party'. Arguably. It can as well be read as an emerging Janus profile: one which admittedly he was eager to keep occluded, but which was to become more pronounced with every shift in hare–hound relations. (Incidentally, both positions seem to have been rather unintelligent as well. Nothing was going to save Labour in 1950–51). Hugh Gaitskell's colossal rearmament budget, announced to meet the supposed exigencies of the Korean War, met with Crossman's unqualified support. But then, so did the subsequent resignations of Aneurin Bevan, John Freeman and Harold Wilson, which were in protest at the immediate consequences of that budget.

There are, to be sure, regular public and private dishonesties, of the kind that every professional politician is expected to commit, and for which he may hope for praise ('a politician to his fingertips'). And there are small venalities, such as the trashy, lucrative lawsuit brought by Crossman and others against the *Spectator*. (The magazine had reported him drunk in Venice: the late Lord Goddard had a bias against the press; and years later I remember Crossman, again in the ghastly Bung Hole, cheerfully admitting that he had been as drunk as — what? Not a lord, perhaps. A skunk?) These sorts of shifting and tacking are small change. What astonishes one continually is the grossness of Crossman's hypocrisy, and the sheer magnitude of his contradictions. As soon as Bevan began to flag, Crossman sought to transfer his own fealty to the more deft and 'flexible' Harold Wilson, who, it seems, had tired of being 'Nye's little dog'. (Bevan had left the Shadow Cabinet on principle over British support for the growing war in Indochina. Is there a premonition, here, of Wilson's later attack on backbench rebels against his own pro-LBJ regime, warning them that every dog was allowed one bite before its licence was revoked?) Yet, seeing that Gaitskell was for the moment impregnable to a challenge from either Bevan or Wilson, Crossman wrote to him as soon as he was elected, saying:

> I am *unqualifiedly* glad that you are now the Leader. I am even gladder that there is now no fence with each of us on his own side. Personally — and because I like Dora very much — it is nice to feel that we can be friends again.
>
> But I want you also to know that I am not a bandwagon kind of person. My value to the Party, so far as I have one, is as an awkward, independent ideas man who can always be relied upon to chase an idea further than is convenient.

Of what is this extreme unction reminding me? The slavish gleam of loyalty in the eye, the wish to be first with assurances, the eager glint of the spectacles, the unstoppable self-regard in the guise of self-deprecation ... Kenneth Widmerpool! Adjustments made for the Wykehamist rather than the Eton style (Gaitskell, too, had been at Winchester), it has the tone of the power-votary and acquaintance-scraper to a T. The act was kept up until Gaitskell died, and its unfolding is not very interesting or instructive, although, if I were Neil Kinnock, I might linger over pages 216–18, where the tale of the 1959 election is told. As Gaitskell's chief of propaganda, Crossman took credit for the Party's widely praised quantum leap in the use of professional advertising, media relations and television technique. Alas, none of this new smoothness availed when Gaitskell made the heinous mistake of bluffing about the cost of his programme. *Caveat.*

Shifting back to Wilson after Gaitskell's death (and now writing to old Bevanites like Anthony Greenwood about 'the hopeless position into which we had sunk under the Gaitskell regime'), Crossman went the whole hog, writing in the *Daily Herald* about Wilson as 'the cleverest man to have led a British political party since Lloyd George' (more apt than perhaps he knew) and as 'at least as professional as Mr Kennedy'. Adoringly, he showed off his intimacy with the new leader by pointing out '*his* chair' when visitors came to the Crossman *casa* in Vincent Square. I doubt that even Widmerpool would have gone that far, but it's easy to imagine him stressing, as did Crossman the intellectual populist, that 'without any affectation' Wilson 'prefers the kind of unassuming, comfortable home life which he shares with millions of ordinary families'. It comes as no surprise to find that he proposed the 'white heat of technology' wheeze to Wilson as a campaign theme for 1964, though Crossman's own ignorance of scientific matters was as near-complete as one could wish. From 1964 to 1970 we all know the story — the fetishization of sterling, the corporate state management style, the getting-rough with the Seamen's Union, the endless cowardice over Rhodesia — though it's true that we know it better in part because of Crossman's jottings. The essence of

British decline, and of the relationship of forces which determined it, is quite well caught by two entries, one for 11 February 1965 and one for 17 June 1966:

Once again we are taking the subsidiary role, the pro-American line, and Michael Stewart as our new Foreign Secretary is following it very faithfully indeed. And in all this Harold is deeply, personally committed.... He just saw that one must either go into Europe or become a subsidiary of the Americans, and he chose the latter.

Undoubtedly it's all a fantastic illusion. How can anyone build up Britain now as a great power East of Suez when we can't even maintain the sterling area and some of our leaders are having the idea of creeping inside Europe in order to escape from our independence outside?

Observe, though, how Crossman embodies rather than diagnoses the contra-dictions here: discontented with the role of permanent junior to America yet surly and resistant in his attitude to Europe. Perhaps knowing when he was licked when it came to opportunism, he stayed grumblingly with Wilson until the last, even though Wilson was by then the most salient example of the tendency he had himself warned against in his celebrated 1963 preface to Bagehot: the tendency of 'Cabinet government' to become prime ministerial, and of the principle of 'collective responsibility' to decay into the decorative. Indeed, Crossman rose to be Lord President of the Council, spending more time with the Queen and on ceremonial matters than any modern Tory would care to. (Incidentally, think how the tone of politics might be altered if the archaic word 'privy' in the title Privy Councillor was given its update to the word 'secret'.)

Trapped in this world of pretend-power, Crossman neither mounted serious criticism of the 'special relationship' nor advocated a European stage on which Labour could recast itself as contemporary and internationalist. This condemned him to the only alternative — a paltry, undemocratic trade-off between the illusions of sovereignty and bargaining with the TUC. Howard says that Crossman opposed the 'In Place of Strife' proposals of 1969, but don't I remember him originating a *New Statesman* editorial defending that policy as an example of 'How Labour stumbled into socialism'? A dank little offshore-barracks socialism that would have been. Crossman's relationship with the *New Statesman*, and with the eventual destruction of an outstanding weekly review, is of a piece with his overall contribution to the British radical scene. Most of the tendencies that put the *NS* out of commission were given a pronounced forward shove by his post-1970 tenure. Having once identified (in *Towards Socialism* in 1963) a morbid Labour condition known as 'ex-ministeritis', he proceeded to invite to the inner editorial meetings the most exploded ex-ministers of Labour's sentimental 'Left' (Barbara Castle) and the most sinister of its unsentimental 'Right' (Lord Chalfont, who, unbelievably, was appointed foreign editor). This guaranteed the identification of the paper with a stultified Westminster and a discredited government.

Casting about for a theme which would unify populist left with reactionary right, Crossman found it in dogmatic opposition to Europe — one conviction he held in common with his predecessor Paul Johnson. To the paper's role as a mouthpiece of party and an organ of faction he added the role of a megaphone for petty chauvinism. Then came the redesign, with empty logos and ill-sorted photographs. Then the utter want of attention to style (Howard is very acute here) and the recruitment of played-out columnists like — well. James Fenton once composed a 'Dick Crossman Blues', to the tune of 'Saint James' Infirmary', a stave of which went:

> Oh we didn't like being beastly
> As we showed him to the door
> But when he brought in J.B. Priestley
> Well it was the final straw.

There was also the politicization of the 'back half' — I remember Crossman refusing to run a spirited piece by Galbraith on a book about the Bernie Cornfeld IOS mutual fund racket, on the fantastic grounds that such exposés were anti-Semitic.

A note, here, on Crossman and *die Judenfrage*. He was intensely Jew-conscious, and once said in my hearing that he could see why people didn't like Jews, so he could see why the Jews needed their own state. His Zionism was of that devious sort. Concerning his famous silence on the Suez war of 1956, Howard writes that Crossman was unwell at the time and that there is, therefore, no mystery about his reticence. But illness never shut Crossman up. And in his neglected book on Israel, *A Nation Reborn*, published in 1960, he described the war as 'a method of pacifying the frontier' which 'did a power of good'. Howard doesn't mention this, or the still more remarkable fact that Crossman referred only to 'the *appearance* of underhand collusion' [emphasis added] between Ben Gurion and Eden. He actually wrote that he doubted 'whether the collusion between these two statesmen went very far', which would have been pretty rich in 1956, never mind 1960. It's clear that Crossman sat out the Suez aggression because, at least with a part of himself, he sympathized with it. His long espousal of the Israeli cause also brought him into contact with Arthur Koestler, who was the real author of Crossman's 1948 pamphlet 'A Palestine Munich?'. Since this partnership evolved into the co-editing of *The God That Failed*, and then into a quarrel, one would like to know more about it than Howard tells us.

In retrospect, it seems evident that the failure of the left to think seriously about Europe was its really great failure: the failure that in effect committed it to upholding and defending the patterns of British backwardness and British dependence. In that wasteful, philistine, *conservative* rearguard action, Crossman played a not inessential part. His end, gratefully accepting a Wilson peerage and then dying before it could be conferred, is too pathetic to speak about. His best legacy — the revelations contained in his Cabinet Diaries — is also the record of his role in the drift and demoralization which he describes. At the Labour Party Conference in 1976, I was at a private dinner given by the Engineers' Union, at which Harold Wilson made a little speech in praise of himself. 'I have', he said, 'been leader of this party for thirteen years.' Even twelve years after they had ended, the 1964 slogan about those 'thirteen years of Tory misrule' still had a resonance. The following day, addressing the full conference and the cameras, Wilson proudly reminded people that he had been 'the leader of this party for twelve and a half years'. That sort of instinct is what gave him his reputation, among admirers and subordinates like Crossman, for political acuity. In 1992, the year of European integration, Thatcherism will have been dominant for thirteen years, and will, not coincidentally, have made Crossman's observations about prime ministerial fiat seem tentative. In these facts, and in the relation between them, the emptiness of an unprincipled gullible Labourism is described. In that sense, Richard Crossman really helped to make the country what it is today.

London Review of Books, October 1990

TOO BIG FOR HIS BOOT·

Alexander reminded me that Black once said that he was prepared to let his editors have a completely free hand except on one subject. He forbade attacks on American Presidents in general and President Reagan in particular.
(Entry for 18 April 1986, *Not Many Dead*)

The success of Michael Moore's film about Roger Smith and General Motors has aroused an envious spirit of emulation in my breast. 'Conrad and Me', a script which I hone and burnish in slack moments, has the following points of mild interest. In the summer of 1985, I wrote an article for the *Spectator* about Ronald Reagan's colon cancer. I said what I believed to be true: that Reagan and certain of his advisers had known of the deplorable state of his health before the 1984 election, and had chosen to cover it up along with much else. I

·Review of Nicholas Garland, *Not Many Dead: Journal of a Year in Fleet Street*, London 1990; Alan Watkins, *A Slight Case of Libel: Meacher v. Telford and Others*, London 1990.

cited some reputable medical writers to this effect. I then allowed myself some very vulgar thoughts about how Reagan, his colon in disrepair, would manage America's affairs in the critical years to come. I'm a bit contrite about those paragraphs now: they were ill-tempered and mean-spirited, and Reagan's astounding moral, mental and physical deliquescence between 1985 and 1988 does not make them any less so. I paid scarcely any attention to a letter that the *Spectator* subsequently published. It was a frothing note from some Canadian business mogul named Black, who evidently hero-worshipped Ronald Reagan. In his closing sentences this entrepreneur spoke of buying up some English newspapers in order to put me, and others like me, out of a job. I had a brief cackle on the telephone with the *Spectator*'s then-editor and filed it away under 'department of empty threats'.

I had much the same reaction after meeting a British financial writer in Washington. He had been in Toronto to interview Black about something, and had found him swirling around his own boardroom, beating the air with the offending copy of the *Spectator*. He repeated verbally the claim he had made in print — that his motive in acquiring a newspaper empire was to cleanse the business of people like me. My friend said the bloke had seemed quite serious, and laughingly added that if Black did acquire complete control of the *Telegraph* I would be held accountable. Black went on to depose the decrepit Berry family entirely. Who cares, I thought. I never wanted to work for the *Telegraph* and they never looked like offering me a job anyway. Then I stopped writing for the *Spectator* in order to accept an offer from the *New Statesman*. At a *Spectator* garden party, in front of my brother and other witnesses, Conrad Black surged up to Charles Moore and congratulated him on firing me. Ever the gentleman, Moore courteously pointed out that there had been a few lines in the magazine thanking me for my services and even regretting my departure. Then Conrad Black bought the *Spectator*.

Well, I reflected, that's still several jumps behind for the tycoon from the Dominions. Another sulphurous letter from Black, rebuking Charles Moore and repeating all the litany against myself, was later published in the *Spectator* and marked the first time, to my knowledge, that a proprietor had helped himself to his own correspondence column. Heigh-ho, I thought, pretty soon Black will be announcing he is a poached egg and shouting for large slices of toast to be laid out in his sanctum whenever he feels the need of a lie-down. Then, this year, when the *Sunday Correspondent* invited me to be its American contributor, Black — or someone with a North American accent calling himself Conrad Black — was on the telephone within hours of my being gazetted, barking that I was a disgrace to the profession and should not be employed. Indeed, he made the very damaging accusation that I was 'a mental case'. A few weeks later, he was boring a dinner table in Georgetown, and loudly announcing that I ought to be 'exterminated'. (If Black reads this — or, as he would probably prefer to say, if he has this 'drawn to his attention' — he may care to know that more than one of the guests gave me separate but identical accounts of his conduct at this soirée. He evidently has a knack of inspiring affection and loyalty in his friends.) Now, I am merely a lone scribe living on my depleted wits. Do I have the right to take offence at this campaign of harassment and defamation from a multimillionaire? I think — I *think* — I shall let it go for now. If Mr Black wishes to know why I may choose to spare him, he will have to read to the end of this article, or pay someone else to read that far on his behalf.

These two books, both by working Fleet Streeters who go on at length about their own lives and times, furnish my excuse for this extended personal intro. In considering the newspaper racket these days, one comes up continually against people and publications who are on the run either from a proprietor or from the laws of libel. (I happen to be travelling in the opposite direction.) More than half of Nicholas Garland's book is given over to an account of demoralization and defection at the *Telegraph*, and the whole of Watkins's effort is an education in the nightmare of the Queen's Bench. Garland approaches the relationship between politics and journalism with an ignorance and a complacency that would almost be refreshing in anyone who wasn't paid to provide a day-by-day comment on the news. At one point, discussing his closing days at the hellhole of the *Telegraph*, he records: 'I interrupted to say that when I'd arrived on the paper I'd never done a political cartoon in my life.' He hasn't done one since, either. Will anyone claim that Garland has ever summarized a political moment or made a truly political observation? He has a fair line and can get a likeness very well indeed, and his Barry Mackenzie stuff was grand, but he is good enough to warn us early on that it was at *Telegraph* leader-writers' meetings that he imbibed 'most of what I knew about British politics', and to amplify this later by saying:

> How on earth does one make up one's mind about anything? I tend to listen to other people's assessments and rely on them to a great extent. There are few issues on which I feel very clear. I once made a list of all the political questions of the day: pay rises, education, Common Market, North Sea oil, inner cities, GLC and so on. I found that I was more or less completely ignorant about the whole lot, and had absolutely no opinion on any of them. All I had was a rough idea of who from the political or journalism world supported which side of any given issue. I also had a clearish idea of which politicians or commentators I usually agreed with. So I make up my mind about things by seeking out who said what about them.

Likeable as this confession is no doubt intended to be, it describes not so much an open mind as an empty mind, and an empty mind in the world of consensus journalism will not stay vacant for long but be swiftly filled up — with platitude. We can take it that Garland has not given us his least favourite cartoons to illustrate this diary. On the first page is a direct comparison of Michael Heseltine with Sidney Carton (Eh?), with the stock quotation incomprehensibly appended as a caption. On page 127 we discover Pickwick's old lady confronting the fat boy who wants to make her flesh creep. The old lady is drawn as Mrs Thatcher. The fat boy has the word 'Voters' emblazoned on his back. Why? What's the point? Where's the pith? Bernard Partridge could have done better in an old *Punch* on a good day. Low and Vicky could have done much better on a bad one. As Garland himself modestly records, of a conversation he had with Max Hastings's secretary:

> She said that she thought my cartoons were very good. 'They're so – political.' She also admitted to being a paid-up member of the SDP and said cheerfully that I should keep up the good work. I don't know how these shyly-stated remarks hung together, but the overall effect was unmistakable. She was being very nice.

If Alice will just pass that sick-bag of hers, we can decode these 'shyly-stated' remarks more accurately. Max Hastings has – or had – a secretary who thinks that Garland's cartoons are in tune with her preferred party: that is, they are expiring from insipidity. The question is: does this tell us anything about the ethos of the *Independent*? The provisional answer appears to be no, which is a distinct relief. The *Telegraph* mavericks who founded the *Independent* wanted a recognizable cartoonist in order to appear both new and familiar – a pardonable desire on the part of a freshly launched daily. What they got for their trouble was, on Garland's own evidence, about eight months' worth of Hamlet-like whinings and haverings about his pension prospects, and a courageous agreement to sign up when it looked as if there were no risks. They also got, by the sound of it, some fairly superior advice on layout and design, which is the field that Garland probably ought to have entered in the first place. Since he doesn't include any samples of the alternative 'dummy' issues he discusses, we have only his turgid recollections to go by, but these do seem persuasive, and his advice must have contributed to that look and feel of authority which the paper possessed from its first day.

I was astonished to learn that many people consider this little book bitchy and indiscreet. Things must be very dull in Fleet Street if so. Garland is out to please everybody if he can, and is no more wounding or incisive in his prose than he is in his cartoons. The absurd figure of William Deedes, for example, is represented thus on page 47:

> I have watched with a strange sort of gloom as the paper has wallowed and yawed and eventually driven herself on the rocks while Bill has grinned and joked at his desk.

> I got a charming letter from Bill today thanking me for the drawing I'd given him. He also amazed and pleased me by saying that in the last turbulent days he'd spent at the *Telegraph* he'd come to look upon my 'reassuring figure as the one anchor in the harbour ...' I was very touched.

As no doubt Mr Deedes now is to read that his steadfast cartoonist even shares the same taste in nautical cliché, as well as the same taste for having it both ways. It's not possible to take offence at anything so innocuous – or rather, the offence is at the surreptitious, invertebrate quality of it all. Garland tries to tell a resentful and misleading story about my opinions on Ireland at one point, but lays off the bet by referring to me as 'Hitch' (which I like) and 'Chris' (which I don't) to show that these things are all part of the general chummery.

If Garland has an opinion of Conrad Black, he keeps it to himself, preferring the safer ground of other people's eavesdropped speech. Charles Moore describes Black at a Downing Street dinner where the guests later watched the Guards beat retreat: 'Conrad Black's act', Garland reports, 'is apparently to be the one who knows everything, and he completely ruined the spectacle with an interminable monologue about the history of the uniforms and the origins of the ritual before them. Charles gave his spluttering laugh. "And it was so boring and pointless".' And Oliver Pritchett tells Alexander Chancellor a middling good yarn ('Perry' is Peregrine Worsthorne):

> He said he'd just seen the most sinister man he'd ever clapped eyes on moving towards Perry's office and was terribly afraid that the man's intention was to murder poor Perry. He was troubled enough by the aspect of this nightmarish intruder to note details of his face and clothes in order to provide the police with a good description: 'He was of South African appearance!' Alexander, on hearing this alarming story, wondered whether under the circumstances they shouldn't call on Perry to see how he was ... Perry was at his desk and greeted them. 'Hello, come in! You'll never guess who has just been to see me.'
> 'Who?'
> 'Conrad Black!'

Garland also supplies a vignette about Black's way of doing business. Again, it is a colleague who finds he is doing the reporting:

> 'It's pathetic isn't it?' said Bernard. 'I heard that at the board meeting where Max's appointment was being discussed Lord H. strongly opposed the choice. After a while someone handed him a bit of paper which he read and fell silent. I think I know what was written on that paper.' He scrawled something on a pad, tore off the page and handed it to me. On it he'd written '80 per cent'. The message to Hartwell was brutal: 'We've got 80 per cent of this place – shut up.'

It's a bit pat – the image of the maundering old peer getting the shaft from the unsentimental capitalists – but precisely because it's such a stark metaphor for the evolution of Fleet Street and Tory Britain, it might be true.

The creation of newspapers like the *Independent* and the *Correspondent* has slightly lessened the journalist's historic fear of the whims of the proprietor, whether Canadian like Beaverbrook, Thompson and Black, Australian-American like Murdoch, or berks or Burkes like most of the rest of them. The other two coercions, of the law of libel and the law of official secrecy, remain as strong as ever. Alan Watkins's book is ostensibly an essay on the intimidating and harassing effects of the libel law. But its subtext concerns the hidden and persistent injuries of the class system as manifested in the person of one mediocre Labour politician. I'm writing this in America, and trying to imagine how I could describe the Meacher case to an educated outsider. How to begin to describe our great country and its sensitivities? I remember, during the debate over the Central African Federation in the 1960s, that Lord Hailsham rose to defend his friend Iain Macleod from the deadly charge of being 'too clever by half'. That jeer, issued by Lord Salisbury, had been amplified in the Lords by the yahoo figure of Angus Graham, Duke of Montrose, later to be a member of Ian Smith's Cabinet. By way of rebuttal, Hailsham mentioned that he had once been bitten by the future Duke of Montrose while playing the Wall Game at Eton. Here was the future of both Rhodesias at stake, and here was our national level of allusion. Wasn't it that sort of thing that brought modernizing, technological Labourism to power in 1964?

Years later, towards the end of the 1970s, an old friend approached me with a look of faint puzzlement. Was it true, he inquired, that Michael Meacher had become a leader of the Labour left? I replied that, without anyone having exactly willed this outcome, it did seem that Mr Meacher, formerly a desiccated Fabian, had evolved into Tony Benn's spear-carrier. Well, said my friend (who, though of sound politics, was not a political man), it seemed jolly rum to him. While at Berkhamsted School, he had been visited with scorching castigations by Meacher, a prefect with a forbidding reputation. 'I can still remember him saying: What you need, X, is a dose of pain. Yes, I think a dose of *pain*. And one of his toadies was there, echoing him like Mr Creakle and saying: Dose of pain.' (Mr Meacher need not excite himself. I possess the relevant affidavits.) Watkins writes: 'There was something of the disciplinarian school prefect about Mr Meacher: that stiff walk, that narrow mouth, those cold eyes, the spectacles!' The *Observer*'s attorney, Richard Hartley QC, asked Meacher about damages: 'That is what you are wanting? The money was to punish the *Observer*?' And Meacher replied: 'A modest punishment, yes. That is right. Because unless people are punished they will do it again. That is one of the bases of psychology.'

It's impossible to summarize Meacher's case against the *Observer* without lapsing into farce and bathos. The best guide for the perplexed is to be found in *Monty Python*'s sketch about the self-made Yorkshire businessmen all loafing around and vying with each other over the hardships of their upbringing. Meacher, in a tussle for the deputy leadership of the Labour Party, gave the impression that his father had been a farm worker. He succeeded in getting several reporters to print this version of his provenance, and never asked them to correct it if it was untrue, which it was. That's it. That's the whole case, which cost almost £200,000 and occupied many a silk. Like Wilde in his incautious pursuit of Queensberry, Meacher found himself having to disclose more about his person and his background than he might have liked, or anticipated. His father had inherited wealth, had owned land, had employed a maid, had sent the lad to a public school. But his father had also suffered a nervous breakdown, and had been compelled to retire to the family farm. In open court, Mr Meacher nearly blubbed, and referred to his father as 'inadequate'.

Watkins has a knowledge of litigation and of Fleet Street, and takes us through it all without overmuch pedantry. Those who like his signature phrases — 'the public stock of harmless pleasure', 'the gaiety of nations', 'the People's Party' — will not be disappointed. Those who found the old Beachcomber column funny will be slightly over-rewarded. Those who recognize the names of certain lawyers — Larry Grant, the firm of Seifert, Sedley and others associated with the National Council for Civil Liberties — will be shocked and depressed to find them on the prosecuting side of this authoritarian and bullying use of a repressive law. I have only one complaint. In describing one of these attorneys, a Ms Sarah Burton, Watkins writes on page 53: 'She was a New York lady, small, dark, intense, of strong socialist convictions.' And on page 100: 'Miss Burton was small, very dark, in her late thirties, with a prominent and masterful nose and a discernible though not pronounced New York accent. She looked Middle Eastern.' Yes, yes, Dr Watkins. Don't waste the time of the court. I think we can all see what you are driving at. On practically every page of both these books, somebody has lunch with Tony Howard. Part-emollient and part-irritant, part-innocent and part-conspirator, he nips to and fro like Osric 'the water fly', fixing a little here and undoing a bit there, always keeping the pot a-boil. Never averse to hearing a bit of bad news or bringing a touch of hot info, he possesses an inexhaustible, directionless energy. Can no one find this man a proper job?

'With the rich and mighty, always a little patience.' This old Spanish proverb still appears to hold as much as ever. In dealing with newspaper proprietors, it is essential to know a great deal about vagary and conceit. In considering any resort to the majesty of the law, it is necessary either to be already rich or (in the case of the libel lottery) plain avaricious as well as rash and vain. In analysing the rise of politically ambitious boys, it still helps to have in mind the diagram of who bit whom in the formative years. In estimating the character of the British and their press (even though Aneurin Bevan once said of Fleet Street and censorship and patronage that there was 'no need to muzzle sheep'), one must have an ear for the rhythms of social nuance and for the class system as crudely summarized in the marketing notion of the A, B and C reader. It's small wonder that Thatcher's version of sado-monetarism has lasted so long and enjoyed such a fair wind from the public prints. Honestly, what a profession. What a country.

London Review of Books, June 1990

P.J. O'ROURKE: NOT FUNNY ENOUGH

In the great arch of Union Station in Washington there is some lapidary, if slightly confusing, advice for the would-be traveller. If you would bring back the wealth of the Indies, it says, you must carry the wealth of the Indies with you. It goes on to add rather lamely that if you hope to gain knowledge by travel, you had better be knowledgeable when you start out.

We all take some intellectual baggage when we set off, but P.J. O'Rourke, whose collected travel writing, *Holidays in Hell*, has just been published, is positively weighed down. O'Rourke has fought to establish a character: that of a crazed sixties refugee who has renounced everything but the craziness. He has to try to see the funny side of the world's trouble spots and plague houses; he has to be chirpily and, of course, 'unpredictably' right wing; and he has to mention California. The first two obligations are part of his contract with Jann Wenner of *Rolling Stone* magazine, who picks up the tab for most of his forays. The third one is, for all I know, self-imposed. But everything reminds him of California. Lebanon reminds him of California: 'The rest of the scenery is also spectacular — Californian, but as though the Sierras had been moved down to Santa Barbara. The mountains of Lebanon rise ten thousand feet only twenty miles from the sea. You can ski in the morning and swim in the afternoon.' El Salvador reminds him of California: 'I thought El Salvador was a jungle. It isn't. El Salvador has the scenery of northern California and the climate of Southern California.' *South Africa* reminds him of California: 'I'd been told South Africa looks like California, and it looks like California — the same tan-to-cancer beaches, the same Granola'd mountains' majesty, the same subdeveloped bush-veldt. Johannesburg looks like L.A.'

This must be a case of travel narrowing the mind. I *knew* that O'Rourke wasn't going to like Nicaragua when he asked himself: Is it 'just a misunderstood Massachusetts with Cuban military advisors?' while still on the plane. Of the nine overseas armpits that O'Rourke infests in these pages — Lebanon, Korea, Panama, Poland, the Philippines, El Salvador, South Africa, Nicaragua, and Israel and the West Bank — I have myself infested seven. He does a better job of trying to be funny about them than I did of trying to be serious. His technique is simple, and it could stand emulation from the more solemn thumb-suckers of the foreign press corps. Rule One: Nix to the big interview. The guerrilla leader and the other *grands fromages* have already been interviewed more times than you have interviewed people. Your attitude should be the same as that towards a sign saying SCENIC VIEW. If it's that hackneyed, it's not worth seeing. Rule Two: Journalists make the best sources. Stay close to the veterans and discover what it is they are drinking (O'Rourke is a specialist at covering the big story from the commanding heights of what we experts call Mahogany Ridge, and I'm impressed at Wenner's patience with his bar bills).

Rule Three: Repress all flickers of compassion. Nobody wants to read: 'As I stand here half-canned and weeping in the burning hell men once called ... the body of a child lay like a broken doll in the street ... one thing is certain, nothing will ever be the same again.' O'Rourke prefers the breezy 'Anyone here been raped and speak English?' school. 'Cut to obligatory squalor,' he sniggers as the cameras move in on a child with limbs like sticks.

Then there is bathos. Here is O'Rourke in El Salvador, visiting the Mercado Central in the capital:

> Coming in from the blinding sunshine, I felt a gestalt hit me, a Jungian race vision – the cruel Pipils and Mayas flaying victims to the sun, strange, hairy man-horse conquistadors, the forced labor *repartimientos*, the Inquisition, the *esquadrones de muerte* – the odor of the charnel house struck me full in the face. But actually I'd walked into a hanging side of beef.

Yeah, yeah. We all want to avoid being thought to take ourselves too seriously. But over the course of several pieces, this tactic stales just a bit. And some of the jokes curled up and died a long time ago, as in: 'Australia is not very exclusive. On the visa application they still ask if you've been convicted of a felony – although they are willing to give you a visa even if you haven't been.' At other times I wasn't certain if our boy was joking or not:

> The larger the German body, the smaller the German bathing suit and the louder the German voice issuing German demands and German orders to everybody who doesn't speak German. For this, and for several other reasons, Germany is known as 'the land where Israelis learned their manners.'

Explain, please, this punch line. On the face of it, as you English say, I am not finding it all that bloody funny.

Still, one must sympathize with somebody who has to be amusing the entire time. And not only amusing, but heartlessly so. There are moments – one of them occurs in a South African black 'homeland' and another in a pitiful bar in Warsaw – when O'Rourke breaks Rule Three and exhibits an unsightly smear of heart on the sleeve. He manages to choke down his larynx, straighten his shoulders, dry his eyes, and fall into the next vat of booze with due aplomb, but at least his guard did slip. (I presume, in fact, that his eyes were blurred with tears when he wrote that Johannesburg is like LA.) This small contradiction comes from a larger one, which he advertises at the very start. He has learned from his trotting and sluicing and fornicating around the globe that 'people are all exactly alike. There's no such thing as a race and barely such a thing as an ethnic group. If we were dogs, we'd be the same breed.' This is one of those humanist *aperçus* that are true and genuine, but make for dull copy. How can you believe it and go on to make jokes about kimchi belches in Korea, informal driving habits in Central America, and people who wear laundry on their heads in the Middle East? You can't, and that's that. And the reading public isn't born that doesn't think foreigners are either funny or faintly sinister. At no point, I must say in his favour, did he employ the old standby: 'As dusk fell, the muezzin wailed, calling the faithful to prayer.' But he did twice commit the amazing solecism of referring to Muslims as 'Mohammedans', the oldest mistake in the book and one of the few insults that he does not utter on purpose.

In previous articles and collections, such as *Republican Party Reptile*, O'Rourke got some mileage out of being a former sixties *enragé* who had turned to democracy, free enterprise, and the American way. Here we have one of those packagings that decays with time rather faster than the contents. In *Holidays in Hell* there are a few half-hearted efforts to keep up the pretence, and a few flashbacks to his obnoxious days as a dope-sodden war hater. Diminishing returns have done the rest, and there just haven't been that many international destinations where Ronald Reagan can be made to look any better than he does at home. Plus which, P.J.'s essentially schmaltzy nature keeps peeping blearily through, like a winking horse thief at some ghastly Irish fair where all hell has broken loose. The most sustained polemic, and the most unbuttoned piece of writing, occurs not in a hellhole or a foxhole but in tranquil, self-regarding Western Europe during the American bombing of Libya. This was the moment when O'Rourke discovered something that comes to us all: you can run down your own country, but you are damned if you will hear the job done by tittering foreigners. A sustained multiparagraph burst of hot invective contains all that he pretends he said, but actually didn't, to a patronizing Brit in a London club. I admired the thrust and verve of the performance, which was worthy of a better cause. But I know the symptoms only too well. When you start taking offence that way and clutching your patriotism like the neck of a bottle ('You say our country's never been invaded? You're right, little buddy. Because I'd like to see the needle-dicked foreigners who'd have the guts to try. We drink napalm to get our hearts started in the morning....'), why, then, it's well past time to go home.

Condé Nast Traveler, 1990

NOT FUNNY ENOUGH (2)

One day, P.J. O'Rourke will make up his mind. Is he Holden Caulfield or Ayn Rand? Until that day, we will be sighing as he writes: 'Also, the Democrats wanted the federal government to solve every one of America's problems, from AIDS to making sure the kids wipe their feet before they come in the house. For chrissake, the federal government can't even deliver mail, and how hard is that? The stuff's got our address right on it and everything.' That's page 31, and in case you were wondering, it's the Caulfield mode. But then, on page 36: 'Barely a weekend passes without some group of people parading in the capital to protest the piteous condition of those inevitable victims of injustice, themselves.... The AIDS Memorial Quilt is unfolded, and the Cancer Sampler and Car-Wreck Duvet are probably coming soon.' These mood swings provide insurance against the dread deformity of being 'predictable', which it is O'Rourke's ostensible stock in trade not to be. Fleeing hectically from boredom and its ugly sister, consistency, O'Rourke feels obliged to be a bad boy. A favoured method is the old one, two, three-*gotcha* construction, as in 'the fact that women suffer discrimination and harassment in the workplace, are paid less than men, are rarely promoted to the highest levels of corporate or professional responsibility and this year's hemlines make their legs look fat'.

I think that Dave Barry does this somewhat better, but there's no doubt that it goes on making some people laugh. In any case, my quarrel with O'Rourke is not his Reaganite chic as much as it is his weakness for an even deadlier virus: even-handedness. Discussing the boring, vulgar hell of modern American politics and viewing it through the last presidential campaign, he writes: 'When you looked at the Republicans, you saw the scum off the top of business. When you looked at the Democrats, you saw the scum off the top of politics.... If you voted for Bush, you'd be robbed blind. If you voted for Dukakis, you'd be too poor to be worth robbing.' This could be one of those 'bipartisan' joke-meisters, like Dennis Miller or Mark Russell, who have a gag for all audiences. O'Rourke is supposed to be a bold young reactionary, for heaven's sake. What gives here?

It's not enough to misquote the Second Amendment on the right to bear arms, as he does. What we want is more stuff like this, on the restoration of military spending cuts: 'Let's hold the Saudi Arabians, Kuwaitis *and whatever Iraqis remain alive* at gunpoint and make them pay the costs.' [Emphasis added.] This is certainly right-wing enough. Trouble is, it suffers from not being in the least bit funny. What is a Tory comedian in the age of Bush and Quayle to do? What O'Rourke ought to do, and sometimes actually does do, is get off his rearguard and go report something. Not something abroad — he tried that in 'Holidays in Hell' and showed that he was a born isolationist — but something all-American. There are two descriptions in this collection, one of a raid on a Washington crack house and one of an expedition with the Guardian Angels, that are very well-wrought and convey the real, rank stench of social despair. Not that O'Rourke would call it that. He is easily embarrassed by words such as 'compassion'. As he says of Mitch Snyder, the man was 'the perennial

*Review of P.J. O'Rourke, *Parliament of Whores: A Lone Humorist Attempts to Explain the Entire U.S. Government*, New York 1992.

homeless advocate and incessant protest-faster who would commit suicide a few months later, thereby obtaining an eternal home, and a warm one at that'.

Better. *Much* better. You can't say *that's* not in poor taste.

The remainder of this salad of pieces takes O'Rourke to the Afghan border, there to have some sport with the towel-heads and to ring every known bell. It takes him to Panama, where he fails to find anyone after the invasion 'with a missing friend or relation', which only argues that he wasn't looking or, alternatively, that he didn't read the Defense Department report on the aftermath. It takes him into the bowels of the S&L scandal, where his *Rolling Stone* colleague William Greider makes a better and more humorous guide. It takes him, in other words, to the outer limits of the conservative ability to find amusement in every human predicament, and well beyond the conservative aptitude for stressing the 'individual responsibility' of all parties except themselves.

New York Newsday, June 1991

WARHOL IN ONE DIMENSION

The intriguing thing about the opening night of the Andy Warhol retrospective in Manhattan was its tameness. MOMA (the Museum of Modern Art) can seldom have looked so respectable while being at the same time, in a faintly macabre way, *en fête*. I could have got in without a black tie, but would have looked wildly conspicuous in mufti and was glad to have observed the protocol of the invitation. The event had the feel of a fund-raiser for the Republicans (or, admittedly, in these days of high-tab politics, the Democrats). Since Warhol had in his time — then just drawn to an end — been sounded out for the post of Jimmy Carter's official photographer, and gone on to grace the glitz-infested dinner table of Ronnie and Nancy, this didn't seem inapposite. The pictures on the walls looked as familiar and predictable as the people. Surely that's Marilyn. And look — there's Jackie. There, reassuringly, is the Campbell's soup can. In fact, there it is again — and again. It's barely even a shock to see the late Andy Warhol himself, holding a small crowd in the angle of the staircase and sporting that unmistakable silver wig. Those who cluster round are careful to betray no sign of excitement, engagement or curiosity. Could this impersonator be the renowned Alan Midgette, who in 1967 'stood in' for Andy at the University of Utah, of all places, and had the students demanding their thousand-dollar fee back? Warhol's hope had been: 'Maybe they'll like him better than me,' but surely there was some faint private relief on his part that this particular con didn't work.

It's a warm evening, and MOMA has thrown open her garden. No sweet scent of the exotic cheroot taints the air; there are scarcely even any smokers, and no one seems to be employing the men's room either to take on fuel or to make a brisk exchange of spermatozoa. It was in MOMA's hitherto demure garden in March 1960 that the Swiss 'happening' artist Jean Tinguely exposed his *Homage to New York*. The exhibit consisted of a vast Heath Robinson or Rube Goldberg device, fashioned from old bike parts, player-pianos, fans, balloons and other detritus. In the presence of Governor Nelson Rockefeller and many other big bananas, Tinguely threw a switch and set the heap on course to clanging, twanging self-destruction. All three networks solemnly recorded the event, which for many people inaugurated the period of 'non-judgemental' art criticism. Marcel Duchamp, Warhol's original Pop guru, commented approvingly that there was merit in the movement to 'destroy art before it's too late'. Warhol's biographer Fred Lawrence Guiles* remarks elsewhere that his subject's Pop creations 'were more Duchampian than anybody's. If a machine could have created silkscreen paintings of coke bottles, soup cans and dollar bills, Andy would have paid its inventor to set the thing up in his studio.' But, back where we started twenty-nine years ago in MOMA's garden, art seems lifeless but by no means dead. On the contrary, it is revered, fetishized, taxonomized – and valued on a scale that Nelson Rockefeller would have gruffly appreciated.

Reporting to lawyers and crime-beat journos about the latest in gang-rape, racial murder or crack-habit dysfunction, the New York City Police Department talks in low tones about something called 'lack of affect'. In this phenomenon, those arrested show no emotion, display no awareness of guilt or shame – in general maintain a scary cool. This in turn leads to worried speculation, much of it profitless, about animal nature, barbarous youth and bad seed. I've often thought that the dense, autistic stare popularized by Warhol was the Ur-type of this amoral, disaffected style. He seems to have tried for a synthesis of the sadomasochism of Dali and Céline, yet to have strained out any relish or abandon from the mixture. He took his pleasures sadly. Impersonalized or even brutalized gay sex, while it had been tried before all right, was something he both cottoned to and helped to proselytize for. The essential figure in the world of the Factory was either a runaway boy or a drifter, joining a Legion where no questions need be asked. That's why William Burroughs was such a tangible influence on Warholism. And speaking of the feral, affectless manner, I can never forget Burroughs telling a film interviewer that when he was a boy mothers would warn their children against playing

*Loner at the Ball: *The Life of Andy Warhol* by Fred Lawrence Guiles.

with him. 'They said I looked like one of them sheep-killing dogs,' he reported, as tonelessly as he dared.

As the *Diaries* show,* however, once AIDS began to stalk his world, Warhol took fright, and distance. He would avoid restaurants where, as he put it, 'fairies' were handling the food. He cold-shouldered friends who tested positive, shunning their society at parties and refusing to ride in taxis with them. His discovery, Ultra Violet,† now born again in a tiresome way, recalls that at their last meeting she teased him without success about his reported meal with Liberace, saying: 'I hope you didn't French-kiss him at lunch.' He writhed away from the subject. Yet it is now given out that Andy was judgemental all along, nipping off secretly to Our Lady of the Perpetual Whatever to abase himself weekly, and helping out with soup-runs and such whenever he wasn't overcommitted elsewhere. At his memorial in St Patrick's Cathedral, some of the better-heeled mourners made much of this life of occluded sanctity, though it was noticeable that they had defended him for his 'do what thou wilt shall be the whole of the law' when he was among the quick. Claus von Bulow was first at the communion rail. 'Amazing Grace' was sung. Warhol's final painting, *The Last Supper*, done all in red, was apparently described by him as having been 'serious'. Thus we have the perfect kitsch of the amoralist who turns to the Cross at the last. As he would have said – Gee. Wow.

Still – and despite his pose of deep-seated indifference – Warhol did have some capacity for love, and for attracting it as well as needing it. It's common-place to hear his circle described as hangers-on, cronies, sponges and nature's damaged dependents. But I'm impressed by the number of people who appear sincerely to miss him, and to stay loyal to him and his memory. This is exactly why the *Diaries* are such a source of fascination. They seem designed to go off like a posthumous stink-bomb in the faces of those who thought them-selves secure in friendship, or at least secure in first-name acquaintance. Jean-Michel Basquiat would not have been thrilled, had he lived anything like his natural span as the handsome, patronized black boy, to read for Tuesday 2 October 1984: 'Jean-Michel came over to the office to paint but he fell asleep on the floor. He looked like a bum lying there. But I woke him up and he did two masterpieces that were great.' Yeah, right. This laconic entry tells you most of what you need to know about the burn-out that overcame Basquiat, yet there is nothing hateful or gloating about it, only the recurrent suspicion that Warhol never quite 'bought' any of the stuff he was apparently marketing.

Otherwise the *Diaries* are a combined exercise in Dada, minor betrayal and the care and feeding of the dreaded Internal Revenue Service, which likes tidy records of incidental expense. 'Bernard went and got lost, talking to Susan Dey at the bar. He's a would-be star-fucker. Susan Dey was emotional about the

---

*The Andy Warhol Diaries, edited by Pat Hackett.
†Famous for Fifteen Minutes: My Years With Andy Warhol by Ultra Violet.

play and said she was protesting war now. I don't know *which* war. Nicaragua, I guess.' 'And Steve Rubell was there and he wasn't that friendly. I mean, he was really friendly, but sometimes he's really really really friendly. So he wasn't friendly enough.' 'Paramount was having a screening of *Mommie Dearest* (cab $6).' Pat Hackett, who devoted so much of her life to getting all this between covers, also edited *The Philosophy of Andy Warhol*, in which appears the thought: 'Some critic called me the Nothingness Himself and that didn't help my sense of existence any. Then I realised that existence itself is nothing and I felt better.' Could this have been put better (as a nihilist statement, I mean)? But then, why the relentless cabbing and socializing and partying and self-publicity? It's too trite to say that he wanted to reassure himself that he *did* exist. As this vast telephone record shows, he could get all that reassurance at home.

It has now become quite impossible to think about publicity as an end in itself without Warhol's name surging into one's mind. The *nada* style of late post-Chabrolian violence, for example, surely owes a great deal to Valerie Solanis's list of 'demands', issued once she had shot Warhol and nearly killed him. The demands were: an appearance on the Johnny Carson show, publication of the SCUM (Society for Cutting Up Men) manifesto in the *Daily News*, $25,000 in cash and a promise that he would make her a star. This got her bail raised. She might conceivably have had better luck if she hadn't pulled her act on the day that Robert Kennedy was murdered in Los Angeles. When Ultra Violet asked Andy the stupid question 'Why were you the one to get shot?' he replied brilliantly: 'I was in the wrong place at the right time.' This ad-man's gift for tags and phrases, perhaps honed by his trainee period as a successful and gifted commercial illustrator, impelled him to propose a tele-vision series, to be hosted by himself and called *Nothing Special*. I would have watched it. (Updike wrote somewhere that the show was one of Warhol's few unfulfilled ambitions.) I'm also not yet bored by the line about fame and however many minutes it is. How many throwaway lines come back to you, perforce, as you read today's newspapers? As I write, there is to be a party at Mr Chow's on West 57th Street, to celebrate the publication of an index to the *Diaries*. (Mr Chow's is mentioned twenty-nine times — the most of any restaurant.) With the appearance of this piece of guerrilla free enterprise, nobody need *read* the book at all. They can just use it as it was meant to be used. The magazine that came up with the idea is called *Fame*, which avoids any ambiguity — at least Warhol's first job was on a magazine modestly called *Glamor*. The invitations to the party have a space for the page number on which the invitee is given a mensh. There is no such thing as notoriety in the United States these days, let alone infamy. Celebrity is all, and Warhol saw it coming even before Tom Wolfe did.

Ultra Violet, to whom I keep on giving menshes, has asked all who were seduced and profaned by the sixties to join her in repudiating drugs, sex and parties. She urges Scripture, and tells us of her dreams. ('Once I broke through to acceptance of God, my immune system rallied and healing began.') She is a drag now, and seems to have been a drag then. But she does tell us something of a topic which gets more and more absorbing as one thumbs through the post-Warhol texts. Did he abolish the concept of the fake? For example, his book *Popism*, also edited by the tireless Pat Hackett, came out in 1980. Ultra Violet told Andy that it contained several errors. He replied: 'Not my fault. I never wrote it, never read it.' She also tells us — perhaps as part of her born-again repentance campaign, but somehow very believably — that:

> authentication is at best nebulous for Andy's silk-screen works, especially since Andy's non-touch policy sometimes disinclined him to put his signature on a canvas. It became normal practice for anyone who happened to be around to sign his (Andy's) name on 'Brillo Boxes', 'Marilyns', various versions of the soup cans. I myself took my turn at signature duty. Gerard, in charge of all the mechanics of the Pop production, ordered the silk-screens, stretched the canvases, applied the screens, mopped on the paint, and, on various occasions, wrote Andy's name.

'Mopped on the paint.' That gives me the same petty thrill as I feel when a wine-label scandal reveals that oenophiles have been savouring the residue of old umbrella-handles and banana skins. Not that even the Factory world can quite dispense with the idea of the genuine. Dorothy Podber, a survivor of the fifties avant-garde, fired a gun in Andy's studio long before Valerie Solanis did. But she only aimed at Warhol before swivelling to the stack of Marilyn Monroe portraits against the wall and pressing the trigger. As Ultra Violet breathily recalls: 'she put her pistol back, pulled on her gloves, gathered her followers, and left. This stylish event was regarded as an art happening.' As she also recalls: 'the bullet penetrated six paintings, which are now called "shot-through Marilyns". They are more valuable than ordinary Marilyns because they are indisputably authentic.' In the context, an odd choice of word.

Postmodernism *à la* Warhol or, indeed, *à la* Baudrillard is very often another way, as if we needed one, of saying 'I don't care' or 'Who cares?' or 'It doesn't matter'. Nothing fresh or original or worthwhile is likely to happen again. A perfect instance of the power of this narcotic but gripping thought occurs in *Loner at the Ball*, when Warhol decides to take a few friends to see his movie *Sleep* at a downtown cinema. The film, which shows John Giorno slumbering almost motionless for six hours, is technically unwatchable. On arrival at the cinema, the party is told that it is empty and that the movie has started, but they press on undaunted. Inside they find the solitary figure of John Giorno, star of the flick, fast asleep. One could hardly get more affectless than that.

London Review of Books, January 1990

8
CRITICAL RESOURCES

SIDING WITH RUSHDIE*

Just as the Muslim world was vibrating to the 'insult' visited on the Prophet Muhamad (Peace Be Upon Him) by an Anglo-Pakistani fictionist of genius and renown, the British and American mass audience was thrilling to the reborn version of David Lean's *Lawrence of Arabia*. The movie, which is the closest investigation most English people have made of their country's long, intense, misunderstood encounter with Islam, is actually rather touching in its attempt to 'understand' the other by means of epic romance. To the fatalism of a subject population, who are serfs to a Turkish empire and captives of a holy book they cannot read, Lawrence cheerily and repeatedly intones: 'Nothing is written.' By this he does not intend any insult to the lapidary, but only a bracing 'Western' injunction against surrender. Yet Islam *means* surrender. The very word is like the echo of a forehead knocking repeatedly on the floor, while the buttocks are proferred to the empty, unfeeling sky in the most ancient gesture of submission and resignation.

In Faisal's tent, eager to conscript his feudal retinue to the service of the Crown, Lawrence waits cunningly until the mullah has spoken a few verses, and then completes the recitation himself. A polite monarch inquires how he knows the Koran, and asks: 'Are you not, then, loyal to England?' Comes the reply: 'To England, and to other things.' The Arabs trust Lawrence for long enough to be betrayed by the Sykes–Picot agreement, and in effect to witness the opening of the present phase of the Middle Eastern calamity. But those mottoes — 'Nothing is written' and 'To England, and to other things' — have now become the blazon of a dozen contradictory banners and the thread, however imperfectly followed, in a labyrinth of competing interpretations. Pluralism, ethnicity, fundamentalism, blasphemy, tolerance, bigotry, enlightenment — there are enough pious key words in play to make anybody spew. An early duty, in the face of this array of sanctimony, is to the obvious. We are not disputing the case of Salman Rushdie because it reminds us of everything else under the sun. We are disputing it because it is unique and unprecedented. I write it down in a verse, before it gets buried in glossary: 'Salman Rushdie was publicly condemned to death, and his murder made a holy obligation upon millions of true believers, by the theocratic and political head of a foreign state, because he had written a work of fiction which allegedly profaned an illiterate seventh-century visionary who had lived on what is now the Arabian peninsula. With the call for Rushdie's death — the *fatwah*, or edict — came a bounty, fluctuating in its value according as to whether the

*Review of Lisa Appignanesi and Sara Maitland (eds), *The Rushdie File*, London 1989; Fay Weldon, *Counter-Blasts No 4: Sacred Cows*, London 1989; Timothy Brennan, *Salman Rushdie and the Third World: Myths of the Nation*, London 1989.

successful assassin was or was not a Muslim. Paradise was promised to any believer dying in the attempt. The contract also covered those "involved in the publication" of the novel.'

In the face of this ukase, which amounts to a life sentence as well as a death sentence on a reflective, autonomous individual, no wonder that people change the subject and take refuge in precedent or analogy. It's natural to do so when faced with a challenge that is so alarmingly singular. Yes, there are other death squads and assassins and proscriptions and archipelagos and all the rest of it. Yes, there are existing campaigns devoted to the release of so-and-so and the freedom of this-and-that. But when last did a head of government *claim* to be soliciting the murder of a citizen of another country, for pay, for the offence of literary production? I have heard great argument about it and about, from reminiscences of the Trotsky assassination to Christopher Hill's recall of the Papal incitement against Gloriana, but evermore came out by the same door as in I went. The Salman Rushdie case *has* no analogue and no precedent. Once that is established, it is fair to ask how it could have, considering the confrontation that, in micro and macro form, it partially represents. Here, it is okay to introduce a few ironies. Until the *fatwah* issued by the late Ayatollah Khomeini (a *fatwah*, we learn, that may be nonrescindable in consequence of his death) anyone who disliked or resented Muslim immigrants in Britain axiomatically disliked Salman Rushdie, who was — and is — one of their stoutest defenders. Until the *fatwah*, the secular left had been reconsidering some of its positions on the anti-Shah revolution in Iran, and at about the time of the *fatwah* the secular right had begun entertaining doubts about the sturdy, incorrigible Afghan *mujahidin*. Everywhere from the West Bank to Bradford those who once explained Islamic fury by easy reference to prevailing conditions and long-nurtured grievances were beginning to wonder if the damn thing didn't possess a hideously energetic life of its own.

But most of this was merely political, or reassuring and analytical. Here the Shia on the march; there the moderate influences: here the long-awaited Muslim 'awakening' in the Soviet southern republics; there the statesmanlike 'accommodation' of the Muslims of Saudi Arabia and Pakistan. There seemed always someone to do business with. And then, suddenly, a near-unanimity about a defenceless novelist, with the 'hard-liners' calling for his immediate dispatch to hell and the 'moderates' like the Saudis confining themselves — as Timothy Brennan usefully reminds us — to no more for now but a holy war or *jihad* against the school known as 'literary modernism'.

Of course religion is a thing of this world rather than the next, and there have always been, since well before *Greenmantle*, 'their' Muslims and 'ours'. Nothing is more ironic than to hear certain liberals and leftists identify Islam and the muezzin with the cry of the oppressed and with anti-imperialism. In British India, Nigeria, Cyprus and elsewhere, the favoured colonial minority was always the Islamic one. Perhaps this was because, as Paul Scott has one of his characters say in *The Raj Quartet*, the British 'prefer Muslims to Hindus (because of the closer affinity that exists between God and Allah than exists between God and the Brahma)'. The character is Harry Coomer or Hari Kumar, ground between the two worlds of the subcontinent and the English greensward. Transplanted to (or is it from?) the mother country and educated at 'Chillingborough' — Salman Rushdie was at Rugby and writes bitingly about the experience in *The Satanic Verses* — Kumar is a misfit in England, and back in Raj-dominated India is grossly treated by a prospective employer: 'You some sort of comedian or something? ... let me tell you this. I don't like bolshie black laddies on my side of the business.' He has no recourse but to become a scribbler, at first for the *Mayapore Gazette*, where he astounds the sahibs by his command of English (Rushdie had to get his start in an advertising agency). In neither world is he considered to be quite sixteen annas to the rupee.

The tension now expressed is not in the first place the usual British resentment of upstarts or hybrids or surrogates. It is the feeling that such a person is necessarily unhappy, incongruous, deracinated. Much depends here upon who is being sorry for whom. Why should the British, who ostensibly worked so hard for the fusion of Indian and English, so much pity — no, *patronize* — the bastard child of the union? And why do the mullahs of Yorkshire so much resent a brilliant pupil who has the *Angrez* themselves waiting upon his dexterous and subtle annexation of their greatest and most treasured resource — their language? It can't just be the politicization of religion, because Rushdie long ago argued by allegory that religion itself can never define a culture or a nationality. In *Shame* he revived the embarrassing but unarguable truth — that the Pakistani Army had done to incipient Bangladesh what even the most fervent emissaries of the Imam could barely dream of doing to him. West Pakistan — 'the west wing' of the novel — was so cruel to the east wing that it set a standard of memory and atrocity even for the Vietnam generation. Later outrages have eclipsed the memory, but they ought not to occlude the fact that Pakistan was the first deliberated modern Islamic republic, that it was created by the British Empire, and that it showed impressively that Islam cannot found the basis of a state or a civil society.

You could object that *religion* alone cannot perform this historic function, and you would be right. But then you would come up against the new and perverse practice of reverse ecumenicism. The reverse ecumenical professes a sort of clerical trade-unionism, where a pretence is made that an injury to one is an injury to all. Those who once denounced each other, and slaughtered each other, are now bound together through an exhausted, insipid, pragmatic opportunism, which boils down to saying that any religion is better than none. See how the cartel of spiritual oligopolies reacted to the publication of *The Satanic Verses*. His Holiness the Pope, the Archbishop of Canterbury, the Chief Rabbi of Israel — all those who compete for the franchise of monotheism — had a solemn declaration to make about the importance of — of all things — tolerance. But cool words like 'tolerance' and 'respect' made their appearance along with older and more minatory terms like 'blasphemy'. It turned out that 'tolerance' and mutuality extended only as far as other monotheists, and not to sceptics, let alone unbelievers. This degradation of concepts caused many an uneasy grimace among the soft-secular, for whom the only commandment is that 'one' — rather than 'thou' — shall not be caught being 'offensive' or 'insensitive' where religion is concerned.

And it was here, rather than in the reflex policy of the religious cartels, that the hypocritical and euphemistic aspect of the Rushdie affair disclosed itself. Reverse ecumenicism gave way to indiscriminate 'sensitivity'. There are, as it happens, many people who regard the origin of the universe as, according to excellent evidence and disinterested inquiry, a black hole. They (we) do not choose to make a black hole an object of worship. They (we) worry about those who do; most especially about those who defend *their* black hole interpretation with thermonuclear devices. They (we) regard all religions as perfectly equal and pardonable revelations of the same fallacy. God did not create man in his own image; man created God in his/her own image. There is only one humanity, but an infinite number of gods. This position may be a mistaken one, but it took a while to evolve and is congruent with quite a lot of what is observable, demonstrable and thinkable. It is, of course, based upon the principle of doubt and revision, and doesn't conform very well to what might be wished by those who yearn for immortality. In theory, therefore, the atheist is proof against the puerile idea of 'giving offence' or inflicting 'deep hurt' about such a question as the origin of species or the cosmos. But, as a humanist, he or she may be offended by man-made authority when it comes in the disguise of the divine. The essence of the Rushdie affair was put to me unintentionally when I was leaving a meeting in his defence in New York City and found myself drawn aside by a radio interviewer for a Muslim station. She had two questions: 'Is nothing sacred?' and 'Where do you draw the line?' The second question might have been coming anyway, but it resulted from my answer to the first, which was, obviously, no. Nothing is sacred. Nothing is written. Only doubt is scientific. Very probably, only doubt is truly artistic. Holy writ may indeed be employed for literary purposes. Holy writ is probably fiction, of a grand sort, to begin with. In the beginning was, if not the black hole, at least the author. If the argument from design asks where the author came from, it must go on asking who created the author of the author until the whole utility of the question dissolves.

As to 'where do you draw the line', I'm not so dumb as not to recognize the father and mother and author of the trick question. One could have answered, even as a foe of all forms of censorship, that the line be drawn at broadcast incitements to murder, especially if the incitement was compounded by the naked offer of cash incentive. Yet, even though the First Amendment might not protect such a definition of 'speech', I would not have jammed or tried to censor that broadcast. It was, though, the false issue of line-drawing that compromised some of our most distinguished 'intellectuals' and noise-makers, many of whom quite obviously found Rushdie's book more 'offensive' than the Ayatollah's lethal anathema, or at least no less so. Faced with *that* astonishing reaction, boring old Voltairean precepts seemed less stale and over-rehearsed. There were radicals, kin to Mr Rushdie, who reprobated him strongly for his lack of closeness to the masses and the concrete. And there were reactionaries, long hostile to him as a person — the 'bolshie black laddie' — who deplored his want of respect for Third World susceptibilities, and (while they were about it) his ability to make money by his pen.

The 'left' critique of Rushdie was — and is — more interesting because it had to *prove* more than the conservative one. (The latter, not merely a knee-jerk objection to blasphemy, however if at all defined, rested itself on a more general bias against making waves and exciting the vulgar.) In the mind of many socialists, cultural relativism has become such an anchor of certainty and principle that it would be physically painful to haul it in. Listen to John Berger, tending the authentic mulch of pig earth and keeping his ear close to his own well-manured ground, as he instructed the readers of the *Guardian* on 25 February:

> The Rushdie affair has already cost several human lives and threatens to cost many, many more.... The affair is about two books. One, the Koran, is a book which has helped, and still helps, many millions of people to make sense of their lives and their mortality. The other, Salman Rushdie's novel, is a rather arrogant fiction about playing at being God and would, in my opinion, have been forgotten in a few years had it not provoked the present furore. The first is a book about responsibility, the second is a story about irresponsibility. The two books at this moment represent two notions of the sacred. The Koran is a sacred book in the most traditional and profound sense of the term, a text dictated to the Prophet by the Archangel Gabriel, an emissary of the One and Only God. Rushdie's book has become a sacred cause to the European world because it represents the artist's right to freedom of expression. In Europe, as has been pointed out before, art has replaced religion. (Art is also a commodity. Rushdie was paid a £850,000 advance for his book.) How to reconcile these two notions of the sacred?

Well, to answer Berger's perfunctory question, it seems that we reconcile them by counting one as literally sacred and the other as profane, irresponsible, avaricious. Berger went on to remember, not a minute too soon, to deplore the death-incitement (I yearn to read a piece against Rushdie that does *not* contain such a disclaimer), before lapsing into self-pity: 'I do not expect many to listen to arguments like mine. The colonial prejudices are still too ingrained.'

There has long been a Berger scale for fatuity, but that piece, even in the judgement of seasoned seismographers, went clear off the graph. Was this, for a start, the same Ayatollah as the one who had gone pimping with Ronald Reagan and Oliver North in order to arm the colonial mercenaries in Nicaragua, who had been so eloquently opposed by Salman Rushdie in *The*

Jaguar Smile? Or was it the other Ayatollah, the genial friend of Kurdistan? The ally of the women of Persia? Who but an effete Westerner would point the finger at Khomeini's use of children as mine-sweepers, or his insistence on the veil, or his pathology about the Baha'i and the Jews? At all costs, one must avoid judging *les damnés de la terre* by 'our' standards. Incidentally, what *are* our standards? How nice it would be to think that Europe and Europeans are defined by their attachment to art and free expression, as Mr Berger, for the first time in his life, seems to maintain. Conversely, I seem to know a number of Iranians who are for the emancipation of women, against the repression of Kurdistan, against the idea of theocracy and in favour of national independence for their proud and much put-upon country. Many of these Iranians fought for these same ideas against the Shah and his Anglo-American backers. It would be impudent of me to say that such people — many of whom took great risks to defend Rushdie — were imposing 'Western' or colonial ideas on Iran. That would be an odd view in any case, since the historically pro-Shah and pro-colonial forces, as represented by politicians like Geoffrey Howe and George Bush and business spokesmen like Lord Shawcross, have found themselves able to resist the allure of *The Satanic Verses* and even to anticipate with a writhe of embarrassment its effect on the tender parts of the Ayatollah.

Anyway, when it comes to values you can't beat people who really believe in the traditional prescriptive stuff. Berger's bleat drew a warm seconding letter from the reliably reactionary Elizabeth Jane Howard and her friend Sybille Bedford. If Berger had slyly blamed all the mayhem on to 'the Rushdie affair', these two went him one better in the business of culpability. The violence was the result not of some artfully displaced 'affair' but of the existence of Rushdie himself: 'The consequences of his choice are no longer private: the people already dead, the hostages in Iran, his own family and the prospect of other innocent people being threatened surely means that he needs to make a moral decision on their behalf?' No mystery here about the roots of atavistic violence. No mystery even about the whereabouts of the hostages: Howard and Bedford say they are in Iran, when all the time we had suspected they were in Lebanon. In any event, the responsibility for all this is clearly Rushdie's. It was by his 'choice' that all this bitterness tore loose. I remember, during the hot days of the Rushdie controversy, that the wised-up remark 'He knew what he was doing all right' was most often made by those with least knowledge of, or curiosity about, the Islamic revolution. I use that last term generally, despite the fact that the campaign against *The Satanic Verses* has confounded all those who write and speak about 'Islam' or 'fundamentalism' without distinction. How did the bizarre campaign against this novel begin?

At least in so far as it was a campaign of physical violence or the threat of same, it originated in South Africa. I can't think how the nervous 'progressives' have missed this salient point. India and Saudi Arabia had already banned the novel by the autumn of last year, while forgoing the demand that the author's head should also be forfeit. (Nobody, incidentally, came forward to say that Rushdie was also the person responsible for the banning.) But it was only when he was embarking for Johannesburg that the physical-force faction took a hand. He had been invited to give the keynote address at an anti-censorship conference organized by the *Weekly Mail*, a doughty anti-apartheid organ, and had cleared himself in advance — what with the writers' and artists' boycott and all — with the African National Congress. His subject, impossibly ironic if you agree to stay with the ironies, was to be 'Wherever they burn books they also burn people' — an attribution to Heine well suited to the apartheid state.

But it wasn't the Afrikaners who lit the pyre. The Muslim establishment in South Africa destroyed the anti-apartheid and anti-censorship conference by announcing a 'holy war' against Rushdie and by threatening the *Weekly Mail* with violence. Not only was the paper itself thereupon closed by government fiat the same week as Rushdie was due to arrive (he prudently cancelled), but the regime also banned *The Satanic Verses* under the well-worn Section 47 (2)(b) of the Publications Act. It's relatively rare for the apartheid state to try and oblige any of its non-white minorities in this way, but as Nadine Gordimer pointed out, the Islamic leadership does agree to sit in the phoney 'Chamber' that is reserved for those who are not quite white and yet not African. I suppose John Berger might find something colonial in Ms Gordimer's cynical suspicion of collusion here, and I feel almost ethnocentric in pointing out that many of the *Weekly Mail* staff are Jewish, and so is Nadine Gordimer, and that this fact, too, featured in the Islamic diatribes. (It's also been known to feature in the Afrikaner supremacist press.) Mind you, Idi Amin represented himself as a spokesman for the oppressed Muslims of Uganda, and please think of the 'deep hurt' caused by attacks on him in the Western press until he sought refuge in Saudi Arabia.

Earlier on, I mentioned the intellectual itch to change the subject away from free speech versus religious absolutism. This was very marked as a tendency in the United States, where the neo-conservative school could not sublimate its glee. Rushdie had written a book of nonfiction which offered critical but decided support to the Nicaraguan revolution. He had also been eloquent about the rights of the ever-relegated Palestinians. What more natural, when he was threatened with assassination by contract, than to jubilate about a terrorist-symp who had been caught in his own logic? I counted some ten newspaper and magazine columns from the Podhoretz school, all making this same point in the same words — demonstrating the impressive Zhdanovite discipline that is the special mark of the faction. All of them seemed to regard the affair as some sort of heavenly revenge for the sin of radical promiscuity; much as they have represented the AIDS crisis as a vengeance on sixties morality. The ethical nullity of these positions never got beyond mere gloating, and will one day help to illustrate the essential distinction between irony and brutish sarcasm. But at least it vented hatred on Rushdie for being anti-colonial rather than colonial.

Meanwhile, the trail lit in Johannesburg had been crackling merrily away. In Bradford, it ignited those forces who want apartheid in the petty sense of separate schools for Muslims and separate schools for boys and girls. How cheering that people can point to such unarguable precedents for their demands, drawn from Ulster and Strathclyde and enforced by law and custom for better-born sectarians. Shift the scene to Karachi, where the Jamaat-Islami Party had just gone down to humiliating defeat in an election which, if Jamaat Islami had had any say in the matter, would never have taken place. Casting about for a salve to emulsify the injury of defeat by a Jewish-backed female socialist (as they both thought and wrote of Ms Bhutto), the fundamentalists took their prompting from South Africa and England. Ungratefully marching on the very US Embassy that had until recently been the prop and stay of their patron General Zia, they managed to draw the first blood. It was the day following the deaths in Karachi that the Ayatollah, several months after the publication of the novel, decided to remind people that nobody — *nobody* — could trump him when it came to defending the faith.

So here is the intriguing problem for reverse ecumenicists and recent Third Worldists and sudden Islamologists and those afflicted by *folie Berger*. In all instances, the 'Islamic' furore has been about something else than — or something more than — religious susceptibility. Tribal jousting in South Africa; a last stand against assimilation in Bradford; a revenge for political eclipse in Pakistan; a last gasp of a frustrated and politically superseded purism in the holy city of Persia. In each case, what Americans call 'the agenda' was determined by rather more than the hermeneutic. Yet once allow these unresolved material dilemmas to define themselves as spiritual, and you get liberal guilt and secular confusion in precisely that wrong apposition for which the extreme conservatives are hoping. Why do *you* think that Peregrine Worsthorne, Paul Johnson and Auberon Waugh are, *pro tem*, in favour of the mosque against secular, brown activists of the Rushdie type?

It is depressing to notice how much of the commentary in this matter depends on the unstated false antithesis between 'the West' and 'Islam'. Some parts of the Muslim world, after all, experienced the presentiments of science and innovation well before what Europeans call 'the Enlightenment'. Other parts of that world got modernism and the Industrial Revolution second hand, as it were, and in the neck in the form of colonialism. As a partial result of that, several former metropolitan powers now experience Islam as a phenomenon of immigrant, uneasy newcomers. This leads to a superiority/inferiority complex on both sides, with many Muslims appalled at the amorality and anomie of the 'host' society, and some of the 'hosts' thunderstruck by the transmission of ritual slaughter, dowries and other Judaeo-Christian relics via the medium of that other monotheism. When Christianity was as old as Islam is now, the Inquisition and the Thirty Years War were still well in its future. On the other hand, it did not have the example of religious toleration in front of it, as fundamentalists of all descriptions now do. Since the migrant is the vector, the register, the sensor of all this contradictory experience and synthesis, it becomes especially important to uphold Rushdie the individual as well as Rushdie the practitioner of cosmopolitan fiction. His decision to occupy and interpret the political and fictional space between two or three worlds is an important resource for both 'host' and 'guest', if they would only see it.

A number of Muslims actually can see it, even if the condescending Western Islamologists (CWI) cannot. The immediate difficulty with the CWIs is that they granted Khomeini his first premiss by assuming that there is something called 'Islam' or 'the Muslim world': something undifferentiated and amorphous that can, like an individual, be 'offended'. What the CWI school fails to notice, or even consider, is that Islam is quite possibly poised on the cusp of its first Reformation, and that this Reformation will be complex and painful precisely because it originates in the displacement of people and values caused by the confusion between modernity and empire. Persia, for example, was a semi-colony of the British until 1953, when it chose a reformist and nationalist regime under Mossadeq. The British enlisted American help in the forcible removal of this modernizer and in his replacement by the Shah. At that time, there was a coincidence of interest between the oil companies and the ayatollahs, because the religious leadership also detested Mossadeq for his secularism. It took decades of Western promiscuity and pillage, indulged by and through the pseudo-dynasty of the Pahlavis, before the theocracy decided against modernism and internationalism *tout court*. This process was not Koran-guided, but was an improvised response to various painful buffetings from the material and external world — as were the disintegration of Pakistan, the decline of OPEC and other phenomena lazily attributed to the capacious generality 'Islam'.

In a brave and spirited essay in the Summer 1989 number of *Grand Street*, Akeel Bilgrami takes upon himself the job of explicating 'moderate Muslim opinion'. He discovers it in a state of crisis and disorder, of the sort that often precedes a new synthesis. His is the essay one had been waiting to read. Written from a perspective that even a CWI would have to respect as genuinely Muslim, it confronts co-religionists with their own contradictions:

> One cannot argue that the Rushdie affair really arises from the conflicting values of the West (more or less officially committed as it is to freedom from censorship) and Islam. As some writers, including Muslim spokesmen in the West, have pointed out, a *world* religion has been attacked by a writer who was born into the religion and wishes to tell the *world* about its failure to cope with the *world*.

Thus — to interpret Bilgrami for a second — the Muslim extremists have, in two vital senses, demanded the impossible. They have asked the slightly lazy but none the less conscious heirs of the Enlightenment to adopt, not the practice (which never dies out, as we know to our cost), but the *principle* of censorship. And they have demanded, for themselves, the smashing of a mirror in which they might glimpse their own reflection. Never mind for a minute the desirability of these demands, or of feeble demands like John Berger's for the banning of 'more or new' editions. It's the *impossibility* of undoing or unpublishing Rushdie that arrests the attention.

This is why it would be nice to hear more about principles and less about ruffled feelings. What thoughtful person has not felt the hurt expressed by the Jews over some performances of *The Merchant of Venice*? A whole anthology of black writing exists in the United States, protesting with quite unfeigned horror about the teaching of *Huckleberry Finn* in the schools, for the good and sufficient reason that the book employs the word 'nigger' as natural. A mature and sensitive response to such tenderness of feeling and consciousness of historic wrong would run much like this, and could be uttered by a person of any race or religion.... We know why you feel as you do, but — too bad. Your thinness of skin, however intelligible, will not be healed by the amputation of the literary and theatrical and musical canon. You just have to live with Shakespeare and Dickens and Twain and Wagner, mainly because they are artistically integral but also, as it happens, because they represent certain truths about human nature. Think for a second. Would prejudice diminish with the banning of Shylock? Concern for the emotions of others cannot license a category mistake on this scale, let alone an *auto da fe*. It was *autos da fe*, if you recall, that were the problem in the first place.

Fay Weldon has no urgent quarrel with the 'free speech first' position. The difficulty with her 'CounterBlast' is that it, too, imports a lot of extraneous matter into the argument, does so before it has made up its mind, and thus fails to arrive at or to argue for any position. *L'affaire Rushdie* reminds her of an astonishing number of 'things', as if the mere pronunciation of his name had become a trigger for word-association or Rorschach blotting. Page Three of the *Sun* (mind you, what *can* one say of a culture that now knowingly capitalizes the words 'Page Three'?); the crappiness of the NHS; computer games; abortion; a trip she once took to Russia; the niceties of feminist precedence — all of these are thrown into the unsorted box of the insoluble and the problematic. The whole is punctuated by the repetitive, rather despairing incantation: 'Sackcloth and Ashes'. At one point, however, Ms Weldon does declare herself as out of sorts with what might be called the consensus of the okay:

> It's ... pleasanter, easier, to be seen on the side of ethnic minorities, all in favour of the multi-cultural, too idle to sort out the religious from the racial, from the political; too frightened of being labelled white racist, élitist, to interfere. Because the best have become frightened of labels; feel they must act and think together: are too frightened of the disapproval of their peers to speak the truth: too abandoned, for a full ten years, to a cosy general disapproval of anything, everything the current government does to be much use to anyone: slaves to liberal orthodoxy. And the black feminists, too put-upon by the black brothers, who insist that any white interference is by definition racist ...

This is confusion raised almost but not quite to the level of eloquence, with its Yeatsian echo of the best and the worst and passion and conviction finally quite drowned in faint moans. At points, it even takes on a tinge of the *Schadenfreude* of the Tory rags and the Podhoretz school: 'See where your permissiveness has got you.' It also contains the ghost or germ of a very dangerous false antithesis — this time between a commitment to pluralism and a commitment to free expression. Imagine the havoc that might result from such antagonism if it became general. Have 'the best' really contributed to such an outcome?

In many ways, Weldon is too pessimistic. A feature of the Rushdie controversy has been the limited but definite emergence of the sort of critical faction envisaged by Bilgrami. This faction is not composed merely of the relatively well-placed, like Tariq Ali and his redoubtable colleagues at Bandung Productions, or Aziz Al-Azmeh at the University of Exeter. It is possessed of a rank and file, including some of the very black feminists whose position Weldon so unfairly represents and who have formed *ad hoc* committees such as Women Against Khomeini. But never mind the sex, look at the politics. As Homi Bhabha put it at the rally of 'Black Voices in Defence of Salman Rushdie': 'We are embattled in the war between the cultural imperatives of Western liberalism, and the fundamentalist interpretations of Islam, both of which seem to claim an abstract and universal authority.' After this formal start, Bhabha went on to pose the central question: 'If there were no doubt, no confusion or conflict, would religion or literature have any place in our lives? Would *The Satanic Verses* have been written?' In other words, it *isn't* 'pleasanter, easier, to be seen on the side of ethnic minorities', but it is a very absorbing and demanding and rewarding *responsibility* to be 'on their side' as they and we confront this question in contrasting ways. And let's not forget that one of the originators of the process of reasoning and combat and exchange that this necessitates was — until his forced removal from the scene — Rushdie himself. The Muslim leadership, seeking to set a term to the education of their own community (at least they don't call it a 'flock'), may have succeeded only in giving that inevitable process an unanticipated spin. All over the country and the world, young Muslim men and women whose names we do not know are wrestling with the heretical thoughts that have been intruded into real life. Good.

Elsewhere in her pamphlet, Weldon shyly and obliquely proposes that perhaps the Bible *is* a little more forgiving and elastic than the Koran, before going on to suggest that we adopt the American 'uniculturist' system. It may not be obvious at first sight, to English readers, how self-contradictory is this position. Leave aside, for the moment, the fact that the Old Testament contains the explicit warrant for slavery, genocide and witch-burning, and that the New Testament contains the justification for passivity in the face of same. (Yes, I know, there are other supposedly more redeeming passages. So, is this stuff the word of God or isn't it?) More to the point, the American Founding

Fathers decided on a 'wall of separation' between Church and state, *whether the Bible was true or not*. In other words, religious and even Christian though many of them were, they wanted to insure against any future religious demagogy and opportunism, and *for that purpose* counted their own faith as one among many. This essential and unprecedented maturity is what marks them off from their forerunners and their successors. I can well remember the shock expressed by many Americans, in principle sympathetic to Rushdie and to his English defenders, when the *New York Times* informed them that the United Kingdom had a blasphemy law that protected only one religion. The most doltish student in the most backward civics class in Grand Rapids could tell you that such a law was flat-out un-Constitutional. This might seem a long way round to the identification of the Weldon error, but it is of some comfort to know that in the land of the holy huckster and the fundamentalist big-mouth the law still states unambiguously that religious pluralism and a secular state amount to the same concept. Given Mrs Thatcher's generally uncritical admiration for all things American, it's noticeable that she has never been able to summon the gusto for this particular transatlantic import.

The Weldon error can, of course, partially license John Berger and (though his articles were much more nuanced and careful) David Caute in detecting post-colonial and ethnocentric bias among 'the best'. But how much does such concern affect the essential issue? The classic Voltairean injunction is a generous one: to defend to the death the rights of one with whom one utterly disagrees. Not by accident, this has achieved the status of a principle of civilization. Is there not an implied corollary — to defend to the death *one's own right* to uphold that other right? If valid, this would hold against all comers, most of all those who employed the threat of death as a weapon of first resort against the imagination. It would override all considerations, however valid, of the other fellow's feelings, even if those feelings were conditioned by genuinely deplorable experiences (Tsarism, the Versailles Treaty, colonialism, the Crusades).

How did the democratic West measure up to this affront, in the bicentennial of the Bastille? *The Rushdie File* is a convenient synopsis, culled mainly from Britain and the United States, of reactions from the thinking classes. Fourth Estate took over its publication when Collins reneged on the original commitment. Next to buckle were the printers, who ratted on their contract at the last moment. The book's main weakness is that it doesn't contain the Berger piece, or give much space to the anti-Rushdie school. Nor does it have Nadine Gordimer's revealing letter from the South African front. But its principal strength is that it does reprint a wide canvass of Muslim and Third World opinion. Its most lasting impression is created, at least for me, by its reproduction of the weasel words, pronounced with no conviction of rectitude or faith, by those who simply wanted a quiet life. The spring of 1989 ought to be remembered for its harvest of sorry evasions.

Do you recall President George Bush, self-styled Leader of the Free World, who had to be prodded into making any statement at all on the murder threat, and then said that he would hold his former hostage-trading partners in Iran responsible for any attacks 'against American interests'? As Susan Sontag said at the PEN meeting held in New York: 'We found this particularly maddening, since from the very beginning fundamental American interests were at stake: our Constitutional rights to write, publish, sell, buy and read books free of intimidation.' But the Bush subconscious (which really *is* colonial) translates 'interests' as tangibles — things like embassies or assets. If a like threat had been made against a corporation president, fleets would have been moved portentously around and White House briefers would have appeared gravely on the nightly news, pointing at maps and 'evaluating options'. In such a case, also, spokesmen for the shopkeeper style like Paul Johnson would not have gone on about the exorbitant cost of police protection, and we would instead have been lectured a good deal about the lessons of appeasement. Conservative eminences such as My Lords Dacre and Shawcross, who blithely accepted the Shah's repeated insults to the Muslim faithful (he styled himself 'Shadow of God', among other obscenities, while looting the treasury), would surely not have given such a high rating to the new-found sensitivities of other cultures. And we might have been spared the sight of Sir Geoffery Howe in the guise of literary critic, solemnly informing an Iranian audience via the BBC that he, too, found *The Satanic Verses* hurtful because it 'compares Britain with Hitler's Germany' — which it doesn't. That was the week when Mrs Thatcher herself came up with a minor classic of reverse ecumenicism by saying: 'We have known in our own religion people doing things which are deeply offensive to some of us and we have felt it very much. And that is what has happened in Islam.' *Our* religion! And one wonders which 'people'. Joyce? Kazantzakis? Perhaps not, since Roman Catholicism and Greek Orthodoxy are not really 'ours'. Spinoza and Luther are obviously far too exotic, as are Voltaire and Diderot for that matter. Still, it would be interesting to know which figure in the distinguished history of blasphemy and heresy 'Mrs Torture' did have in mind. Surely not her sheep-faced foe Dr Runcie, who deplored *The Satanic Verses* with the best of them?

The political Establishment has interests to protect and deals to make and weighty responsibilities to ponder. Those who live by language and ideas, not to say principles, have rather less excuse to temporize. *Raison d'état*, no doubt, impelled the political bosses of glasnost to seize the Rushdie moment by having high-level Soviet meetings with Rafsanjani. But the unofficial Soviet world, just emerging from decades of bullying and mendacity and being permitted its first independent PEN club, took the same opportunity to declare solidarity with Rushdie as one of its first orders of business. The contrast could hardly be better illustrated.

This is an all-out confrontation between the ironic and the literal mind: between every kind of commissar and inquisitor and bureaucrat and those who know that whatever the role of social and political forces, ideas and books have to be formulated and written by individuals. The unwavering defence of Salman Rushdie and his rights is therefore mandated, not just for those who believe in fair play for individual and minority rights, or for those who profess pluralism and tolerance, or for those who prefer scientific detachment to magic and superstition, but for those who suspect that all these things are interdependent. It is absurd for any one 'civilization' to claim this insight; the 'West' would not be the West if it had not persecuted Dreyfus and Galileo. That is why this confrontation has been fought out on every continent. It happens to be the occasion, in our time and place, for the traditional enmity between the imaginative and the literal to be dramatized. And, complex though it all is, it has elements of simplicity too. One must side with Salman Rushdie not because he is an underdog but because there is no other side to be on.

London Review of Books, October 1989

GOYA'S RADICAL PESSIMISM

Despite its many painterly glories and its bolts of brilliant humour and bitterness, the exhibition on 'Goya and the Spirit of Enlightenment' at the Metropolitan Museum of Art in New York City suffers from the appearance of having been edited to suit a liberal sensibility. There are plenty of satires on monarchy, clergy and stupidity — in one study, a grinning donkey proudly displays a family tree of long-eared, braying likenesses to show the purity of his pedigree — but the total effect is almost cheerfully defiant, like a successful lampoon. Whereas if one spends a few hours in the Prado in Madrid, which for so long consigned Goya's best work to an archive, the effect is one of sobering pessimism and occasional despair. Nothing could be more 'modern' than *The Disasters of War*, engraved with an almost sadistic attention to detail at a time when *Guernica* was still more than a century in the future.

One should never miss an opportunity to celebrate the Enlightenment or to mock priestcraft and the worship of mediocre princes and tycoons. And probably there has never been a finer vial of scorn than the one that Goya emptied so gracefully over the clowns and toadies and witch doctors who made up the Spanish 'restoration of traditional values'. In the *Caprichos*, the series that forms the centrepiece of this exhibition, Goya could hardly bring himself to represent such people as human. The etchings pullulate with freaks: depraved, slobbering bats and goblins and ghouls. It is not surprising that the Inquisition was so quick to try to repress them. The etching titled *The Sleep of Reason Brings Forth Monsters* is almost expressly intended to infuriate those who believe that evil spirits hover about us, bringing with them the necessity of the protection of Mother Church. Long before the Vienna school, also, Goya appears to have guessed at the latent connection between sexual repression and the other kinds. There is an awful lubricity and hypocrisy on the faces of his monks and friars, and a definite and felt relationship between those qualities and the uses of torture and slavery. Very little about the atrocities of our great twentieth century would have astonished this artist. The choice of the donkey as the prime symbol of stupidity is an intriguing and unsettling one, however. Goya's *burros* are everywhere, and it's clear that though they stand for the irredeemable and the benighted, they also represent in some measure their more traditional metaphoric counterpart, which is the common people, the millennial peasantry. It was a cliché of feudalism to say that it treated men like horses and horses like men; in the more rugged versions of this mode of production, such as we know the Spanish to have been, there were many serfs who would have been glad of the consideration that a property-owner lavished on a mule.

Goya was one of those who identified 'enlightenment' with privilege and refinement. He was, whatever his private opinions, a court painter. Moreover, he was one of a considerable group of Spaniards who could identify the cause of the Enlightenment only with the cause of France — which happened, at crucial times in his life, to be also the enemy of Spanish independence. He was not the first sympathizer of revolution to be accused of being, by way of his sympathy, both a snob and the agent *de facto* of a foreign power. This is what gives *The Disasters of War* and *The Third of May* their terrible quality. Many Spaniards, often the most humble, fought with desperate bravery and ferocity against a French presence which, at least in its proclaimed ideas, was more 'enlightened' than any native Spanish regime aspired to be. For Goya, who had factions to contend with and self-preservation to think about, this tension between country and cause was acute, and could in the end be solved only by voluntary exile in France. For him, the Spanish mob was at least as often an instrument of reaction as it was the cry of the oppressed. The frenzies of superstition and the occult, the great carnivals of cruelty and credulity that attended the witch trials of the Inquisition, were frequently the demonstration of authentic popular feeling.

In one of his albums, not represented in this exhibition, Goya shows a peasant groaning under the weight of a squat, bloated friar — and captions the picture: 'Will you never learn what you are carrying on your back?' He saw the rule of the unenlightened as a fraud in which the powerless colluded, and a form of sadomasochism in which they could be actively enlisted if things went sufficiently wrong. This is a prefiguration of modern fascism, evidently registered by a very lonely man who had finally to ask whether it was he who was mad, or everybody else. Lasting, too, are the pictures of individual rather than mass victims of authority. Their offences are detailed as they stand, appallingly meek, before the cowled figures of the Inquisition: *For Being a Jew*; *For Wagging His Tongue in a Different Way*; *For Discovering the Movement of the Earth*; *For Having Been Born Elsewhere*. In *For Being a Liberal?*, one of the most harrowing of these, Goya depicts a woman fettered by the neck and suggests the imminence of that special symbol of Spanish reaction, the *garrote*. Here outrage was being expressed by someone who saw no great hope for justice, and could bear witness against injustice only as a fortunate, if nervous, individual.

Goya did not idealize 'the people' and was more inclined to notice savagery than nobility in human nature. The 'human nature' argument has been allowed to waste a lot of liberal time, and keeps emerging as the subtext of contemporary arguments about crime, race, evil and other areas where reactionaries feel that the instinctive gives them the upper hand. It is the special achievement of Goya to have been a radical pessimist; to have forced our attention upon the base and the ghastly aspects of the human personality while not surrendering to them or ceasing to protest their official instatement. He had few illusions to lose – fewer, perhaps, than many liberals of today, whose optimism would have buckled if forced by a circumstance like that of Spain in 1812.

The Nation, June 1989

DEGENERATE ART

Describing a riot of vicious Oxford upper-class 'hearties' against weedy 'aesthetes' in his *Decline and Fall*, Evelyn Waugh depicted the mob as it 'tore up Mr. Partridge's sheets, and threw the Matisse into his water jug; Mr. Sanders had nothing to break except his windows, but they found the manuscript at which he had been working for the Newdigate Prize Poem, and had great fun with that.' The image came back to me after visiting an exhibition titled 'Degenerate Art', which detailed the fate of the avant-garde in Nazi Germany and made its way, via Los Angeles and Washington, around the country before moving on to Berlin. Here were paintings and sculptures that the Hitlerites themselves had once exhibited, like carcasses on hooks and without their cultural context, to gratify the philistinism of an outraged public. Even the word for art was placed in heavily sarcastic inverted commas (*Entartete 'Kunst'*) on the 1937 advertising posters, as if to confirm the opinion of any *Kleinburger* who has ever said: 'Call this art? My three-year-old could do better.' The original exhibition was the result of organized theft from German museums, presided over by something called the Ziegler Commission, which was appointed by Goebbels. Count Klaus von Baudissin was one of its members – he had distinguished himself by cleansing the museum in Essen of 'offensive' modern art – and it was his figure that reminded me of the saturnalia of yahooism sketched by Waugh. What fun they must have had!

When this exhibition opened in Washington last fall, the responsible newspapers and critics cautioned us at once. It was a fine and sobering thing, they said, to see the extent of pillage and desecration inflicted upon German culture by the National Socialists. No doubt some facile people would try to draw parallels between this and the mean, stupid campaign of Jesse Helms and others against the National Endowment for the Arts. On no account was one to fall for anything as propagandistic as that comparison. I went to the gallery with an almost prophylactic reluctance to make any such trite analogy. But the interesting thing is the near-perfect symmetry between the Nazi critique of modernism and the American chauvinist one. Once Goebbels had made his two general critiques of modern art – which were that it was 'incomprehensible and elitist' and that art criticism should therefore be forbidden because it stood in the way of a healthy public making up its own mind – and once Hitler at Nuremberg had warned that 'anyone who seeks the new for its own sake strays all too easily into the realm of folly', certain specific offences began to be defined. Among those were: 'Insolent Mockery of the Divine'; 'Deliberate Sabotage of National Defence'; 'An Insult to German Womanhood'; and 'Crazy at Any Price', a reflection of the Nazi loathing of psychoanalysis. By those criteria, Ludwig Gies's *Kruzifixus* carving, for example, was twice damned. First, because it threw Calvary in the spectator's face as few things had since the paintings of Grünewald; second, because it had been used as a First World War memorial in Lübeck.

Like most people who hadn't seen his work before, I came out of the exhibition wanting to know more about Otto Dix. His etching series *Der Krieg* alone was worth the price of the ticket, and a Berlin retrospective of his stuff, which I have since visited, is on its way to these shores and must be seen at any cost. Although he was associated with the Dada school, his work on the trenches and gas warfare makes even the most untutored critic say 'Goya' almost at once. It is interesting to learn that the young Konrad Adenauer, later the conservative hero of the Cold War, stopped the acquisition of Dix by a museum in Cologne as early as 1925. Like the rest of the German right – like the right at all times and in all places – Adenauer could not tolerate attacks on religion or anything else that might lead to the questioning of blood sacrifice in war. Once let that happen, and there would be free love and legal homosexuality. This overt and latent connection is present throughout the 'Degenerate Art' exhibition, which is particularly obsessed with 'family values' and gay life, and quite warrants the contemporary connection that we are not supposed to be making. So does the red sticker affixed by the Nazi philistines to many of the purloined artifacts. *Bezahlt von den Steuer-groschen des arbeit-enden deutschen Volkes*, it reads. 'Paid for by the taxes of the German working people.' Of course, there's nothing like the inciting phrase 'taxpayers' money'.

E.M. Forster gave two lectures on Nazism in which he correctly pointed out that you had to see what the Nazis had done to Germany if you wanted to imagine what they would do to 'us'. I had expected the exhibition to be heavily racist and nationalist, which it was, but not in the way I had anticipated. Most of the artists who were held up to hatred in the *Entartete 'Kunst'* campaign were, so to say, 'pure' Germans, accused of race treason by virtue of their attitudes to war, piety, morality and loyalty. Only six of the 112 artists in the exhibition were Jewish. Perhaps that's less surprising at a second consider-ation, since the author of the concept of *Entartung* ('Degeneration') in German and Western culture was Max Nordau, who published a windy and nasty book by that name in 1892. Ridiculing the Symbolists as much as the Pre-Raphaelites, Zola as much as Ibsen, Nordau asserted the superiority of the Germanic culture and wrote that a breakdown was coming, which meant: 'To the voluptuary, unbridled lewdness and the unchaining of the beast in man. To the withered heart of the egotist, disdain of all consideration for his fellow-men.... To the believer it meant the repudiation of dogma, the negation of a super-sensuous world. To the sensitive nature, yearning for aesthetic thrills, it meant the vanishing of ideals in art.' George Bernard Shaw wrote quite a lampoon on Nordau, mocking him and saying: 'This theory of his is, at bottom, nothing but the familiar delusion that the world is going to the dogs.' Dis-appointed as a cultural critic, Nordau went on to become, with Herzl, one of the founders of political Zionism. I have no idea how the Nazis reconciled their annexation of his concept of degeneracy, but it teaches one to beware strenuous art critics who know what they like.

The Nation, February 1992

JAMES BALDWIN: HUMANITY FIRST[*]

James Baldwin always described himself as a cat — sometimes, but not always, as a black cat — and the loveliness of the term falls happily on the inner ear amid the clanking of politicized euphemism ('African-American' has now supposely replaced 'black', which definitively deposed 'negro' and supplanted 'coloured') and the snarling of bigotry ('Nigger' is back in white inner cities these days). The word happened to fit Baldwin like a skin: silky, jumpy, contemptuously independent, poised for flight or fight, sensual and vain. Cats make things look easy, and have an exquisite sense of balance. Baldwin desperately desired to avoid or escape the strenuous, the boring and the fanatical aspects of life. Listen to this, from *Notes of a Native Son*:

> I hazard that the King James Bible, the rhetoric of the store-front churches, something ironic and violent and perpetually understated in Negro speech — and something of Dickens' love for bravura — have something to do with me today; but I wouldn't stake my life on it.

That was his tone at its best. When asked by tiring interviewers if he was a 'spokesman' for his people, he would repress a twinge of irritation at the dullness of the word and allow as how he preferred to be thought of as a 'witness'. He didn't mistake being laconic for being languid: several demotic versions of *carpe diem* — 'go for broke', 'let it all hang out' — recurred in his talk. He also adored Lambert Strether's counsel in *The Ambassadors*: 'Live all you can; it's a mistake not to.'

The Price of the Ticket may be the most apt of Baldwin's invariably well-wrought titles; better than *Blues for Mr Charlie, Just Above My Head, The Fire Next Time* and even, arguably, better than *If Beale Street Could Talk*. It expressed, as W.J. Weatherby details in this first-rate portrait, the mixture of apprehension and resignation that he registered when his feline balance was disturbed or invaded or upset. Much as he may have yearned for an emancipated, various and keen existence, he was to be thwarted by sexual self-doubt, racial hostility and ambiguity, a permanent credit squeeze, and the bottle. Ever conscious of the price of the ticket, he strove not to lapse into rancour or self-pity, and was aware of the lapses he did permit. He had a trick of self-knowledge, turning his big Louis Armstrong grin to himself as well as others:

> One of the reasons I had fought so hard after all was to wrest from the world fame and money and love. And here I was at thirty-two finding my notoriety hard to bear, since its principal effect was to make me more lonely; money, it turned out, was exactly like sex, you thought of nothing else if you didn't have it and thought of other things if you did.

*Review of W.J. Weatherby, *James Baldwin: Artist on Fire*, London 1990.

Though Baldwin's first published piece was a very assured article on Maxim Gorky in the *Nation*, it's curious to remember that Norman Podhoretz at *Commentary*, in commissioning him to write about the black Muslims, was present at the conception of what became *The Fire Next Time*. Podhoretz was to write of his later disappointment with Baldwin in *Doings and Undoings*, saying that 'Baldwin, who speaks so passionately of the white man's need for the courage to know the Negro and the heterosexual's need to know the homosexual, is himself unable to summon the courage to know and respect those who live in that other country usually designated as normal.' This seems especially inapposite on the evidence of Weatherby's portrait, which is full of telling and saddening episodes such as this one:

> 'I sometimes don't understand white people' — his voice rose, was the volcano about to erupt and Baldwin catch fire? — 'but I'm working on it, and I've always understood them a lot more than they've ever understood *me*.' He touched my hand impulsively. 'Don't take what I say personally.'

Baldwin's 'working on it' was part of the price of his ticket; a sense of obligation to humanity that axiomatically transcended colour. He might have preferred to do without anything so effortful as an obligation, but he did not wish to dodge it. To him, an admirer of Henry James's fineness of distinction, racialism and tribalism were, above all, offensively *stupid*. Hyacinth Robertson, in *The Princess Casamassima*, was never a real individual to the Princess, merely 'an opportunity for her to discharge a certain kind of rage, anguish and bitterness'. This line caught Baldwin's eye. He was faithful enough to the idea, and to James, to preface *Another Country* with a quotation from him, reprobating inarticulacy and inhumanity. There is a fashion, in American black studies these days, for running down the DWEM — the Dead White European Male who is held to dominate the study of literature and civilization. It would have been good to have Baldwin's caustic reaction to any such vulgar mauling of his James — the DWEM *par excellence*.

The origins of this new Third World philistinism can actually be sought and found in a book that was overrated at the time and has been unfairly forgotten since — Eldridge Cleaver's *Soul on Ice*. In this diatribe, Cleaver (who is now a Moonie and a Reaganite) lacerated Baldwin for a kink in his make-up 'which corresponds to his relationship to black people and to masculinity'. To be more direct about it, Cleaver accused Baldwin of 'the most gruelling, agonising, total hatred of the blacks, particularly of himself, and the most shameful, fanatical, fawning, sycophantic love of the whites'. Baldwin could have chosen to posture, to say that this lunge from a black ultra equalized the pained critiques of white ex-liberals and conferred the cherished status of impartial man in the middle. Instead, he was calm and ironic in his riposte, just as he had been in his earlier exchanges with Elijah Muhammad on racial theology. On that occasion, though he realized that 'a bill is coming that I fear America is not prepared to pay', he decided: 'I cannot make allegiances on the basis of colour.' There was a residuum of Harlem Christianity in this decision; of the boyhood faith and testimony that had once nearly taken him to the ministry. Baldwin had seen his stepfather (he was illegitimate as well, completing his outsiderhood) eaten up by the carcinoma of racial loathing and self-loathing. He was determined not to allow himself this toxic and destructive revenge. On his father's coffin he took an oath of sorts, saying: 'It had now been laid to my charge to keep my own heart free of hatred and despair.' The cadences of King James were in there somewhere, as they were — often mediated through the gospel song and the Spiritual — in titles like 'My Dungeon Shook' and *The Evidence of Things Not Seen*. E.L. Doctorow, one of his editors at Dial, here reveals that Baldwin would start from the title and then build the story or the narrative. There is an obvious debt to the notion of a text, allowing the elaboration of — well, not a sermon exactly, but sometimes an address or a call.

Biblical and religious imagery has its converse, of course. While it may license compassion or universalism, it is no less likely to warrant intolerance or feeble mysticism. In 1948, in *Commentary*, Baldwin wrote: 'just as society must have a scapegoat, so hatred must have a symbol. Georgia has the Negro and Harlem has the Jew.' In this mature observation he prefigured some of the squalid jealousy and resentment that was to arise between black and Jewish congregations. But he was to become less mature about this, saying in a lecture in 1983 that Jews were nothing more than 'white Christians who go to something called a synagogue on a Saturday rather than church on Sunday'. He spoke these words in a time of illness and creative frustration, and also a time of political meanness and sectarianism, but it's painful to have to make this excuse. At least it may be said that he can be shown, in such moments, to have been untrue to himself; catty rather than feline. Similarly, in *The Evidence of Things Not Seen* — a suspiciously elastic borrowing from St Paul's justification by faith — he had a maundering and almost paranoid tendency to compress the complex evidence of the Atlanta murders into a heroic, mythologized Georgia past. It just didn't work, and it embarrassed him and his friends. Weatherby's account recalls the impression one had at the time that Baldwin was running on empty. Not long before this, I had myself tried to talk to him about the growing crisis in the homosexual world, and yearned to hear his view of what would happen to Rufus and Vivaldo (of *Another Country*) in the age of unsafe congress. My disappointment was in his apparent reluctance to acknowledge that there might be a quandary here. Baldwin had been fond of Robert Frost's line about not being a radical when young for fear of becoming a conservative later. He avoided this wretched terminus, but in decline seemed like a repetitive and querulous version of his more youthful and daring self.

There were still bursts and bolts of the old form. During the making of a film in 1981, at the annual meeting of the African Literature Association in Gainesville, Florida, Baldwin's opening speech was interrupted by a vigilante voice over the public-address system. Sneering threats and abuse crackled into the hall. Baldwin froze *exactly* like a cat, and then, nervously but with

mounting courage and scorn, threw back the taunts of the anonymous inter-
jector. Chinua Achebe, who was present and made 'Jimmy' laugh by saying 'Mr
Baldwin, I presume' at their first meeting, was to say at his death:

> Principalities and powers do not tolerate those who interrupt the sleep of their
> consciences. That Baldwin got away with it for forty years was a miracle. Except
> of course that he didn't get away; he paid dearly every single day of those years,
> every single hour of those days. What was his crime that we should turn him into
> a man of sadness, this man inhabited by a soul so eager to be loved and to smile?

Black America seems these days to be leading an inward and grievance-
burdened life: preoccupied not just with ancient wrongs but with fresh resentments against newly arrived Koreans, Mexicans and Cubans, and exhibiting
various kinds of Cleaverite machismo. Baldwin's weary but strong voice,
insisting on certain human verities, is much missed. He never forgot that
racialism is America's great test, and he battled most of his life, not merely to
exhort other people to pass it, but to pass it himself.

Times Literary Supplement, June 1990

UPDIKE ON THE MAKE·

The snakelike sibilant is not rendered in scarlet here, even though its female
bearer is on the run from Puritan New England, has an ancestor named Prynne
and is (Updike's punning can be infectious) also a mother of Pearl. Her ex-
husband's signature, she writes in her note of desertion to him, has been
'branded into me, I wouldn't be surprised to see it burned into my flank if I
looked down'. Of her new man, the plausible guru Shri Arhat Mindadali, MA,
PhD ('the Arhat'), she records that his hypnotic speech has 'the strangest,
longest, "s"s'. Her letters are all signed with different names, or letters. To her
ex-husband she is 'S'; to her various bankers she is Sarah P. Worth (the P is for
Price and, as the ashramites might say, 'Ko Veda?' – who knows? – about price
and worth). To her banal contacts in the routine, literal-minded, material
world, who are respectively the dentist Dr Podhoretz and the unscrupulous,
manipulative chum Midge (and why not?), she is Sarah Worth. But for much
of the narrative she is Ma Prem Kundalini, an adept and initiate at the alternatively sinister and goofy ashram, established by the Arhat to milk the adage

·Review of John Updike, S. London 1988.

about fools and their money. The real-life setting of this place was Antelope, Oregon, renamed Rajneeshpuram by the acolytes of the discredited Bhagwan, but here it finds itself in the desert of Arizona — in order, perhaps, to supply the faint Lawrentian and Huxleyan flavours of mescal and soma.

Recurring key words are 'play' and 'playful', as Updike conscripts the Yogic concept of Lila for his own antic purposes. As often as he ridicules the life of the ashram, he asks the question — what's so great about the unexamined life of the surrounding 'rational' culture? This is a poser he is fond of setting. Rabbit had his encounters with the world of supernatural speculation. The ladies of Eastwick found life insupportable without it. In *Roger's Version* one can only be touched by the God-bothering computer hacker, whose very absurdity and quixotry afford a contrast with the staunchly selfish and complacent society that mocks him. Best of all, in *The Coup*, there was the *tour de force* diatribe against American mediocrity and consumerism by a putative Islamic fundamentalist crusader. It's always with a very slight effort that Updike plucks himself back from these exotic temptations, and lets the nonmagical world reassert itself. In this case he has also chosen the mode of *anima* to illustrate his tale, making himself still more protean by impersonating a woman of many moods and guises. She can be kittenish to her mother, shrewish to her daughter and plain bitchy to her old man. These inventions probably didn't tax Updike's invention overmuch, but Ma Prem Kundalini can also find the Arhat's sexual wavelength, which involves her in accommodating a certain determined passivity on his part. Though there is nothing androgynous about the guru — he shows himself to be a strict tits'n'ass type when the groaning need is upon him — a residual desire for the female part prompts Sarah to experiment with love among the ochre-clad vestals of the blessed one's *équipe*. In these ways she tries to live up to her ashram name. *Kundalini* is a karmic version of the polymorphous perverse; incarnating the feminine principle which is possessed by all and is located at the base of the spine. (Later, and on another subject, we are reminded that this is also where the syphilis germ bides its own sweet time.)

Released to experiment as she will with Sapphism in the evenings and man's work during the day, Sarah looks back on her respectable and anodyne past. She makes withering observations about her former husband and cleverly crafted ones about the vanity of men in general ('the gay ones have that gay way of walking so there's no up and down to their heads, just this even floating even when they're moving along very briskly'). She continues to squirrel away money with lawyers and bankers, and I think we have to conclude that some of it is embezzled from the credulous who have already been well fleeced by the Arhat. A feline war of manoeuvre is meanwhile conducted with the striped shirts hired by a vengeful hubby. At a certain point, Updike seems to have realized that he did not have the patience and application that are required for the epistolary style. When people compose letters they do not write, as does 'S' in her first missive to the abandoned Charles: 'Your dignified useful life, of which I was an ever smaller and less significant adornment, surely will forbid any ugly vulgar furor of detectives and lawyers and warrants.' Nor do they write: 'I didn't mind fatally the comical snobbish brusque callousness that comes when you've processed enough misery.' They don't *write* like that, but they may conceivably *talk* like it. So we start to get tapes, where the free association and stream of consciousness is more believable, and elements of the off-stage action can be overheard. This rather clumsy device at least means that some of the ashram life, complete with gunplay and drugs, can be heard in its own voice instead of Sarah's original contrivance of reported speech.

The motif is bathos. This is true of the dialogues and monologues: 'But the *suffering* a woman endures for the same mute Shiva, the same stony linga over and over! My entire subtle body aches; I awake to this ache and fall asleep impaled upon it. Also, I have caught a cold, as I tend to do when I travel.' And it is true of the action. The Arhat turns out to be Art Steinmetz, a chancy kid from a borderline district in Boston, Massachusetts, with enough swarthiness to 'pass'. And this discovery reminds Sarah that she always really yearned for Myron Stern, who also hailed from those parts but was judged catastrophically unsuitable by her parents. With this, the spell is broken and we are released from any more nonsense about *prakriti* and *purusha* — terms that Updike has mastered but not really made the effort to deploy. This is one of his lighter efforts and left me in no doubt, after some false trails and Sanskrit gags, that S — $, and did so all along.

Times Literary Supplement, April 1988

P.G. WODEHOUSE IN LOVE, POVERTY AND WAR*

The choice of one's first Wodehouse is frightfully important. How often one runs across a soul practically dead, who claims 'not to see the funny side', only to discover that fate had slipped the lead into the boxing glove by dealing him one of the golfing stories first crack out of the box. My invariable practice with young people starting out in life is to hand them *Archibald and the Masses*, or

*Review of Frances Donaldson (ed.), *Yours, Plum: The Letters of P.G. Wodehouse*, London 1990.

Right Ho, Jeeves in the case of the better element, and then to shoot my cuffs and sit back; a confident smile playing about the lips. As you see, the real stuff really is inimitable. But at a tender age I myself first clicked with *Joy in the Morning*. I suppose I already knew dimly that Wodehouse composed this especially ripe one while interned by the Wehrmacht, but it is good to be reminded of that astonishing and vaguely encouraging fact by Frances Donaldson, who has also unearthed for *Yours, Plum* the following letter written to Guy Bolton upon publication:

> I don't think it's bad, considering that it was written during the German occu-
> pation of Le Touquet, with German soldiers prowling about under my window,
> plus necessity of having to walk to Paris Plage every morning to report to a
> German Kommandant with a glass eye.

This is good fun in itself, but contains no clue or trace worth following. One of the addictive ingredients of this collection — a loosely sorted box of widely spaced and various correspondence — is the occasional nugget of matter that actually *corresponds*. For example, in a letter written to his pal Denis Mackail in 1954: 'As I often say, I am never happier than when curled up with Trevisa's translation of *De Proprietatibus Rerum*.' Here is the perfect echo of 'You'll usually find me curled up with Spinoza's latest', which got Bertie into such trouble when found purchasing the *Ethics* by — was it Florence Craye? I leave all that sort of thing to my man Usborne, even though he overdoes the buff business and has encouraged the trying practice of referring to 'The Master'. Not that it's without interest to find Wodehouse writing, to Usborne in 1955 in response to one of his interminable inquiries:

> My parents were in Hong Kong most of the time, and I was left in charge of
> various aunts, many of them vicars' wives who paid occasional calls on the local
> Great House, taking me with them. Why, I can't imagine, as I had no social gifts.
> But those visits made me familiar with life in the Servants' Hall, as I was usually
> sent off there in the custody of the butler, to be called for later.

This makes dullish reading, but the picture of 'aunt calling to aunt like mastodons bellowing across some primeval swamp' is in there somewhere. So is 'ice formed on the upper slopes of the butler'. And thus one persists, fascinated; rewarded by an occasional unforced usage of 'foul', 'footer', 'bilge', 'blighter' or 'I say'.

One of Wodehouse's editors told me years ago that he'd been to visit 'Plum' on Long Island, and discovered the old boy scarlet with embarrassment at having just read *A Spy in the Family* by Alec Waugh. 'Is this sort of stuff *common* in England now?' he had inquired shyly about that mild comedy of spanking and blowing. 'It's the filthiest thing I have ever read.' Not only does this image of Wodehouse seem essential to his biographers; it also acts as a sort of guarantee of the innocence of Blandings and the Drones. Yet in 1937, writing from Beverly Hills, 'Plum' reports:

Scandal about Henry Daniell and wife. Apparently they go down to Los Angeles and either (a) indulge in or (b) witness orgies – probably both. Though don't you feel there's something rather pleasantly domestic about a husband and wife sitting side by side with their eyes glued to peepholes, watching the baser element whoop it up? All it needs is the kiddies at *their* peepholes. And what I want to know is – where are these orgies? I feel I've been missing something.

Golly. It's as if Jeeves had been caught flashing his Hampton ('the contingency is a remote one, Sir'). And this letter was to Wodehouse's adopted daughter, Leonora ('Snorky'), to whom he sent some of his most spiffing reports of work and leisure. Elsewhere, 'Plum' writes to his co-conspirator Guy Bolton, saying: 'for a stage play I doubt if you can get by with a story that doesn't deal primarily with sex relations. My type of story is apt to be thin on the stage. So why don't we try and get something sexy for a Jeeves play?' I reeled and clutched the lemon. Why don't we try to get something what for a *what*? 'Not all the soda, Jeeves.'

Wodehouse was as notoriously hopeless about politics as about sex. I thought there was nothing more to be said about the absurd episode of the German broadcasts, but there is one interesting footnote here, which is that in later life Plum became quite a pal of W.D. Connor ('Cassandra') who had launched such a vulgar, hateful attack on him in 1941. Connor had made game of Wodehouse's upper-crust-sounding names, curling his lip mightily at 'Pelham Grenville', and in return Wodehouse had expressed the hope that W.D. stood for 'Walpurgis Diarmid or something of that sort'. By the early 1960s, the milk of human kindness was sloshing around so freely in his system that Plum was writing to Connor as 'Dear Walp'. He even urged Evelyn Waugh to go easy on the old brute when Waugh made his beautiful restitutive broadcast on the BBC in 1961. As against this, given the generosity of George Orwell's *In Defence of P.G. Wodehouse*, which was written at a time when Plum's stock was in the cellar, it is sad to find P.G.W. writing ungraciously about him eleven years later: 'George Orwell. Why do the eggheads make such a fuss of him? He's quite good of course, but surely not so good as all that? Weird fellow. I think he genuinely enjoyed being unhappy.' Coming back to the *res*, I may have said that Plum's grasp on public affairs was dashed shaky, but here again – not so fast. Admittedly the stuff written in April 1939 is pretty priceless ('Do you know, a feeling is gradually stealing over me that the world has never been farther from a war than it is at present'). But never forget the prescience Wodehouse displayed when he drew the figure of Sir Roderick Spode, Leader of the Black Shorts. His instinct for spotting the sinister phoney in public life stayed with him, as here in 1936 and about the Abdication:

> Over here, the Hearst papers, of course, took a very yelling attitude about the thing, trying to stir up feeling on the ground that wasn't a pure, sweet American girl a fitting mate for the highest in the land, but the others were all right, and Mencken wrote a very good article, putting the thing very sanely and showing what an ass Edward was.

A significant thing, I thought, was that when I went to the pictures the other night and Mrs Simpson came on the news reel there wasn't a sound. Nobody clapped. It showed once more how futile the Hearst papers are when it comes to influencing the public. He roasted Roosevelt day after day for months, and look what *he's* done.

Shrewd, that. In lighter vein, but displaying good form, a letter about another vile big-mouth in 1954:

Are you following the McCarthy business? If so, can you tell me what it's all about? 'You dined with Mr X on Friday the tenth?' 'Yes, sir.' (keenly) 'What did you eat?' 'A chocolate nut sundae, sir.' (Sensation) It's like Bardell vs Pickwick, which reminds me. Do you like Dickens's stuff? I can't read it.

Wodehouse may not have liked Dickens, but he certainly read him. He read like a fiend. In 1920 he is giving Leon Feuchtwanger a whirl. H.G. Wells's auto-biography (a mixed report here) in 1934. An excellent critique of *A Handful of Dust* in the same year. Trenchant observations about Kipling, Du Maurier, Le Carré. This intense reading must bear some relation to 'Plum''s prodigious application and productivity. He seems never to have wasted anything. A report from the adored Snorky on girls' schools is pressed into service for *Bertie Changes His Mind*. Repeated failure at the *Times* crossword, reported to Denis Mackail, must be a clue to the running gag about 'large Australian bird, three letters, first letter E and last letter U'. Six years before his first Jeeves novel, he writes to William Townend that Edgar Wallace employs 'a day butler and a night butler, so that you can never go into his house and not find a butler. That's the way they live. But why not two day butlers and two night butlers, so that they could do cross-talk and perhaps a song?'

Disparagement of Dickens to one side, his feeling for tripe was a sure one. The gruesomeness of *Gone with the Wind* ('After an eternity of it Clark Gable and Vivien Leigh fell into the embrace and I was just reaching for my hat when blowed if they didn't start an entirely new story'). The bloodiness of *My Fair Lady* ('I had always considered Professor Higgins the most loathsome of all stage characters, but I never realised how loathsome he could be till I saw Sexy Rexy playing him'). All the letters to his showbiz collaborators show his relent-less insistence upon zip, brio, snap and *espièglerie*. 'Get on with it' was his motto; succeeding in making the arduous seem natural. Two letters rebuking the slothful lines of Cole Porter, and making very handy suggestions for improvement, show his address and perfectionism. But there is nary a trace of mean spirit here. Even the letters about reviews and reviewers, which oscillate wildly between gloom at stinkers and joy at raves, are self-mocking. (A rugged, anonymous notice in the *TLS* makes him feel 'as if someone had flung an egg at me from a bomb-proof shelter'.) And when writing about the quotidian and the mundane, and throughout showing a very lively and informed interest in the needful and the readies, he tried always to keep his timing:

Just got statements from my publishers. My books have sold five million in England and four million over here. And presumably another million in the European countries, including Japan. Not so bad, what? It cheered me up. I am going deaf in the left ear, blast it.

Like Lady Donaldson, I have saved the last, ghastly news *for* the last. It seems that 'Plum' was a secret spiritualist. Talk about a swift slosh to the upper maxillary bone. We all have to cope with the impending doom, of course, but not, surely, by believing that the stars are God's daisy chain. ('All rot of course. They're nothing of the sort.') Yet here, as inescapable as the minutes of the Junior Ganymede, is the incriminating drool about mediums, planchettes and wistful missives from the beyond. How perfectly foul.

Times Literary Supplement, September 1990

GREENE: WHERE THE SHADOW FALLS·

The poetic cinema, it is worth remembering, can be built up on a few very simple ideas, as simple as the idea behind the poetic fictions of Conrad: the love of peace, of country, a feeling for fidelity ...

'Peace, Country, Fidelity' — these read like a triptych of non-Greene virtues and assets, as blazoned on some doltishly pious sampler, perhaps, or on a postage stamp issued by Vichy France. They appear in a consideration of the film industry written in 1937, when it seems that Greene regarded Conrad as a stout, simple soul (and when he praised the staunch cinematic virtues of D.W. Griffith).

Kim Philby, they say, was never happier than when receiving his edition of *Wisden*, his airmail copy of *The Times* or his consignment of cat-food from Fortnum and Mason. James Cameron, radical globetrotter, was given to saying that he himself was conservative about everything except politics. George Orwell, in a series of sardonic comments on Greene (he was especially repelled by the sickliness of morality in *The Heart of the Matter*), always claimed to detect a devout little reactionary behind the experimenter. Is there any necessary contradiction between the image of the proper, continent Greene and the widespread impression of Greene the friend of the Sandinista, Greene the connoisseur of the third pipe, Greene the novelist of the Index-linked matters

·Review of Graham Greene, *Reflections*, ed. Judith Adamson, London 1990.

of culpable doubt, adultery and fornication; Greene the special literary interpreter of treason? Greene's abiding brilliance and fascination arise or derive from the fact that he contains this multitude without, apparently, being fully aware of it. He can discard and dissociate: he can break threads and celebrate inconsistencies. While reading his last, rather tepid fiction, *The Captain and the Enemy*, I noticed that the plot was a direct 'lift' from a dream which he had experienced and recorded in Vietnam before Dien Bien Phu and set down years ago in *Ways of Escape*. As with the forgotten and recovered script of *The Tenth Man*, he seemed oblivious of the fact that he had this occult capital upon which to borrow. In the marinade of the unconscious, resolution occurs. Lucky him. As he writes here, in a description of the floating world of the haunter of second-hand bookshops:

> There was a shop in London which occurred very frequently in my dreams: I can remember clearly its façade but not its interior. It stood somewhere in the region behind Charlotte Street before you come to the Euston Road. I never went inside, and I am sure now that there never was such a shop. I would always wake from such dreams with a sense of happiness and expectation.

This is in every sense a gift, which might dissolve upon any too-minute examination. And it helps to account for the amazing discrepancies in his ways of seeing.

The early pieces in this anthology begin with undergraduate reportage from the Rhineland in 1924, and show a vivid sense of outrage at the French deployment of colonial — all right, *black* — troops to control post-Versailles Germany. We are told, by Greene and by his editor Judith Adamson, that this visit was financed by the German Embassy. But spin forward the spool of memory to 1945, to discover Greene writing in praise of a book which justified the policy of unconditional surrender. He recalls with sarcasm and scorn the anti-occupation protests of the Germans in 1924, saying that on his visit then he 'was only an undergraduate, but was not beneath the organizers' notice'. Presumably not, since he was a sponsored guest of those organizers. But of his earlier writings and attitudes he seems, even now, to have no recollection whatever. There is no great trick in catching him out here, because he supplies all the incidental detail himself. In a beguiling early review of R.K. Narayan in 1937, he innocently maps for us his yearning for scope and endeavour by comparing the villagers of Malgudi to the thwarted aspirations of Chekhov's characters:

> The huge Indian spaces into which friends disappear to take up railway clerk-ships and never to write letters ... the same wasted intellectual effort ... the same Siberian distances ... a waving handkerchief, a departure, a looking back to something beautiful, a looking forward to something which we know will never happen.

This seems to me to be a seminal review, with its curious but pregnant melancholy and the marvellous diffidence with which it says, of Narayan's Malgudi: 'I was going to say tragedy, but that word is too blatant for a pathos as delicate as the faint discoloration of ivory with age.' It contrasts very well with the slightly hollow breviary maxims, often and necessarily contradictory, which dot the reportage. Thus, in a practice raid with the RAF in 1939: 'One always prefers the ruled to the rulers, and the servants of a policy to its dictators.' In a real raid with the French rulers over very much ruled Vietnam in 1954: 'One does not visit a disaster except to give aid.' In an essay, again from the French side, in Indochina the following year: 'If one is writing about war, self-respect demands that occasionally one shares a very small portion of the risk.' In a rumination on Shakespeare in 1969: 'The writer should always be ready to change sides at the drop of a hat. He stands for the victims, and the victims change.' In a report from Allende's Chile in 1972: 'I suppose pessimism is the doubtful privilege of an outsider with a return ticket.'

There is a kind of continuity to these statements, which are of opinion rather than conviction. In another book altogether, Greene told his inter-locutor Marie-Françoise Allain that he would never agree to exploit the suffer-ings of others for literary purposes. But as Judith Adamson points out in her introduction here, in *A Sort of Life* Greene records the scene of a mother with a dead child and justifies himself by saying: 'There is a splinter of ice in the heart of a writer. . . . This was something which one day I might need.' Such a protean morality, adaptable to exigency while always striving to retain something of its same character, would be either unfathomable or uninteresting if it were not linked to Greene's Catholicism. It must be so linked; though many critics fight shy of the subject lest they be accused of sectarianism. Yet to skip the RC stuff is to decline an invitation which Greene himself relentlessly extends. He has, for example, included two quite preposterously bigoted attacks on Shakespeare, in both cases for being insufficiently Catholic. A 1951 review of John Gerard's Elizabethan *Autobiography* says:

> One might have guessed from Shakespeare's plays that there was a vast vacuum where the Faith had been – the noise and bustle of pilgrimages have been stilled: we come out of the brisk world of Chaucer into the silence of Hamlet's court after the Prince's departure.

It is then suggested that Shakespeare would have gained great insight by witnessing Gerard's fortitude under interrogation. In a 1969 address upon accepting a Shakespeare prize in Hamburg, Greene goes even further, quoting John of Gaunt to the extent of 'This happy breed of men, this little world – This blessed plot, this earth, this realm, this England', and adding:

> These complacent lines were published in 1597. Two years before, Shakespeare's fellow poet Southwell had died on the scaffold after three years of torture. If only Shakespeare had shared his disloyalty, we could have loved him better as a man.

'We all learned the lines at school,' says Greene smugly, thus blackening the name of Berkhamsted if it failed to give him old Gaunt's conclusion about the tenement and pelting farm, the shameful conquest and his remaining, very far from 'complacent', valediction. This sort of vulgarity does not even rise to the Chesterbellocian.

Greene's attitude to Communism can also be read against his relatively mindless attitude to Holy Mother Church. To take the most frequently cited instance of his prescience, namely the war in Vietnam, it is interesting to find that he sympathized in general with the French occupation — which was, after all, a *mission civilisatrice* — and in 1952 proposed a specially fatuous version of the domino theory. ('If Indo-China falls, Korea will be isolated, Siam can be invaded in twenty-four hours and Malaya may have to be abandoned.') His reporting is full of credulity about pro-French, clerical-led comebacks in remote areas. Once the Diem gang had been shot out of its priest-hole by its American sponsors, Greene seems to have felt free to criticize rather than satirize foreign intervention. In the Poland of the 1950s, Greene is able to indulge the Stalinist regime to the precise extent that it runs a collaborationist Catholic front (the old 'Pax') to whose agonies of balance and contradiction he lends a tender ear. In Cuba in 1963 he repeats every boast of the government, praising Castro's attention to the Nuncio and the catechism and writing: 'There is no inherent opposition between Marxist economics and Catholicism, and in Cuba co-existence with the Church has proved easier than in Poland (Cuba is less strictly Catholic than Poland, just as Marxism here is less philosophical).' One loves that last parenthetical *aperçu*, even as one remembers the Catholic origin of the word 'apologetics'. Finally, in a frankly and toe-curlingly embarrassing address to Gorbachev, delivered in Moscow in 1987, we learn that: 'There is no division in our thoughts between Catholics — Roman Catholics — and Communists.' Apparently: 'We are fighting together against the Death Squads in El Salvador. We are fighting together against the Contras in Nicaragua. We are fighting together against General Pinochet in Chile.' It does no good to point out that the death squads, the Contras and the General all likewise claimed — and received — Catholic blessing. The Haiti of Papa Doc is the only government to receive no quarter or compassion or 'context' from Greene but after all, though Mother Teresa went on to become the patron and defender of the Duvalier family, the old man himself was an excommunicated blasphemer.

As T.S. Eliot wrote, and as Greene more than once reminds us, 'Between the conception and the creation / Between the idea and the reality / Falls the Shadow.' In Greene's case, the shadow of creativity and imagination has often mercifully interposed between his morality and his writing. The beauty and clarity of his observations about Narayan and Chekhov are matched when he writes about 'the awful tiredness of hospitality — the strain of politeness and friendliness in the absence of companionship'. They are more than matched when he says (of ghastly but Faithful Paraguay) that 'to live here one would be charged in the quite small currency of the conscience'. Take away the cloying sanctimony, and thank God that on so many occasions Greene has shown that he can write like an atheist.

Times Literary Supplement, September 1990

KAZUO ISHIGURO

When I read Kazuo Ishiguro's novel *An Artist of the Floating World*, I had already heard that he was about to publish *The Remains of the Day*. All I knew about the impending book was that it took a minute interest in English social relations. It turns out to be an advantage to read the books in this order, close together, because they disclose an intriguing latent similarity.

The resemblance is superficial to begin with. Both novels take the form of unmediated retrospective monologue. In *An Artist of the Floating World*, the narrator is Masuji Ono, a Japanese painter from a bourgeois background. In *The Remains of the Day*, the raconteur is 'Stevens' — we never learn his first name — a devoted butler in an English country house. Both men are in the evening or autumn of their days, the point at which Minerva's owl is supposed to take wing. Both are coming to recognize their inability to alter the past or to influence the present, and both are visited by the uneasy suspicion that their lives have been spent on the wrong course, and in the wrong cause. Both, consequently, are great prosaic rationalizers. Here is each at his respective conclusion:

> For however one may come in later years to reassess one's achievement, it is always a consolation to know that one's life has contained a moment or two of real satisfaction such as I experienced that day up on that high mountain path. (*Artist*)

> What is the point in worrying oneself too much about what one could or could not have done to control the course one's life took? Surely it is enough that the likes of you and I at least *try* to make our small contribution count for something true and worthy. (*Remains*)

Each narrator has lived according to strict codes of etiquette and order: the ethos of actively and passively 'knowing one's place', and adhering to protocol and precedent. Masuji Ono is formed by the practice of giving and receiving deference of the kind due to 'masters', both in the aesthetic and the imperial hierarchy. Stevens is loyal and obsequious to his master, Lord Darlington, while maintaining a sternly measured distance from the underservants and the junior staff. Both men, too, inhabit a universe in which women are governed almost exclusively by marriage prospects and the duties and sadnesses attendant upon them.

It occurs to me that Ishiguro's developed sense of social rank and nuance makes him a potentially acute fictional miniaturist whether he chooses England or Japan. Both nations have an ingrained, antique response to caste, class and station. Both are island peoples, at an angle to the nearest continental landmass. Both are former imperial powers who held dominion over populations that far outnumbered them. And both are maritime; people forget that the Anglo-Japanese naval treaty of 1902 was an agreement between effective superpowers.

Crucial to the tone and texture of both novels, therefore, is the memory of imperialism and war. Ono, as emerges gradually from his reminiscences and encounters, is a former partisan and propagandist for Tojo and Hirohito. Stevens has to admit that his own feudal commander was active in the cause of Munich and appeasement, and even of domestic British fascism. Moreover, both Ono and Stevens have suffered family losses in the pursuit of military and national grandeur:

> 'There seems to be no end of courageous deaths,' he said, eventually. 'Half of my high school graduation year have died courageous deaths. They were all for stupid causes, though they were never to know that. Do you know, Father, what really makes me angry?'
> 'What is that, Suichi?'
> 'Those who sent the likes of Kenji out there to die these brave deaths, where are they today? They're carrying on with their lives, much the same as ever.'
> (*Artist*)

> I should explain here that I am one of two brothers — and that my elder brother, Leonard, was killed during the Southern African War while I was still a boy. Naturally, my father would have felt this loss keenly; but to make matters worse, the usual comfort a father has in these situations — that is, the notion that his son gave his life gloriously for king and country — was sullied by the fact that my brother had perished in a particularly infamous manoeuvre ... at the close of the Southern African conflict, [his] general had been discreetly retired, and he had then entered business, dealing in shipments from Southern Africa. (*Remains*)

Registering these and other echoes, one is tempted to elaborate upon them. Surely there is an element of Bushido in Stevens's notions of honour and 'dignity', which allow him to be dauntlessly unemotional in the face even of his father's death? Is there not an unremarked comparison to be made between his rhapsody on the intricacies of silver polish and the renowned Japanese punctilio about interior design and tea service? Do not both societies rely heavily, as does Ishiguro, on the effect of cutting manners, ruthless courtesy and deadly euphemism?

Finally, there is the dating. *An Artist of the Floating World* is set in 1948–50, and *The Remains of the Day* in 1956. The dates mark the period when each former empire came to accept, however grudgingly, the American dispensation: during occupation in the first instance and just before Suez in the second. Ono finds the American style deposing the old Japanese tradition wherever he turns to look, and Stevens is adjusting (not at all well) to a buyout of his old employer's ancestral country seat by a jaunty American businessman.

Ishiguro has lived in England much longer than he has in Japan, but like other London novelists of Asian birth (Rushdie) or parentage (Kureishi), he has at least subliminally imported an element of perspective that lends depth and distance to the picture. Since the English weakness is for irony, just as the Japanese obsession is said to be with miniaturization, it would be satisfying to think that he had enriched these tiny portraits without really intending to do so.

The Nation, June 1990

VICTOR SERGE

People argue endlessly about Auden's intention when he wrote, commemorating Yeats, that 'poetry makes nothing happen'. They tend to forget that he put it like this:

> For poetry makes nothing happen: it survives
> In the valley of its making where executives
> Would never want to tamper ...

'It survives.' Not a very grand claim on the face of it. But mark the implicit idea that it survives actively as well as passively; that it outlives its prosaic and banal enemies. The thought recurs while reading *Resistance*, the poetry of Victor Serge, newly translated from the French by James Brook and published by City Lights Books in perfect time for next year's centenary of Serge's birth. By the single term 'executives', Auden obviously meant the bureaucratic, the commercial, the literal-minded and the repressed. Victor Serge's entire life was a confrontation, in word and action, with those forces. His *Memoirs of a Revolutionary* is part of the core record of the interwar drama of fascism and Stalinism, and his novels — *The Case of Comrade Tulayev; Birth of Our Power* —

have an advantage over Arthur Koestler's fiction of revolution and betrayal by virtue of a superior purity and intensity. Still, what a shock to find a shuddering anticipation of *Darkness at Noon* in his 1938 poem 'Confessions', about the Moscow Trials:

> If we roused the peoples and made the continents quake,
> shot the powerful, destroyed the old armies, the old cities, the old ideas,
> began to make everything anew with these dirty old stones,
> these tired hands, and the meager souls that were left us,
> it was not in order to haggle with you now,
> sad revolution, our mother, our child, our flesh,
> our decapitated dawn, our night with its stars askew,
> with its inexplicable Milky Way torn to pieces.

Although much of Serge's poetry bears the marks of the place and time in which it was written — an outpost of the gulag during the extermination of the Bolshevik old guard — it is by no means didactic or political verse. In 'Trust', for example, he is almost lyrical ('I've seen the steppe turn green and the child grow') about the natural and human symphony. And in 'Boat on the Ural River', you do not have to know that his companions on the voyage are fellow-deportees, because the poem is about friendship and hardship:

> *Kiss the girl you fancy ...*
>
> Jacques lightly purses his thin lips
> like a wise Jew who will live to grow old.
> Boris with the profile of a hungry wolf
> drinks in the sadness of a night without drink.

Serge occupied that fragile and fascinating span that extended between the Surrealist Manifesto and the platform of the Left Opposition; between André Breton and the betrayal of Barcelona. His internationalism was as natural to him as his breathing. He hated backwardness and servility, whether political or artistic, and he hated it most of all when it was manifest among so-called revolutionaries. He saw Yesenin, Mayakovsky, Mandelstam, either destroyed or demoralized by the crushing pressure of a brutal pseudo-realism, and he also saw the cowardice of many writers and intellectuals in the face of this pressure. His defiance of conformism and time-serving is best evoked in his poem on the death of Panait Istrati:

> You lay upon your press clippings, like Job upon his ashes,
> quietly spitting the last bit of your lungs
> in the faces of those copy-pissers,
> glorifiers of profitable massacres,
> profiteers of disfigured revolutions ...

Yeats used to speak of 'a book of the people': a record of tradition, precept and insight that was transmitted invisibly and independently of the doings of high culture and politics. The importance of poems and songs to this metaphorical 'book' is obvious. They can be learned and treasured even by the poor and illiterate, as Homer was preserved in antiquity. Poetry, in other words, is morally proof against censorship. Serge's own work is a nice instance of this quality. When he was finally deported from the Soviet Union in 1936, the goons at the border confiscated his manuscript. But once in Paris he was able to recompose the poems from memory, a sterling proof of the strength of poetry as against the executives. As he put it in his fragment 'Be Hard':

> In time flesh will wear ot chains,
> In time the mind will make chains snap.

When Serge died, an impoverished and neglected exile in Mexico, he had tasted every variety of disillusionment and defeat. But he never degenerated into cynicism or permitted himself a flirtation with any variety of reaction. That would have been despair, and it was despair that his poems so beautifully, and with dignity and humour, kept at bay.

In later life he would tell his son to keep clear of the anti-Soviet cult that was spreading with such meretricious ease through the Western intelligentsia. It was important, he said, to keep up great hopes. And now it has been announced that the literary magazine *URAL* will publish *The Case of Comrade Tulayev*, thus bringing to a Soviet readership a novel about the reality of the purges that anticipated Solzhenitsyn by several decades. Moreover, the Foundation for Soviet Culture has agreed to institute a search for the original manuscript of Serge's confiscated poems. But that is all secondary and antiquarian. Serge's poetry has already stayed true to Auden's injunction. In fact, it may even have improved upon it. The poetry has survived. And by surviving, as part of the residue of a tragic but incomplete struggle, it has contributed to making something happen:

> Let's get to work so that one day, perhaps, a passerby might see
> in the lines ripening at this moment, as I too haul in my net in the pond
>   of useless days,
> some traces of a reassuring sky that I cannot see there.
>
>   ('On the Ural River' [Orenburg camp, summer 1935])

The Nation, October 1989

C.L.R. JAMES

There is an old, tenacious and widely ridiculed idea that all people (and all peoples, for that matter) are at least intrinsically capable of the same appreciation of philosophy, poetry and beauty, and are not just to be measured by their attitude to political economy or — as we have further degraded the proposition — by the attitude of political economists to them. There had better be something to this idea. During a utopian interlude in the utilitarian nineteenth century, men like William Morris and John Ruskin attempted to give expression to the yearning for wholeness, an ambition that in other quarters prompted the founding of a working-class college, separated from the High Church- and empire-minded university in Oxford. It was in a hall of this institution, Ruskin College, that I first heard C.L.R. James speak, and first began to think that utopianism was too feeble and colourless a term for those few who have the courage to talk of a future we cannot yet fully imagine.

His actual or ostensible subject was Vietnam. This was the fall of 1967, and the fantastic web of official lying and bluff about the war had already been torn irreparably apart. (Don't you hate it, incidentally, when revisionist historians date the awakening of 'concern' to the later events of Tet and My Lai? Anyone who cared to know the truth about Indochina knew it well before those crises.) James did not waste any phrases on the revelations of atrocities that were beginning to disturb even Cold War liberals. He was a historian of imperialism, and he knew all he needed to know about free-fire zones and strategic hamlets. He understood them by analogy, from his rigorous study of the French in Haiti, the Spanish in Cuba, the British in South Africa and the Italians in Ethiopia. Such conduct towards lesser peoples scarcely rated a raising of the voice. What was impressive about the Vietnamese, he said coolly, was the proven fact that they wouldn't put up with it any longer, and had taken the decision to endure anything. This was how history was made. He was already old by then, with a nimbus of silver surrounding his anthracite features. He had taken decades to evolve his balanced, synthesized combination of the heart on fire and the brain on ice. From early youth in Trinidad, where he made himself master of Greek classics, Shakespeare and the novel, he had progressed along an astounding number of paths, accepting the role of chance just as he strove to detect the workings of history. He had debated Bertrand Russell on dialectics; had been detained on Ellis Island and deported; had inspired the leadership of at least one Caribbean independence movement; had been the most fluent writer on cricket in the English language; had been the severest and bravest Third World polemicist against Stanlinism; had been an example to a nascent generation of immigrants fighting for a place in 'the old country'.

The real test of a radical or a revolutionary is not the willingness to confront the orthodoxy and arrogance of the rulers but the readiness to contest illusions and falsehoods among close friends and allies. This crux occurred in James's life in the late 1930s, when the Communist International made a cynical decision to discard anti-colonial activity in order to woo imperial Britain and France. With George Padmore and a handful of others, James declared that the struggle of the colonized was not the political property of any party or apparatus. His early critique of this cynicism had a presentiment of the Hitler–Stalin Pact, and you can intuit the same point in a different way from his historical masterpiece *The Black Jacobins*, which shows that metropolitan France and its revolution helped to emancipate the slaves, but also shows decisively that Toussaint L'Ouverture's fighters had to rely on their own sinews. This stand, and others like it, condemned James to spend decades among the fragments of the independent, quasi-Trotskyist left. I say 'condemned' because the experience was null as far as any definite gain in politics or organization went. But James did not waste even these locust years. He remained in touch with small but significant internationalist groupings, and before the end of his life, which came on 31 May, he was celebrated in Africa and the Caribbean in a way that his former detractors of the Stalin period could never hope to be. His last public speech in America was a vindication of Solidarity in Poland and an affirmation of the unguessed-at capacity of an educated working class.

In Paul Buhle's admirable book *C.L.R. James: The Artist as Revolutionary* there is a moment from one of James's early cricket columns, written for the *Manchester Guardian* in the 1930s by the only black correspondent then allowed to comment on the great game. James had decided to challenge the quotidian reader with a comparison to the ancient Olympiad:

> What would an Athenian have thought of the day's play? Probably that the white-flannelled actors moving so sedately from place to place were performing the funeral rites over the corpse of a hero buried between the wickets.

James had a developed sense, derived partly from Hellenism, of the symmetry and grace latent in art and work. He makes an excellent guide to the increasingly one-dimensional argument over 'Western civilization'. He needed no instruction about slavery and ethnocentricity. But he had no tolerance either for callow, sectarian diatribes, and shuddered at the philistinism that reduces Shakespeare to 'a white male'. Some have seen in his early short stories from Trinidad a premonition of the best of Naipaul. Both men benefit by the comparison, if it is honestly made.

In old age he made his home in London, on the Railton Road in Brixton, 'front line' between the two declensions of Thatcherism. I called on him there last summer, and found him infirm and rather deaf, but still engaged. Handing him my copy of *The Black Jacobins* for an inscription, I was asked what I'd like him to write. 'If you just put "fraternal greetings" I'll be honoured.' He gave me a searching look. 'I do not', he said, 'believe in the eternal.' To conflate eternity with fraternity seemed a most elegant mistake for a man of his years and of, in every sense, his history.

The Nation, July 1989

IN DEFENCE OF DANIEL DERONDA

In the course of her lifetime, George Eliot had always to confront those who distrusted or suspected her seriousness. If this seemed an ironic reception for a respectable and educated woman at the height of the Victorian age, how much more so should it seem to us, equipped as we are with all the glib means of decoding the unacknowledged contradictions of that epoch. We are supposed to smile knowingly when we read John Fiske, American disciple of Herbert Spencer, as he writes home to his dear wife, having met the lady authoress just after her fifty-fourth birthday in 1873:

> I never before saw such a clear-headed woman. She thinks just like a man, and can put her thoughts into clear and forcible language at a moment's notice. And her knowledge is quite amazing. I have often heard of learned women, whose learning, I have usually found, is a mighty flimsy affair. But to meet a woman who can meet the ins and outs of the question, and not *putting on any airs*, but talking sincerely of the thing as a subject which has deeply interested her — this is, indeed, quite a new experience.

This little demonstration of the limits of positivism comes down to us — doesn't it? — as an example of period condescension. Yet the tendency to condescend to the wife of Mr G.H. Lewes outlived the 1870s and in many respects persists to our own time. Virginia Woolf, perhaps thinking that Mrs Lewes needed more money and at least one room of her own, anxiously wrote that her early life of filiality and connubiality had cut her off from experience, and that 'the loss for a novelist was serious'. Added Mrs Leonard Woolf, as if sighing for what might have been: 'She is no satirist.'

Marcel Proust, in his *Contre Saint-Beuve*, achieved magnificences of unbending, awarding George Eliot many points for moral *hauteur*, dwelling upon her affinity for the humble in station and her sense of duty before electing to praise her for 'A conservative spirit; not too much book-learning, not too many railways, not too much religious reform.' He also approved her 'sense of the uses of suffering'. Dr F.R. Leavis, the incarnation of that collision between English literature and high tasks and values which has left so many shattered bodies by the wayside, took longer to uncurl his neck and made, as ever, tremendous use of the awesome 'we' and the inclusive 'us'. Giving George Eliot a beta alpha for her sympathetic rendering of the mental atmosphere at Cambridge (an atmosphere that she had had, as a woman, to imbibe at second hand by close questioning of Sir Leslie Stephen), he calls the evocation 'characteristic of the innumerable things, by the way, that even in George Eliot's weaker places remind us we are dealing with an extremely vigorous and distinguished mind, and one in no respect disabled by being a woman's'. Leavis penned this qualified encomium as part of his very reserved treatment of *Daniel Deronda*, George Eliot's last novel and the one which the critics have been most united in deploring — for its alleged vices of affectation, contrivance, strenuousness, and even piety ('the wastes of biblicality and fervid idealism' — F.R. Leavis). I think that the novel can and should be defended from the faint praise and outright sneering which have been directed at it, and I believe that George Eliot's right to be serious can be upheld without any implication of the tedious or the merely didactic.

In his terrible book *Victorian Novelists*, Lord David Cecil reviews George Eliot without one single mention of *Daniel Deronda* but none the less manages to say of her: 'like all Victorian rationalists, she is a Philistine.... Constructed within so confined an area of vision, it is inevitable that her criticism of life is inadequate. Compared to Tolstoy, it seems petty, drab, provincial.' The last sentence here is like the clutch of a drowning and floundering man. Compared to *Tolstoy*, after all, even the whinnyings of the endless Cecil family seem provincial. To be *comparable* to Tolstoy, who regarded even Shakespeare as a buffoon, is not the disgrace that Lord David seeks so hastily to imply. In point of fact, George Eliot was neither a moralist — in the sense intended by Lord David — nor a philistine. She is the instance *par excellence* of a woman who took religion too seriously to take it seriously — of what might now be called a freethinker or agnostic. She found the discovery that religion and morality are ill-connected a shattering and disturbing one, and she operated as a sort of register of this well-known contradiction. In *Felix Holt, The Radical*, she deals in the first few chapters with book-learning, the coming of the railways, and the essence of religious reform (notice that if Proust doesn't get her, Lord David will); and when Harold Transome comes home from a spell of primitive accumulation in the Middle East (at Smyrna, then still the home of Greeks, Jews and Armenians) and repudiates the Tory ticket, his stricken mother takes it poorly: 'There were rich Radicals, she was aware, as there were rich Jews and Dissenters, but she had never thought of them as country people.'

In other words, George Eliot had taken the measure of the moralists and philistines of her day by 1866. It was precisely those who, privileged as they were, yet chose to remain 'constructed within so confined an area of vision' who aroused her scorn and impatience. By the time that she undertook *Daniel Deronda* she was equipped for a far more thorough settlement of accounts than had been necessary to see off Mrs Transome. I suggest the words 'under-taking' and 'equipment' with a perfect awareness that these are ponderous terms connoting worthy and weighty purposes. But although she hoped to accomplish something in the world of thought with *Daniel Deronda*, George Eliot was by no means prepared to sacrifice her art to the bearing of a message. In the figure of Gwendolen Harleth, she has provided a central character of uncommon depth and versatility. One is forever being impressed by the resources of this young woman, as she confronts the inescapable dilemma of all Victorian heroines — her marriageability. See how she varies her stratagem and her rhetoric:

> 'I am aware of that, uncle,' said Gwendolen, rising and shaking her head back, as if to rouse herself out of painful passivity. 'I am not foolish. I know that I must be married sometime — before it is too late. And I don't see how I could do better than marry Mr. Grandcourt. I mean to accept him, if possible.' She felt as if she were reinforcing herself by speaking with this decisiveness to her uncle.

And then, being both more and less artful with her mother than she had been with the good Rector:

> The cheque was for five hundred pounds, and Gwendolen turned it towards her mother, with the letter. 'How very kind and delicate!' said Mrs. Davilow with much feeling. 'But I should really like better not to be dependent on a son-in-law. I and the girls could get along very well.'
>
> 'Mamma, if you say that again, I will not marry him,' said Gwendolen, angrily.
>
> 'My dear child, I trust you are not going to marry only for my sake,' said Mrs. Davilow deprecatingly.
>
> Gwendolen tossed her head on the pillow away from her mother, and let the ring lie. She was irritated at this attempt to take away a motive.

These moments, in which a young woman has to face her own lack of resources while retaining pride and strength of mind, are imperishable. Gwendolen's consciousness, furthermore, is very much that of a woman *who knows what she may be missing* — an insight that Virginia Woolf, perhaps, credits too little in the life experience of the author.

The portrayal of Gwendolen is not, of course, objected to by any of *Daniel Deronda*'s critics. In fact, Leavis suggests that the novel should be retitled *Gwendolen Harleth*, and all the tiresome Jewish and religious material excised from it. Henry James, in the person of Constantius in his *Daniel Deronda, A Conversation*, made a similar plea: 'I say it under my breath — I began to feel an occasional temptation to skip. Roughly speaking, all the Jewish burden of the story tended to weary me....' 'Roughly speaking' is not a habitual Jamesian mode of address, to put it no higher. But it seems intended here to be the approximation of James's own reaction. Constantius goes on: 'All the Jewish part is at bottom cold; that is my only objection.' Having professed himself so unmoved and so uninterested, he nevertheless adds, after some fairly wretched verbal fencing with the ladies:

The universe, forcing itself with a slow, inexorable pressure into a narrow, complacent and yet after all extremely sensitive mind, and making it ache with the process — that is Gwendolen's story. And it becomes completely character-istic in that her supreme perception of the fact that the world is whirling past her is the disappointment not of a base, but of an exalted passion. The very chance to embrace what the author is so fond of calling a 'larger life' seems refused to her. She is punished for being narrow and she is not allowed a chance to expand. Her finding Deronda pre-engaged to go to the East and stir up the race-feeling of the Jews strikes me as a wonderfully happy invention. The irony of the situation, for poor Gwendolen, is almost grotesque, and it makes one wonder whether the whole heavy structure of the Jewish question in the story was not built up by the author for the express purpose of giving its proper force to this particular stroke.

Here James stumbles on the point, but picks himself up as if nothing had happened. It is precisely the Deronda dimension that exposes, not just the confined world of Gwendolen, but the constriction and smugness of English society. Yet, confronted with this new horizon, James wastes himself with a snigger about Deronda's being 'pre-engaged' — almost as if his dance card were to be too improvidently filled.

It is essential to realize that Gwendolen means it, and so does her creator, when she thinks of Deronda as an 'outer conscience'. The choice of words is rather a lovely one, bearing the connotation of 'outsider' as well as that of a wider sphere of intellectual and moral action. It may owe something to George Eliot's work in translating German philosophy. If its aim was to make the gentry feel slightly uncomfortable with the trammelled lives that they led and celebrated, and ordained for others, it seems to have succeeded. Sir Leslie Stephen took an early opportunity of exercising the classic English veto of heavy sarcasm:

> As we cannot all discover that we belong to the chosen people, and some of us might, even then, doubt the wisdom of the enterprise, one feels that Deronda's mode of solving his problem is not generally applicable.
>
> (*George Eliot*, 1902)

What would be the point of its having general applicability? Sir Leslie adds the second classic English veto — that of saying, in effect, that something is boring or solemn:

> George Eliot's sympathy for the Jews, her aversion to anti-Semitism, was thoroughly generous, and naturally welcomed by its objects. But taken as the motive of a hero it strikes one as showing a defective sense of humour.

Like Sir Leslie (whose use of the term 'objects' above is admirable in its intended charity and revealing in its presumption of exclusiveness), many of George Eliot's critics reveal their weakness and want of sympathy by inventing a mystery where none exists. How can she sketch a character as risible as Herr Klesmer, inquire Messrs James and Leavis and Stephen, and not see that Daniel Deronda himself is a dry old stick? Before I make the obvious retort to this, let me show, *pace* Virginia Woolf, why Herr Klesmer is a demonstration of the satirical gift as well as the grace of deft humour. Here is Gwendolen at his mercy — or is he at hers?

> 'One may understand jokes without liking them,' said the terrible Klesmer. 'I have had opera books sent me full of jokes; it was just because I understood them that I did not like them. The comic people are ready to challenge a man because he looks grave. "You don't see the witticism, sir?" "No, sir, but I see what you meant." Then I am what we call ticketed as a fellow without *esprit*. But in fact,' said Klesmer, suddenly dropping from his quick narrative to a reflective tone, with an impressive frown, 'I am very sensible to wit and humour.'

After this, Gwendolen teases him skilfully, 'which made them quite friendly until she begged to be deposited by the side of her mamma'.

Julius Klesmer, in other words, lightens the picture in accordance with the wishes of the critics. What else does he do? We find out when he has a slight confrontation with the MP Mr Bult, who represents the roast beef of old England, 'the general solidity and suffusive pinkness of a healthy Briton on the central table-land of life'. Mr Bult mistakes the *timbre* of one of Herr Klesmer's after-dinner perorations:

> 'You must have been used to public speaking. You speak uncommonly well, though I don't agree with you. From what you said about sentiment, I fancy you are a Panslavist.' 'No, my name is Elijah. I am the Wandering Jew,' said Klesmer, flashing a smile at Miss Arrowpoint, and suddenly making a mysterious wind-like rush backwards and forwards on the piano. Mr. Bult felt this buffoonery rather offensive and Polish, but — Miss Arrowpoint being there — did not like to move away.
> 'Herr Klesmer has cosmopolitan ideas,' said Miss Arrowpoint, trying to make the best of the situation. 'He looks forward to a fusion of races.'

In this almost hilarious dialogue, George Eliot hints at the central contrast of the book, which is between the pallid certainties and unsmiling rules of the well-to-do English, and the exotic, occluded world of the cosmopolitan — or what was then known, significantly, as the Bohemian. Of Klesmer we learn that he grew up 'on the outskirts of Bohemia; and in the figurative Bohemia too he had had large acquaintance with the variety and romance which belong to small incomes'. Some have seen in Klesmer the figure of Liszt, whom George Eliot met in Weimar in 1854, but Liszt was a Hungarian Catholic and Gordon Haight's biography makes it pretty clear that the real model was Anton Rubinstein, also encountered in Weimar, who kept up his acquaintance with her, and to a performance of whose devotional opera *The Maccabees* George Eliot went late in life.

Klesmer is, of course, the long-maned, emotional, histrionic type; almost a *Punch* cartoon image of a MittelEuropean. Even George Eliot more than once employs the verb 'flash' to describe his smiling. His role, coming as he does from haunts of Jews and gypsies, is one of *épater*. Clearly, then, her other

Jewish characters could hardly be stereotypical without being – stereotypical. Her purpose was also to show the melancholy, millennial aspect of Jewish existence. It is perhaps to be regretted that this has never been done by any author in such a way as to make Henry James or Sir Leslie Stephen feel that they have had their money's worth of entertainment.

George Eliot did not come by chance to her educated interest in Judaism. It evolved from her deep early commitment to Christianity and the gospels. In 1838, during a week spent in London, she forwent the frivolities of the theatre and stayed indoors during the evening immersed in Josephus's *History of the Jews*. The impression this may have created in the short term is uncertain; a little later we find her writing to a fellow-evangelical in deprecation of a concert at which Mendelssohn's new oratorio *Paul* had been performed by John Braham. Her objection was partly to the showy use of scriptural text, but she added to Marian Lewis: 'For my part I humbly conceive it to be little less than blasphemy for such words as "Now then we are ambassadors for Christ" to be taken on the lips of such a man as Braham (a Jew too!).' But these and other pettinesses appear to have evaporated with her self-emancipation from Anglican orthodoxy, her empirical observation that Dissenters were as moral as the Established churchmen, and her discovery from reading Sir Walter Scott that even Papists might have fine characters. Meanwhile, she had been translating the theological work of D.F. Strauss, which had a distinctly rationalist tone, and studying Hegel. In a suggestive letter which may prefigure Klesmer's exchange with Mr Bult, she wrote in 1848 of the positive effects of intermarriage and of her rejection of the theory of 'pure' race. Interestingly, this 'pure race' theory was associated in England with the name of Benjamin Disraeli, who wrote grandly of the 'Hebrew-Caucasian' species, as well as staking his claim to Tory leadership and an Earldom by writing:

> The native tendency of the Jewish race is against the doctrine of the equality of man. They have also another characteristic – the faculty of acquisition. Thus it will be seen that all the tendencies of the Jewish race are conservative. Their bias is to religion, property and natural aristocracy, and it should be the interest of statesmen that their energies and creative powers should be enlisted in the cause of existing society.

Disraeli became England's first Jewish Prime Minister in the year – 1876 – that *Daniel Deronda* was published. Within a few years he had persuaded Queen Victoria to crown herself Empress of India. The writing of the novel took place against a background of expansion and innovation – especially the opening that resulted from the digging of the Suez Canal. That is why its action can, for the first time, comprehend a world outside England.

George Eliot's evolution on the Jewish question took three forms. It took, first, the form of an intense interest in the Jews as a biblical and scriptural people. It took, second, the form of a commitment against religious, particularly Christian, intolerance. And it took, third, the form of an education – an encounter with the cosmopolitan and with the wider horizons of Europe and the East as these became accessible to a woman of formerly insular temperament. But 'religion, property and natural aristocracy' – Disraeli's ministering terms – are not presented as unambiguous goods in *Daniel Deronda*, either in so far as they affect Gwendolen Harleth or Mirah Cohen. The tributary stream in Jewish thought which most influenced George Eliot was that which originated from the writings of Spinoza, writing which she was translating into English at the time of the great European emancipation movement of 1848. (She found the exercise of rendering the *Tractatus Theologico-Politicus* 'such a rest to my mind', which makes me foolishly want to recall Bertie Wooster's claim, in *Thank You, Jeeves*: 'You'll usually find me curled up with Spinoza's latest.')

During her 1854 tour of Europe with George Henry Lewes, she made a point of visiting the Jewish world. In Frankfurt she was very struck by the *Judengasse*, returning two decades later to refresh her memory of it and to employ it as the setting of Deronda's premonitory meeting with Joseph Kalonymos. Returning to England, she busied herself with the study and translation of Heinrich Heine, another non-Jewish Jew of genius who also plays his part, it seems to me, in rounding the character of Julius Klesmer. In an article on Heine's wit, George Eliot drew a distinction between humour and *esprit*, with some reflection on this distinction as it occurs among Teutons, which plainly recur in the dialogue with Gwendolen quoted above.

In Prague in 1858, she wrote in her journal:

> The most interesting things we saw were the Jewish burial ground (the *Alter Friedhof*) and the old Synagogue. We saw a lovely dark-eyed Jewish child here, which we were glad to kiss in all its dirt. Then came the grimy old synagogue with its smoky groins, and lamp forever burning. An intelligent old Jew was our cicerone and read us some Hebrew out of the precious old book of the Law.

This is a slightly painstaking and self-conscious progress towards tolerance, but it is a definite one. And it's of interest that Mirah escapes from her father in Prague in the action of the novel. The old Prague synagogue – the *Altneuschul* – incidentally supplied the title for Theodor Herzl's Zionist novel *Altneuland*, or 'Old-New Land', which is the only utopian fiction ever written by the moral father of an actual state. The novel was published in 1902 and has as one of its central characters a brutal, arrogant misogynist named – Kingscourt. I wonder....

As one looks at George Eliot's later development, everything seems to press towards the realization of *Daniel Deronda*. In the mid 1860s she and her husband began to broaden their social circle, meeting Mr and Mrs Robert Browning and being shown by the latter 'her Hebrew bible with notes in her handwriting'. At the Monckton-Milnes salon in Upper Brook Street, where Lewes and Eliot were frequent guests, Matthew Arnold observed that one could meet 'all the advanced liberals in religion and politics, and a Cingalese in full costume; so that, having lunched with the Rothschilds, I seemed to be passing my day among Jews, Turks, infidels and heretics'. In 1864 George Eliot became friendly with Mr and Mrs Frederick Lehmann, and through them with a set of confident, worldly, 'cosmopolitan' painters, musicians, and writers. This essential detour brings us to a little-known intersection — the writing of *The Spanish Gypsy*. Immediately preceding *Middlemarch*, this verse drama is set in medieval Spain. Let me quote the sarcastic account of its plot given by Sir Leslie Stephen. On the eve of her wedding to a Spanish aristocrat, the heroine is visited by a gypsy who:

> explains without loss of time that he is her father; that he is about to be the Moses or Mahomet of a gypsy nation; and orders her to give up her country, her religion, and her lover to join him in this hopeful enterprise.

'Why place the heroine in conditions so hard to imagine?' inquires the suddenly realist Sir Leslie, as if he had never hit upon or roared over a Dickensian or Shakespearean coincidence. In fact, George Eliot gave the answer to this question in her own lifetime:

> Nothing would serve me except that moment in Spanish history when the struggle with the Moors was attaining its climax, and when there was the gypsy race present under such conditions as would enable me to get my heroine and the hereditary claim on her among the gypsies. *I required the opposition of race to give the need for renouncing the expectation of marriage.* [Emphasis added.]

What could be plainer? The 'Jewish' part of Daniel Deronda, which the gentleman-critics want to heave over the side in order to give unobstructed play to the internal wrenchings of Miss Harleth, is the necessary counterpoint to these emotions, and to the awful scale of their disappointment. Moreover, for George Eliot the Jewish issue had come, after long study and reflection, to stand for an entire range of matters that came under the general heading of 'emancipation'.

Emancipation never comes cheap — it had cost George Eliot considerable emotional strain herself. And she scored it very deep into Gwendolen Harleth:

> The world seemed getting larger round poor Gwendolen, and she more solitary and helpless in the midst. The thought that he might come back after going to the East, sank before the bewildering vision of these wide-stretching purposes in which she felt herself reduced to a mere speck. There comes a terrible moment to many souls when the great movements of the world, the larger destinies of mankind, which have lain aloof in newspapers and other neglected reading, enter like an earthquake into their own lives — when the slow urgency of growing generations turns into the tread of an invading army or the dire clash of civil war, and grey fathers know nothing to seek for but the corpses of their blooming sons, and girls forget all vanity to make lint and bandages which may serve for the shattered limbs of their betrothed husbands.

Here are the punishments that fall on the inattentive or the careless; those who are content to remain within a small compass of the imagination; those who are not prepared for the worst. Deronda's discontent and restlessness appear, by contrast, not as a 'pre-engagement' but as something daring and worthwhile even if, as Henry James objects, he does continually signal his seriousness by grasping his lapel and going on a bit.

In the passage above, which combines some of the fiercer passages of the Old Testament with the periods of a Marx or a Luxemburg, Gwendolen's awakening to loss is made more poignant by the fact that Jewish life has always been part of the warp and woof of English society, only she has not been educated to realize it. In George Eliot's essay 'The Modern Hep! Hep! Hep!', written at about the same time as *Daniel Deronda* and published in *The Impressions of Theophrastus Such* in 1879, she took the old crusader battle-cry as a slogan by which to examine and criticize anti-Semitism in England. She compared it directly to the rationalizations for modern slavery:

> And this is the usual level of thinking in polite society concerning the Jews. Apart from theological purposes, it seems to be held surprising that anybody should take an interest in the history of a people whose literature has furnished all our devotional language; and if any reference is made to their past and future destinies some hearer is sure to state as a relevant fact which may assist our judgement that she, for her part, is not fond of them, having known a Mrs. Jacobson who was very unpleasant, or that he, for his part, thinks meanly of them as a race, though on inquiry you find that he is so little acquainted with their characteristics that he is astonished to learn how many persons whom he has blindly admired and applauded are Jews to the backbone.

George Eliot's scorn was seldom less than splendid and thoroughgoing. In a letter replying to warm praise for the novel from Harriet Beecher Stowe, she later adumbrated the same point in more detail:

> As to the Jewish element in 'Deronda,' I expected from first to last in writing it, that it would create much stronger resistance and even repulsion than it has actually met with. But precisely because I felt that the usual attitude of Christians towards Jews is — I hardly know whether to say more impious or more stupid in the light of their professed principles, I therefore felt urged to treat Jews with such sympathy and understanding as my nature and knowledge could attain to. *Moreover, not only towards the Jews, but towards all oriental peoples with whom we English come in contact, a spirit of arrogance and contemptuous dictatorialness is observable which has become a national disgrace to us.* [Emphasis added.]

'There is nothing I should care more to do,' she continued, 'if it were possible, than to rouse the imagination of men and women to a vision of human claims in those races of their fellow men who most differ from them in customs and beliefs.' But this was no generalized humanitarian emotion. It had a specific object as well: 'Towards the Hebrews we Western people who have been reared in Christianity have a peculiar debt and, whether we acknowledge it or not, a peculiar thoroughness of fellowship in religious and moral sentiment.' This comes near to 'fiction with a message', but it can also be seen as suiting the internal needs of the novel very well. Gwendolen is beset by stultification; she and we must discover the fallacies of regnant assumptions; for this an exotic (in the Greek sense) character is necessary. The Harleth and the Jewish halves of the story, then, can and must be seen not as opposites or antitheses but as a symmetry and, at their most finely realized, a synthesis.

I have posponed two final critics to the last, one because of his silliness and one because of his gravity. In his 'Literature and Social Theory: George Eliot', which appears in his volume *Representations*, Professor Steven Marcus commits himself to the following proposition:

> Deronda's identity is a mystery to himself and has always been. It is only when he is a grown man, having been to Eton and Cambridge, that he discovers he is a Jew. What this has to mean — given the conventions of medical practice at the time — is that he never looked down. In order for the plot of *Daniel Deronda* to work, Deronda's circumcised penis must be invisible, or nonexistent — which is one more demonstration in detail of why the plot does not in fact work. Yet this peculiarity of circumstance — which, I think it should be remarked, has never been noticed before — is, I have been arguing, characteristic in several senses of both George Eliot and the culture she was representing.

This requires the razor of Occam, which can accomplish in a simple deft stroke what the *mohel* has failed to do for the author of *Sex and the Victorians*. When Deronda confronts his mother, in Chapter 51, and surprises her by saying that he is 'glad' to hear her revelation of his Jewishness, she replies, 'violently': '"Why do you say you are glad? You are an English gentleman. I secured you that."' As one who has spent more time than most critics in the schools which prepare English gentlemen, and the frigid showers in which these schools abound, I think we may take it that Deronda *mère* knew what she was about when she decided his future in his infancy. Professor Marcus has got no nearer the nub than the schoolmen who debated the hypothesis of an earthly foreskin of the Nazarene, left behind for the reliquaries of the pious.

Professor Edward Said does not complain that *Daniel Deronda* is humourless, or unduly bifurcated, or indifferent to the special sensitivity of those who are averse to fictional coincidence. He focuses, with some insistence, on something that is not present in the novel but is absent from it. With his usual mordant sense of the crux, he notices that neither the humane and generous George Eliot, nor any of her characters, pays the least attention to, or shows the slightest concern for, the native inhabitants of that yet-to-be redeemed Palestine which they make the internal and external object of their multifarious yearnings. I suppose that it could be objected that Said is viewing the novel through a retrospective optic. Yet George Eliot herself writes, in the opening section of the novel:

> A human life, I think, should be well-rooted in some spot of a native land, where it may get the love of tender kinship for the face of the earth, for the labours men go forth to, for the sounds and accents that haunt it, for whatever will give that earthly home a familiar, unmistakeable difference amidst the future widening of knowledge.

No Palestinian or Zionist, writing of 'The Land', has put it much more satisfyingly than that. But Said is on slightly weaker ground when he attributes this to a generalized callousness on the author's part:

> The few references to the East in *Daniel Deronda* [he writes in *The Question of Palestine*] are always to England's Indian colonies, for whose people – as people having wishes, values, aspirations – Eliot expresses the complete indifference of absolute silence.

This is true as far as it goes (George Eliot's statement of sympathy for 'all oriental peoples with whom we English come in contact' does not appear in the novel), but does not quite bring off the implication that she could not care less about the colonial subjects of the British Crown. She could not write with any direct experience of the Indians, but she could catch out Mr Bult who, if you remember, 'rather neutral in private life, had strong opinions concerning the districts of the Niger, was much at home also in the Brazils, spoke with decision of affairs in the South Seas'.

In *Theophrastus Such*, and her defence of the Jews against Christian obtuseness and cruelty, George Eliot expressed herself rather forcefully about the hypocrisies of empire. To select a few of her choicest incisions into the contented hide of the Bults:

> We do not call ourselves a dispersed and a punished people; we are a colonising people and it is we who have punished others.

> Are we to adopt the exclusiveness for which we have punished the Chinese?

> He [Mixtus] continues his early habit of regarding the spread of Christianity as a great result of our commercial intercourse with black, brown and yellow populations; but this is an idea not spoken of in the sort of fashionable society that Scintilla collects around her husband's table, and Mixtus now philosophically reflects that the cause must come before the effect, and that the thing to be striven for is the commercial intercourse, not excluding a little war if that also should prove needful as a pioneer of Christianity.

> ... the Irish, also a servile race, who have rejected Protestantism though it has been repeatedly urged on them by fire and sword and penal laws, and whose place in the moral scale may be judged by our advertisements, where the clause 'No Irish need apply' parallels the sentence which for many polite persons sums up the question of Judaism – 'I never *did* like the Jews.'

This scarcely supports a finding of indifference towards the colonized. Even the speec of the fierce and solipsistic Mordechai, cited by Said, speaks only of a land with 'debauched and paupered conquerors' and, when it defames the East, is directed only at that ancient and familiar despot, the unfeeling Turkish *pasha*, common foe of Christendom, Jewry, and the Arabs. Though this does not automatically contradict Said, who concedes: 'curiously, all of Eliot's descriptions of Jews stress their exotic "Eastern" aspects', it both qualifies and perhaps intensifies his essential critique. George Eliot, like quite a few writers who have had their fill of a stolid, hypocritical, self-satisfied England, had come to an unusual empathy with the agile, versatile, vociferous, ingenious peoples. There is something almost Byronic, mingled with a little German idealism, in her fellow-feeling for Armenians, Jews, gypsies, Bohemians, and all the others for whom her posterity prepared such a frightful relegation. I think it is certain that she had no prejudice — rather the reverse — against the swarthy and the silken. To the question 'Had she no room in her heart for the Palestinian Arab?' the reply must be that she was, like most of her contemporaries, quite unaware that any such people, or 'problem', existed. This would be a criticism in itself, whether or not it reflected general ignorance, or the propaganda about 'a land without a people for a people without a land'.

George Eliot was most influenced by Emanuel Deutsch, a Silesian Jew who had come to London and worked at the British Museum. Encountered at the Lehmanns, he proved to have an infectious enthusiasm and a store of recondite scriptural knowledge. He made a trip to Palestine in 1869, writing with passion about the Wailing Wall and his 'wild yearnings'. His presence in the figure of Mordechai is evident, and it seems clear that he embodies the religious Zionist rather than the colonizing, state-building sort. Deutsch's friend and patron Lady Strangford, whose husband is thought to have furnished the model of Disraeli's Coningsby, gave George Eliot information about the Near East (as it was then known), telling her: 'Since 1863 the "Israelitish Alliance" (chiefly of Paris), shamed by the efforts of Christians to promote colonies and agricultural occupations in Palestine, have endeavored to found a colony at Jaffa.' She added that this task was made more difficult by rabbinical teaching that Jews in Palestine should be supported by the faithful elsewhere, holding that 'it is irreligious of a Jew in Jerusalem to work, so to say.' Lady Strangford also urged that George Eliot make the voyage, which she was never strong enough to do. Who knows? Like some of the characters in S.Y. Agnon's *A Guest for the Night*, she might have discovered at first hand that the word 'colony' had double meaning, and that Palestine was not an unpeopled wilderness for spiritual contemplation. She could certainly have found out the falsity of a letter from Haim Guedalla, of the London *Jewish Chronicle*, who wrote thanking her for *Deronda* and mentioning his hectic 'vision of Syria again in the hands of the Jews'.

In denying herself the usual conventions of the love story — the overcoming of unjust opposition or of difference in station; the whole apparatus of what

Barbara Hardy calls 'moral rescue' — George Eliot set herself a more rigorous standard than that of showing up, say, the sinister etiolation of a Grandcourt, the deference of a rural Rector, or the complacency of a Mr Bult. Poor Gwendolen is made to face a challenge to happiness that she is not equipped to understand. This is the indirect realization of a pledge made in one of George Eliot's letters:

> The day will come when there will be a temple of white marble where sweet incense and anthems shall rise to the memory of every man and every woman who has had a deep *ahnung*, a presentiment, a yearning, or a clear vision of the time when this miserable reign of Mammon shall end.

But as she strove, without the prop of orthodox religion, to convey the Greek sense of *entheos* — enthusiasm that is 'possession' without ceremony — she never scorned the earthbound and the banal, the plain realization that is contained in the closing passage of her penultimate novel, *Middlemarch*: 'The growing good of the world is partly dependent on unhistoric acts; and that things are not so ill with you and me as they might have been, is half owing to the number who lived faithfully a hidden life, and rest in unvisited tombs.' This counterpoint — between the rising incense and the dying cadence, the triumphant and the modest, the prophetic and the quotidian — is nowhere more boldly confronted than in the chapters of *Daniel Deronda*, which have already easily outlived the distinctly earthbound, confining objections made to them.

Lecture in the *Art of Criticism* series delivered at
Berkeley, reprinted in *Threepenny Review*, Fall 1989

INDEX